Global Perspectives on Human Migration, Asylum, and Security

Christina M. Akrivopoulou
Hellenic Open University, Greece

A volume in the Advances in
Human Services and Public Health
(AHSPH) Book Series

IGI Global
DISSEMINATOR OF KNOWLEDGE

Published in the United States of America by
IGI Global
Information Science Reference (an imprint of IGI Global)
701 E. Chocolate Avenue
Hershey PA, USA 17033
Tel: 717-533-8845
Fax: 717-533-8661
E-mail: cust@igi-global.com
Web site: http://www.igi-global.com

Library of Congress Cataloging-in-Publication Data

Names: Akrivopoulou, Christina, editor.
Title: Global perspectives on human migration, asylum, and security / Christina M. Akrivopoulou, editor.
Description: Hershey PA : Information Science Reference, [2018]
Identifiers: LCCN 2017010786| ISBN 9781522528173 (hardcover) | ISBN 9781522528180 (ebook)
Subjects: LCSH: Emigration and immigration--Cross-cultural studies. | Emigration and immigration--Government policy--Cross-cultural studies. | Immigrants--Social conditions. | Asylum, Right of. | Globalization. | Security, International.
Classification: LCC JV6035 .G573 2018 | DDC 362.87--dc23 LC record available at https://lccn.loc.gov/2017010786

This book is published in the IGI Global book series Advances in Human Services and Public Health (AHSPH) (ISSN: 2475-6571; eISSN: 2475-658X)

British Cataloguing in Publication Data
A Cataloguing in Publication record for this book is available from the British Library.

All work contributed to this book is new, previously-unpublished material.
The views expressed in this book are those of the authors, but not necessarily of the publisher.

For electronic access to this publication, please contact: eresources@igi-global.com.

Advances in Human Services and Public Health (AHSPH) Book Series

ISSN:2475-6571
EISSN:2475-658X

Editor-in-Chief: Jennifer Martin, RMIT University, Australia

MISSION

The well-being of the general public should be a primary concern for any modern civilization. Ongoing research in the field of human services and public healthcare is necessary to evaluate, manage, and respond to the health and social needs of the global population.

The **Advances in Human Services and Public Health (AHSPH)** book series aims to publish high-quality reference publications focused on the latest methodologies, tools, issues, and strategies for managing the health and social welfare of the public. The AHSPH book series will be especially relevant for healthcare professionals, policy makers, government officials, and students seeking the latest research in this field.

COVERAGE

- Public Welfare
- Access to Healthcare Services
- Social Work
- Medicare and Medicaid
- Health policy
- Healthcare Reform
- Youth Development
- Domestic Violence
- Poverty
- Assistance Programs

IGI Global is currently accepting manuscripts for publication within this series. To submit a proposal for a volume in this series, please contact our Acquisition Editors at Acquisitions@igi-global.com or visit: http://www.igi-global.com/publish/.

The Advances in Human Services and Public Health (AHSPH) Book Series (ISSN 2475-6571) is published by IGI Global, 701 E. Chocolate Avenue, Hershey, PA 17033-1240, USA, www.igi-global.com. This series is composed of titles available for purchase individually; each title is edited to be contextually exclusive from any other title within the series. For pricing and ordering information please visit http://www.igi-global.com/book-series/advances-human-services-public-health/102256. Postmaster: Send all address changes to above address.

Titles in this Series

For a list of additional titles in this series, please visit:
https://www.igi-global.com/book-series/advances-human-services-public-health/102256

Health Information Systems and the Advancement of Medical Practice in Developing ...
Kgomotso H. Moahi (University of Botswana, Botswana) Kelvin Joseph Bwalya (University of Johannesburg, South Africa) and Peter Mazebe II Sebina (University of Botswana, Botswana)
Medical Information Science Reference • ©2017 • 350pp • H/C (ISBN: 9781522522621) • US $200.00

Examining the Role of Environmental Change on Emerging Infectious Diseases and Pandemics
Maha Bouzid (University of East Anglia, UK)
Information Science Reference • ©2017 • 327pp • H/C (ISBN: 9781522505532) • US $200.00

Sexual Misconduct in the Education and Human Services Sector
Christopher Schwilk (Shippensburg University, USA) Rachel Stevenson (Shippensburg University, USA) and David Bateman (Shippensburg University, USA)
Information Science Reference • ©2017 • 291pp • H/C (ISBN: 9781522506577) • US $190.00

Public Health Genomics and International Wealth Creation
E. William Ebomoyi (Chicago State University, USA)
Information Science Reference • ©2015 • 463pp • H/C (ISBN: 9781466685598) • US $235.00

Transforming Public Health in Developing Nations
Mohamud Sheikh (The School of Public Health and Community Medicine, The University of New South Wales, Sydney, Australia) Aziza Mahamoud (Sidra Medical and Research Center, Qatar) and Mowafa Househ (King Saud Bin Abdul Aziz University for Health Sciences, College Of Public Health and Health Informatics, Saudi Arabia)
Information Science Reference • ©2015 • 416pp • H/C (ISBN: 9781466687028) • US $215.00

Innovative Collaborative Practice and Reflection in Patient Education
Jennifer Lynne Bird (Florida Atlantic University, USA)
Medical Information Science Reference • ©2015 • 308pp • H/C (ISBN: 9781466675247) • US $225.00

For an enitre list of titles in this series, please visit:
https://www.igi-global.com/book-series/advances-human-services-public-health/102256

IGI Global
DISSEMINATOR OF KNOWLEDGE

701 East Chocolate Avenue, Hershey, PA 17033, USA
Tel: 717-533-8845 x100 • Fax: 717-533-8661
E-Mail: cust@igi-global.com • www.igi-global.com

Table of Contents

Detailed Table of Contents

Based on the contributions of Jean Baudrillard, a French well known philosopher who exerted a radical criticism to the mass-media and its position respecting to migration and terrorism, Korstanje alluded to a neologism, "Thana-Capitalism", which situates as a new stage of production where the suffering of others is the main commodity exchanged among classes. In times of Thana Capitalism, though we horrify from refugees and their miseries or the latest terrorist blow in CNN, we have doing nothing to change reality. This begs an interesting question, how does perception form in times of thana capitalism? what is the concept of reality in the age of pseudo-reality? is the media and the spectacle of disasters disorganizing social ties? This chapter centers on the role of reality in times where others` death crystalized as a criterion of consumption.

As refugees / immigrants are forced to cross the border, the member states of European Union are trying to manage mobile populations or the new labor force in various ways. Under the over-accumulation crisis, what kind of policies are drawn; or are denizens be punished as they question the stability of borders, state sovereign and supranational policies? When social contradictions are intense, in bourgeois democracy human rights are shrunk and the process of fascistisation is activated. Ultimately, maybe it is noticeable to understand that refugees /migrants become mutatis mutandis an allegorical figure of Muselmanner.

Based on the recently-dated terrorist attacks perpetrated in Europe, where terrorists weaponized classic forms of transport against civilian targets, one might speculate that likely mobilities and terrorism would be inextricably intertwined. In the mid of this mayhem, this chapter centers on the mobilities-paradigm as an ideological platform that keeps the interests of ruling elite, inasmuch as only 1% of mankind is legally authorized to travel worldwide. It is vital for social scientists to interrogate on the cultural effects of 9/11, in a world which is characterized by serious economic imbalances. In this world of full contrasts, while first world tourists are encouraged to move from one point to another without any restriction, migrants, asylum-seekers and vagabonds are energetically pursued, jailed or exiled by nation-state.

The existing European legislative frameworks seem to be unable to deal with the huge amount of refugees. Greece failed to fulfil its obligations according to the European Union Dublin Regulation and allowed refugees to move on a country of their choice. Therefore, taking into account the difficulties that the European states have to face regarding the increasing flow of refugees, the present chapter reviews the existing jurisprudence of the European Court of Human Rights regarding the protection of refugees, in order to explain whether the CoE Member States have obligation to protect and promote the rights of refugees. Moreover, it focuses on the contribution of the Council of Europe in the harmonisation of national policies towards the treatment of refugees. Finally, it assesses the Greek policies with regard to the treatment of refugees and suggests improvements in accordance with the Council of Europe's recommendations.

Children have always been a part of the war for millennia but child soldiering is often portrayed as something rather new, as a side product of the Post-Cold War in most of the fragile states in the world. Underdevelopment is a feature of the fragile state and especially political violence is a common figure in such states. This paper argues that, children's role changes in fragile states, and further focuses on children in Syrian war and their changing role in the society. While the conflict was turning into a war the role of the children both in the society and in the conflict of which increasing tension was turning it into a war. And when the country, one of the fragile states in the world, collapsed, the government lost control and the children took the sides as terrorists. Given the brief information about the changing roles of Syrian children in this dynamically violent environment, this article will examine the transformation of the role of the children in the fragile state Syria.

Following the Arab Spring, the Middle East is in chaos with ongoing wars in Yemen and Syria. There are millions of Syrians seeking refuge in neighboring countries like Turkey and Lebanon, and in European countries like Greece, Hungary, and Germany. Nonetheless, the largest proportion of Syrian refugees in hosted by neighboring countries needing continuous support of the international community. As the issue of Syrian refugees is transnational, there is a need to look for multilateral options for dealing with the crisis. Thus, the role of the Organization of Islamic Cooperation (OIC) becomes crucial. Irrespective of being labelled as a 'talk fest', there is no denying of the fact that OIC has significant potential for tackling grave challenges facing the Muslim world. The problems range from extremism and radicalization to poverty and illiteracy. Now there is the emergent challenge of refugees from the Middle Eastern crisis. This paper evaluates the role of OIC with reference to the Syrian refugee crisis in the Middle East and beyond.

The aim of this study is to examine the hate speech in the reader comments towards Syrian refugee s in Turkey. Within the framework of this purpose, the reader comments made on the news about the violence towards a Syrian child, which took place on the web page of national newspaper Hürriyet, are analysed. It is hoped that, this study will help reveal the concerns or motives which lie behind the negative point of views and opinions towards Syrian refugees. Thus, it may make a contribution to determining the counter-strategies against the intolerance and hostility towards the refugees.

Preface

INTRODUCTION

Over the past two years, from 2015, the matters of asylum and migration have been moved up in the hierarchy of the world political agenda. The main reason was the Syrian refugee crisis which still remains and unresolved problem for the EU. Though the EU is applying the Geneva Convention of 1951 in the case of Syrian asylum seekers and refugees, still the number of flows is large and the problem of their accommodation, proper health care, education and integration remains unsolved. At the same period that the EU is putting all it's efforts in providing the Syrian refugees with humanitarian assistance, a series of terrorist attacks in many European cities, such as Paris, Brussels, Munich, Manchester and London serves as the basis for an uprising rhetoric against refugees and migrants in many European countries.

ORGANIZATION OF CHAPTERS

In this pressing framework, the book that follows examines many of very important issues related to the current Syrian refugee crisis from a theoretical and empirical perspective. Thus, in the first chapter of the book, "Thana-Capitalism and the Sense of Reality: Lessons Unlearned," the author examines the link between the media coverage of the refugee drama with the actual care and protection offered to them. Based on the work of Jean Baudrillard, a French well known philosopher who exerted a radical criticism to the mass-media and its position respecting to migration and terrorism, the author reflects on the neologism of "Thana-Capitalism," a new stage of production where the suffering of others is the main commodity exchanged among classes.

The second chapter of the book, "Refugees or Migrants: Fascistisation and Punishment," provides with a critical understanding of the current EU policies on migrant and refugee integration. The author examines a series of very important issues, such as the 'stability' of the EU borders and the combination between national and supranational policies that the EU is putting into effect during the Syrian refugee crisis. Nevertheless, the most important issue for the author is to examine how this crisis is connected to the fascistisation of society and possible limitations to human rights in the name of preserving the security of the public.

The third chapter of the book, "How Can World Leaders Understand the Perverse Core of Terrorism? Terror in The Global Village," reflects on the recently dated terrorist attacks perpetrated in Europe, where terrorists weaponized—among others—classic forms of transport against civilian targets, one might speculate that likely mobilities and terrorism would be inextricably intertwined. The author is connecting the paradigm of mobility to the terrorist attacks to the terrorist attacks as a model of class division and economic imbalances. He further highlights this points by underlining that while first world tourists are encouraged to move from one point to another without any restriction, migrants, asylum-seekers and vagabonds are energetically pursued, jailed or exiled by nation-state.

The fourth chapter of the book, "Providente Asylum vs. the Council of Europe: The Case of Greece," reflects on the recent refugee and migration flow towards Europe in order to analyze especially the role of the Council of Europe in the resolution of the crisis. As it is pointed out by the authors, since 1949, the Council of Europe has made an outstanding progress in the harmonization of the national policies in the field of democracy, rule of law and human rights, especially when it concerns the Geneva Convention of 1951 obligations. In this framework, the authors examine the recent case law of the Strasburg Court in cases where the member states of the Council of Europe have failed to provide with quick and sufficient procedures in relation to asylum process and the inhuman conditions of the reception centres. In this framework, this chapter reviews the existing legislation of the Council of Europe and jurisprudence of the European Court of Human Rights regarding the protection of refugees, in order to explain whether the Council of Europe member states have the obligation to protect and promote the rights of refugees. Moreover, it focuses on the contribution of the Council of Europe in the harmonization of national policies towards the treatment of refugees with a specific focus to the Greek policies regarding the treatment of refugees.

The fifth chapter of the book, "Supporter, Activist, Rebel, Terrorist: Children in Syria," deals with the many aspects of war violence against children. As it is pointed out, children are rather neglected in the international relations though throughout history their presence in military conflicts is characteristic, e.g., the British Navy recruited young boys to serve as cabin boys and cannon prepping throughout the 18th and 19th centuries, while substantial numbers of children fought on both sides in the U.S. Civil War, from 1861 to 1865. Of the 31 countries where there were armed conflicts in 1998, 87% used children soldiers below the age of 18 years. The present paper faces the crucial question of what can be done to prevent the existence and practices of using child soldiers in armed conflicts. The author is trying to develop a comprehensive understanding for the correlation between the notion of a fragile state and the children in conflict, more specifically in the framework of the Syrian war.

The sixth chapter of the book, "Middle Eastern Refugee Crisis and the Role of the Organization of Islamic Cooperation," examines the role of the Organization in the current Syrian refugee crisis. As it is pointed out there are millions of Syrians seeking refuge in neighboring countries like Turkey and Lebanon, and in European countries like Greece, Hungary, and Germany. As the issue of Syrian refugees is transnational, there is a need to look for multilateral options for dealing with the crisis, thus deeming the role of the Organization of Islamic Cooperation as extremely crucial. In this direction, the present paper evaluates the role of the Organization of Islamic Cooperation with reference to the Syrian refugee crisis in the Middle East and beyond.

The seventh chapter of the book, "Hate Speech Towards Syrian Refugees in Turkish Online Reader Comments," examines the hate speech comments developed in the reader comments towards Syrian refugees in Turkey. The present analysis reveals the problems of racism and xenophobia connected to the move of Syrian refugee flows to other countries and more specifically in Turkey. The author attempts to illustrate the concerns or motives which lie behind the negative point of views and opinions towards Syrian refugees in order to make a contribution to determining the counter-strategies against the intolerance and hostility towards the refugees.

The eighth and last chapter of the book, "The LGBT Right Activism and the Risk of Chistianophobia in Nigeria," reflects on the ideological conflict between LGTB activism and the christianic religion in Nigeria. The author reflects on the Nigerian conservatism and doctrinaire religion that have been cardinal forces behind the adoption of a homophobic legislation in Nigeria as the explanation for the rise of a "Christianophobic" rhetoric. The paper highlights indexes pointing to a future "Christianophobia" in Nigeria, driven by a "Christianophobic" gay activism and finally argues that any pro-gay advocacy rooted in the de-Christianization of Nigerians unarguably proffers the disrespect of religious freedom.

CONCLUSION

The current global problems regarding migration, asylum and security are many and complex. The present book is covering only some of these many and complex issues on which the dialogue remains still open, aiming in providing with some answers and guidance or policy making solutions. Thus, the present book attempts in illustrating the connection between migration and asylum flows with the role of international organizations, such as the European Union, the Organization of Islamic Cooperation and the Council of Europe, to critically evaluate their role, to reveal problems of xenophobia and racism occurring from the move of refugee flows to Turkey and Europe, as well as to understand their connection to terrorist actions. Hopefully it will serve as a useful tool for the academics, the policy makers and the global citizens in the ongoing international dialogue regarding migration, asylum and security.

Christina Akrivopoulou
Hellenic Open University, Greece

Chapter 1
Thana-Capitalism and the Sense of Reality:
Lessons Unlearned

Maximiliano Emanuel Korstanje
University of Palermo, Argentina

ABSTRACT

Based on the contributions of Jean Baudrillard, a French well known philosopher who exerted a radical criticism to the mass-media and its position respecting to migration and terrorism, Korstanje alluded to a neologism, "Thana-Capitalism", which situates as a new stage of production where the suffering of others is the main commodity exchanged among classes. In times of Thana Capitalism, though we horrify from refugees and their miseries or the latest terrorist blow in CNN, we have doing nothing to change reality. This begs an interesting question, how does perception form in times of thana capitalism? what is the concept of reality in the age of pseudo-reality? is the media and the spectacle of disasters disorganizing social ties? This chapter centers on the role of reality in times where others` death crystalized as a criterion of consumption.

INTRODUCTION

During my studies on terrorism, amid 2007-2009 and my fellowship in Leeds by 2015, an interesting argument struck to me to revisit the specialized literature. Not only we have found evidence enough to confirm "terrorism was mobilities by other means", which explained fascination for terrorists to target innocent travellers worldwide (Akrivopooulou, 2012; Korstanje, 2015), but we realized the world of

DOI: 10.4018/978-1-5225-2817-3.ch001

risks, as known, has certainly changed forever by 9/11 (Howie 2010; Korstanje & Clayton, 2012; Bauman & Lyon, 2013). After this traumatic event, natural disasters, lethal virus outbreaks and any other apocalyptic dangers made us believe we were living in a world out of control (Sunstein 2003, 2005; Kelly 2009; Beck 2009; Innerarity 2013; Korstanje 2015).

In 2016, we published two seminal texts, *The Rise of Thana Capitalism and tourism* (Routledge, UK) and Tourism and Terrorism (Studium Press, India). In these books, we discussed the thesis that risk society as it was imagined by Giddens or Beck sets the pace to a new stage of production, where death played a vital role mediating between citizens and their institutions. Thana-Capitalism was a term coined to denote "an uncanny need to consume "the others` death" to reinforce sentiments associated to "chauvinism", some of them crystalized in BREXIT, or "narcissism", as it can be found in plots as Hunger Games, where social Darwinism imposes. Participants of *Hunger Games* are not interested to cooperate with the others in quest of better results, because they are over-valorised in their skills to be proclaimed as the only winner. Immersed in the culture of Narcissism, what they ignore, is that they have little probabilities to defeat president Snow, unless they work together. In times of *Thana Capitalism*, consuming disasters allows an aura to sightseers which leads to feel they are special, outstanding, respecting to the victims. Than-capitalism reminds the needs of modern citizens to consume the others` suffering to feel they are outstanding, special and superior to those who have died (Korstanje 2016a). This is the reason why, although terrorism disgusts us, we are unable to let watching media coverage (Korstanje 2016b). While risk society started in post Chernobyl society, Thana Capitalism was inaugurated after 9/11. At some extent, this argument resonates very well within sociological circles in Europe, but the problem of reality was not dully addressed in that occasion until this chapter. We feel that somehow, the section dedicated to reality leaves many questions open. Since each stage of capitalism, which was perpetuated according to a specific pervading narrative that moulded social behaviour, the sense of reality varied on changes happened at the core of system of production. This begs some intriguing questions, how 9/11 changed our culture?, is terror a result of mass-consumption?, in what forms changed the sense of reality in times of Thana Capitalism?, are we a more sadist society?.

Initially, Manuel de Landa (2006) proposes an innovative model to understand social change. Society seems to be an abstract idea, which is adapted according to individual needs. What is clear, is that from small groups to nation-states two contrasting forces converge. While territorialization tends to structure rules and politics within the hegemony of territory, a deeper trend towards deterritorialization effaces the old structures which are not economically functional to production. Based on Assemblage theory, he contends that the social order combines conflict with cooperation. In this vein, globalization offers an illustrative clarification on de Landa`s theory because at the time, capitalism cements its authority depositing over nation-states the legitimacy over their geographies, globalization blurs such borders (by means of mobilities, even tourism) which produces a global climate that undermines the control of governments by enhancing the credibility of states.

THE SENSE OF REALITY

It is very difficult to cite and discuss all epistemologists and their development in this chapter. The concept of reality was historically touched in more than two thousand years by different fields and academic disciplines. Rather, it is preferably to tackle on the original concerns of some of them who have focused on the sense of reality as the pre-condition to sociality and reciprocity. Well, the point of entry in this discussion is given to the following dilemma: if we are individuals whose crave is independent of others, how can explain the needs to live in companion?, in what way society is structured?, how does society keep united?

To these questions formulated above, Thomas Hobbes (2006; 2013), who was inspired in a revolutionary climate in England, would respond two contrasting but influential drives coexist in human soul. The needs of disposing the others of their properties are fitted against the needs of protection, in order not to be disposed from own property. Since humans seek to avoid the war of all against all, the authority is endorsed in a third-party, known as "Leviathan" who monopolizes the use of force to impose the law. The question whether the world of Hobbes is pre-determined by a necessary violence which is only regulated when peoples from nature to civilization, no less true is that Lockean thesis appeals to "the division of labour", as the main criterion that precedes culture. Locke (1988) claims that the right of land possession is not given by conquest (as Hobbes noted) but by the capacity of enhancement, which is crystalized by labour. Since the founding parents of sociology found in language, customs and religion some commonalities conducive to the formation of reciprocity and morality (Sahlins, 2013; Durkheim, 2014), some hints suggested their followers that economy (or production) was the touchstone of social scaffolding. In view of this, if Marx (1973) explored the concept of *Grundisse* as a philosophical platform for the creation of capital, and consequently the acceptance of ideology while Mauss developed his notion of giving-while-receiving as a clear answer to the question detailed on the introduction. The society works because of two main reasons. The gift-exchange opens the doors for creating circuits which found the economic production. Secondly, Mauss (2000) adds, the act of giving while receiving allows not only the necessary reciprocity to classify interpretations, but produces "the sense of reality" expressed in the worlds of stories and myths. The European discourse aimed at subordinating non-western cultures by the injection of a so-called inferiority respecting to European Lords. In view of this, scholars precluded that Europe in its inception was similar to aboriginals in Australasia, but the power of law conjoined to the expansion of trade paved the ways for Europeans to launch to more evolved forms of life and production. It was until the process of deconstructionism where structuralists as Levi-Strauss showed amply the commonalities between modern citizens and aboriginals in their manner of reasoning (Levi-Strauss, 2013). After all, humans keep similar patterns to develop their sense of reality, which oddly depends on the means of production adopted by each society or human group. In economic terms, professor Thomas Sugden from East Anglia University UK, alerted that society does not evolve from "the means of production", as planned programs or policies top-down imposed; rather, there is precedent "spontaneous order", which is previously conditioned by many negotiations and pacts. Starting from this earlier-noted premise, people do not move to maximize their profits as pro status quo theorists suggest, but sacrificing their aims to achieve their goals. This happens because a societal order encompasses three basic tenets which explain "the cooperation", a) conventions of coordination, b) property and c) reciprocity. As Sugden noted, reciprocity plays a crucial role producing a counter-reaction to do the same the other did. This represents the onset of social cooperation (Sugden 2005).

As the previous argument given, one might speculate that if reciprocity is the vital force that engenders the social bondage, the sense of reality changes according each society. Pierre Bourdieu & Loic Wacquant in their classic work, *An Invitation to reflexive sociology* argue that the dilemma of reality adjoined to French sociology from its onset. The antinomy of individualism vs. collectivism not only casts some reasonable doubts in scholars as Emile Durkheim, or Marcel Mauss, but also appealed to further discussion respecting to the meaning of experience. Since the aims of sociology are to uncover "the buried structures", which are orchestrated to ensure the reproduction of social order, institutions are created according to a system of classification. As this backdrop, humans behave in view of their individual desires, but following much deeper structural rules.

The conservation of social order is decisively reinforced by the orchestration of categories of perception of the social world, which being adjusted to the division of the established order (and therefore, to the interests of those who dominate it) and common to all minds structured in accordance with those structures, impose themselves with all appearance of objective necessity (Bourdieu & Wacquant, 1992: 13)

To wit, Bourdieu & Wacquant clarify from the bias of intellectuals to understand reality, the tendency to make a spectacle for the world is the most influential one. Though the conception of reality was widely addressed by many academic circles, little attention was given to the fact that the produced knowledge advances by means of "the dialectic of thought". Professor Geoffrey Skoll has discussed this point in his book *the Dialectics of Social thought.* Per his outcomes, we need to think the intersection of agency and society from another angle. Skoll reminds that any sense is based on a triadic interpretation where definitions lack of any meaning without its opposite. In the same way, workers are situated in dialectics with elite, the society is pitted against the agent. Any negotiation between two parts allude to a third-leg, which legitimates "dialectics" as an invisible force; from Freud towards modern social scientists, dialectics still remains a symbolic bridge that mediates between mind and reality. Particularly, this doctrine was conducive to "war on terror" simply because Bush administration not only used a third-object (as scapegoat) not to face the charges for bringing economy into collapse, but diverting attention from real problems. Skoll goes on to say,

Security and terrorism are bound together in a dialectical process of mutually defining each other; they create each other in economic and environmental turmoil. What the process produces is the national security state, continual terrorist incidents, and an ever growing market for security goods and services. Despite its apparent self-generating dynamic, the terrorism dynamic is part of a larger whole with links to the economic process and the biophysical environment. Terrorism, like anti-Communism and crime fighting are political faces of larger social processes. (p. 116)

As we will discuss later, Skoll pivots on the idea that 9/11 would have taken place in the moment and society where it did. There are a lot of indicators that cemented the possibility capitalism and terrorism would be inevitably entwined. This was the point ushered Baudrillard in the polemic phrase, "the war of Gulf never took place", a point which will be debated in next section.

THE HYPER-REAL

The notion of hyper-real was originally coined by Jean Baudrillard (2006) to refer the excess of the real, which means the disappearance between imaginary and reality. In other terms, hyper-reality seems to be associated to the inflation of simulation, which corresponds with the lack of intensity. It is as though lay-people are obsessed by personal achievements, prefer to avoid hard work to accomplish their tasks. Though misunderstood by many of their critics, Baudrillard was a pioneer signalling that "the spectacle of disaster" would inevitably lead towards "the emptiness of meaning". For Baudrillard, technology plays a crucial role configuring a hypothetical scenario enrooted in the future, with ends of disciplining practices and behaviour in present. This process not only was accelerated by 9/11 but also divided a parallel reality where pseudo-events prevail. In this respect, he contends the film of S. Spielberg Minority Report synthesizes his thesis about the convergence of the future with present. In a time located in the future, human beings can recognize the crimes before they occur and of course neutralize criminals efficiently. The ethic question here lies in how a crime can be punished whenever it had never committed. A similar case follows with September 11 admits Baudrillard. Terrorism is legitimating in advance a set of policies related to the geopolitical control of the World. Fear is paving the pathway towards a broader paranoia product of the multiplication of information and the hegemony of object-sign (Baudrillard, 2006). In terms of Douglas Kellner

In Baudrillard view, the 9/11 attacks represented the clash of triumphant globalization at war with itself and unfolded a fourth world war: the first put and end to European Supremacy and to the era of colonialism; the second put an end to Nazism; and the third to Communism. Each one brought us progressively closer to the single world order of today, which is now nearing its end, everywhere opposed, everywhere grappling with hostile forces. This is a war of fractal complexity, waged worldwide against rebellious singularities that, in the manner of antibodies, mount a resistance in every cell (Kellner, 2005: 3).

In digital times, Baudrillard acknowledges, events happen first at screens than in reality. One of the key factors that distinguish Baudrillard`s thought is "reversibility", which suggests the possibility the system weakens its core while functioning. From this viewpoint, reversibility not only echoes "Greek irony", which leads to tragedy, but places "dialectics" understanding that "nothing can be said or interpreted from reality. At the time, mass-media disseminates news where appearances replace meaning, audience witnesses "a vertigo of interpretations", where each image is eaten by a next one to come. The violence of interpretation consists in the impossibility to divide reasons from causes. News and images of terror are portrayed without a reasonable explanation of why these happen. In retrospect, Baudrillard adamantly insists western rationality which was historically rested on the dichotomy between truth and fake, in the society of consumerists this logic has changed to a monopoly of the code instead of veracity. In several of his text, he resolves the philosophical dichotomy modern society rests on "an absence of truth" since reality and fictions have merged into the same form, *the hyper-real.*

Most certainly, the best ways of understanding hyper-real are the examples of Minority Report, where Precogs anticipate crimes before they to be committed. Though crimes were real only through images and screens, they remain enrooted in the future, not present. The excess of credibility on forecasting not only is a double-edge sword, but eradicates present to the extent any image is allegorically imposed from future, externally fabricated to discipline the bodies of citizens (Baudrillard 1994; 1995; 2001; 2006; Baudrillard & Evans 1991). As stated, this was the reason behind he declared, 9/11 never took place.

9/11 and the Rise of Thana Capitalism

Although terrorism attacked American targets in different zones of third world during years, nothing was similar to events to come, when three civilian airplanes were crushed against World Trade Centre and Pentagon respectively. In view of this, Al-Qaeda, a terrorist cell which years earlier were supported by US, showed to the world two important assumptions. First and foremost, the icons of western supremacy as leisure and mobility can be used against the most powerful nation of the world, in which case it deduces there is no safe place any-longer. Secondly, terrorism ignited a new culture, which centered on witnessing, provided to the necessary oxygen to perpetuate. Professor Luke Howie (2010) explains that that terrorism is something else than a tactic of violence, but a form of intimidation where witnessing is the key factor. Terrorist do not want a lot of people dying, they want a lot of people watching!

The witness is a central figure of this book. I base my arguments in this book on the assumption that no witness terrorism is to be a victim of terrorism since, as Jenkins has argued, terrorist want a lot of people watching, not just a lot of people dead. Those who watch, those who bear witness, are the intended targets of terrorism (Howie 2010: p 7).

Allegorically, the media reproduced not only a biased image of 9/11 but animates, in terms of Baudrillard, a simulacra, to locate the discussion in the angles of celebrity-terrorism. Howie, in this vein, introduces readers in a new theory for understanding this slippery matter, but also reminds that terrorists are in pursuit of the same logic of attention, celebrities do. For a climate functional to terrorism unfolds, we need two things. The first is a division between us and them, but secondly, the possibility to label the others, as evildoers, or as "the axis of evilness".

Howie, who combines an interesting argument with 105 qualitative interviews and stories of life, understands that "the concept of theatre" or trauma-escape is of paramount important to explain why an event, as 9/11, remains enrooted in a site resisting the passing of time. We live in a culture of witnessing which evokes our own vulnerability as city dwellers, but in so doing, many racist practices emerge to point on Muslim collectives. Indeed, one of the main risks consists in "islamophobia", or any other related chauvinist expression of racism. All lies in the same Pandora box. What remains clear, is that without witness terrorism would never exists.

The spectacle of terrorism depends of the co-existence of witnesses, images of terrorism, and – in contemporary times- cities. 9/11 happened, it happened on 11 September 2001 in New York City, Washington DC and a field of Pennsylvania. The image, however, is not bound to this temporal and geographic logic. 9/11 was an atemporal event that can be understood in time and space in apparently unlimited coordinates of temporality and spatiality. It resides in the desert of the real of the contemporary city (p. 60).

Methodologically speaking, he creates a new "phenomenology of terrorism", which is expressed not by their real effects, but to "the recreation of the media", modern consumption emulates. Frightening people not only are Americans but the entire world. Even, so distant cities as Melbourne, or even Buenos Aires are more frightful than American cities. The power of amplification of media terrorism is based on the needs of captivating audience in order for enhancing further profits. Just there, where observers or pundits see terrorism as a great evil for West, Howie sees another point in the discussion. As social field-workers, we will never understand terrorism if we reject the idea that 9/11 was a founding event that forged "a culture of witnessing", which worked as a conduit of terror. Instead of speculating on where the next blow will take place, specialists should explore the effects of terrorism in our daily life. Doubtless, the war on terror declared by Bush`s administration accelerated many of the changes worker unions face today, or even the climate of paranoia, through neoliberal programs are introduced within societies. Howie unfolds an interesting point of view which is combined with higher-erudition on the legacy of Jean Baudrillard, and his theory of Simulacra. Citing the Matrix Saga, Howie sheds light on how 9/11 posed as an "leading event" that obscured many other similar acts of terrorism in other peripheral cities. At some extent, we think that 9/11 was the first declaration of terrorism against our civilization, and not only this, we reply that they "hate us" simply because we living in comfortable conditions dotted of technology and prosperity. Well, confirming this caveat, we are ignoring that the same strongholds of urban zones such as media communication, information, or transport system, is used for terrorism to instil fear. 9/11 represented point of rupture, a gap, between witnessing and a screen culture of terrorism. The culture of celebrities, as it was studied by scholars concerned by dark tourism sites where visitors consume spaces of mass death, endorse notoriety not only to cities whipped by terrorism, but to survivors and even "pseudo-academicians" whose opinions are on the head of journalist corporation. This uncanny obsession for witnessing created a new terrorism-as-celebrity culture:

Through 9/11, the Twin Towers and NYC have attained a renewed celebrity status. In a post 9/11 world, NYC and the Twin Towers share something in common with Paris Hilton, Brad Pitt and Britney Spears – people want to see them, people want to know about them, and when their image appear on television and in other media spaces it is difficult for witnesses to look away (p. 70)

The contribution of Howie to our theme consists in focusing on 9/11 not only as a founding event, but also as the end of causality, which ruled the life of risk society. In earlier decades, scholars as Giddens (1991; 1999; 2009) and Beck (1992; 2002) agree that the net of experts played a vital role bringing certainness to a complex world. Lay-people believed that external threats not only can be controlled by scientific reason, but also risks found and finally mitigated. This raises the question, what has changed with 9/11?.

Over decades, in developed societies the spectorship was disciplined to believe the only truth is what be watched in TV or media entertainment. As Howie puts it, it forged a culture of witnessing which escaped from real (hostile) world. William Irwin (2002) calls the attention to the plot of Matrix, where the mission of Neo to salve human race associates to the fact he should face "the desert of the real", which means avoiding any logic oriented to pleasure-maximization; from Plato onwards philosophy interrogated to the conception of reality and suffering, but after 2000s decade, the needs of pushing imagination towards the borders of reality became stronger. Doubtless, Matrix as 9/11 represents an attempt to re-discuss "the epistemology of western capitalism", appealing to the problem of pain; which still remain unresolved by Protestant ethos. Following this, Carolyn Korsmeyer (2005) sheds light on this problem reminding that Anderson lives a predictable life, with a job, but he feels something is unreal. His quest finally leads to Trinity and Morpheus who do not promise a world of pleasures, but give Neo the possibility to make the right decision. He opts for taking the read pill, breaking in this way, with the illusory realm fabricated by Matrix. Cypher, goes on the opposite direction betraying his friends to leave reality behind. Not only Cypher does not bear the reality but he needs to forget the past. This suggests that the sense of conformity may be very well an election as the needs of discovery. Korsmeyer writes

Cypher has been seduced by food, but he has additional reasons to abandon the fight, for he has come to believe that the world of the matrix is more real than the one outside. (as he puts it, real is just another four-letter word). His conclusion

proceeds not only from his own valuation of pleasurable sense experience but also from a perspective voiced earlier by Morpheus himself: all sense experience is just interpreted stimulation of nerve reception (Korsmeyer, 2005: 50)

In the middle of this mayhem, terrorism first and 9/11 later introduced the germen of distrust in a world where the contours between reality and fake were already blurred. To put this in other terms, West has constructed a wonderland, which served as shelter, to protect denizens from the dangers coming from environment. The same strongholds that determined the supremacy of Europe and US over other cultures, are used now by terrorists to instil panic within these societies. The "culture of witnessing" not only is conducive to terrorism, but to the rise of a new class, "death-seekers" which are obsessed to consume "the others` death".

CONSUMING DEATH: UNDERSTANDING THIS WORLD

It is tempting to say that after pragmatism which posed a serious doubt on the meaning of reality, no other philosophical school developed a culture of scepticism as Americans. Even, Richard Rorty (1982) brilliantly reviewed the consequences of Pragmatism in American Philosophy as a result of the rise and advance of capitalism. Not only Pragmatists and their programs were not interested in considering reality as a philosophical issue, but it was enrooted in the logic of instrumentalization. To put this in bluntly, Rorty clarifies, if we start from a premise that indicates reality only comes from our internal questions, which move the necessary ends towards a convincing answer, it equals to admit the concept of reality cannot be divorced from personal achievements. Not surprisingly, pragmatism was envisaged in a culture that made from meritocracy a cultural mainstream value. He toyed with the idea reality for pragmatists was a question of subjectivism.

In consonance with Rorty, British Geographer, David Harvey, found a correlation between postmodernity and centralization of economies. For him, postmodernism emerged from 1972 oil embargo in post Arab-Israeli war. The question of truth (and reality) as it was understood by Enlightenment, fractured in many individual interpretations of the real. This means that totalizing narratives sets the pace to fragmented view of reality which coincides to the new capitalist modes of production, more decentralized and adjusted to specific segments (Harvey, 1989; 1999). As Helen Longino confirmed, far from being objective scientific knowledge is previously conditioned by contextual dynamics and many factors. From the arrival of Social Darwinism, which crystalized in cloning or DNA manipulation, science played a crucial role in the orchestration of politics and authorities within society. Everything we think or question never escapes to the paradigm fabricated by science. However, this does not mean that the quest for truth equals to "reality". The production of knowledge corresponds with *the cultural environment* while *constitutional values* indicates the acceptance or accuracy of used methodology (Longino, 1990). Paul Virilio (2010) alerts that science has been dominated by the logic of liberal-market, focusing on risks that threaten economic order, instead of discovering the reasons behind of such risks. Nowadays, science and theories, no matter than its family, protect the interest of financial elite, even if current policies compromises the planet. The scientific knowledge produced in XIXth century was aimed at discovering the truth, for enhancing the citizens` quality of life. Rather, this new postmodern science, which receives funds from greatest financial poles of the world, is formatted to research only for investors to gain further profits. Scientists are educated to face, locate and mitigate risks by protecting the interests of profit-organizations (Virilio, 2010).

In times of Thana-Capitalism, the concept of reality as it was imagined by Enlightenment has substantially changed to a commodity sold and exchanged by media. In his book *Diario de Guerra,* French ethnographer Marc Augè (2002) dissects the intersection of terrorism and media. Our obsession for consuming news of disasters and violence is not conducive to truth. Far from understanding the real causes of events, audience is bombarded relentlessly by atemporal images which are organized through the screen. Since reasons and effects of events are blurred, people are far from a real understanding of what they are watching. In consonance with others scholars as Baudrillard, Virilio and Howie, Auge argues convincingly that "the war on terror" inaugurates "an internal globalization" which erodes the conceptual tenets of epistemology respecting to time and space. To put this in bluntly, though we are subject to a great complex of information (coming from different sources), we are unable to distinguish why things happen. Here two assumptions should be done. Even if Auge-Virilio did not recognize it, the solipsism of capitalism to adjust reality to subjective interpretation depended on the success of pragmatism as philosophical project. Secondly, for some reasons, saying in passing, English Speaking countries seem to be culturally concerned by a closed-conception of future. This sentiment of predestination engendered a frightening culture where "otherness" who is not like-me represents a danger for community (Korstanje 2015).

Furthermore, one of the examples of how reality works in times of Thana Capitalism can be very well found in dark tourism sites. In this spaces of consumptions, visitors interrogate on their own death by witnessing others' death. In fact, these spaces of mass-death not only are recycled to accelerate the post recovery times in post disaster contexts, but also confers to community a message that explains why disasters took hit (Seaton, 1996; Miles 2009; Stone, 2012; Raine 2013). However, as Joy Sather-Wagstaff (2011) noted, the transmitted message can be tergiversated whenever politicians are involved. While we are prone to witness an allegory of 9/11, probabilities of being further from the truth turns higher (Korstanje 2016). Visitors of dark tourism sites consume fabricated spectacle of disasters whose messages are aimed at perpetuating the interests of status quo. Here is where our conception presents as a fresh alternative to the epistemological crisis. The concept of reality does not start from discovery as some epistemologists feel, it comes from the figure of death. We will explain better this in the next lines.

Neither visitors of ground-zero keep unfamiliar with the roots of Al-Qaeda, nor "death-seekers" understand the background from where Media operates. This happens simply because in times of Thana-capitalism, life is perceived as a cruel trace where only the strongest ones will survive. The medieval man lived a life fraught of dangers, but he was hopeful, death was a mean towards eternal life. Science has expanded the expectancy of life in modern societies, but at a higher cost: the death of God(s). Following this argument, we may add, in secularized societies, death is contemplated as a sign of weakness, which should be eradicated. At a closer look, modern consumers not only do not want aging but what is unnatural, they resist to die. The concept of life, as we know, is imagined as a great race, where all should struggle against all to be the only one. Since the others` death wakes up a solipsist happiness because one continues in the competition, cooperation is discarded as a potential course of action. Thana-Capitalism, which not only commoditizes death but produces an insensible citizen, was feasible only from Protestant Cosmology where salvation was originally reserved by few souls (who appears in the Book of Life). The sense of predetermination that characterized the epistemology of English speaking countries was conducive to the formation of modern capitalism. Quite aside from this, only once social Darwinism was adopted as a mainstream cultural value, capitalism was replaced by society of risk and later by Thana-Capitalism. The notion of reality was instrumentalised according to "the discovery" of the book of life, which means that technology and science were oriented to future in basis on a precautionary platform. In English speaking nations, understanding was the condition to prevent the worse to come. Unlike Catholics who lives in present, Protestant are co-determined by the future (Korstanje 2015; 2016a).

As this backdrop, the excess of technology opens the doors for the advance of paradoxical conditions of existence. This is the world of Giddens and Beck, known as the *risk society*. If Chernobyl proved something, it was that the same technology used to make safer this world, becomes in the reason of a future nuclear disaster. This cosmology posed a notion of reality which was out of any human control. The inflation of global risk paved the pathways for the rise of a new class of citizens, death seekers. Disasters were not remembered to be prevented by next generations, but commoditized to gain further profits or recycled the effaced lands in post of future capital-investment. Events and their causality blurred into what Baudrillard dubbed as "the Spectacle of Disaster". Death transformed not only the human relations, but situated as the touchstone of a society where material asymmetries enlarged. Examples of this cultural tendency can be found in films as Hunger Games or even in Realities as Big Brother. In these plots, participants do not cooperate simply because they know only one can win. In this climate of social Darwinism, they embrace narcissism. They over-estimate their real probabilities of reaching the glory, welcoming others` death as dotted by the sign of exemplarity. As Protestants, citizens of Thana capitalism were educated in the doctrine of "uphill city" or "theory of exemption", where their world is presented as the best of possible many others worlds. Therefore, consuming death through TV, Media, Films, tourism or any other cultural entertainment industry serves as an ideological instrument to perpetuate the idea of "chosen peoples", where Thana capitalism was constructed from.

Last but not least, one of the postmodern thinkers who has theorized on suffering and capitalism, Slavoj Zizek alludes to the genesis of Christianity as the ideological foundation of submission. In a seminal book, published some years ago, *The Dwarf and the Puppet* Zizek exerts a radical criticism against Christianity, because it is the only religion which promotes "betrayal" as a platform for redemption. In fact, in the Christology, Christ not only should be killed but betrayed by Judas in order for him to become in God. From that moment onwards, Zizek claims, Paul`s doctrine not only cemented the hegemony of Catholic Church but introduced the suffering as a possibility, a precondition to be salved. Since God does not intervene for Job in his tragedy, he still remains hand-tied to do the same for Christ. Christianity evolved thanks to a perverse core, which is enrooted in the ideology of capitalism, where God asks humankind to be abandoned, inverting Job`s disgrace into hopes. Far from what some theologizes precludes, suffering is in Christianity the necessary platform to operate. For example, while academicians disgust from the death of thousands migrants who are pressed to enter in Europe, they need profoundly nothing in capitalist system will be given to change their situation. The policies and programs in favour of migrants, promoted by left-wind scholars not only are cynic, but used to reinforce their own status quo (from a paternalist viewpoint). Well, Zizek (2003; 2016) is one of the first to bring the problem of pain into foreground, and of course for that merits recognition. However, some caveats in his argument should highlighted. First and foremost, as Korstanje (2016) amply showed, the problem of death (suffering) is present in precedent myths than Christ`s Crucifixion. The founding events of Thana Capitalism stems from Noah`s Ark, where God angry from humankind asked Noah to build an ark. God, in this narrative, disposed of a universal flood to eliminate the sin for earth, but forgiving the life of Noah and his family. This act of selection paved the ways for the introduction of social Darwinism, at the same time, Noah was pressed to keep his task in secrecy. Undoubtedly, this mythical event was the first genocide, the original genocide, which divided the world in two, victims and witnesses. Secondly, of course Christ`s martyrdom revitalized this already-existent logic reminding that the Sons of the Lord live forever. At some extent, if the medieval soul waited for death as the necessary step to reach eternity, modern citizens acquired an extreme fear to death. Since the society of risk has gone to a new type, Thana Capitalism, risk any more is the meditator among workers. In Thana Capitalism, the figure of death plays a guiding role mediating between fiction and reality to the extent, consuming others` suffering through Magazines, Cinema, newspapers and so forth, confers an aura of exemplarity to sightseers. Beyond betrayal as Zizek insists, the asymmetries of Thana Capitalism are legitimated by the doctrine of Social Darwinism, where few survives while the rest perishes. Not surprisingly, the intersection of terrorism and media goes under the same logic. While news on terrorism, migrants who are found dead at European coasts shock us, nobody can let witnessing these tragedies.

ORIENTATION FOR FUTURE RESEARCH

In this difficult word, what can we do with mass migration?. Rodanthi Tzanelli calls the attention to the problem of Thana-Tourism as a reified form of former colonialism. Doubtless, if terrorism is sold as a form of entertainment for millions of rich citizens in first world, the inaction of central nations provokes a forced migration from Syria towards Europe in quest of better opportunities to survive. Tzanelli recognizes that dark tourism surfaced over decades as a trend of leisure consumption precisely in zones where promises of development diluted. Exegetes of Capitalism has serious limitation to explain why some few gathers huge profits while many others are pressed to live with basic condition of subsistence unmet. It is important not to lose the sigh that the expansion of capitalism worldwide, produced zones of extreme poverty and ghettoization, which today are exploited by international tourism. The inflation of different risks which oscillates from natural disasters to terrorism, evinces that the holiday-making and leisure practices as tourism are next to disappear but paradoxically, dark tourism still revitalizing the gift-exchange process that made capitalism feasible. In retrospect, the instrument of surveillance orchestrated by capitalism appeal to the metaphor of *undesired guests* where working-migrants are stereotyped as zombies, monsters, terrorists or even viruses which may very well threaten the current civilized social order. Since the concept of risk which is theatricalized by the film-related industries allows the imposition of allegories to see the capitalist ethos as one of the best possible worlds, entrepreneurship surfaces as a vehicle to invest first world citizens of an exceptional aura. She holds the following interesting thesis, slum and dark tourism are central places where spectorship aesthetically enlarges the gap between have and have-nots. Expiating their burdens to be part of a society which exploited "Others", dark tourists reify a commoditized version of colonialism tailored for white and western subjectivities. This exactly represents the dystopia of fiction, which covers the reasons why Colonialism subordinated the periphery to an economy of exploitation (Tzanelli 2016). She masterfully anticipates to a new concept to understand capitalism, where death plays a vital role mediating between citizens and their institutions. As Korstanje puts it, these are times of indifference and extreme competition, it is Thana Capitalism and its concept of reality never escapes from screens (Korstanje 2016a; 2016b).

CONCLUSION

Epistemologically speaking, we have in this chapter discussed the notion of reality though the lens of postmodern theorists as Jean Baudrillard, Marc Auge, Paul Virilio and so forth. We coined the term "Thana capitalism" to explain the uncanny obsession for consuming death in order to remind how special we (the witnesses) are. Centered on the thesis that the consumption of disasters, and human suffering where migrations offer fertile ground, accelerates the already existent decomposition of social ties, leading society towards a climate of social Darwinism and solipsism. The consuming of others` suffering seems to be something more complex than a sadist trend as psychologists suggest, but a clear indicator the mode of production of capitalism are changed into new forms. Take the example of our grand-parents who travelled to paradisiacal destination to enjoy from their holidays. Their concept of apollonian beautiness which was associated to landscapes has been replaced by new emergent segments, where visitors are fascinated by episodes of mass-death, suffering, pain and desolation. New uncanny destinations offer visitors to gaze cities effaced by quakes or any other disasters, abandoned prions, coasts where thousands of migrants are found dead or even camps of concentrations refurbished in museums. The society in Thana Capitalism has developed a pathological resistance to die, which ushers it into happiness for others` pain. In this context, the causality of events is not significant any-longer unless it can be transformed in a great show for richer classes. An ideological reminder pour classes do not perish because the condition of production turned unequal, but they lack of the necessary eagerness to engage with progress.

REFERENCES

Akrivopoulou, C. M. (Ed.). (2012). *Human Rights and Risks in the Digital Era: Globalization and the Effects of Information Technologies: Globalization and the Effects of Information Technologies*. Hershey, PA: IGI Global.

Augé, M. (2002). *Diario de Guerra: el mundo después del 11 de Septiembre*. Barcelona: Gedisa.

Baudrillard, J. (1994). *Simulacra and simulation*. University of Michigan press.

Baudrillard, J. (1995). *The Gulf War did not take place*. Indianapolis, IN: Indiana University Press.

Baudrillard, J. (2001). The spirit of terrorism. *Telos*, *121*, 134-142.

Baudrillard, J. (2006). Virtuality and Events: The hell of power. *Baudrillard Studies*, *3*(2), 1–4.

Baudrillard, J., & Evans, A. B. (1991). Simulacra and Science Fiction (Simulacres et science-fiction). *Science Fiction Studies*, *1*, 309–313.

Bauman, Z., & Lyon, D. (2013). *Liquid surveillance: A conversation*. New York: John Wiley & Sons.

Beck, U. (1992). *Risk society: Towards a new modernity* (Vol. 17). London: Sage.

Beck, U. (2002). The terrorist threat world risk society revisited. *Theory, Culture & Society*, *19*(4), 39–55. doi:10.1177/0263276402019004003

Beck, U. (2009). *World at risk*. Cambridge, UK: Polity Press.

Bourdieu, P., & Wacquant, D. (1992). *An Invitation to reflective Sociology*. Chicago, IL: Chicago University Press.

De Landa, M. (2006). *A new Philosophy of Society: assembling Theory and social complexity*. London: Bloomsbury.

Durkheim, E. (2014). *The rules of sociological method: and selected texts on sociology and its method*. New York, NY: Simon and Schuster.

Giddens, A. (1991). *Modernity and self-identity: Self and society in the late modern age*. Stanford, CA: Stanford University Press.

Giddens, A. (1999). Risk and responsibility. *The Modern Law Review*, *62*(1), 1–10. doi:10.1111/1468-2230.00188

Giddens, A. (2009). *The politics of climate change*. Cambridge, UK: Polity Press.

Harvey, D. (1989). *The postmodern condition: An enquiry into the origins of cultural change*. Oxford, UK: Blackwell.

Harvey, D. (1999). Time-space compression and the postmodern condition. *Modernity: Critical Concepts*, *4*, 98–118.

Hobbes, T. (2006). *Leviathan*. London: A&C Black.

Hobbes, T. (2013). *Elements of law, natural and political*. Abingdon, UK: Routledge.

Howie, L. (2010). *Terror on the Screen Witnesses and the Re-animation of 9/11 as Image-event, Popular Culture and Pornography*. Washington, DC: New Academia Publishing.

Innerarity, D. (2013). Power and knowledge: The politics of the knowledge society. *European Journal of Social Theory*, *16*(1), 3–16. doi:10.1177/1368431012468801

Irwin, W. (2005). Computers, Caves and Oracle: Neo and Socrates. In W. Irwin (Ed.), *The Matrix and Philosophy* (pp. 5–15). Chicago, IL: Open Court.

Kellner, D. (2005). Baudrillard, Globalization and Terrorism: Some comments in recent adventures of the Image and Spectable on the occasion of Baudrillard's 75th birthday. *Baudrillard Studies*, *2*(1), 1–18.

Korsmeyer, C. (2005). Seeing, Believing, touching, Truth. In W. Irwin (Ed.), *The Matrix and Philosophy* (pp. 41–52). Chicago, IL: Open Court.

Korstanje, M. E. (2015). *A Difficult World: examining the roots of Capitalism*. New York, NY: Nova Science Pubs.

Korstanje, M. E. (2016a). *The Rise of Thana Capitalism and tourism*. Abingdon, UK: Routledge.

Korstanje, M. E. (2016b). *Tourism and Terrorism*. New Delhi: Studium Press LCC.

Lévi-Strauss, C. (2013). *Myth and meaning*. London: Routledge.

Locke, J. (1988). *Locke: Two treatises of government student edition*. Cambridge, UK: Cambridge University Press. doi:10.1017/CBO9780511810268

Longino, H. (1990). *Science as a Social Knowledge*. Princeton, NJ: Princeton University Press.

Marx, K. (1973). *Grundrisse: Foundation of the critique of political economy.Trans. Martin Nicolaus*. Harmondsworth, UK: Penguin.

Mauss, M. (2000). *The gift: The form and reason for exchange in archaic societies (No. 378)*. New York: WW Norton & Company.

Miles, W. (2002). Auschwitz: Museum interpretation and Darker Tourism. *Annals of Tourism Research*, *29*(4), 1175–1178. doi:10.1016/S0160-7383(02)00054-3

Raine, R. (2013). A Dark Tourism spectrum. *International Journal of Culture, Tourism and Hospitality Research*, *7*(3), 242-256.

Rorty, R. (1982). *Consequences of pragmatism: Essays, 1972-1980*. Minneapolis, MN: University of Minnesota Press.

Sahlins, M. (2013). *Culture and practical reason*. Chicago, IL: University of Chicago Press.

Sather-Wagstaff, J. (2011). *Heritage that hurts: Tourists in the memoryscapes of September 11* (Vol. 4). California, CA: Left Coast Press.

Seaton, A. V. (1996). Guided by the dark: From thanatopsis to thanatourism. *International Journal of Heritage Studies*, *2*(4), 234–244. doi:10.1080/13527259608722178

Skoll, G. (2014). *The Dialectics of Social thought*. New York, NY: Palgrave-Macmillan. doi:10.1057/9781137387066

Stone, P. R. (2012). Dark tourism and significant other death: Towards a model of mortality mediation. *Annals of Tourism Research*, *39*(3), 1565–1587. doi:10.1016/j.annals.2012.04.007

Sugden, R. (2005). *The Economics of Rights, Cooperation and Welfare*. Hampshire, UK: Palgrave Macmillan. doi:10.1057/9780230536791

Sunstein, C. R. (2003). Terrorism and probability neglect. *Journal of Risk and Uncertainty*, *26*(2), 121–136. doi:10.1023/A:1024111006336

Sunstein, C. R. (2005). *Laws of fear: Beyond the precautionary principle* (Vol. 6). Cambridge, UK: Cambridge University Press. doi:10.1017/CBO9780511790850

Virilio, P. (2010). *The University of Disaster*. Cambridge, UK: Polity Press.

ADDITIONAL READING

Biocca, M. (2005). Risk communication and the precautionary principle. *Human and Ecological Risk Assessment: An International Journal*, *11*(1), 261–266. doi:10.1080/10807030590920097

Bowman, M. S., & Pezzullo, P. C. (2009). Whats so darkabout dark tourism?: Death, tours, and performance. *Tourist Studies*, *9*(3), 187–202. doi:10.1177/1468797610382699

Brunsma, D., & Picou, J. S. (2008). Disasters in the twenty-first century: Modern destruction and future instruction. *Social Forces*, *87*(2), 983–991. doi:10.1353/sof.0.0149

Bryant, W. C. (1948). The Genesis of Thanatopsis. *The New England Quarterly*, *21*(2), 163–184. doi:10.2307/361747

Cohen, E. H. (2011). Educational dark tourism at an in populo site: The Holocaust museum in Jerusalem. *Annals of Tourism Research*, *38*(1), 193–209. doi:10.1016/j.annals.2010.08.003

Debord, G. (2012). *Society of the Spectacle*. London: Bread and Circuses Publishing.

Hofstadter, R. (1963). *Anti-intellectualism in American Life.(3. Print.)* (Vol. 713). New York, NY: Vintage books.

Jameson, F. (2002). The dialectics of disaster. *The South Atlantic Quarterly*, *101*(2), 297–304. doi:10.1215/00382876-101-2-297

Kelly, K. (2009). *Out of control: The new biology of machines, social systems, and the economic world*. New York, NY: Basic Books.

Klein, N. (2007). *The shock doctrine: The rise of disaster capitalism*. New York, NY: Macmillan.

Korstanje, M. E. (2011). Detaching the elementary forms of dark-tourism. *Anatolia*, *22*(3), 424–427. doi:10.1080/13032917.2011.620800

Korstanje, M. E. (2014). Chile helps Chile: Exploring the effects of earthquake Chile 2010. *International Journal of Disaster Resilience in the Built Environment*, *5*(4), 380–390. doi:10.1108/IJDRBE-01-2012-0002

Korstanje, M. E., Tzanelli, R., & Clayton, A. (2014). Brazilian World cup 2014: Terrorism, tourism, and social conflict. *Event Management*, *18*(4), 487–491. doi:10.3727/152599514X14143427352391

Lennon, J. J., & Foley, M. (1999). Interpretation of the unimaginable: The US Holocaust Memorial Museum, Washington, DC, and dark tourism. *Journal of Travel Research*, *38*(1), 46–50. doi:10.1177/004728759903800110

Mead, G. H. (2009). *Mind, self, and society: From the standpoint of a social behaviourist* (Vol. 1). Chicago, IL: University of Chicago press.

Nassar, J. R. (2009). *Globalization and terrorism: The migration of dreams and nightmares*. New York, NY: Rowman & Littlefield Publishers.

Reijnders, S. (2009). Watching the Detectives Inside the Guilty Landscapes of Inspector Morse, Baantjer and Wallander. *European Journal of Communication*, *24*(2), 165–181. doi:10.1177/0267323108101830

Tzanelli, R. (2013). *Olympic Ceremonialism and the performance of national character*. Hampshire: Palgrave-Macmillan. doi:10.1057/9781137336323

White, L., & Frew, E. (2013). *Dark Tourism: place and identity: managing and interpreting dark places*. London: Routledge.

Žižek, S. (2003). *The puppet and the dwarf: The perverse core of Christianity*. Cambridge, MA: MIT Press.

Žižek, S. (2016). Is God dead, unconsciouss, Evil, Impotent, Stupid… or just Counter-factual? *International Journal of Zizek Studies.*, *10*(1), 1–31.

KEY TERMS AND DEFINITIONS

Media: Combination of media dispositiffs and technologies aimed at producing and disseminating information to an audience.

Migration: Physical movement where subject looks something which cannot be found at home. Many migrants abandon their nations in quest of better opportunities of life.

Reality: Denotes the state of things as they actually exist beyond the hegemony of interpretation or appearances.

Suffering: Similarly to pain, is an emotional disposition of displeasure associated with the perception of harm.

Terrorism: Violent crime defined by the use of illegal force against innocent civilians, who are hosted to negotiate with stronger state.

Thana Capitalism: It is a new stage of capitalism where death situates as the main commodity that keeps the economic system functioning.

Chapter 2
Refugees or Migrants:
Fascistisation and Punishment

Anastasia Pitsou
Aristotle University of Thessaloniki, Greece

ABSTRACT

As refugees / immigrants are forced to cross the border, the member states of European Union are trying to manage mobile populations or the new labor force in various ways. Under the over-accumulation crisis, what kind of policies are drawn; or are denizens be punished as they question the stability of borders, state sovereign and supranational policies? When social contradictions are intense, in bourgeois democracy human rights are shrunk and the process of fascistisation is activated. Ultimately, maybe it is noticeable to understand that refugees /migrants become mutatis mutandis an allegorical figure of Muselmanner.

INTRODUCTION

Jamel is a tiny German village, where a street sign ab initio declares in gothic script that this community is "free, social, and national". In this village with little welcome for strangers the residents are members or voters of the far- right NPD political party (National Democratic Party of Germany), which was founded as the only significant patriotic force, as successor to the German Reich Party (Paterson, 2010). A signpost proclaims the direction of Adolf Hitler's birthplace, children give Hitler's salutes in the street, guests sing "Hitler is my Fuehrer", photos of German Jewish or woods are used as targets for shooting practice and anti- Nazi couple live under police protection after burning down their barn (Popp, 2011 & Anti-Nazi couple's barn, 2015).

DOI: 10.4018/978-1-5225-2817-3.ch002

In February 2016, members of the German neo-nazi organization Der Dritte Weg, in which participate former members of NPD and of Nazi organization "Freies Netz Sud", visited the offices of Golden Dawn and the Greek parliament not only for Imia crisis[1] anniversary but mostly for anniversary of Adolf Hitler's ascent to the Chancellery (The flag of the German Reich, 2016 & Der III. Weg, 2016). During their visit, they paid homage at nazi soldiers in German military cemetery Dionysus – Rapentozis and the next day, they raised next to the flag of their party the flag of Third Reich in Acropolis (German neo-Nazis raised, 2016 & Der III. Weg, 2016). Simultaneously, the movement of Patriotic Europeans Against the Islamisation of the West, (Pegida) protested in Dresden for the dangers associated with Europe refugee crisis and for the entry of Islamic extremist, while counter-demonstrators rallied under the motto "Solidarity instead of exclusion" and "No Place for Nazis", in many cities across Europe (Anti-Islam movement, 2016).

What is the meaning of "refugee crisis"? The use of the term crisis refers to a governmental category, to the role of the state as manager of fear- which expressed at collective level by fear of terrorism and by sense of insecurity (Katsiaounis, 2016) - of capital, concealing class characteristics. Moving to Security State, securitization as a tactic creates the conditions under which subjects receive disproportionate amount of attention compared to real cause of human repression. Thus, in "disciplinary societies", apparatus of security and juridico-legal techniques are used not as mechanism of preventing, but as mechanism of governance to the direction shown profitable (Foucault, 2009:45).

According to Frantz Fanon in his book "The Wretched of the Earth":

Let us not lose time in useless laments and sickening mimicry. Leave this Europe where they are never to stop talking of man, yet massacres him/her at every one of its street corners, at every corner of the world. For centuries it has stifled virtually the whole of humanity in the name of a so-called "spiritual adventure"... Look at them today swaying between atomic and spiritual disintegration...Europe undertook the leadership of the world with ardour, cynicism and violence (Fanon, 2004:235).

YESTERDAY REFUGEES, TOADY MIGRANTS, TOMORROW?

The United Union Convention in Geneva 1951, the recommendations of the United Nations High Commissioner for Refugees and of the Council of Europe are now largely incorporated into European Union Law (Palazzani, 2012:6). According to Article 1 of the Convention, as amended by the 1967 Protocol, defines a refugee as this: "a person who owing to wellfounded fear of being persecuted for reasons of race, religion, nationality, membership of a particular social group or political opinion, is outside the country of his nationality and is unable or, owing to such fear, is unwilling to avail himself of the protection of that country; or who, not having a nationality and being outside the country of his former habitual residence as a result of such events, is unable or, owing to such fear, is unwilling to return to it"(UNHCR,2010). Many states have incorporate the UNHCR's position that the source of threat of persecution has minor importance[2] and that cannot be restricted to persecution coming only from the state institutions or state organs (Maiani, 2008 & UNHCR, 2001).

Refugees should not be identified with alien who can enjoy diplomatic protection from the country of nationality, with stateless persons, with refugee sur place, with crypto-refugees and with migrants (Naskou- Perraki, 1991:62, 63). Migrants pass the borders to work and reside permanently or temporarily in a country other than their country of birth or citizenship and they have always the possibility to return (Inter-Parliamentary Union, 2015). The 1951 Convention was drawn up in the wake of Second World War, thus, this definition of refugee could be characterized as generic, but de facto it could not predict and include new categories of refugees like boat-people, massive refugee movements, refugees in orbit (Naskou- Perraki, 1991:89, 90).

The 1951 Convention and the 1967 Protocol are not mentioned in the process by which Member States are obliged to recognize refugee status (UNHCR, 2015:11). Each national legislation are responsible for setting the stages, the demanded guarantees mainly on individual basis. In cases of mass movements of refugees, the United Nations High Commissioner for Refugees put into force the process of collective recognition (group-based refugees), for example when war breaks out in country of origin, UNHCR often provides refugee status to members of a particular group on a prima facie basis (UNHCR, 2015:12). However the European Union (EU) established common rules for all Member States in providing temporary protection to persons fleeing their country, in case of mass outputs of displaced persons. The Council Directive 2001/55/EC mentioned in Article 1 that "The purpose of this Directive is to establish minimum standards for giving temporary protection in the event of a mass influx of displaced persons from third countries who are unable to return to their country of origin and to promote a balance of effort between Member States in receiving and bearing the consequences of receiving such persons" (Perrakis, Mastakas, 2005:561) and "Persons enjoying temporary protection shall be granted: a. the right to engage in employed or self-employed activities, and in educational opportunities for adults, vocational training and practical workplace experience, b. the right to have access to suitable accommodation, c. the right to receive necessary assistance in terms of social welfare and means of subsistence if they do not have sufficient resources, as well as medical care, d. the right for children under 18 years of age to access the education system under the same conditions as nationals of the host Member State (European Union: Council of the European Union, 2001)".

One of the most important principles in the 1951 Convention is non-refoulement (Art33), according which "no contracting state shall expel or return ("refouler") a refugee in any manner whatsoever to the frontiers of territories where his life or freedom would be threatened on account of his race, religion, nationality, membership of a particular social group or political opinion" (Naskou- Perraki, 1991:152). This basic provision constitutes part of others conventions at global and regional level, as United Nations Declaration on Territorial Asylum (1967,Art3), UN International Convention against the Taking of Hostages (1979), Hague Agreement Relating to Refugee Seamen (1957,Art10), Convention Governing the Specific Aspects of Refugee Problems in Africa (1969,Art11), American Human Rights Convention (1969,Art22), Caracas Convention on Territorial Asylum (1954, Art3), European Convention on Extradition (1957,Art3), European Convention on the Suppression of Terrorism (1977), Resolution on Asylum to Persons in Danger of Persecution (1967), Status and Treatment of Refugees- AALCC (1966,Art3). However, this provision is relativized many times and finally is not implemented as specified by the 1951 Convention. This means that apart from phenomena of abuse incidents and rights violations, it is obviously that institutional decisions are infected by fascistisation seeds.

Particularly, juxtaposition and perusal of different incident reports shed light on Greek and European tactic -among others- constitutes of using weapons in order to stop smugglers' boats, sometimes injuring or killing migrants/refugees (Campbell, 2016). These reports refer to the 20-month period, exactly from May 2014 to December 2015 (Hubert, 2016). Under the 1951 Convention, the contracting states undertake not to send refugees to a country, where there is a real threat for her/him, even if this country is not the one of origin. Making reference to the case of M.S.S. v. Belgium (Application No. 30696/09) and Greece, in the Case Sharifi and others v. Greece and Italy (Application No 16643/09), the Court also held clearly that "If a state carries out a return, it is obliged to make sure that the country of destination offers satisfactory guarantees in respect of the law and the rights of individuals protected by the Convention, including the Principle of Non-Refoulement"(Case of Sharifi and Others v. Italy and Greece, 2014). Moreover, the Thrace Court of Appeal has delivered convictions for illegal entry of foreigners such as the 405/23 July 1986, the 563 / 14.11.1988, the 304 / 05.24.1989, according to which most defendants had declared that they came to Greece for political reasons (Naskou-Perraki, 1991:180-182).

Equally important events of the 1951 Treaty infringement considered the meeting in Zagreb and the EU-Turkey agreement. In Zagreb, on 18 February 2016, the Heads of Police Services of the Republic of Austria, of the Republic of Slovenia, of the Republic of Croatia, of the Republic of Serbia, of the Republic of Macedonia, decided to adopt measures in order to close essentially Western Balkans Route, from where refugees/ migrants were passing (ecre, 2016). Thus, among other they underlined that "on humanitarian grounds, the entry of third country nationals may be authorized to those persons who do not fulfil the conditions referred, but who are arriving from war-torn areas and are in need of international protection (for example from Syria, Iraq) provided that they can prove their nationality and are in possession of the registration form issued by Greek authorities (Joint Statement of Heads of Police Services, 2016)". Essentially, these state authorities rejected refugees based on their nationality, namely they introduced a discriminatory border policy, only allowing Syrian, Iraqi to enter their borders (Prifti, 2016).

The relativization of the concept of refugee in the sequel reproduces a dominant binary "deserving / undeserving" discourse based on prioritization of certain nationalities. On 7 March 2016, EU heads of state or government held a meeting with Turkey in order to strengthen their cooperation to address the refugee and migration issues. The EU-Turkey joint action plan constitutes "a historic blow to rights (Amnesty International, 2016) ". According to this agreement, which reinforces the democratic deficit in the EU, as the European Parliament has not been consulted for the sake of political efficiency, its main points are considered the following (European Council, Foreign Affairs& International Relations, 2016): Firstly, the return of "irregular migrants" crossing from Turkey to islands after March 20, secondly, the "one for one deal" principle, namely, "for every Syrian being returned to Turkey from Greek islands, another Syrian will be resettled from Turkey to the EU, taking into account the UN Vulnerability Criteria the EU. Given priority for resettlement in the EU to Syrians from Turkey and not from Greece, since the EU gives priority to migrants who have not previously entered, or attempted to enter (European Council, Foreign Affairs& International Relations, 2016)". Thirdly, preventing measures for reducing of sans papiers' arrivals from Turkey to EU and fourthly, recognition of Turkey as a safe country. Last and not least, all "irregular migrants" will be held in closed detention centers, and asylum seekers will be accommodated in open reception centers (European Commission, Factsheet on the EU-Turkey Agreement, 2016). It is obviously under this agreement, the overlapping of two distinct legal categories "migrants" and "refugees", as a vast majority of those 'irregular migrants' mentioned are actually asylum seekers from Syria.

THE GRADUALLY FASCISTISATION

Process of fascistisasion is developed inside bourgeois democracy during the period of economic crisis. This process is associated with dynamic sharpening and aggravation of contradictions between the dominant class and the dominated class (Poulatzas, 2006:77). However, apart from economic level, these contradictions expand and crystallize to the political and ideological level. Thus, fascistisation is not derived only from economic crisis, but also from political and ideological crisis (Poulatzas, 2006:78). Namely, class contradictions cause repercussions in the heart of the state apparatus. The process of fascistisation related with the State of Emergency, under which the legalization of the delegalisation is actualized and rules are formatted as an exception of economic and social regulation.

Political crisis, which resides in social relations, acquires different aspects of institutional dysfunctions through the state apparatus (Poulatzas, 2008: 295). Specifically, the state form of government remains presidential parliamentary democracy, but some serious institutional changes are evident. For example, there is a representation gap between parties in power and citizens, because parties do not comply with the will of the people and they are unable to transfer represented people's requests to parliament. Parties in power are concerned only with economic problems, by circumventing even constitutional rights due to the condition of emergency, the financial crisis. Thus, both intense financiarisation of constitutional function and bourgeois democracy and circumventing rights entail militarization, consolidating methods of state repression and strengthening bureaucratic decision-making networks in the name of national interest.

Economic and political crisis articulates a crisis of dominant ideology (Poulatzas, 2008:301). The intense contradictions among different segments of the bourgeoisie contributes usually to the use of the parliamentary solution of "cooperation" in order to achieve greater assault against the working class. The large intensity of relation capital- labor seeks a formation of social democratic loyalism with neo-Keynesian logic and nationalist rhetoric, as a determinant factor to proletariat's defeat. Thus, gradually this cooperation submit to the interest of bourgeois class segments, to imperatives of neoliberal policy and further it disabuse proletariat's delusions, causing extensive disaffection. During the process of fascistisation, passivation is obviously reflected through every action and aspect of life, because after so many defeats of proletariat's mass political action, political reactions could be characterized as defensives, frangmentals and non assertives (Poulatzas, 2006:197).

The process of fascistization cannot mean that it will end up with mathematical, linear path to the establishment of a fascist regime, but certainly it removes constraints of the nationalist rhetoric and violence. Dominant narrative of national unity, which is structured anew in front of the "danger of cultural alteration" with the refugee/

migrant entry, attempts to homogenize the already fragmented social relations and to dampen the class contradictions. Nevertheless, it is essentially to underline that the naturalization of racism occurs as a social relationship which is produced from the capitalist mode of production, and it is combined with supremacy of dominant nationalism identity and patriarchy. Under post-political biopower (Kioupkiolis, 2014:143-158), it is necessary in this case to discuss fascistisation elements pertaining to enclosures, Islamophobia and rape culture.

ENCLOSURES

According the "Schengen acquis", article 5 entitled "Entry conditions for third-country nationals", refers to the entry prerequisites of third country nationals. Among the others it defines the following: "a. they are in possession of valid travel document or documents authorizing them to cross the border, b. they are in possession of a valid visa" (Official Journal of the European Union, 2006). Also, article 7 clarifies that "on entry and exit, third- country nationals shall be subject to thorough checks" and article 12 conjoins virtually asylum policy with the policy related to "irregular" migration, namely "The main purpose of border surveillance shall be to prevent unauthorized border crossings, to counter cross- border criminality and to take measures against persons who have crossed the border illegally" (Official Journal of the European Union, 2006). Thus, the Greek immigration policy, developed in the axis of a wider European policy, linked to concepts such as policing, security, crime, while leaving narrow margin for an approach based on human rights.

Since 2012, the Greek authorities strengthened the Greek- Turkish land border, which at that time was the main point of entry migrants/refugees 'irregularly' into Greek territory and tried to reduce the population residing 'illegally' in the country (Vafiadis, 2014). On the occasion of statements by European Commission Representative, M. Cercone, about the Greek border fence in Evros with Turkey[3], the Minister of Citizen Protection, C. Papoutsis, mentioned the following: "The Greek Government decided on 06th of September to fund the construction of the fence from the National Public Investment Program" (Hellenic Republic Citizen Protection Ministry, 2012). Along with the construction of the border fence was completed in December 2012 and cost 5.5 million Euros, authorities used enhanced electronic surveillance, including thermal cameras and helicopters and implemented the "Aspida" and "Xenios Zeus" operations (UNHR, 2013)[4]. Certainly, these policies infringe on the Geneva Convention 1951 and abuse human rights because are based on logic of migrant/refugee entry deterrence and on zero tolerance of those who put into question the state sovereignty. Prohibiting entrance to refugees in a country is linked with the non-refoulement principle (Naskou- Perraki, 1991:156), "whether it was a question of closing the frontier to a refugee who asked admittance, or of turning him back after he had crossed the frontier, or even expelling him after he had been admitted to residence in the territory, the problem was more or less the same" (UNHCR, 2007). In December 2013, the leader of the Greek police N. Papagianopoulos characteristically was reported to have said: "We need to make their life unbearable" (Fotiadis, 2015:37). However, after closing the Evros, migrants/ refugees turned to Aegean Sea passages.

Because of massive migrants/refugees arrivals, EU countries decided to upgrade the Eurosur system and the role of Frontex, to create a high tech Panopticon system, strengthening the security industry (Fotiadis, 2015:55, 56), and some of them proceeded to closure their borders. Moreover, apart from the militarization of borders, some EU countries made efforts and agreements with countries outside EU, identified as transit country, in order to establish in their territory new control structures about the entry of migrants/ refugees (Fotiadis, 2015:70, 71). Essentially, the golden rule of each state power is condensed to following: the moment the sanctity of national sovereignty and of the Europeans colonial powers are desecrated by passage the borders, then "the sanctity could be only restored with the offender's death (Menninghaus & Gunn, 2008:35)" or punishment. Therefore, system of the legal code capture a binary division between the permitted and the prohibited, and a coupling between prohibited action and punishment (Foucault, 2009:20). Migrants, as offenders, are under legal code and out of it at the same time, but in the latter case, are punished and are put under surveillance. This means that migrants at the same time included and excluded.

While the traditional sense of enclosure is defined as the transformation of common land into private property, primitive accumulation remains crucial to how capitalist system works, which based on division, on reconfiguration and on demolition of various forms of public life. Enclosure can be designated as "a process of erosion and seizure of the commons" (Sevilla- Buitrago, 2015: 829-1100). However, it is not only that "the price of the supposedly unified world of capital is the brutal division of human existence into regions separated by police dogs, bureaucratic controls, naval patrols, barbed wire and expulsions (Badiou, 2008)", but also the relationship of the space must be linked with the dispossession process. This process seeks to "subsume and homogenize diverse non-commodified, self-managed social spaces under capitalist value-regimes (Sevilla- Buitrago, 2015: 829-1100)".

In this particular case, on May the Greek authorities completed the operation of evacuation from Idomeni, from the hotel Xara and from EKO gas station, where refugees were settled in makeshift cities (Labropoulou & Hunt, 2016). These refugees were transferred to organized structures operating in former industrial sites as migration transit accommodation centers or centers of deportation. For this operation to take place 30 platoons of YAT in cooperation with groups of YMET, Groups of

Crime Prevention and Suppression (OPKE), plainclothes officers from the Security Services of Northern Greece and helicopter Police were deployed (Souliotis, 2016). Homogenization of a social situation, which is element fascistisation, contains the idea that there is no life outside the institutional recognition and therefore actions of migrants must obey to institutional guidelines.

The "successful" police operation has contributed to the preservation and strengthening of national identity, and the state apparatus showed that activated effectively, as authorities ensure security inside the country and defend the interests of Greece and European Union, guarding maritime borders in cooperation with NATO[5] and Frontex. For a refugee to be recognized institutionally and be subject of rights and duties, must be determined to pass the physical boundaries and fences, to have physical and mental strength, to face the administrative enclosures[6], to submit to state violence and to discipline under the depreciation of their dignity. It is obviously that during the process of fascistisation authorities can used the threat of death or of imprisonment in order to force them to fall to their knees (Menninghaus & Gunn, 2008:79). Thus, after devaluing ignominiously labor force of refugees, bourgeois class "will use them as a tool of their trade expansion (Mixail, 1999:41)". Essentially, the development of a national-racist logic is used to support national capitalist interests, excluding and including refugees/migrants as cheap labor force.

ISLAMOPHOBIA

Islamophobia means anti-Muslim racism, as a national dominant west identity imposed on group of people in order to widening their power by defining a scapegoat who be under exclusion from the resources and rights (Bayrakli & Hafez, 2016:7). Thus, it is attributed negative content to Muslim identity and it reproduces stereotypes which are reflected in using descriptive words like fanatic, violent, phallocrat, obscurantist or irrationalist. Particularly, governmental officers, assisted by willing commentators, analysts, etc., do not lose opportunity to pinpoint Muslims as the number one threat to our lives, reinforcing the process of fascistisation. Apart from the known attacks of "inconceivable enemy [7]", ISIS, in Paris, Brussels, Lebanon, Libya, in Buckland, in Turkey, Egypt, Yemen etc - on support that behind every woman with headscarf and each immigrant or refugee hiding a possibility of attack by Muslim jihadists. For example, the Greece's defense minister P. Kammenos accused the EU and warned of massive influx of irregular immigrants and jihadists in Europe, if Greece collapsed (Waterfield, 2015) and a year later adds that he try to "build stability shaft against Islamic fundamentalism" in the Mediterranean (The Athens News Agency - Macedonian Press Agency, 2016). Moreover, others thought that "the new migratory flows contain a great risk, the Islamization of Greece (Fragkoulis,

2016)" and "through refugees Islam threatens to alter the Christian synthesis of the Greek and European populations (Bayrakli & Hafez, 2016:208)".

The plan for the construction of central mosque in Athens dates back to 1890, since when there have been at least five laws on this issue (Bayrakli & Hafez 2016:205). Due to intense debate in the public sphere[8] and in parliament and also due to legal and bureaucracy complications, the implementation of this project has been blighted. Thus, Muslims as trying to find places to worship, go into private home or rent places. Javed Aslam, president of the main Pakistani community organization, raised a question: "If the Greek constitution says everyone has religious rights, where are my rights (Hague, 2016)"? Indeed, according to Article 13§1, 2 of the Greek constitution: "Freedom of religious conscience is inviolable. The enjoyment of civil rights and liberties does not depend on the individual's religious beliefs. All known religions shall be free and their rites of worship shall be performed unhindered and under the protection of the law. The practice of rites of worship is not allowed to offend public order or the good usages. Proselytism is prohibited (The Constitution of Greece (1975/1986/2001/2008)". Providing that the law protect the freedom of religion and the rites of Islam worship is not offend public order or the good usages, why have the authorities been so far incapable to implement the construction of central mosque?

Greece "recognizes only one minority, the Muslim religious minority in Western Thrace, which is protected by the terms of the Lausanne Peace Treaty of 1923" (Organization for Security and Co-operation in Europe & Office for Democratic Institutions and Human Rights, 2009:17). Since electoral law 1907/1990, the introduction of three per cent (3%) threshold, namely a minimum of 3% of the national votes that a party needs to receive in order to be entitled to any parliamentary representation (Lyrintzis & Nikolakopoulos, 2004:93). The aim of this prerequisite is not only to avoid the parliamentary fragmentation, thus strengthening governmental stability, but also the presence of independent Muslim candidates in Western Thrace (Spyropoulos, 2006:187). This means that Muslim candidates could be Member of Parliament only with the major parties, and not as local/minority party like 'Independent Trust List" and Friendship and Equality Party or as independent candidate (Küçükcan, 1999:63). It is no coincidence that nowadays immigration minister Mouzalas declares that in region of Thrace the houses rental project for the settlement of refugees will not be implemented, because this area is characterized as a "sensitive area" (The Ministry Immigration, 2016). It is obviously, that authorities seek to avoid the augmentation of percentage Muslims in the region 'for reasons of the national interest'.

When a national community builds and reproduces stereotypes focusing religious and cultural practices of a minority, then there is the possibility of being confronted with institutionalized discrimination or institutional fascistisation. Nationalism -because of colonial imaginary supremacy- conform to the defense of Western identity in visage of the alleged clash of civilizations (Traverso, 2011:20). For example the threat of the Islamic headscarf, of minarets, of dangerous criminals' immigrants activate the mechanism of exclusion and stigmatization (Traverso, 2011:21). In a number of European Countries the ban of wearing scarves, face veils, body veils violates right to freedom of thought, conscience and religion, which is enshrined not only in the European Convention on Human Rights but also in many other national, international and European instruments.

According to Article 9 of the European Convention on Human Rights, "Everyone has the right to freedom of thought, conscience and religion; this right includes freedom to change his religion or belief and freedom, either alone or in community with others and in public or private, to manifest his religion or belief, in worship, teaching, practice and observance. Freedom to manifest one's religion or beliefs shall be subject only to such limitations as are prescribed by law and are necessary in a democratic society in the interests of public safety, for the protection of public order, health or morals, or for the protection of the rights and freedoms of others (European Court Of Human Rights & Council of Europe)". The religious freedom provision in the Article 18§4 of the International Covenant on Civil and Political Rights mention also that: "The States Parties to the present Covenant undertake to have respect for the liberty of parents and, when applicable, legal guardians to ensure the religious and moral education of their children in conformity with their own convictions (UNHR, 1996)".

In most of the decisions of the ECHR like Dahlab v Switzerland (Application no 42393/98), Sahin v Tutrkey (Application no 44774/98), Kervanci v France (Application no 31645/04), Dogru v France (Application no 27058/05) etc, it becomes clear that the wearing of religious clothing constitute a religious manifestation and if necessary it may be subject to limitations in a democratic society in favor of the interests of public safety, for the protection of public order, health or morals, or for the protection of the rights and freedoms of others. This is explained formally by its reliance on the "margin of appreciation" doctrine. The application of this doctrine in the case law of ECHR depends –among other- on the importance of the national interest at jeopardy must be balanced against the individual rights (Yuval, 2006:927), as rights limiting law is justified due to national authorities' interests. Thus, Islamic religious practices are perceived as an inherent factor of threat to public order and safety in secular European state[9], where authorities ought to protect religious harmony, neutrality and peaceful coexistence. The notion of secularism and homogenization includes elements islamophobia and fascistisation. It is very important to underline that this neo-colonial logic of paternalism was appeared again during the Algerian war, where the French occupiers organized a ceremony for Algerian women in order to celebrate their liberation from the shackles of headscarves (Costra-Kostritsky, 2012).

RAPE CULTURE AND NATIONALITY

On New Year's Eve (2015-2016) in Cologne mass sex attacks took placed by an unknown group of men the appearance of whom described as immigrant from Arab or North African countries (Porter, 2016). However, "what is of interest [for those in power] is only in what way sexualised violence can be instrumentalised for other topics; in this case it means what the sexist incidents can mean for the acceptance of refugees and the legalities of Schengen. Just like narratives about an imported anti-Semitism or homophobia, women's rights are also a site for the consolidation of the claim that the 'Muslim Other' imports dangerous values (Younes, 2015:194)". Indeed, these sexual attacks provoked an intense anti- refugee's rhetoric in spite the fact that there was not clear evidence of the identities of the perpetrators (Connolly, 2016). However, the key figure for these attacks is not the national identity but the patriarchal logic. In Germany (New Year's Eve, Oktoberfest and general during festivities), according to Terre des Femme, formally recorded 160,000 rapes per year with around 8,000 complaints to the police and 1,000 convictions (Younes, 2015:194). Thus, in this case the dominant narrative is constructed ground on national identity of refugees, and therefore it presented as threat which ostensibly cannot be conform to west identity of cultural and secular states of Europe. It is remarkable how methodologically the myth of black rapist is renewed nowadays.

In the United States between 1930 and 1967, from the 455 men who executed on the charge of rape, the 405 men of them were Black (Davis, 2014:104), although rape of Black women had naturalized so much that after the abolition of slavery, it considered as essential dimension of the social relations. Racism constitute provocation to rape for example during the Vietnam War, US soldiers raped Vietnamese women as being a military "duty" and also they could "search the women with their penises" (Davis, 2014:109). This myth is activated if by magic as convincing justification racist incidents violence. In this case, the message which is reproduced defines that uncivilized, underdeveloped men (refugees/immigrants) are a danger (Politico, 2016), because they express their sexual appetite to unwilling white women. This myth of uncontrollable male sexual desire namely acquires a national and a class sign character, seeking the stigmatization and persecution of Other, of uncanny (unheimlich). Thus, nowadays, the myth of "Black Peril" is shifted into "Muslim Peril".

The German parliament voted overwhelmingly the new rape law "No means No", which broadens the definition of sexual assault (Germany rape law, 2016). According to previous law a victim must prove that try to resist physically against rapist in order to be punishable (Huggler, 2016). It is obviously that No Model is preferable to a traditional force-resistance approach. Moreover, in wake of New Year's Eve assaults on women, the new law allow the easier deportation of refugees/ migrants with criminal convictions from Germany. This means that deportation comes into force for committing sexual assault by people granted or seeking asylum if they are sentenced to one year in prison (in the past to three years) without parole and suspended sentences (Thomas, 2016). It is pointed from above the capacity of law to produce punishment and violence as form of beyond state sovereignty but which simultaneously captured within it. This law namely, create a distinction and works as a counter of gravity of anomie and also more punitive for person who is not under benefits of Western identity. Essentially, it is a violent domination which manifests through the law, reaffirms the legalization of state power and responds to such challenges with a demonstration of itself. The act of law-preserving violence contains elements of lawmaking violence so that the legitimated authority of state re-posits itself as such (Benjamin, 1986:284-295). Through law it takes place in disguise a kind of anew legitimation of Western domination. Could remember one that in the 19th century at the time colonialism, the West countries often proceeded to anew instrumentalization of the female body in order to legitimize repression.

Rape is a very serious form of gender-based violence mostly against women, "but most rapists are not convicted" (Directorate General For Internal Policies Policy Department C: Citizens' Rights And Constitutional Affairs & Gender Equality, 2013:27). In spite that the United Nations Universal Declaration of Human Rights entrenches rape as a violation of human rights, that the Convention of Belem do Para defines violence against women "any act or conduct, based on gender, which causes death or physical, sexual or psychological harm or suffering to women, whether in the public or the private sphere", that the Istanbul Convention, which the Council of Europe adopted in 2011 (the first legally binding regional instrument) criminalizes various forms of violence against women, some member States like Austria, Hungary, maintain the gaps between their national and international standards in this field (Directorate General For Internal Policies Policy Department C: Citizens' Rights And Constitutional Affairs & Gender Equality, 2013:77).

Moreover, the Convention on the Elimination of all Forms of Discrimination against Women (CEDAW) recognizes gender-based violence, highlights that states should take measures for preventing, investigating and punishment sexual assaults and reaffirms the enjoyment for several rights[10]. However, The European Court of Human Rights (ECHR) has clarified that limited force-based definitions provide inadequate protection for women against sexual violence, whereas consent-based definitions are closer to the human rights principle of protecting bodily integrity and human dignity. Especially, the ECHR underlines that rape violates the rights under articles 3 prohibition of torture and 8 right to privacy (Case of M.C. v. Bulgaria, Application no. 39272/98). On the other hand, the Istanbul Convention underline that a non-consensual act of sexual nature is violence and should be criminalized (The European Women's Lobby, 2013:7). Thus, criminal justice systems (CJS) should eavesdrop carefully the victims, not only avoiding secondary victimization, because are frequently "mise en abume" as they experience humiliation within a humiliation, but also because the consent could be stem from threat, drugs, alcohol, as law is unambiguous about consent.

The feminist movements focused their attention on to the subject itself that suffered rape, moving away from the rhetoric concerning parents (Hufton, 2003:311) and social environment, they made visible sexual violence that took place within marriage or family[11], in prisons (or by police officers like Salmanoglu & Polattas v Turkey application no.15828/03), in war and they emphasized that rape of women can be verbal, psychological, physical, but certainly it happens in everyday life under the perpetual onslaught of masculinity. Therefore, rape is not related to culture or national identity, but with patriarchy and with masculinity. Nowadays, in England, all incidents of misogynistic abuse can be reported and be investigated by Nottinghamshire police (Samuels, 2016). The misogyny hate crime is defined as: "Incidents against women that are motivated by an attitude of a man towards a woman and includes behavior targeted towards a woman by men simply because they are a woman (Teale, 2016)".

CONCLUSION

Migrants/refugees, crossing the borders desecrating sovereignty and simultaneously the colonial political practice, experience the punishment of detention, which should only be applied *under certain conditions* (Case of Saadi v. United Kingdom, Application no13229/03) • namely, detention is considered as extreme measure, which should be used only when there is a fear that the person will abscond in a view of deportation, or when there is a well-founded fear that the person will commit a crime (Case of Saadi v. United Kingdom, Application no13229/03). According to Directive 2008/115/EC, the use of detention should be limited and is justified if the application of less coercive measures would not be sufficient. Also, it must be applied for the shortest time and the "third-country nationals in detention should be treated in a humane and dignified manner with respect for their fundamental rights and in compliance with international and national law. Without prejudice to the initial apprehension by law-enforcement authorities, regulated by national legislation, detention should, as a rule, take place in specialised detention facilities" (Official Journal of the European Union, 2008). In practice, however the policy of detention constitute not only as a punitive measure aiming to deter future arrivals, but also is an effective way to control and reduce of asylum claims.

Greek authorities in spite the fact that was convicted by the European Court of Human Rights for conditions of migrants/refugees detention[12], announced "our aim is that every illegal immigrant if the relevant officers consider not entitled to international protection, to be detained until they return home (Minister of Public Order and Citizen Protection, 2013) ". Moreover, Law 4075/2012 refers that "persons suffering from communicable disease or at increased risk of transmission because of circumstances in their country of origin, or because they live in poor sanitary conditions, or because they sex workers or because they make intravenous drug used, are considered "dangerous to public order" and may be detained" (Journal of the Hellenic Republic Government, 2012). The Committee about the conditions of detention of persons deprived of their liberty, made it clear that "detaining "irregular migrants" for weeks or even months in very poorly furnished and inadequately lit and/or ventilated premises, without offering them either the possibility of daily outdoor exercise or a minimum of activities with which to occupy themselves during the day, is unacceptable and could even amount to inhuman and degrading treatment (European Committee for the Prevention of Torture and Inhuman or Degrading Treatment or Punishment, 2011)".

Migrants/refugees seems as a gated community invisible people in which the bio-political control and management of migration ground on the sense of fear. The product of fear demands that the management policy of refugees/migrants will be based on biometric technology in order to strengthen securitization of western countries. For example, during registration process in Jordan refugee centers, the Iris Recognition Technology was implemented and in some camps supermarket have been set up in which refugees buy their products using iris scan technology (Iris-Scanning, 2014). UNHCR used for the first time biometric technology to Afghan refugees in 2002 and it was experimental (Jakobsen, 2015:145). Since January 2016, 260,000 Syrian refugees has already participated to the biometric registration program in Jordan, and nowadays UNHCR aim to expand the use of iris scanning in other countries (Nillasithanukroh, 2016). Certainly, of the late 1990s many Western countries – UK proceeded to overhaul of the 1971 migration legislation and German advanced a 'green card' program for 20,000 high-skilled workers- take shift to the skilled migrants/refugees who can reinforce their production base and their economy (Spencer, 2003:34). This means, new process surveillance, setting restrictions criteria to low-skilled migrants and to asylum seeker. However, EC Regulation 380/2008 refers that "the purpose of this Regulation is solely to set the security features and biometric identifiers to be used by the Member States in a uniform format of residence permit for third-country nationals"(Official Journal of the European Union, 2008).

Use of biometric technology for the migration management is essential core of contemporary securitized politics, which related to internal homeland security, to the securitization of borders and the bodies. It is obviously that biometric technology overcame the line between domestic security and foreign policy, creating a permanent state of emergency in order to manage crisis, refugee crisis. As the basic principle of state activity is considered security, every migrant/refugee is viewed as a potential terrorist, criminal, who must discipline to Western culture. Docile bodies under securitization/ criminalization must be transformed to good, obedient, peaceable workers. The logic of fascistisation established behind registration of racial profiling of refugees and asylum seekers under biometric surveillance and control of geopolitical borders, set in danger human dignity and human rights.

Challenging their invisibility, noncitizens (denizens) react and self-organized in order to gain their life, beyond their temporary legal situation which lead either to naturalization or to repatriation. Refugees try not to be acculturated or/and not to be denationalized their cultural characteristics but to resists against dominant discourse of integration and assimilation. However, both the mechanism of production and the management by a state/ transnational bureaucratic center, which constructed by human, are became the subject, as a false and inverted pseudosubject (Kosik, 2003:169). This means that the true subject becomes an object as mere merchandise. The fragmentary thought and the subjectivism - result of the mode production- permit and facilitate impose of power of pseudosubject over disciplined object- human. It is true albeit that "not all people exist in the same Now. Of course all living people at any given time may be said to co-exist physically" (Bloch, 1977:22-38). Essentially, nonsynchronous contradictions exist alongside synchronous contradictions which condense to migrants/refugees.

REFERENCES

Agelidis, D. (2015). *Asylum- seeking only through Skype and not always.* Retrieved from http://www.efsyn.gr/h-istoria-tis-efsyn accessed on 14/06/2016

Aggeli, D., Dimitriadi, A., & Triantafilidou, A. (2014). *Evaluating the cost – effectiveness control policies irregular migration in Greece.* Midas Report, ELIAMEP, 10/2014. Retrieved from http://www.eliamep.gr/wp-content/uploads/2014/11/MIDAS-REPORT-GR-1.pdf

Amnesty International. (2016). *EU-Turkey refugee deal a historic blow to rights*. Retrieved from https://www.amnesty.org/en/latest/news/2016/03/eu-turkey-refugee-deal-a-historic-blow-to-rights/

Anti-Islam movement PEGIDA stages protests across Europe. (2016). Retrieved from http://www.reuters.com/article/us-europe-migrants-protests-germany-idUSKCN0VF0P4

Anti-Nazi couple's barn burned down in eastern Germany. (2015). Retrieved from http://www.bbc.com/news/world-europe-33928047

Athens News Agency - Macedonian Press Agency (ANA-MPA). (2016). *Greece calls NATO to remain in the Aegean*. Retrieved from http://www.kathimerini.gr/863741/article/epikairothta/politikh/yper-ths-paramonhs-toy-nato-sto-aigaio-tassetai-h-ellada accessed on 14/06/2016

Badiou, A. (2008). The communist hypothesis. *New Left Review, 49*. Retrieved on https://newleftreview.org/II/49/alain-badiou-the-communist-hypothesis

Bayrakli, E., & Hafez, F. (2016). *European Islamophobia Report 2015*. Istanbul: SETA.

Benjamin, W. (1986). *Reflections essays, aphorisms, autobiographical writing Walter Benjamin*. New York: Schocken Books.

Bloch, E. (1977). *Nonsynchronism and the Obligation to Its Dialectics. New German Critique No. 11*. Duke University Press.

Campbell, Z. (2016). *Shoot First. Coast Guard Fired at Migrant Boats, European Boarder Agency Documents Show*. Retrieved from https://theintercept.com/2016/08/22/coast-guard-fired-at-migrant-boats-european-border-agency-documents-show/

Case of Dahlab v Switzerland, 15/02/2001, Application no. 42393/98. (n.d.). Retrieved from http://hudoc.echr.coe.int/eng?i=001-22643#{"itemid":["001-22643"]}

Case of Dogru v France, 04/03/2009, Application no. 27058/05. (n.d.). Retrieved from http://hudoc.echr.coe.int/eng?i=001-90039

Case of Islam (A.P.) v. Secretary of State for the Home Department Regina v. Immigration Appeal Tribunal and Another Ex Parte Shah (A.P.), 25/03/1999, House of Lords. (n.d.). Retrieved from www.parliament.uk

Case of Kervanci v France, 04/03/2009, Application no. 31645/04. (n.d.). Retrieved from http://hudoc.echr.coe.int/eng?i=001-90047

Case of M.C. v. Bulgaria, 04/03/2004, Application no. 39272/98. (n.d.). Retrieved from https://www.coe.int/t/dg2/equality/domesticviolencecampaign/resources/M.C.v.BULGARIA_en.asp

Case of Minister for Immigration and Multicultural Affairs v. Haji Ibrahim, 26/08/2000 HCA 55,SI57/1999, Australia: High Court. (n.d.). Retrieved from http://www.refworld.org/docid/3deb737f7.html

Case of Rahimi v. Greece, 05/07/2011, Application No. 8687/08. (n.d.). Retrieved from http://www.asylumlawdatabase.eu/en/content/ecthr-rahimi-v-greece-application-no-868708-1

Case of R.U. v. Greece, 07/09/2011, Application no. 2237/08. (n.d.). Retrieved from http://www.asylumlawdatabase.eu/en/content/ecthr-ru-v-greece-application-no-223708

Case of Saadi v. United Kingdom, 29/01/2008, Application no13229/03, Council of Europe: European Court of Human Rights. (n.d.). Retrieved from http://www.refworld.org/docid/47a074302.html

Case of Sahin v Tutrkey, 10/11/2005, Application no 44774/98. (n.d.). Retrieved from http://www.tjsl.edu/slomansonb/SahinTurk.pdf

Case of Sharifi and Others v. Italy and Greece, 21/10/2014 no 16643|09. (n.d.). Retrieved from http://hudoc.echr.coe.int/eng?i=001-163391

Connolly, K. (2016). *Tensions rise in Germany over handling of mass sexual assaults in Cologne*. Retrieved from www.theguardian.com/world/2016/jan/06/tensions-rise-ingermany-over-handling-of-mass-sexual-assaults-in-cologne

Constitution of Greece. (1975). *Article 13 §1, 2*. Retrieved from http://www.hri.org/docs/syntagma/artcl25.html#A13

Convention on the Elimination of all Forms of Discrimination against Women (CEDAW Convention). (n.d.). Retrieved from http://www.iwraw-ap.org/cedaw/what-is-cedaw/cedaw-principles/

Costra-Kostritsky, V. (2012). *France and the veil – the dark side of the law*. Retrieved from https://www.opendemocracy.net/5050/valeria-costa-kostritsky/france-and-veil-%E2%80%93-dark-side-of-law

Davis, A. (2014). *Women, Race and Class*. Athens: Arxeio 17 migada.

Debord, G. (1988). *Comments on the Society of the Spectacle*. Athens: Eleutheros Tipos, thesis 9.

Der I. I. I. Weg beim Imia-Gedenken in Athens, 06/02/2016. (n.d.). Retrieved from http://archive.is/2MMnP#selection-173.0-173.154

Directorate General For Internal Policies Policy Department C. Citizens' Rights And Constitutional Affairs & Gender Equality. (2013). *Overview of the worldwide best practices for rape prevention and for assisting women victims of rape*. European Parliament. Retrieved from http://www.europarl.europa.eu/RegData/etudes/etudes/join/2013/493025/IPOL-FEMM_ET(2013)493025_EN.pdf

ecre. (2016). *Joint Statement: European leaders should keep the borders open and allow access to asylum*. Retrieved from http://www.ecre.org/joint-statement-european-leaders-keep-the-borders-open-and-allow-access-to-asylum/?option=com_downloads&id=1078

Esteves, O. (2015). *Islamophobia in France, National Report 2015* (E. Bayrakli & F. Hafez, Eds.). Istanbul: SETA.

EU refuses to fund Greek border fence with Turkey. (2012). *Daily News*. Retrieved from http://www.hurriyetdailynews.com/eu-refuses-to-fund-greek-border-fence-with-turkey.aspx?pagrlID=238&nID=13346&NewsCatlID=338

European Commission. Factsheet on the EU-Turkey Agreement. (2016). Retrieved from http://europa.eu/rapid/press-release_MEMO-16-963_en.htm

European Committee for the Prevention of Torture and Inhuman or Degrading Treatment or Punishment (CPT). (2011). *Public statement concerning Greece*. Retrieved from http://www.cpt.coe.int/documents/grc/2011-10-inf-eng.htm

European Council. Foreign Affairs & International Relations. (2016). Retrieved from http://www.consilium.europa.eu/en/press/press-releases/2016/03/18-eu-turkey-statement/

European Court of Human Rights & Council of Europe. (n.d.). *European Convention of Human Rights*. Retrieved from http://www.echr.coe.int/Documents/Convention_ENG.pdf

European Union: Council of the European Union. (2001). *Council Directive 20 01/55/EC of 20 July 2001 on Minimum Standards for Giving Temporary Protection in the Event of a Mass Influx of Displaced Persons and on Measures Promoting a Balance of Efforts Between Member States in Receiving such Persons and Bearing the Consequences Thereof, 7/08/2001, OJ L.212/12-212/23; 7.8.2001, 2001/55/EC*. Retrieved from http://www.refworld.org/docid/3ddcee2e4.html

European Women's Lobby (EWL). (2013). *EWL Barometer on Rape in the EU 2013*. Retrieved from file:///C:/Users/spiros/Downloads/ewl_barometre_final_11092013.pdf

Fanon, F. (2004). *The Wretched of the Earth*. New York: Grove Press.

Fotiadis, A. (2015). *Border Merchants*. Athens: Potamos.

Foucault, M. (2009). *Security, Territory, Population. Lectures at the College de France 1977-1978*. New York: Picador- Palgrave Macmillan.

Fragkoulis, F. (2016). *The gradual Islamisation of Greece*. Retrieved from http://www.kathimerini.gr/850302/opinion/epikairothta/politikh/h-proioysa-islamopoihsh-ths-elladas

German neo-Nazis raised the flag of the Third Reich in Acropolis. (2016). Retrieved from http://www.skai.gr/news/greece/article/306395/germanoi-neonazi-sikosan-simaia-tou-g-raih-stin-akropoli/

Germany rape law: "No means No" law passed. (2016). Retrieved from http://www.bbc.com/news/world-europe-36726095

Hague, B. (2016). *Athens Muslims worship underground in absence of official mosque*. Retrieved from http://www.abc.net.au/news/2016-06-11/muslims-forced-to-worship-in-underground-mosque-in-athens/7501488

Hellenic Republic Citizen Protection Ministry. (2012). *Statement by the Minister for Citizen Protection and former Commissioner, Mr. Christos Papoutsis, about the fence in Evros, following the statements made today by the Spokesman for the European Commission, Mr. Michele Cercone*. Retrieved from http://www.minocp.gov.gr/index.php?option=ozo_content&lang=perform=view&id=4080&ltemid=529?option=ozo_search&lang=EN accessed on 03/06/2016

Hubert, P. (2016). *Frontex -Greece- unredacted Original Documents*. Retrieved from https://www.documentcloud.org/documents/3013909-Frontex-Greece-unredacted.html

Hufton, O. (2003). *History of Women in Europe 1500-1800*. Athens: Nefeli.

Huggler, J. (2016). *Germany passes 'no means no' rape law*. Retrieved from http://www.telegraph.co.uk/news/2016/07/07/germany-passes-no-means-no-rape-law/

Inter-Parliamentary Union. (2015). *Migration, human rights and governance*. Retrieved from http://www.refworld.org/docid/57b6e1697.html

Iris-Scanning Technology streamlines Refugee Registration Process. (2014). Retrieved from http://www.growthgate.com/Iris-scanning-technology-streamlines-refugee-registration-process

Jakobsen, L. K. (2015). Experimentation in humanitarian locations: UNHCR and biometric registration of Afghan refugees. *Security Dialogue*, *46*(2).

Joint Statement of Heads of Police Services from the Meeting Held in Zagreb, Croatia, on 18th February 2016. (n.d.). Retrieved from http://www.mup.hr/UserDocsImages/topvijesti/2016/veljaca/migranti_sastanak/joint_statement.pdf

Journal of the Hellenic Republic Government. (2012). *Law 4075, no.89, par 59, 11/04/2012*. Retrieved from http://www.tapit.gr/attachments/nomoi/fek89-N4075.pdf

Katsiaounis, N. (2015). *Crime and immigrant: Interview with Stefanos Rozanis*. Retrieved from http://www.kenosfakelos.blogspot.gr/2015/10/blog-post.html

Kioupkiolis, A. (2014). Towards a Regime of Post-political Biopower? Dispatches from Greece, 2010-2012. *Theory, Culture and Society, 31*. Retrieved from http://www.tcs.sagepub.com/content/31/1/143.abstract

Kosik, K. (2003). *The Crisis of Modernity*. Athens: Psichogios.

Küçükcan, T. (1999). Re-claiming Identity: Ethnicity, Religion and Politics among Turkish-Muslims in Bulgaria and Greece. *Journal of Muslim Minority Affairs, 19*(1). Retrieved from http://s3.amazonaws.com/academia.edu.documents/36047675/Re-claiming_Identity__Ethnicity__Religion_and_Politics_among_Turkish-Muslims_in_Bulgaria_and_Gree.pdf?AWSAccessKeyId=AKIAJ56TQJRTWSMTNPEA&Expires=1467821530&Signature=ips1%2FW6wJvt3ESw%2FS18jAo4KcKA%3D&response-content-disposition=inline%3B%20filename%3DRe_claiming_identity_ethnicity_religion.pdf

Labropoulou, E., & Hunt, K. (2016). *Greece starts clearing Idomeni migrant border camp*. Retrieved from http://edition.cnn.com/2016/05/24/europe/greece-clears-migrant-camp/

Lyrintzis, C., & Nikolakopoulos, E. (2004). *Political System and Elections in Greece*. Retrieved from http://video.minpress.gr/wwwminpress/aboutgreece/aboutgreece_political_system.pdf

Maiani, F. (2008). *The Concept of "Persecution" in Refugee Law: Indeterminacy, Context-sensitivity, and the Quest for a Principled Approach*. Retrieved from https://dossiersgrihl.revues.org/3896#bodyftn24

Mandrou, I. (2016). *The Council of State dismissed appeal for building mosque*. Retrieved from http://www.kathimerini.gr/866601/article/epikairothta/ellada/to-ste-aperriye-prosfyges-gia-temenos

Menninghaus, W., & Gunn, J. (2008). *Benjamin's Theory of Myth and Benjamin's Magic*. Athens: Ipsilon.

Minister of Public Order and Citizen Protection. (2013). *Reply of the Press Office of the Minister of Public Order and Citizen Protection Mr. Nikos Dendias the statement of the Press Office of SYRIZA for events in Amygdaleza*. Retrieved from http://www.yptp.gr/index.php?option=ozo_content&lang=GR&perform=view&id=4736&Itemid=579?option=ozo_search&lang=EN&lang=GR?option=ozo_search&lang=EN&lang=GR

Mixail, S. (1999). *Forms of Messianic*. Athens: Agra.

Naskou-Perraki, P. (1991). *The legal status of refugees in international and Greek law*. Athens-Komotini, Ant.N. Sakkoulas.

Nillasithanukroh, S. (2016). Rethinking the Use of Biometric Systems for Refugee Management. *Chicago Policy Review*. Retrieved from http://chicagopolicyreview.org/2016/02/24/rethinking-the-use-of-biometric-systems-for-refugee-management/

Official Journal of the European Union. (2006). *Legislation: Regulation (EC) No 562/2006 of the European Parliament and of the Council of 15 March 2006 establishing a Community Code on the rules governing the movement of persons across borders (Schengen Borders Code), L 105, vol 49, 13/04/2006*. Retrieved from http://www.eur-lex.europa.eu/legal-content/EN/TXT/HTML/?uri=OJ:L:2006:105:FULL&from=EN#L_200605EN.01000101.doc

Official Journal of the European Union. (2008a). *Council Regulation (EC) No 380/2008 of 18 April 2008 amending Regulation (EC) No 1030/2002 laying down a uniform format for residence permits for third-country nationals*. Retrieved from http://eur-lex.europa.eu/LexUriServ/LexUriServ.do?uri=OJ:L:2008:115:0001:0007:EN:PDF

Official Journal of the European Union. (2008b). *Directive 2008/115/EC of the European Parliament and of the Council of 16 December 2008 on common standards and procedures in Member States for returning illegally staying third-country nationals*. Retrieved from http://eur-lex.europa.eu/legal-content/EN/TXT/PDF/?uri=CELEX:32008L0115&from=en

Organization for Security and Co-operation in Europe & Office for Democratic Institutions and Human Rights (OSCE/ODIHR). (2009). *Greece, Early Parliamentary Elections 4 October 2009, OSCE/ODIHR Election Assessment Mission Report.* Retrieved http://www.osce.org/odihr/elections/greece/41001?download=true

Palazzani, L. (2012). *Gender in Philosophy and Law.* London: Springer.

Paparriga-Kostovara K. (2007). *Rape: The crime, trial, law and social perceptions.* Athens: Metaixmio.

Paterson, T. (2010). *Germany's neighbors from hell.* Retrieved from http://www.independent.co.uk/news/world/europe/germanys-neighbours-from-hell-2110303.html

Perrakis, S., & Mastakas, P. (2005). *Asylum- Refugees. Legislative Policy of International Organizations (UN High Commissioner for Refugees - EU - Council of Europe, etc.).* Athens: Ant.N.Sakkoula.

Politico. (2016). *Imbalance of refugee.* Retrieved from http://www.kathimerini.gr/846091/article/epikairothta/kosmos/anisorropia-apo-to-prosfygiko

Popp, M. (2011). *Right- Wing Extremism: The Village Where the Neo-Nazis Rule.* Retrieved from http://www.spiegel.de/international/germany/right-wing-extremism-the-village-where-the-neo-nazis-rule-a-737471.html

Porter, T. (2016). *Germany: Refugees hand out flowers to women in protest against New Year's Eve mass sex attacks.* Retrieved from http://www.ibtimes.co.uk/germany-refugees-hand-out-flowers-women-protest-against-new-years-eve-mass-sex-attacks-1538407

Poulatzas, N. (2006). *Fascism and dictatorship: The Third International and the Problem of Fascism.* Athens: Themelio.

Poulatzas, N. (2008). *The Poulatzas Reader, Marxism, Law and the State* (J. Martin, Ed.). London: Verso.

Prifti, K. (2016). *Why the Macedonian movement to close the border to Afghans can only be the first step of the "hard" European strategy.* Retrieved from http://www.huffingtonpost.gr/2016/02/25/afganoi-pgdm-synora-giati_n_9297546.html

Samuels, G. (2016). *Nottinghamshire Police to record misogyny and harassment against women as hate crimes.* Retrieved from http://www.independent.co.uk/news/uk/home-news/nottinghamshire-police-to-record-misogyny-and-harassment-against-women-as-hate-crimes-a7134306.html

Sevilla-Buitrago, A. (2015). Capitalist Formations of Enclosure: Space, and the Extinction of the Commons. *Antipode, 47*(4), 829-1100. Retrieved from http://www.onlinelibrary.wiley.com/doi/10.1111/anti.12143/epdf

Souliotis, G. (2016). *The Idomeni evacuation plan*. Retrieved from http://www.kathimerini.gr/860810/article/epikairothta/ellada/to-sxedio-ekkenwshs-ths-eidomenhs

Spencer, S. (2003). *The Politics of Migration: Managing Opportunity, Conflict and Change*. Oxford, UK: Blackwell Publishing.

Spyropoulos, K. F. (2006). *Introduction to Constitutional Law*. Athens: ANT. N. SAKKOULAS.

Teale, S. (2016). *Nottinghamshire Police records misogyny as a hate crime*. Retrieved from http://www.bbc.com/news/uk-england-nottinghamshire-36775398

The flag of the German Reich was raised in the Acropolis by the "German tourists" of Golden Dawn. (2016). Retrieved from http://jungle-report.blogspot.gr/2016/02/simaia-reich.html

The Ministry Immigration Policy. (2016). There will be no rental housing for refugees in Thrace, The area is Thrace is expressly excluded from the specific program. *Ethnos*. Retrieved from http://www.ethnos.gr/koinonia/arthro/yp_metanasteutikis_politikis_den_tha_ginei_enoikiasi_katoikion_se_prosfyges_sti_thraki-64329404/

Thomas, A. (2016). Germany Plans to Make It Easier to Deport Migrants. *The Wall Street Journal*. Retrieved from http://www.wsj.com/articles/germany-plans-to-tighten-deportation-rules-1452620702

Traverso, E. (2011). Populism and Islamophobia. ENEKEN, 19.

UNHCR. (2001). *Interpreting Article 1 of the 1951 Convention Relating to the Status of Refugees*. Retrieved from http://www.refworld.org/pdfid/3b20a3914.pdf

UNHCR. (2007). *Advisory Opinion on the Extraterritorial Application of Non-Refoulement Obligations under the 1951 Convention relating to the Status of Refugees and its 1967 Protocol*. Retrieved from http://www.unhcr.org/4d9486929.pdf

UNHCR. (2010). *Convention and Protocol relating to the Status of Refugees*. Retrieved from http://www.unhcr.org/protection/basic/3b66c2aa10/convention-protocol-relating-status-refugees.html

UNHCR. (2015). *Refugee Status Determination, Identifying who is a refugee*. Office of the UNHCR.

UNHR. (1996). *International Covenant on Civil and Political Rights*. Retrieved from http://www.ohchr.org/en/professionalinterest/pages/ccpr.aspx

UNHR. (2013). *Addendum-Mission to Greece, 2013 23rd session HRC, A/HRC/23/46/ Add.4*. Retrieved from http://www.ohchr.org/EN/Issues/Migration/SRMigrants/ Pages/AnnualReports.aspx

Vafiadis, N. (2014). *The Evros is no longer "an unfenced vineyard"*. Retrieved from http://www.kathimerini.com.cy/index.php?pageaction=kat&modid=1&arti d=179753

Waterfield, B. (2015). *Greece's defence minister threatens to send migrants including jihadists to Western Europe*. Retrieved from http://www.telegraph.co.uk/news/ worldnews/islamic-state/11459675/Greeces-defence-minister-threatens-to-send-migrants-including-jihadists-to-Western-Europe.html

Younes, A.-E. (2015). *Islamophobia in Germany, National Report 2015* (E. Bayrakli & F. Hafez, Eds.). Istanbul: SETA.

Yuval, S. (2006). Toward a General Margin of Appreciation Doctrine in International Law?. *The European Journal of International Law, 16*(5). Retrieved from http:// www.ejil.org/pdfs/16/5/330.pdf

KEY TERMS AND DEFINITIONS

Asylum Seeker: Is someone who yearns to granted refugee status, but yet she/ he is not be recognized as a refugee.

Fascistisation: Concerns the process of re-contextualisation of fascist features by political forces during economic crisis in bourgeois democracy.

Islamophobia: Is an unfounded fear or prejudice against Islam or Muslims.

Migrant: because of their status in the country origin, people move from one country to another in order to find job or to join family members.

Nonsynchronism: According with E. Bloch, it refers to a given historical moment as a co-presence of social and cultural elements or structures of the past with contemporary capitalist ones and those seeing in the future.

Rape Culture: Describes a complex of beliefs that encourages male sexual aggression and violence against women with any direct or indirect way, physically and emotionally, condensing thus the normalization of sexual assault in a society.

Refugee: Is the person who has been forced to seek international protection because he suffered from violation of human rights.

ENDNOTES

1 A military crisis related to sovereignty between Greece and Turkey for small uninhabited islet, Imia, in the Aegean Sea in 1996.

2 For example: Case of Minister for Immigration and Multicultural Affairs v. Haji Ibrahim, (26/08/2000) HCA 55, Australia: High Court, Retrieved from http://www.refworld.org/docid/3deb737f7.html, accessed on 29/08/ 2016, Case of Islam (A.P.) v. Secretary of State for the Home Department. Regina v. Immigration Appeal Tribunal and Another Ex Parte Shah (A.P.), 25/03/1999, House of Lords, Retrieved from www.parliament.uk, accessed on 20/08/2016.

3 "The commission has decided not to follow up the Greek request because it considers it pointless. Fences and walls are short term measures that do not solve migration management issues in a structural way". *EU refuses to fund Greek border fence with Turkey*, 09/02/2012, Daily News, Retrieved from http://www.hurriyetdailynews.com/eu-refuses-to-fund-greek-border-fence-with-turkey.aspx?pagrlID=238&nID=13346&NewsCatlID=338, accessed on 02/06/2015.

4 "Aspida": 1.800 policemen are guarded the Greek-Turkish border land. "Xenios Zeus": sweep operations have led to massive arrests and detention of immigrants, even they were asylum seeker. Aggeli D, Dimitriadi A & Triantafilidou A (2014), *"Evaluating the cost –effectiveness control policies irregular migration in Greece"*, Midas Report, ELIAMEP, 10/2014, Retrieved from http://www.eliamep.gr/wp-content/uploads/2014/11/MIDAS-REPORT-GR-1.pdf, accessed on 04/06/2016.

5 The Greek side considers that the NATO presence in the Aegean has contributed to the reduction of refugee flows and seeks the cooperation of the EU and NATO through the combination of Endeavor business and Sophia. The Athens News Agency - Macedonian Press Agency (ANA-MPA)(2016), *Greece calls NATO to remain in the Aegean*, Kathimerini, 14/06/2016, Retrieved from http://www.kathimerini.gr/863741/article/epikairothta/politikh/yper-ths-paramonhs-toy-nato-sto-aigaio-tassetai-h-elladaaccessedon14/06/2016.

6 "The only way to access anyone in the asylum process, is through Skype, however, this procedure presents enormous problems. Access is limited to three hours per week for each language and often the system collapses from the number of calls. Thus, those that manage to connect through Skype are enumerable compared to those who try". Agelidis D (2015), *Asylum- seeking only through Skype and not always...*, Ef.Syn., 26/05/2015, Retrieved from http://www.efsyn.gr/h-istoria-tis-efsynaccessedon14/06/2016.

7 "This perfect democracy fabricates its own inconceivable enemy, terrorism. It wants, actually, to be judged by its enemies rather than by its results. The history of terrorism is written by the State and it is thus instructive. The spectating populations must certainly never know everything about terrorism, but they must always know enough to convince them that, compared with terrorism, everything else seems rather acceptable, in any case more rational and democratic". Debord G (1988), *Comments on the Society of the Spectacle,* Athens, Eleutheros Tipos, thesis 9, pp25.

8 The Council of State rejected the appeals of some residents, allowing work to continue to build the mosque. Mandrou I (2016), *The Council of State dismissed appeal for building mosque*, Kathimerini, 08/07/2016, Retrieved from http://www.kathimerini.gr/866601/article/epikairothta/ellada/to-ste-aperriye-prosfyges-gia-temenos, accessed on 08/07/2016.

9 «State Secretary for Women's Rights Pascale Boistard publicly stated on 2 March, 2015: *I am not sure the veil belongs in higher education*". Esteves O (2015), Islamophobia in France, National Report 2015, Bayrakli E & Hafez F(ed), Istanbul, SETA, pp164.

10 The UN General Assembly adopted the CEDAW Convention on 19th December 1979. The Convention on the Elimination of all Forms of Discrimination against Women (CEDAW Convention), Retrieved from http://www.iwraw-ap.org/cedaw/what-is-cedaw/cedaw-principles/, accessed on 04/07/2016.

11 Until 2006 in Greece "domestic violence" was not recognized as a separate offense according to the Criminal Code, while "domestic rape" also until 2006 could not be typesetting. The legislative bill 25 / 11.2005 entailed not the protection of women but the protection of the family. In the explanatory report of the law is mentioned: "The State does not intervene in the privacy sphere of family members and does not affect morals, values and principles, as reflected in the Greek society". The legal form of the crime of rape before the n. 3500/2006 determined that: """ anyone with physical violence or threat .... forces another into illegitimate sexual intercourse…". Paparriga- Kostovara K (2007), *Rape: The crime, trial, law and social perceptions*, Athens, Metaixmio, pp174.

12 For example: Case of R.U. v. Greece, 07/09/2011, Application no. 2237/08, Retrieved from http://www.asylumlawdatabase.eu/en/content/ecthr-ru-v-greece-application-no-223708 & Case of Rahimi v. Greece, 05/07/2011, Application No. 8687/08, Retrieved from http://www.asylumlawdatabase.eu/en/content/ecthr-rahimi-v-greece-application-no-868708-1 accessedon02/09/2016.

Chapter 3
How Can World Leaders Understand the Perverse Core of Terrorism?
Terror in the Global Village

Maximiliano E. Korstanje
University of Palermo, Argentina

ABSTRACT

Based on the recently-dated terrorist attacks perpetrated in Europe, where terrorists weaponized classic forms of transport against civilian targets, one might speculate that likely mobilities and terrorism would be inextricably intertwined. In the mid of this mayhem, this chapter centers on the mobilities-paradigm as an ideological platform that keeps the interests of ruling elite, inasmuch as only 1% of mankind is legally authorized to travel worldwide. It is vital for social scientists to interrogate on the cultural effects of 9/11, in a world which is characterized by serious economic imbalances. In this world of full contrasts, while first world tourists are encouraged to move from one point to another without any restriction, migrants, asylum-seekers and vagabonds are energetically pursued, jailed or exiled by nation-state.

INTRODUCTION

The paradigm of mobilities as it was formulated to date emphasizes on the rights of citizens to move wherever as a sign of democratic spirit and technological supremacy over other cultures where the freedom from want is unknown. In this sense the allegory of mobilities as an inalienable right for all free persons seems to

DOI: 10.4018/978-1-5225-2817-3.ch003

be associated to an ideological disposition instead a reality in the world (Cresswell 2006; Farrington 2007; Germann-Molz & Gibson, 2012). Only 1% of total global population can travel or make expensive travels abroad as first world citizens often do (Korstanje 2015). In the capitalist ethos, a privilege class is legally authorized to move, while peripheral workforce is discouraged to abandon their homeland, or at least when they did it, are traced, trapped and exiled (Zizek, 2001; Diken 2001). These noted asymmetries in the fields of mobilities were expressed when three civil airplanes where directed against one of the most important skyscrapers of the world (WTC) in New York city. This major event noted not only the vulnerability of Westerners to anticipate terrorism, but also how the main prides of West which are expressed in mobilities, freedom and consumption were used to instill panic in the US and the rest of the World. Shocked by this sad event, public opinion and media will understand nobody will feel safer any longer and in any place. If 9/11 kicked off the start of a new era where terror governed by the individual minds of consumers, the United States of America reacted energetically in two led invasions in Afghanistan and Iraq. Although the first was widely accepted by international popular parlance, even some scholars emphasized on how just was the invasion that ended the Taliban regime, no less true was that Iraq Campaign was a complete disaster. Bush`s administration received not only several strong criticisms but it paved the ways for the necessary political chaos that facilitated the rise of ISIS in Middle East. Dotted with crueler tactics than Al-Qaeda, ISIS formally declared the Jihad against leisure centers, tourist destinations and any spot Centre characterized by consumption and hedonism. The successive attacks in Paris and Brussels showed how places of night cultural entertainment or nexus of transport as airports were the main targets of native-born Frenchmen weary from the humdrum routine of their societies. In this chapter, we place the paradigm of mobilities as peace-maker process under the lens of scrutiny, holding the polemic thesis that mobile tourism is terrorism by other means. The expansion of globalization would have liberated terrorism from its iron cage, but what would be interesting to discuss is the ways hospitality is being affected by terrorism. While nineteen-century imperialism developed the interest for meeting with others, not only with the ends of expropriating their lands, but subduing them into imperial eye, globalization facilitated the expansion of extortion as the main vehicle towards terrorism. As a result of this, the sacred-law of hospitality was undermined by the fear engendered in main economies.

CONCEPTUAL BACKGROUND

From an anthropological point of view, we discuss in this chapter not only the rise and expansion of terrorism, as a form of instrumentalization of others` pain, but also the effects on 9/11 in the worlds of hospitality and mobilities. The specialized literature in mobilities issues focus on the material aspects of globalization, as well as the radical shifts prompted by the use of high-technology. One of the main authorative voices in mobilities and migration studies, John Urry (2002), claims that mobilities have reformulated the cosmology of Western societies to the extent to embrace aesthetical cultural values, which led to a new way of perceiving modernity. Geographical displacements, as tourism, or the industry of hospitality, depends on the available technological background which achieved a substantial rupture between tradition and future. While the "tourist gaze" expropriates "the otherness" by the usufruct of technological dispositiffs, which helped people to travel faster than other times, the world of labour has been precaritized in view of a more mobile capital which presses to workforce to renounce many of their rights. This paradoxical situation results in a grim landscape, that today combines mass consumption with a deterioration of environment and the working conditions of workers. (Urry 2002; 2007; Lash & Urry, 1993; Sheller & Urry, 2004; Urry & Larsen 2011; Hannam, Sheller & Urry, 2006).

As this backdrop, Jennie Germann Molz (2014) theorizes on the current patterns of travels in her recent book, *Travel Connections*. At a first, we must accept the wide-spread belief that technology changed our ways of being together, and for that, our ways of traveling. Today the blogs, Facebook and other social networks allow uploading pictures while touring. This not only defies the current literature respecting to the dichotomy home-destination, but also altered the methodologies ethnographers use to understand this types of issues. From its inception, the sociology of tourism developed a pejorative connection around leisure as an alienatory activity, which is opposite to human freedom. In fact, far from being true, this position reinforced the thesis that tourist-gaze commoditizes landscapes, cultures and peoples under the obsession for authenticity. The importance of social networks, which are used today as platform to enhance social ties, may be very well prone to produce new forms of hospitality. She cites the example of couchsurfing, a software platform where users give lodge to other members of the network asking nothing in return. Originally developed by Australian surfers, couchsurfing as many other blogs, ensures free cost lodging when traveling abroad. In perspective, Germann Molz`s argument rests on a deep quandary. Are mobile technologies making a more sociable world, or rather, are they conducive to an irreversible social bond declination?

To this question, she will answer that, the new mobile sociality, engendered by the media are being organized in a set of controversies and paradoxes. The performance of traveling debates between two contrasting forces, anxiety and aspiration. While Technology has been embraced to foster desires of escapement, from postindustrial society, they produce "togetherness", combining psychological needs of moving but resting. What is more than important to discuss is the fact that travel connections "do not just hold distant friend together, they also hold together (and are held together by) competing spatial and social positions" (p. 178).

This happens simply because, in our mobile society, the possibility of escapement has diluted. The emergence of internet, and social platforms promised a more cohesive society, however the ties are more fluid than other times. Ultimately, Geoffrey Skoll situates globalization as the main cause that explains the unabated inflation of risks the world experiences today. With focus on terrorism, Skoll adds, Americans developed a culture of fear to exert a stricter control over other ethnicities, in order for elite to monopolize the means of production and wealth concentration in economy. While US opted to become as the main empire, post-Soviet collapse, this fear expanded to the four corners of the world. Historically, Marxism has discussed capitalism reproduces by its growth, substantial inequalities that enlarge the gap between bourgeoisie and rank-and-file workers. The media portrays an archetype of terrorists as hatred-filled hears, maniacs or demons who threaten the spirit of democracy. But we ignore that the act of governing through fear, which was stimulated by government from the inception of America, not only created a climate of mistrust, but passed unpopular laws which otherwise would be rejected. Not surprisingly, neoliberal program enthralled terrorism as a main ally internally and in the international affairs. At the time, capital and American Empire expanded to colonize new worlds, a much deeper sentiment of fear accompanied the politics. Therefore, it is safe to say we live in a world characterized by a "global fear" which is functional to a particular way of making politics. One of the aspects facilitated the expansion of capitalism was the idea that citizens live in the best of the possible worlds. Based on two ideological mechanisms as repression and fear, American Empire, in post 9/11 context, established an all-encompassing control over periphery focusing on the state of exception doctrine. The discourse of fear was widely adopted by main economies to discipline their respective workers, leading governments to implement what specialists called, "the securitization process" (Skoll 2016).

TERRORISM AND THE END OF LEISURE

The pervasive roles played by globalization and the war on terror have revealed a cynical dynamic. Liberal markets facilitate the circulations of goods and trade but constraining the mobilities of Workforce, which travel to centre in quest of better opportunities. Capital replicates worldwide producing serious asymmetries which pave the ways for the rise of resentment (Powell 2010). The state of conflicts produced by capitalism represents a fertile ground for terrorism to recruit new comrades. However, a linear correlation between poverty and terrorism has recently come under scrutiny (Enders & Hoover, 2012). Though interesting studies have been advanced on the economic nature of terrorism (Enders & Sandler 2011), they fail to explain the way economic theories conceive of pleasure and wealth maximization. As Luke Howie (2010) puts it, terrorists do not want all people dead, but they need all peoples witnessing. In a symbiosis with the World of celebrities, terrorism appeals to the attention captivated by the media in order to perpetuate worldwide. While nations devote considerable resources in struggling against terror, less are the probabilities to reach success. This suggests that instrumentality is a key factor that leads towards "terrorism".

In *The Economics of Justice,* Richard Posner acknowledges that utilitarianism as it was formulated by Jeremy Bentham engenders two types of monstrousness. If society is based on the maximization of pleasure for all their members, we must assume that torture is a good option to enhance security. One type of monstrosity arises whenever we valorise peoples by the degree of pleasure they develop instead by effects of their decisions. Suppose that A is very fond of killing animals, and B is prone to feed them. Following utilitarianism, A is a better person than B irrespective of ethical conduct. A second type of monstrousness is these types of societies where the collectivity leads to the sacrifice of innocent persons on the altar of social need (Posner 1983).

In a seminal work, David Altheide offers a radical critique on the criteria used by journalism to select what news is published. American and British newspapers are prone to cover news related to crime and terrorism as if both were determined by the same factors. Terrorists are portrayed as the main *Threat for West*, while local crime is disciplined by the cultural values of society. Local offenders, after all, are framed as individuals who have adapted to society whereas terrorists had no such luck. Terrorists are treated as psychopaths whose behaviour still remains irreversible (Altheide, 2009). This explains not only their degree of "dangerousness", but also how the law is orchestrated as an apparatus of repression. The liberal scholar, Michael Ignatieff (2013), declared that terrorism is the lesser evil in view of the dangers democratic societies face. One of the troublesome aspects of democracy in its struggle against terrorism, is how can we ethically see torture. Ignatieff argues that "the war on terror" is the lesser evil. The West should devote all its resources to eradicate terrorism, and of course, in this process torture should be limited to legal controls (Skoll 2008). This suggests that the current meaning of terrorism should be at least revisited.

People feel extreme fright whenever events are going beyond their control. This is exactly what happens with terrorism. No matter that states enhance their security homeland, nobody knows when and how the next attack will take form (Altheide 2009; Sunstein, 2002a; 2002b; Skoll 2007). It is unfortunate that ethnographers who are interested in getting a hold of terrorists face serious legal problems not only because terrorism is an illegal activity, but is globally repudiated. This seems the reason why today the research, as M. Sageman (2014) anticipated, reached a stage of stagnation. In recently published paper, he argues that mass media concentrates the opinions of many "pseudo-analysts" who create a barrage of speculation, biased ideas, or commentaries that feedback the policies of governments. Instead of expanding the current understanding of this issue, it increases the ethnocentrism of the West. The lack of valuable investigation relates to the impossibilities of making contact with terrorists, since they are considered maniacs, demons, or psychopaths almost impossible to re-educate. Richard Bernstein (2013) argues convincingly that if terrorists are stereotyped as evil-doers or demons, why their actions are adamantly criticized and medicatically condemned. As formulated this question has no response. However, psychology teaches that terrorism is a human activity, performed by people who embrace radical tactics at a specific time of their lives. Since all we are all potential terrorists, research should explore the factors that determine how the terrorist mind is formed. Demonization is contrary to understanding.

Neither the monopoly of the state nor the attempts of insurgents to pose their message by means of violence, terrorism should be defined as a dialectics of hate in which case both parties are involved in an atmosphere of conflict and violence. Nation-states exert considerable power over populations (sometimes violating essential human rights), but the problem lies in the fact that terrorists are indeed hidden within the population. Beyond their technologies, nation-states are unable to forecast when and where the next attack will be. Under some conditions, torture plays a crucial role by interrogating some suspects. However, terror cells work disconnected from other cells, which means that tortured persons have no idea or key information that can be used by state to protect society. The concept of normalcy of terror is one of the troubling aspects that should be discussed by specialists and pundits (Howie, 2011).

Beyond the responsibilities of religion, terrorism justifies violent actions against vulnerable persons using discourses that lead toward self-victimization. In so doing, religion serves as an excuse but never as the real reason behind it. James Piazza commented that it is common terrorist groups once participated in democratic processes to some extent but were forced to go underground for many reasons. Political atomization conjoined to weaker autocracies is one of the key factors that pave the way for the rise of terrorism. The focus placed by some scholars on poverty or psychological frustration does not explain at a macro-sociological level the influence of politics in the configuration of the necessary instability that sooner or later leads to terrorism. Whenever groups are pressed to clandestine action because of a lack of democratic channels, terrorism rises as an option (Piazza 2007; 2008).

Over recent decades, some voices emerged to find commonalities or shared lines of actions in different terror organizations which range from the IRA to Al-Qaeda.

At first blush, no matter than their religion, culture, or class, a psychological profile may be addressed.

We may use psychology to delineate two contrasting profiles: *offenders and terrorists*. While the former signal a disordered, deviant behaviour to social rules, the later one emulates a law-abiding attitude to the extent of sacrifice of their lives. Let´s clarify first that criminals deny their crimes, but this happens because they belong or want to belong to society. The same does not apply to terrorists, who are rewarded by captivating the attention of society. Terrorists often adopt their reactions in view of a mythical struggle against injustice or some other broader targets such as "Westernization," Rationality," or Mass Consumption. Re-channeling their hatred towards a much deeper process of victimization, the discourse of terrorism lacks from any rational basis. Nonetheless, once questioned, they vindicate their crimes by alluding to higher positive ideals such as freedom, the struggle against injustice, or the restoration of a lost moral order. Far from being considered as evil-doers, they perceive themselves as "disinterested" freedom fighters. In inculcating terrorists, terror groups employ a sentiment of radicalization, which was widely studied by McCauley & S. Moskalenko (2008; 2011) & Moskalenko & McCauley (2009). For these psychologists, radicalization corresponds with a system of beliefs which are products of history or certain bad personal experiences. However, terrorists are fewer than those who can share the same sentiment of disappointment, experts add. What is important is that this process of radicalization only prospers in small groups, where interactions with others seem to be reduced to the leaders` viewpoints.

TERRORISM, GLOBALIZATION AND COLONIALISM

Undoubtedly, the problem of terrorism stems from the process of colonization as it happened during XIXth centuries and even earlier. This point was brilliantly addressed by lecturer from University of Leeds, UK, Rodanthi Tzanelli in her recently-published book, *Thana tourism and Cinematic Representation of Risk*. The question whether dark tourism surfaced over recent decades as one of the trends of leisure consumption in zones of extreme poverty or areas of ghettoization resulted from decades of an exploitative logic exported during the facet of colonization during XIXth and XXth centuries. However, instead of provoking a collective awakening, cinema offers a biased diagnosis to the material asymmetries produced by the expansion of capitalism. It is important not to lose the sight that in these new global. The inflation of different risks which oscillates from natural disasters to terrorism, evinces that the holiday-making and leisure practices as tourism are next to disappear but paradoxically, dark tourism still revitalizing the gift-exchange process that made capitalism feasible. In retrospect, the instrument of surveillance orchestrated by capitalism appeal to the metaphor of *undesired guests* where working-migrants are stereotyped as zombies, monsters, terrorists or even viruses which may very well threaten the current civilized social order. Since the concept of risk which is theatricalized by the film-related industries allows the imposition of allegories to see the capitalist ethos as one of the best possible worlds, entrepreneurship surfaces as a vehicle to invest first world citizens of an exceptional aura. Put the problems in these terms, Tzanelli adheres to confirm the legacy of colonialism still remains in the core of Western consumption, for example not only in slumming peripheral places characterized by extreme poverty, but also in zones of disasters as Ground Zero in NY. What these visitors look seems to be the exemplary aura constructed and crystalized by old colonialism. Besides, instead of assuming the legal charges for what their human right violations their respective states committed in pastime (as the Belgium genocide started in Congo), European nations developed an uncanny paternalism for strangers. Thousands of visitors travel to former colonial countries to inspect on poverty or the ways people live in these destinations, ignoring or leaving behind the responsibilities of Europe in producing these apocalyptic landscapes of misery (Tzanelli 2016). In terms of Korstanje, the fear of Terrorism comes from the repression over the neglected liabilities from modern States in the bloodshed during colonialism. Those anxieties waken up by mass destruction weapons in hands of terrorist cells seems to be reinforced by the lack of repentance of US for bombing Hiroshima and Nagasaki, major event which violated all human rights (Korstanje 2010; 2013; 2015).

As Frederick Buell puts it, we need to foster a new theory of globalization to discuss again the role of Europe in a post-colonial world. The role of culture was historically oriented not only to highlight the supremacy of civilized whiteness, but also to question the "non-European others" (Buell 1994). The quest for heritage and authenticity stems from an old need of colonize the difference, to control to those who are not like us. the process of decolonization post WWII created the inverse stage. However, the meaning of culture never was questioned. Today, culture is sold by tourism and global industries. The merits in Buell`s work consisted in discussing critically the belief that late-modernity commoditizes cultures. Not surprisingly, culture as an invention of colonial West expanded globalization to worldwide (Buell, 1994). The concept of tourist-gaze as well as the idea of a mobile world appeals to the old colonial stereotypes; Buell acknowledges that the efficacy of capitalism consisted not only in transcending the market, introducing the concept of cultures through post-war period, but creating a hierarchy of the world (three worlds) where first one was in the superior ladder than the other two. The third world represented the sign of deficiency but was morally authentic. The "inauthentic" west, which was characterized by greed, anomie and conflict, should help under-developing countries to reach modernization and rationality.

Culturally, there is still stronger tendency toward hierarchy in the three worlds theory. This cultural hierarchy, however, has proven as brittle as is has been tenacious. Thanks to a vigorous survival of cultural attitudes from Euro-colonial Past, the first World sees itself and is seen as the source of high modern culture and scientific rationality, of universalism and universal literary and artistic genius (Buell 1998: p. 23).

If John Urry was in the correct side, Dean MacCannell adds, it was because he envisaged the exhaustion of economic sources in hands of capitalism but not for the role given to tourist-gaze. Unlike Urry, MacCannell formulates that sightseeing corresponds with a cultural structure, which is co-determined by the current means of production. Since the totems are significant allegories to guide the life in aboriginal tribes, tourism did the same in secularized societies (MacCannell, 1973; 1976; 1984; 1988; 1992). While tourists gaze others, they too are becoming in commodities which are observed by others (Gillespie 2006; Germann-Molz 2014; Dann & Jacobsen 2003). Last but not least, as Bauman put it, postmodern made extensive the belief we dwell a mobile world whenever only few privilege peoples are legally allowed to travel and move freely. This modern world offers two type of mobilities which correspond with two types of treating strangers. While some are legally encouraged to travel worldwide, others are impeded to pass the national borders. Thousand millions of workers that are pauperized by the existent capitalist-machine are unable to travel (Bauman 1998a; 1998b), as Urry precludes. Modern terrorism opens the doors of already-existent dichotomies to construct and perceive "the otherness" in European allegories.

THE PROBLEM OF HOSPITALITY

One of the sad metaphor how the right of hospitality undermines by action of terrorism seems to be the tragedy of Aylan (Kurdi), a 3 years old Syrian boy found death at the cost of Turkey together his brother and mother. This reflects the reality of thousands of Syrian refugee who daily seek shelter trespassing the boundaries of Europe. Once Europe, shocked by this tragedy, acceded to reformulate the quota of immigrants in a temporal basis, ISIS jihadist announced the infiltrations of some of their warriors as Trojan horses to put "Europe on its knees". Unfortunately, Police suspected one of the involved terrorist in the massacre of Paris was infiltrated within Syrian contingents. It sooner resulted in a strengthening of border surveillance as well as the reduction and rejection of many refugees and desesperated migrants in quest of asylum. This suggests that effects of terrorism impact directly on the world of mobilities, but undermining the European hospitality as it was formulated two thousand years ago.

In this respect, Jacques Derrida postulated his theory of hospitality taking into consideration absolute hospitality is never possible. Over centuries, hospitality not only accompanied the rise of Europe and its final expansion in colonialism but also forged the spirit of Western nations. As Derrida puts it, though hospitality intersects with strangers, not all strangers are accepted in invocation of hospitality rule. In this vein, two types of hospitality surfaced: *the absolute and conditioned*. While the former demands any host to open the doors of their home asking nothing in return, the latter signals to a much deeper right which calls for reciprocity. I will only welcome those who can do the same for me. Since, this counter-balanced reciprocity demands a return, Derrida dubbed as "conditioned hospitality". Starting from the premise the rights of foreigners are within hospitality itself, Derrida adds, it confers to the needs of protection (Derrida 2000). To what extent this protection is legally manipulated to kill the guest or any host is one of the issues present in ancient tragedy (as Helen of Troy or Macbeth) or even in horror movie genre. In fact, Korstanje & Olsen and Korstanje & Tarlow explored the synopsis of some horror films to understand that the roots of hospitality. While the rout of tourists run in remote lands, beyond the control of state, the problem arises since they meet with villains, who never reveal their real interests. Seduced to enjoy from banquets, and their hospitality, these monsters plan to kill or torture the innocent guests. The outcome of this investigation holds the thesis that the corruption of hospitality-law allows the rise of evilness (Korstanje & Olsen 2011; Korstanje & Tarlow 2012). At a closer look, the question whether hospitality reduces the fear at meeting with an "unknown other", no less true is that both, hosts and guests should compromise not to attack the others in vulnerable conditions. Julia Kristeva denoted to the dark side of hospitality as the precondition for evilness to reveal its face. This type of "sinister hospitality" allows the guest to vulnerates the integrity of hosts (Kristeva, 1991).

At some extent, Jihadism saw in the industries of leisure a fertile ground to perpetrate its attack against Europeans and Americans. It reflects not only the axis of liberality where it is very hard to control the mobile other, but also erodes one of the tenets of capitalist societies, the conditioned hospitality. Although many politicians and policy makers have devoted considerable time and resource to expand a climate of securitization to First World, less attention was given to the fact, many of jihadists are natives from the societies they attack. As one of the scourges of West, terrorism seems to be enrooted in the core of capitalism, in means as extortion or instrumentalization that feeds from the other`s suffering. This raises a more than interesting question, what is the connection of terrorism and leisure industries?

As Korstanje (2015) noted, terrorism and democracy seem to be inextricably intertwined. One of the pillars of terrorism is based not only on how much fear they can instil in populations, but also in the hope of extortion directed towards nation-state. During 19th century Europe faced one of the most serious crises in its history. It triggered forced migration of the impoverished workforce towards peripheral countries such as United States, Australia, Brazil, and Argentina where those economies experienced a sudden growth. However, the conditions of work in these hosting nations were far from optimal. European migrants were subject to long hours of work and otherwise exploited by the owners of capital. Some of these newcomers adopted ideologies coming from socialism and anarchism. In their struggles to gain better working conditions some planned bombings against government officials and notorious industrialists and their property. These anarchists were labelled as terrorists, and were promptly jailed and deported. However, the core of their ideological discourse remained in the organization of anarcho-syndicalists, a more moderate group that adopted the ideals of anarchism to be materialized in improvements for workforce. A few of their claims were finally accepted by the elite, and unions gained the right to strike in furtherance of improved wages and working conditions. Thus disciplined into forms of leisure consumption, terrorism became settled into the core of Westernization. Not only the fear, which is a touchstone, lingers in the heart of our civilization but also interesting commonalities between the strike, unionization, and terrorism converge. From that moment on, cultural industries such as tourism, museums, or various cultural entertainments, as the case of Paris evinced, become targets for international terrorism. As Korstanje argues, we have to consider the thesis that tourism is terrorism by other means. These intersections are based on three common factors: *surprise, the instrumentalization of the Other, and extortion*. At a first glance, the latter two are appeals to sudden blows against State where citizens are unethically hosted. The surprise factor supports state in accepting claims that otherwise would be neglected. In so doing, the Other is not only instrumentalzed as a means to achieve goals, but disseminates a message of terror to society. The point of entry in this discussion seems to be that mass media plays a vital role by amplifying the effects of terrorism in post-industrial societies (Howie 2012; Eid 2014).

FUTURE RESEARCH HORIZONS

In Witnesses To Terror Luke Howie (2012) noted, terrorists do not seek to destroy entire civilizations, but by the introduction of fear they seek to dismantle the interests of state. Despite its complex algorithms and mathematical models, one of the frightful dilemmas of the West consists of the incapacities to forecast the next attack. Starting from the belief that the *innocent* is harmed to show the impossibility of the state to protect ordinary people, the credibility and legitimacy of officialdom plummets. It seems worth discussing whether terrorists channel their hate against particular or broader targets. In fact, victims are aleatory; they are selected to cause a psychological shock to society, and terrorists do not have previous knowledge of their victims they will kill. The targets are things are symbolic and abstract like Capitalism, Democracy or Secularism. Following secular logics more associated to means-ends models than religious pursuits, *the discourse of terrorism* feeds back from perceived global injustices that have taken place in the past and which nourishes a mythical archetype. Normally, terrorists are co-active and prone to minimize the risks whenever the safety of community is in jeopardy. Terrorists are ordinary people who at some moment of their lives were subject to radicalization that isolated them from society. In this vein, one should not lose sight of the fact that terrorists are indifferent to other´s suffering for two main reasons. First, they consider their goals as superior to personal life or any other individual desires. Second, the Other is used as a means to fulfill the own objectives. The question whether others are instrumentalized explains why terrorists are insensible to their pain. Whenever, they (terrorists) feel that states are not handling their claims, extortion surfaces as the necessary instrument to impose their agenda. On this point, terrorists, union leaders and businessmen are not so different. Beyond the fear, a more than interesting approach is to discuss is to how much the pillars of terrorism are rationality and extortion.

Throughout his vast bibliography, Zygmunt Bauman has analysed to what extent the logic of instrumentality remains rooted in the ideology of capitalism. The West valorised security over other cultural values, and that means that people (consumers) debate between the fear of abandonment and the need to belong. Those persons who harmonize a comfortable life-style paradoxically need the technological background to protect their home. At the same time, it serves as a sign of distinction with respect to others who are unable to consume, and the derived sentiment of fear is rechannelled towards mass consumption. Unlike animals, humans develop "a type of derivate fear" which is socially constructed. Because this sentiment has the possibility to transcend the boundaries of time and space, it makes more terrible and diffuse than a real threat. Our imagination is our staunch enemy. Doubtless, the Titanic symbolizes what would happen with Western civilization if the radicalized Other is not accepted. This luxurious cruise that embodied the pride of civilized nations met a simple iceberg. The inflation of risk that leads to paranoia facilitates a much deeper process of securitization which permeates the social environment. The vulnerability of humankind is neglected in view of an allegory of consumption, where the maximization of happiness persists. Our terror of death is rooted in the logic of market (Bauman, 2001; 2006; Bauman y Lyon, 2013).

CONCLUSION

The culture of Occident rests on the needs to figure "the Others" who does not look like us in order to legitimate its overseas expansion. The history of colonialism witnessed how several mercantile projects launched to the unknown world to colonize "other lands". As a result of this, capitalism becomes in one of the most leading cultural project worldwide, indexing economies in Asia, Africa and Latin America. In terms of Hardt & Negri (2001), *The Empire* monopolized not only the law-making, but also the rights to expropriate territories to strengthen the proper means of production. In a seminal book, entitled *The Lonely Crowd,* David Riesman (1961) showed amply how this interests for others which paved the ways for the rise of novels, science, and all wonders that characterized by the life of Europeans during years, in the bottom was legitimized by a bloody conquest over the bodies of colonial natives. In this context, the right of hospitality was conducive to the expansion of capitalism, under the original shape of colonial law. However, after 9/11 and the attacks to World Trade Centre, not only where a bunch of terrorists showed how vulnerable the main power of the world is, but manipulating the symbolic bulwark of Western spirit as real weapons, things changed a lot. The intersection of terrorism with hospitality accelerated not only a military escalate in the world to colonize autonomous countries but curtailing individual rights within US soil. This reminds as Mahmoud Eid brilliantly discussed, one of the most troublesome aspects of terrorism is the obsession to cover terrorism-related news. If modern terrorism surfaced from the core of European mobilities, as it was evinced by Korstanje (2015), now it is mining the pillars of democracy and capitalism.

REFERENCES

Altheide, D. (2006). *Terrorist and the Politics of Fear*. Oxford, UK: Altamira Press.

Bauman, Z. (1998a). *Globalization: The human consequences*. New York: Columbia University Press.

Bauman, Z. (1998b). On glocalization: Or globalization for some, localization for some others. *Thesis Eleven, 54*(1), 37-49.

Bauman, Z. (2001). Consuming life. *Journal of Consumer Culture, 1*(1), 9–29. doi:10.1177/146954050100100102

Bauman, Z. (2006). *Liquid Fear*. Cambridge, UK: Polity Press.

Bauman, Z., & Lyon, D. (2013). *Liquid surveillance: A conversation*. New York: John Wiley & Sons.

Bernstein, R. J. (2013). *The abuse of evil: The corruption of politics and religion since 9/11*. New York: John Wiley & Sons.

Buell, F. (1994). *National Culture and the New Global System*. Baltimore, MD: John Hopkins University Press.

Cresswell, T. (2006). The right to mobility: The production of mobility in the courtroom. *Antipode*, *38*(4), 735–754. doi:10.1111/j.1467-8330.2006.00474.x

Dann, G., & Jacobsen, J. (2003). Leading the tourist by the nose. In G. M. S. Dann (Ed.), *The Tourist as a metaphor of the social World*. New York: CABI.

Derrida, J. (2000). Of Hospitality: Anne Dufourmantelle Invites Jacques Derrida to Respond (R. Bowlby, Trans.). Stanford, CA: Stanford Univ. Press.

Diken, B. (2001). Immigration, multiculturalism and post politics after nine eleven. *Third Text*, *15*(57), 3–12. doi:10.1080/09528820108576937

Enders, W., & Hoover, G. A. (2012). The nonlinear relationship between terrorism and poverty. *The American Economic Review*, *102*(3), 267–272. doi:10.1257/aer.102.3.267

Enders, W., & Sandler, T. (2011). *The political economy of terrorism*. Cambridge, UK: Cambridge University Press. doi:10.1017/CBO9780511791451

Farrington, J. H. (2007). The new narrative of accessibility: Its potential contribution to discourses in (transport) geography. *Journal of Transport Geography*, *15*(5), 319–330. doi:10.1016/j.jtrangeo.2006.11.007

Germann Molz, J. (2014). *Travel Connection: tourism. Technology and togetherness in a mobile World*. New York: Routledge.

Germann Molz, J. (2014). *Travel Connection: tourism. Technology and togetherness in a mobile World*. New York: Routledge.

Gillespie, A. (2006). tourist photography and the reverse gaze. *Ethos (Berkeley, Calif.)*, *34*(3), 343–346. doi:10.1525/eth.2006.34.3.343

Hannam, K., Sheller, M., & Urry, J. (2006). Editorial: Mobilities, immobilities and moorings. *Mobilities*, *1*(1), 1–22. doi:10.1080/17450100500489189

Hardt, M., & Negri, A. (2001). *Empire*. Harvard University Press.

Howie, L. (2010). *Terror on the Screen*. Washington, DC: New Academia Publishing.

Howie, L. (2011). The were created by Man... and they have a plan: Subjective and objective violence in Battlestar Gallactica and the War on terror. *International Zizek Studies.*, *5*(2), 1–19.

Howie, L. (2012). *Witnesses to Terror: Understanding the Meanings and Consequences of Terrorism*. Hampshire, UK: Palgrave Macmillan. doi:10.1057/9781137271761

Ignatieff, M. (2013). *The lesser evil: Political ethics in an age of terror*. Princeton, NJ: Princeton University Press.

Korstanje, M. (2015). *A Difficult World, examining the roots of Capitalism*. New York: Nova Science Publishers.

Korstanje, M. E. (2010). Ironman. *Cultura International Journal of Philosophy of Culture and Axiology*, *7*(2), 188–203. doi:10.5840/cultura20107214

Korstanje, M. E. (2013). The archetype of terrorism: how 11/9 changed the world?. *Sincronía*, (63), 8-22.

Korstanje, M. E., & Olsen, D. H. (2011). The discourse of risk in horror movies post 9/11: Hospitality and hostility in perspective. *International Journal of Tourism Anthropology*, *1*(3-4), 304–317. doi:10.1504/IJTA.2011.043712

Korstanje, M. E., & Tarlow, P. (2012). Being lost: Tourism, risk and vulnerability in the post-9/11entertainment industry. *Journal of Tourism and Cultural Change*, *10*(1), 22–33. doi:10.1080/14766825.2011.639455

Kristeva, J. (1991). Extranjeros para nosotros mismos, trad. de X. *Gispert, Barcelona, Plaza & Janes Editores (Hombre y Sociedad).*

Lash, S. M., Urry, S. L. J., & Urry, J. (1993). *Economies of signs and space* (Vol. 26). London: Sage.

MacCannell, D. (1973). Staged authenticity: Arrangements of social space in tourist settings. *American Journal of Sociology*, *79*(3), 589–603. doi:10.1086/225585

MacCannell, D. (1976). *The tourist: A new theory of the leisure class*. Berkeley, CA: University of California Press.

MacCannell, D. (1984). Reconstructed ethnicity tourism and cultural identity in third world communities. *Annals of Tourism Research*, *11*(3), 375–391. doi:10.1016/0160-7383(84)90028-8

Maccannell, D. (1988). Turismo e Identidad [Tourism & Identity]. In Teodorov Tzvetan. Madrid: Juncar Edition.

MacCannell, D. (1992). *Empty meeting grounds: The tourist papers*. London: Routledge. doi:10.4324/9780203412145

McCauley, C., & Moskalenko, S. (2008). Mechanisms of political radicalization: Pathways toward terrorism. *Terrorism and Political Violence*, *20*(3), 415–433. doi:10.1080/09546550802073367

McCauley, C., & Moskalenko, S. (2011). *Friction: How radicalization happens to them and us*. Oxford, UK: Oxford University Press.

Molz, J. G., & Gibson, S. (Eds.). (2012). *Mobilizing hospitality: The ethics of social relations in a mobile world*. Hampshire, UK: Ashgate Publishing, Ltd.

Moskalenko, S., & McCauley, C. (2009). Measuring political mobilization: The distinction between activism and radicalism. *Terrorism and Political Violence*, *21*(2), 239–260. doi:10.1080/09546550902765508

Piazza, J. A. (2007). Draining the swamp: Democracy promotion, state failure, and terrorism in 19 Middle Eastern countries. *Studies in Conflict and Terrorism*, *30*(6), 521–539. doi:10.1080/10576100701329576

Piazza, J. A. (2008). Incubators of terror: Do failed and failing states promote transnational terrorism? *International Studies Quarterly*, *52*(3), 469–488. doi:10.1111/j.1468-2478.2008.00511.x

Possner, R. A. (1983). *The Economics of Justice*. Cambridge, MA: Harvard University Press.

Powell, J. (2010). Neo-liberalism and Globalization: repetitious inequalities and the implication for a global social theory. In *Sincronia: a journal of Social Sciences and Humanities*. University of Guadalajara.

Riesman, D. (1961). *The Lonely Crowd: A Study of the Changing American Character. 1950*. New Haven, CT: Yale UP.

Sageman, M. (2014). The Stagnation in Terrorism Research. *Terrorism and Political Violence*, 1-16.

Sheller, M., & Urry, J. (2004). *Tourism mobilities: Places to play, places in play*. London: Routledge.

Skoll, G. (2011). Travel Insecurity in North America: the Mexico-US border. *International Journal of Safety and Security in Tourism, 1*(1), 44-63.

Skoll, G. (2016). *Globalization of American Fear Culture: The empire in the Twenty-First Century*. New York: Palgrave-Macmillan.

Skoll, G. R. (2007). Meanings of terrorism. *International Journal for the Semiotics of Law-Revue internationale de Sémiotique juridique, 20*(2), 107-127.

Skoll, G. R. (2008). Torture and the Fifth Amendment Torture, the Global War on Terror, and Constitutional Values. *Criminal Justice Review, 33*(1), 29–47. doi:10.1177/0734016808315585

Sunstein, C. R. (2002a). *Risk and reason: Safety, law, and the environment*. Cambridge, UK: Cambridge University Press.

Sunstein, C. R. (2002b). Probability neglect: Emotions, worst cases, and law. *The Yale Law Journal, 112*(1), 61–107. doi:10.2307/1562234

Tzanelli, R. (2016). *Thana tourism and Cinematic Representation of Risk*. Abingdon, UK: Routledge.

Urry, J. (2002). *The Tourist Gaze*. London: Sage.

Urry, J. (2007). Introduction: Mobile cultures. *Viajes y Geografías*, 17–32.

Urry, J., & Larsen, J. (2011). *The tourist gaze 3.0*. London: Sage. doi:10.4135/9781446251904

Žižek, S. (2001). Have Michael Hardt and Antonio Negri rewritten the Communist Manifesto for the twenty-first century? *Rethinking Marxism, 13*(3-4), 190–198. doi:10.1080/089356901101241875

ADDITIONAL READING

Bauman, Z. (2001). Consuming life. *Journal of Consumer Culture, 1*(1), 9–29. doi:10.1177/146954050100100102

Bauman, Z. (2006). *Liquid Fear*. Cambridge: Polity Press.

Bauman, Z., & Lyon, D. (2013). *Liquid surveillance: A conversation*. New York: John Wiley & Sons.

Eid, M. (Ed.). (2014). *Exchanging Terrorism Oxygen for Media Airwaves: The Age of Terroredia: The Age of Terroredia*. Hershey: IGI Global. doi:10.4018/978-1-4666-5776-2

Korstanje, M. E. (2013). Preemption and terrorism. When the future governs. *Cultura (Asociación de Docentes de la Universidad de San Martín de Porres), 10*(1), 167–184.

Korstanje, M. E. (2015). The spirit of Terrorism: Tourism, Unionization and Terrorism. *Pasos: Revista de turismo y patrimonio cultural, 13*(1), 239-250.

Korstanje, M. E., & Clayton, A. (2012). Tourism and terrorism: Conflicts and commonalities. *Worldwide Hospitality and Tourism Themes, 4*(1), 8–25. doi:10.1108/17554211211198552

Korstanje, M. E., & Skoll, G. (2016). Estados unidos y el principio de extraordinariedad. *Revista de Sociales y Jurídicas*, (11), 390-422.

Korstanje, M. E., Tzanelli, R., & Clayton, A. (2014). Brazilian World cup 2014: Terrorism, tourism, and social conflict. *Event Management, 18*(4), 487–491. doi:10.3727/152599514X14143427352391

MacCannell, D. (2001). Tourist agency. *Tourist Studies, 1*(1), 23–37. doi:10.1177/146879760100100102

MacCannell, D. (2009). "Dmitri Shalin Interview with Dean

MacCannell, D. (2011). *The ethics of sightseeing*. Berkeley: University of California Press. doi:10.1525/california/9780520257825.001.0001

MacCannell, D. (2012). On the ethical stake in tourism research. *Tourism Geographies, 14*(1), 183–194. doi:10.1080/14616688.2012.639387

MacCannell about Erving Goffman entitled "Some of Goffman's Guardedness and Verbal Toughness Was Simply a Way of Giving Himself the Space and Time That He Needed to Do the Work That He Really Loved". *Bios Sociologicus: The Erving Goffman Archives* 1-37.

MacFarlane, J. S. (2014). Desperate times and desperate measures: False-representation and distortion of terrorism in post-9/11 superhero films. *Critical Studies on Terrorism, 7*(3), 446–455. doi:10.1080/17539153.2014.956460

Marx, K., & Engels, F. (1952). *Kapital* [manifesto of communist party]. Chicago: William Benton Publisher.

Sayyid, S. (2014). A measure of Islamophobia. *Islamophobia Studies Journal, 2*(1), 10–25. doi:10.13169/islastudj.2.1.0010

Skoll, G. R., & Korstanje, M. E. (2013). Constructing an American fear culture from red scares to terrorism. *International Journal of Human Rights and Constitutional Studies, 1*(4), 341–364. doi:10.1504/IJHRCS.2013.057302

Soyinka, W. (2005). *The Climate of Fear: the quest for dignity in a dehumanized World.* New York: Random House.

Tzanelli, R. (2006). Not My Flag!Citizenship and nationhood in the margins of Europe (Greece, October 2000/2003). *Ethnic and Racial Studies, 29*(1), 27–49. doi:10.1080/01419870500351217

Tzanelli, R. (2007). *The cinematic tourist: Explorations in globalization, culture and resistance.* Abingdon: Routledge.

Tzanelli, R. (2010). Mediating cosmopolitanism: Crafting an allegorical imperative through Beijing 2008. *International Review of Sociology–Revue Internationale de Sociologie, 20*(2), 215–241.

Tzanelli, R. (2014). Embodied art and aesthetic performativity in the London 2012 handover to Rio (2016). *Global Studies Journal, 6*(2), 13–24. doi:10.18848/1835-4432/CGP/v06i02/40885

Tzanelli, R. (2015). *Mobility, Modernity and the Slum: The Real and Virtual Journeys of'Slumdog Millionaire.* Abingdon: Routledge.

Veblen, T. (2007). *The theory of the leisure class.* Oxford: Oxford University Press.

Virilio, P. (2006) Speed and Politics: An Essay on Dromology [Velocidad y política: Ensayo sobre dromología]. Polizzotti, Mark (trad.). Los Ángeles: Semiotext (e).

Watson, S. (2012) "Review, the Ethics of Sightseeing". *Enlightening Tourism. A pathmaking Journal,* 2, 1, 66-69.

Wilson, M., Bradford, E., & Lemanski, L. (2013) "The role of group process in terrorism" In. Wood, J. L., & Gannon, T. A. (Eds.). (2013). Crime and Crime Reduction: The importance of group processes. Abingdon, Routledge, pp 99-117.

Wood, J. L., & Gannon, T. A. (Eds.). (2013). *Crime and Crime Reduction: The importance of group processes.* Abingdon: Routledge.

Zimbardo, P. (2007). *The Lucifer effect: Understanding how good people turn evil.* New York: Taylor and Francis.

KEY TERMS AND DEFINITIONS

Culture of Fear: A concept ignited to incite fear in population for political peruses.

Estate of Exception: Signals to the act of legislating or governing beyond the authority of law.

Globalization: Socio economic process that integrates internationally nations and economies into the same network.

Mobilities: Act of moving freely without restrictions

Risk: Is the potential harm or loss perceived or real any person faces.

Terrorism: Is defined as the illegal use of violence to achieve goals beyond democratic system.

Tourism: A modern industry which exploits the visitation to destination and leisure goals beyond home for more than 24 hours and less than one year.

Violence: Understood as the use of physical coaction in order to discipline others.

Chapter 4
Providente Asylum vs. the Council of Europe:
The Case of Greece

Zafeiris Tsiftzis
University of Bolton, UK

Iliana Kynigopoulou
National and Kapodistrian University of Athens, Greece

ABSTRACT

The existing European legislative frameworks seem to be unable to deal with the huge amount of refugees. Greece failed to fulfil its obligations according to the European Union Dublin Regulation and allowed refugees to move on a country of their choice. Therefore, taking into account the difficulties that the European states have to face regarding the increasing flow of refugees, the present chapter reviews the existing jurisprudence of the European Court of Human Rights regarding the protection of refugees, in order to explain whether the CoE Member States have obligation to protect and promote the rights of refugees. Moreover, it focuses on the contribution of the Council of Europe in the harmonisation of national policies towards the treatment of refugees. Finally, it assesses the Greek policies with regard to the treatment of refugees and suggests improvements in accordance with the Council of Europe's recommendations.

DOI: 10.4018/978-1-5225-2817-3.ch004

INTRODUCTION

The recent report of the International Organization of Migration (hereinafter as IOM) showed that in 2015 more than 1.000.000 people crossed the Mediterranean borders of Europe (International Organization for Migration, 2015), followed by more than 230.000 people in the first semester of 2016 (International Organization of Migration report for the first semester of 2016). In addition, specialists are expecting the flows to increase until the end of 2016 and during 2017. In these numbers two main categories are included: the economic immigrants and the refugees (Art. 1 United Nations Convention relating to the Status of Refugees, 189 U.N.T.S. 150, entered into force April 22, 1954).

Having in mind the extremely massive immigration flows, the European States still make significant efforts to handle with their huge demands. Towards this direction, the European States are assisted by the guidelines of two most important regional organizations in Europe; the European Union (hereinafter as EU) and the Council of Europe (hereinafter as CoE). Both have already set the named 'refugee crisis' on the top of their agendas in order to address it as well and sufficiently as possible.

More significantly, the matter of refugees has drawn the attention of the CoE with regards to their protection and the elimination of any kind of action that opposes to their rights being on the center of any negotiation in which CoE takes part. Besides, the CoE, in order to protect and promote the human rights of refugees, attempts to harmonize the national standards in relation to the asylum procedures and the reception conditions (European Union Agency for Fundamental Rights, 2014).

Since 1949, the CoE has made an outstanding progress in the harmonization of the national policies of its -up-to-this-date- 47 Member States in the field of democracy, rule of law and human rights. The 47 Members States have enriched with the obligation to protect each and every person that lives within their national territory/jurisdiction regardless their nationality, sex, color and beliefs. A distinct example of the strict human rights protection is the obligations that the Strasbourg institutions create for the States and particularly for these States that have already ratified the European Convention of Human Rights (hereinafter as ECHR).

In addition, the CoE does not operate on its own for the protection of human rights. The established human rights monitoring system; such as the European Court of Human Rights (hereinafter as ECtHR) was created in order to supervise the States Parties in compliance with the ECHR provisions. In the event of any alleged human rights violation, the States and the individuals can bring their case in front of the ECtHR. Further, the ECtHR does not only vindicate the victims of any violation of their rights may be occurred by a State, but also imposes on the States the obligation to comply with its judgments. Therefore, someone could easily conclude that the ECtHR's role is largely transcendental as it mandates the adaptation of its decisions by the national law; the States are forced to comply with the judgement and provide remedies to the victims (Brems and Gerards, 2013).

To continue with, since many refugees become victims of human rights violations occurred by States, the case-law of the ECtHR is referring to the phenomenon of immigrating and asylum seeking. To that extend, the ECtHR found in most of the cases that States Parties to the ECHR failed to provide with quick and sufficient procedures in relation to asylum process and the inhuman conditions of the reception centres. Yet, the main question is why States still violate fundamental human rights and freedoms of the refugees nevertheless the existing international and regional frameworks?

To answer the abovementioned question, someone could take into account different and countless factors; however, nowadays these factors differ because of armed borders and conflicts that are taking place near the European borders and in conjunction with the current economic and social crisis. These factors lead to a general humanitarian crisis that is difficult to be coped with. Moreover, there are several examples from European practices which are not very friendly for the rights of refugees that create a hostile environment for the asylum seekers and refugees.

To this point, the Greek case could be an interesting example as Greece belongs to those countries that – because of the geographical position - welcomes on a daily basis the most refugees rather than any other Member State of the CoE. Moreover, the economic and - as a consequence- social crisis in Greece, the huge refugee flow and its European neighbors' national policies against immigration on their national grounds (Dearden, 2016) may indicate a deep and sharp problem which could shed light on the enormous existing gaps in the European legislative framework. By examining and analyzing the difficult position of Greece and the Greek policy in relation to the asylum seekers and refugees, this chapter aims to give possible answers to an already existing problem that is expected to become permanent during the following years within Europe.

Taking into account all the above, the present chapter reviews the existing legislation of the Council of Europe and jurisprudence of the European Court of Human Rights regarding the protection of refugees, in order to explain whether the CoE member states have obligation to protect and promote the rights of refugees. Moreover, it focuses on the contribution of the Council of Europe in the harmonization of national policies towards the treatment of refugees. Finally, it assesses the Greek policies, as an instance, with regard to the treatment of refugees and suggests improvements in accordance with the CoE's recommendations.

THE ROLE OF THE COUNCIL OF EUROPE IN THE PROTECTION OF THE RIGHTS OF THE REFUGEES

Introduction to the Purpose and Structure of the Council of Europe

Set up on the ruins of the World War II, the main purpose of the CoE was the reconstruction of the European continent on common values (Wassenberg, 2013). These values required decisions by the European States in a sense of good faith and solidarity. However, the outset was made when the leaders of a number of European countries signed the Statute of CoE (Statute of the Council of Europe, 87 U.N.T.S. 103, E.T.S. 1), where the values of the newborn organization had already been placed. In particular, 'the human rights, the democracy and the rule of law' (Art. 3 of the Statute of the Council of Europe, 87 U.N.T.S. 103, E.T.S. 1) are the undeniable principles which have always been examined for any candidate member. On the other hand, if an already Member State has to deal with issues regarding human rights protection, rule of law and democracy, the CoE enacts specific procedures depending on the importance, the events and the continuance of the problems.

In addition, the CoE has a significant number of organs which contribute further to the fulfillment of its purpose. Before arguing their contribution to the refugee crisis, it is worth to point out some key features of these organs. First of all, the Committee of Ministers comprises the ministers of foreign affairs of all Member States. The Committee of Ministers is responsible for the organization's decision making. Whenever the Committee of Ministers reaches a decision, all Member States have to comply with it (Royer, 2010).

Following the Committee of Ministers, Parliamentary Assembly of the CoE (hereinafter PACE) is the first international parliament in history, established in 1949. Its decisions, in contrast to those of the Committee of Ministers, do not impose obligations on the national policies. Still they play a significant and supportive role to the CoE as a whole (Royer, 2010).

Thirdly, the Secretariat has responsibilities in relation to the managing of the Organization's guidelines which assist the Council's organs and bodies in their function.

To conclude, the ECtHR is the CoE's permanent judicial body. What makes ECtHR unique is the fact that any individual has the ability to claim a violation of its human rights against a CoE's Member State, irrespectively of the person's nationality or origin. The contribution of the ECtHR in the refugee's crisis will be extensively discussed below.

The Contribution of the CoE's Organs to the Refugee' Crisis

As the present chapter is discussing the current situation in relation to granting asylum to refugees, it could be beneficial to further demonstrate not only the contribution of the overmentioned organs, but also the assistance of a number of specialized agencies which were established in order to specifically cope with the overdemanding tasks in accordance to the human rights and the refugees within the European jurisdiction.

To begin with, the Commissioner for Human Rights was established in 1999. The Commissioner deals with human rights violations committing among Europe. The Commissioner has to draw the attention of the other CoE's organs on serious human rights violations in the continent (O'Flaherty, Kędzia, Müller and Ulrich, 2011). In relation to the refugees, Mr Nils Muižnieks –the current Commissioner for Human Rights-, carried out a number of visits in the countries that welcome refugees such as Turkey, Greece, Italy, Spain and Former Yugoslav Republic of Macedonia (hereinafter as FYROM). He discussed also with the national authorities, and he received recommendations of the representatives of asylum seekers. Finally, he proposed some specific/special measures for the best interest of the refugees.

The Commissioner for Human Rights does not have the authority to establish obligatory measures to national authorities. However, he has to address a matter to the Committee of Ministers. Moreover, his reports, comments and recommendations push the States to act (Council of Europe, 2016a). To that extent, his reports are taken into consideration by the CoE's organs and the member States while deciding and acting in specific topics; the management and organization of these topics take place in a way oriented on his reports and recommendations. Most of the times, the prestige of the CoE organs and States' is damaged when acting without taking into account the Commissioner's work. That happens because first, the Commissioner has the ability to mention publicly any member's measures against his recommendations and act in a way that puts these measures on the European spotlight; in addition, some of the CoE's organs may address directly a member for opposing to a Commissioner's comment or suggestion. An example could be the current cancel, followed by public announcement of the Commissioner's working visit to the Russian Federation due to restrictions that the Russian authorities put in his investigation in accordance to human rights issues within the country (Human Rights Commissioner Cancels Russia Visit, 2016, October 11).

On the other hand, an important example of the Commissioner's for Human Rights contribution is his comment titled *"Human rights of refugee and migrant women and girls need to be better protected*" (Commissioner for Human Rights, 2016a).

This comment focuses on the female migration and the risks that many women and girls face as they are much more vulnerable than men to human trafficking, exploitation, discrimination and any kind of abuse while entering in the European region. Mr Muižnieks underlined the fact that women and girls who are victims of the above events, should have effective access to the national system of justice. About the asylum seeking procedures, the Commissioner mentions that more female interviewers should be included in the national authorities to service the female asylum seekers. To conclude, Mr Muižnieks suggested that national authorities have to take measures for better and faster service of the female asylum seekers and for the observation of the female refugees and the record of any act against their rights.

Additionally, a distinct example of Commissioner's recommendations is the report entitled as "Time for Europe to get migrant integration right" (Commissioner for Human Rights, 2016b). The recommendation refers, among others, to the right for family reunion, chiefly for the unaccompanied minors and states that the procedures and the waiting periods should be shorter for each and every applicant. Furthermore, as the recommendation suggests, refugees should have equal access to the national education and employment, facts that could easily take place by following some measures which are mentioned in the recommendation's text.

To continue with, since 2016, the Special Representative of the Secretary General on Migration and Refugees was established. At the time, Mr Tomáš Boček has the responsibility to collect and receive information about the situation of migrants and refugees' rights throughout Europe and suggests measures for the prevention of any kind of violation or discrimination against them. Similar to the Commissioner for Human Rights, the Special Representative travels to regions where migrants and refugees enter or live either temporarily or permanently, discusses with the local authorities, notes asylum seekers' testimonials and sees by first hand their conditions of living, health, education etc. His task is completed when he publishes reports and action plans on specific topics such as the issue of the refugee and migrant children's rights, an issue which Mr Boček addresses at present (Council of Europe, 2016).

Migrant and refugee children are particularly vulnerable to sexual exploitation and abuse. During my fact-finding missions I have seen evidence of this.In the Council of Europe action plan that I am preparing to protect these children, we will be proposing assistance to the member states on how to combat this phenomenon (Bocek. 2016)

At the same time, the *"Report of the fact-finding mission by Ambassador Tomáš Boček Special Representative of the Secretary General on Migration and Refugees to Greece and the Former Republic of Macedonia"* (Council of Europe, 2016c) constitutes a significant example of the contribution of this organ to the refugee crisis. Following his visit to refugee camps in Greece and FYROM, he discussed the issue with the relevant ministers of each country, representatives of United Nations' (hereinafter as UN) specialized bodies such as United Nations' High Commissioner for Refugees (hereinafter as UNHCR) in Greece, representatives of Non-Governmental Organizations (hereinafter as NGOs) which offer assistance to refugees and asylum seekers in Greece, delegations of refugees and asylum seekers in the camps, centers for unaccompanied children or hotspots where they have been placed in both countries. In the report's conclusion the Special Representative points out a number of measures that should be taken by each one of the two countries and by the Council of Europe in order to help the national authorities. On the one side, as Mr Boček mentions, the national framework should have some changes in order to follow in a better way the universal standards on the procedures of asylum seeking, but on the other side, the CoE should assist the national authorities in their efforts to modernize and humanize their law. Not only the national authorities do need to get informed and expertise in specific procedures, but also the Council has the obligation to provide the knowledge and the information to the national personnel. The above proposals are only two between an extensive numbers of suggestions that are written down in the Special Representative's report.

For instance, the Special Representative's work could be presented by mentioning, as well, his "*Report on Turkey: Migrant children and refugees living precariously outside camps*", in which he recorded the refugees' situation within the Turkish borders and the challenges that the Turkish authorities meet because of the large refugees' number and as a result its demands. While concluding, Mr Boček suggests the better as possible application of the international obligations that Turkey has to fulfill, such as the United Nations Convention Relating to the Status of Refugees, and the modernization of the Turkish law according to refugees' matters to serve their fundamental rights and demands (Council of Europe, 2016d). Last but not least, the Special Representative's "*report of fact-finding mission on the situation of migrants and refugees in Calais and Grande-Synthe, France*" comes to stress out the living conditions in the so-called "jungle" camp in Calais, placed in the borders of United Kingdom and France. In its concluding remarks, it is proposed the improvement of the accommodations' conditions and the strengthening of the French law on the protection of unaccompanied children.

At the same time with the aforementioned activities, there are several specialized bodies that include in their daily agenda the issue of refugees and asylum seekers, even in a more general way. For instance, the European Committee for the Prevention of Torture and Inhuman or Degrading Treatment or Punishment (hereinafter as CPT). The CPT investigates across the European region how the national authorities treat people who are deprived of their freedom due to a number of reasons. CPT visits prisons, immigration detention centers, psychiatric clinics etc, places where people are obliged to live even for a while (Council of Europe, 2016e). As it could be easily understood, the detention centers for immigrants are places where, in some cases, asylum seekers are forced to live until the procedures for their acceptance as refugees come to an end.

Legal Regulatory Framework in Relation to the Asylum Seekers and Refugees

Considering the above analysis, the present chapter now focuses on the legal framework that fully applies on refugees and asylum seekers. To this point, before proceeding, it could be wise to mention two legal documents of universal significance and application; the Universal Declaration for Human Rights (hereinafter as UDHR) and the International Convention relating to the Status of Refugees.

To begin with the UDHR, it is the first time in the whole history there were recorded the most fundamental human rights and there was underlined the fact that all people have these rights without any discrimination at all. The UDHR – as a cornerstone - has always been the only paradigm for each and every human rights legal document worldwide (Schabas, 2013, Obokata and O'Connell, 2010). It includes articles that also asylum seekers and/or refugees are able to recall in front of any national authority; these articles are 1 – 10, 12, 13, 16 (para. 3), 25 and 26 (para. 1) and - last but not least - the article 14 which addresses specifically asylum seekers and refugees and their right for *"asylum from persecution"* (Chetail, 2014). The UDHR, as its title shows, does not create any obligation to States, but, as mentioned above, it has been existing on the preambles of any conventional document that deals with human rights' issues.

Moreover, what follows is the United Nations Convention Relating to the Status of Refugees and its Protocol - also known as the 1951 Refugee Convention and the 1967 Refugee Protocol respectively - which have been ratified by the total of the 47 member countries of the CoE (Edwards, 2014).

The 1951 Refugee Convention first of all clarifies the exact meaning of the word "refugee" (Art. 1) and right after introduces their basic and inviolable rights which are referred subsequently. Beginning with the right to non-discrimination (Art. 3), next comes the right to religion and the parents' privilege to provide religious education to their children (Art. 4), followed by the exemption from exceptional measures against foreigners and their property (Art. 8), the respect by the host authorities of refugees' movable and immovable property (Art. 13), the provision of the same protection with indigenous people in accordance to their artistic rights and their industrial property (Art. 14), the right of association with some restrictions that have the same effect to everyone living on the national territory (Art. 15), the fundamental right of free access to the national courts and of free providence of legal assistance (Art. 16), the favorable access to employment in contrast to other foreigners who are not refugees, with few exceptions in specific circumstances (Art. 17), the right to set up and run a business (Art. 18), the recognition of their diplomas (Art. 19), the common with the nationals right to rationing (Art. 20), the right to housing, as at each alien person (Art. 21), the right to education and the recognition of any obtained diplomas (Art. 22), the same with the indigenous access to public relief and public assistance (Art. 23), the same with the nationals access and treatment in the labor market and the social security (Art. 24), the administrative assistance to the public paperwork in the case that some of their documents cannot be identified or sent by the national authorities of their origin (Art. 25), the freedom of movement in the national territory where they live as refugees (Art. 26), the provision of identity (Art. 27) or travel documents, with a number of restrictions concerning the travel documents (Art. 28), the exemption of any penalty to those who enter the host country illegally and directly from a territory where their life or liberty are in danger (Art. 31), the national obligation of non-return of refugees or asylum seekers to countries where their life is in danger (Art. 33) and finally their right of access to naturalization (Art. 34). Between all the above rights and liberties, refugees and asylum seekers face a number of specific limitations such as the obligation to obey the law of the host country and its measures for the public order (Art. 2), the acceptance of provisional measures in exceptional cases such as a war situation (Art. 9) and the host authorities' decision for their expulsion, in which case they have the right to submit appeal request (Art. 32). Regarding the Protocol, it introduces a number of articles which relate to the signatories' obligation of informing UN about their national measures on the refugee issue and their commitment of sending reports in specific period of time to the UNHCR Office.

Even if the above legal documents are not adopted within the CoE's framework, it is a matter of great importance that all CoE Member States have signed and ratified them. Moving forward, we will analyze the legal framework of the CoE that applies on the refugee matter (Council of Europe, 1999).

First of all, the ECHR focuses in a way on the refugee and asylum seeking matter (Mole and Meredith, 2010). According to its articles, all the signatories have the obligation to recognize the rights, as they are mentioned in the ECHR, of all the people who depend on their jurisdiction (Art. 1), therefore the rights of refugees and asylum seekers. Moreover, all humans living within the jurisdiction of the European States have the undeniable right to life (Art. 2) and to personal freedom and safety (Art. 5). Additionally, the obligation to refrain from any form of torture, inhuman or degrading treatment (Art. 3) and slavery or forced labor (Art. 4) applies to all States. Furthermore, each person not only does have the right to respect of private and family life (Art. 8), but also, they have the right to their freedom of thought, conscience and religion (Art. 9). Furthermore, the Convention clarifies that everyone has the right to effective remedy (Art. 13) without any discrimination, as a general ban is set on any kind of discrimination against each person (Art. 14).

The ECHR came into force in 1953 and since then it has been amended by 14 Protocols (ETS 5), two of them may also be applied over cases of refugees and asylum seekers; the First Protocol to the ECHR points out the right to education for everyone (Art. 2) and the Forth Protocol underlines the strict ban on collective expulsion of aliens (Art. 4). To conclude with the ECHR, several number of cases that had to do with violations of the above articles were brought before the ECtHR; some cases will be mentioned in the following sections; such as *Cruz Varas v. Sweden* and *Soering v United Kingdom.*

What is next, the European Convention on Extradition (Paris, 13/12/1957, ETS No.024.) refers to any probable case when a State, receiving a request for extradition by the authorities of another state, has substantial reasons to believe that this request has as main purpose the prosecution or punishment of a person because of his/her race, religion, nationality or political opinion (Art. 3, para. 2). In this case the person has the right to seek asylum and live as a refugee in the State whose authorities received the extradition's request.

Moreover, in 1959 the CoE introduced the European Agreement on the Abolition of Visas for Refugees, which came into force in 1960 (Strasbourg, 20/04/1959, ETS No.031). In accordance with its content, the refugees who stay legally within the borders of one of the 47 Member States and have valid travel documents are able to travel without visas up to 3 months in the territory of all the States that are signatories to the Agreement without carrying out any gainful activity on their territory (Art. 1). However, States still have the right to refuse the entrance or the stay to people that are considered as undesirable by their authorities (Art. 4 para. 2) and in specific cases, for the public order, safety or health, a country has the right to temporarily suspend the Agreement's application (Art. 7).

Continuing with the European Social Charter (hereinafter as ESC), it was introduced in 1961, came into force in 1965, amended by 3 Protocols and finally revised in 1996 (Strasbourg, 03/05/1996, ETS No.163). According to its Appendix where there are mentioned the protected persons whom the ESC addresses, refugees should be treated equally by the national authorities in relation to occupation, health insurance, salary, as well the aspects of the rights that the ESC highlights.

Furthermore, in 1972 the CoE was presented the European Convention on Social Security (hereinafter as ECSS) (Strasbourg 14/12/1972, ETS. 078), which gave high attention to the social security law of the Member States, defined the rights of the secured people and the obligations of their employers and also illustrated - among others - the occasions on which the secured are able to get allowances. On its 4th Art., the ECSS specifies the people on whose cases focuses, including the refugees, who, as a consequence, are able to use the ECSS before their employers and the national authorities of the country where they live. The Convention came into force in 1977.

Additionally, the European Agreement on Transfer of Responsibility for Refugees (hereinafter as EATRR) (Strasbourg 16/10/1980, ETS No.107) refers to the transfer of responsibility from a first country to a second, after an uninterrupted period of two years of a refugee's residence to the second's territory, with the consent of its authorities; there is also the case that the authorities of the second state agree earlier than the two-year period with the refugee's residence on the second state's grounds, permanently or for a period that exceeds the specified on the travel document length of his/her stay (Art. 2).

Until the responsibility's transfer takes place, the authorities of the first state have the obligation to extend or renew the refugee's travel document (Art. 3). In case of acceptance by the second country to transfer the responsibility, the second state ought to inform the first about the fact and hereinafter, has the total responsibility for the refugee (Art. 5), something that suggests the second country's obligation to facilitate the refugee's family reunification with his/her wife/husband, their children and any person that is under the refugee's protection (Art. 6). On the other side, in case of non-acceptance, the refugee is obliged to return to the first country after the expiry of his/her travel documents (Art. 4).

As there are many recorded cases of refugees staying in a country after the expiry of their travel documents, the EATRR comes to underline that the second state's authorities submit a readmission application to the first state within six months of the travel documents' expiry date, providing that they know the exact place of refugee's residence on their territory. Is the refugee missing, the authorities are not able to submit the application; do two years pass after the expiry date, the refugee is able to submit residency permit to the authorities of the second country (Art. 4).

Moreover, the European Convention on Nationality (hereinafter as ECN) (Strasbourg, 6.XI.1997, ETS. No. 166) essentially gives the right to refugees to apply for citizenship to the country where they have been officially accepted as refugees. As the ECN mentions, all people who live legally on the territory of a country, have the right to apply for citizenship (Art. 6, para. 3), between these people are the recognized refugees who "lawfully and habitually" are state's residents (Art. 6, para. 4). As for the period of applications' processing, it should be reasonable (Art. 10), followed by the decision which ought to contain written justification (Art. 11). In case of a negative decision there should be the choice of administrative or judicial review for the applicant (Art. 12) with reasonable fees that everyone may afford (Art. 13). Last but not least, there shouldn't be as a condition for obtaining nationality the resignation or the loss of any other preexisting (Art. 16).

To conclude with the legislative framework in relation to refugees and asylum seekers, it is worth to be mentioned that the Council of Ministers and the PACE have to present an extensive and massive number of recommendations on the refugee problem. Even if they do have a non-binding character, in many occasions on which CoE has led to a specific, optional direction for a number of reasons, including the preparation of the member States for a future obligatory decision. To that extent, in 1967 the Council of Ministers made a proposal about the asylum granting to people that are threatened with persecution, something that was legally covered years later. Another example is the recommendations on the use of effective remedy by the refugees, a fact that also took conventional form afterwards. Bearing in mind the above incidents, the Council's future legislative framework could be very well established on the recommendations that the two bodies make currently.

The Contribution of the European Court of Human Rights

Following the analysis of the contribution of the CoE's organs and the conventional framework to the promotion of the rights and freedoms of the refugees and also to respond to the current and emerge situation, it is crucial to highlight the important role of the ECHR towards this direction. Even the ECHR does not provide an explicit framework with regards to the protection of refugees, the interpretation of its provisions through the jurisprudence of the ECtHR makes the conventional framework of the CoE priceless in relation to refugees' issues (35 East African Asians v. United Kingdom. (1979). (DEC.) [GC] No. 4626/70, ECHR; Cruz Varas v. Sweden. (1991) [GC] No. 15576/89, ECHR; Soering v United Kingdom (1989) 11 EHRR 439; Chahal v. United Kingdom. (1997) 23 EHRR 413. See also D. v. United Kingdom (1997) 24 EHRR 42).

The same was emphasized by the ECtHR in *Vilvarajah and Others v. the United Kingdom.* It argued that the right to asylum is not provided by the provisions of the ECHR (Vilvarakah and Others v. the United Kingdom, 1991: para. 102). However, the ECHR has a strong impact on States regarding the refugees and the asylum seekers. For instance, Art. 3 obliges State Parties to refrain from any form of ''torture or inhuman or degrading treatment or punishment' ' (Art. 3 of the ECHR) in relation to those who are living within their jurisdiction –including the refugees. This prohibition is absolute (de Wet, 2004).

To that extent, in the most of the cases in relation to refugees and their status, Art. 3 and Art. 1 of the ECHR are read together in order to emphasize that State Parties hold responsibility for any violation of the ECHR for any event that takes place outside of their jurisdiction. Since 1960, the European Commission of Human Rights (EComHR) and later the ECtHR considered cases of extradition, expulsion, or deportation to a country where the life of the individual is at risk (Cruz Varas v. Sweden, 1991; Soering v United Kingdom, 1989; N. v. the United Kingdom, 2008).

The most known case of this matter is *Soering v. the United Kingdom.* In this case, the ECtHR examined in detail the application of the ECHR on a case of extradition. Briefly, the United States of America decided to extradite Soering from the United Kingdom in order to attend a trial on capital charges. However, the ECtHR found that this constituted a serious violation of Art. 3 of the ECHR with regards to inhuman and degrading treatment. In particular, it also illustrated that one of the primary purposes of the ECHR is to "search for a fair balance between the demands of the general interest of the community and the requirements of the protection of the individual's fundamental right" (Soering v United Kingdom, 1989: para. 89). So as, in extradition cases, the ECHR should be considered under the light of the inhuman and degrading treatment or punishment.

Following the *Soering v. the United Kingdom*, the first case in relation to the refusal of the asylum status to an asylum seeker was brought in front of the ECtHR. The *Cruz Varas v. Sweden* states that the principles set out in *Soering Case* fully applied to decisions to expel and/or to extradite (Cruz Varas v. Sweden, 1991: para. 108). It is worth mentioning that the same approach is adopted by the ECtHR in *Vilvarajah v. the United Kingdom* (Vilvarakah and Others v. the United Kingdom, 1991: para. 103). Therefore, the applicability of Art. 3 to expulsion cases is a very well established practice in the cases regarding refugees. However, in 1995, the United Kingdom was arguing the contrary. For instance, in *Chahal v. the United Kingdom* (Chahal v. United Kingdom, 1997), the EComHR reaffirmed the principle laid down in *Vilvarajah v. the United Kingdom* and denoted that:

[...] expulsion by the Contracting State of an asylum-seeker may give rise to an issue under Art. 3, and hence engage the responsibility of that State under the Convention, where substantial grounds have been shown for believing that the person concerned faced a real risk of being subjected to torture or to inhuman or degrading treatment or punishment in the country to which he was returned [...]. (Chahal v. United Kingdom, 1997: para. 74; Vilvarakah and Others v. the United Kingdom, 1991: para. 103)

Besides, Art. 3 is not the only provision which is relevant to asylum seekers. In some instances, refusing to grant asylum to a refugee may raise significant questions in relation to Art. 2, Art. 5 and Art. 8 of the ECHR.

Currently, in many European States, asylum-seekers are held in detention while their status is being examined by the national authorities. This is often a longstanding process, even the governments elaborate hard to reduce the length of time taken to consider asylum applications. The ECtHR had examined whether the detention of persons pending removal violated the obligations under Art. 5 of the ECHR reads as follow:

1. Everyone has the right to liberty and security of person. No one shall be deprived of his liberty save in the following cases and in accordance with a procedure prescribed by law:
   a. The lawful detention of a person after conviction by a competent court;
   b. The lawful arrest or detention of a person for non-compliance with the lawful order of a court or in order to secure the fulfilment of any obligation prescribed by law;
   c. The lawful arrest or detention of a person affected for the purpose of bringing them before the competent legal authority on reasonable suspicion of having committed an offence or when it is reasonably considered necessary to prevent them committing an offence or fleeing after having done so;
   d. The detention of a minor by lawful order for the purpose of educational supervision or their lawful detention for the purpose of bringing them before the competent legal authority;
   e. The lawful detention of persons for the prevention of the spreading of infectious diseases, of persons of unsound mind, alcoholics or drug addicts or vagrants;
   f. The lawful arrest or detention of a person to prevent their effecting an unauthorised entry into the country or of a person against whom action is being taken with a view to deportation or extradition. You can not have below text citation, everything should be either incorporated in the text or gone.
2. Everyone who is arrested shall be informed promptly, in a language which they understand, of the reasons for their arrest and of any charge against them.
3. Everyone arrested or detained in accordance with the provisions of para. 1(c) of this Art. shall be brought promptly before a judge or other officer authorised by law to exercise judicial power and shall be entitled to trial within a reasonable time or to release pending trial. Release may be conditioned by guarantees to appear for trial.
4. Everyone who is deprived of their liberty by arrest or detention shall be entitled to take proceedings by which the lawfulness of their detention shall be decided speedily by a court and their release ordered if the detention is not lawful.
5. *Everyone who has been the victim of arrest or detention in contravention of the provisions of this Article shall have an enforceable right to compensation*".

In *Louled Massoud v. Malta* ([GC] No. 24340/08, ECHR), the ECtHR held that:

[...] the Court has grave doubts as to whether the grounds for the applicant's detention – action taken with a view to his deportation – remained valid for the whole period of his detention, namely, more than eighteen months following the rejection of his asylum claim, owing to the probable lack of a realistic prospect of his expulsion and the possible failure of the domestic authorities to conduct the proceedings with due diligence [...] (Louled Massoud v. Malta, 2010: para. 60; Muminov v. Russia, 2008).

Similar approach was adopted by the ECtHR in *R.U. v. Greece* ([GC] No. 2237/08. ECHR). The ECtHR emphasized that in case that the national authorities have to deprive the liberty of a person, it should be done in accordance with the domestic law which should be feasible in this regards. Therefore, in order to avoid the detention of a person *"[...] to prevent his effecting an unauthorised entry into the country or against whom action is being taken with a view to deportation or extradition [...]"* (R.U. v. Greece, 2011) must be done in good faith.

At the same time, it is important to notify that Art. 18 of the ECHR provides with the restrictions permitted under the ECHR shall not be applied for any purpose other than those for which they have been prescribed, the detention of a proposed deportee can only be justified under Art. 5, para. 1 (f), if it is related to the deportation proceedings and not for any other purpose.

In particular, in *Caprino v. the United Kingdom* (No. 6871/75, 4 E.H.R.R. 97), the EComHR had concluded that there was an adequate relationship between the detention and the deportation proceedings (Caprino v. U.K., 1978). However, the EComHR never focused in the way in which the British law safeguards the effective implementation of the provision of Art. 5, para. 4. That happened because the British Courts had a very limited jurisdiction over the review of this case (Mole and Meredith, 2010: p. 44). It is also a matter of significance that in *Chahal v. the United Kingdom* did not examine any alleged violation with regards to Art. 5, as the EComHR did in the *Caprino* case. Yet, it preferred to consider the lawfulness of the detention under Art. 13, where the EComHR found a violation.

Furthermore, the decisions of the EComHR are focused on the way in which the proceedings are conducted. For instance, the *Kolompar v. Belgium* held that a violation of Art. 5, para. 1 occurred since five years was excessive and that the proceedings had not been pursued with the requisite speed (Kolompar v. Belgium, 1994: para. 123). On the other hand, in *Chahal v. the United Kingdom*, the EComHR found no violation of Art. 5, para. 1. The reasoning was because the case was very complicated due to the long period of detention – twenty one days- and to a statement made by a panel that is used in national security cases provided *"an important safeguard against arbitrariness"* (Chahal v. United Kingdom., 1997: para. 122). It also re-affirmed that "it is immaterial, for the purpose of Art. 5 (1) (f), whether the underlying decision to expel can be justified under national or Convention law" (Chahal v. United Kingdom., 1997: para. 112). In contrast, at the present case, the ECtHR held that there was a clear violation of Art. 5, para. 4.

In continuance, several asylum-seekers arriving in Europe are not in possession of the relevant identity documents. If the national authorities reject their claims there is the fear that they will be detained or abscond. Further, the ECtHR stipulated that in *Bozano v. France* (Merits, App No 9990/82, A/111, (1991) 9 EHRR 29: para. 8) the detention took place in order to set aside the standard requirements of the extradition procedure. However, in *Ali v. Switzerland* (28 E.H.R.R. 304, ECHR), the detention was a clear violation of Art. 5, para. 1. That happened because the Swiss authorities did not manage to expel the applicant, since he had not the necessary travel documents.

In relation to extradition cases, Art. 8 of the ECHR plays an equity important role. For instance, in *Gül v. Switzerland* (1994) (22 E.H.R.R. 93.), the ECtHR raised concerns with regards to the family life of a person who has already been unlawful or unreasonable to expel. This case was about a Turkish-Kurd who claimed asylum in Switzerland and left his family behind. However, his wife was brought in Switzerland and the government gave her a humanitarian residence permit on the grounds that her health and her life would be endangered if she were returned back to Turkey. Later, they applied for permission in order to bring their older child who was living in Turkey, but they were refused because they were only resident, not domiciled, in the country.

So as EComHR and the ECtHR had to examine first if there was any "interference" with the right to respect for family life, and secondly to determine whether that interference is justified under Art. 8 (2). The ECtHR stated that, since "it has not been proved that she could not later have received appropriate medical treatment in specialist hospitals in Turkey" (Gul v, Switzerland, 1994: para. 41) there was no interference with the right to family life. Similarly, the ECtHR held that their older child grew up in the "cultural and linguistic environment" (Gul v, Switzerland, 1994: para. 42) of Turkey. Even the fact that he was Kurdish, he lived with Kurdish families and never attended a Turkish school. So as, in relation to this matter, the ECtHR found that there was still no interference with the right to respect for family life since there was no obstacle for them to conduct their family life in Turkey.

However, in *Bulus v. Sweden*, the ECtHR argued that family life could not be conducted in the state of origin (Abdulmassih Bulus v. Sweden, 1984: para. 75). The case was about Syrian adolescents threatened with expulsion when their mother and sister were permitted to remain. Yet, the European Commission on Human Rights declared inadmissible the case of *Askar v. the United Kingdom* ([GC] No. 26373/95.

ECHR) on the grounds of the refusal to admit the extended family of a Somali with refugee status in the United Kingdom and the delays in processing the application.

Moreover, the ECtHR had connected the cases of expulsion with Art. 4 of the Protocol No 4 to the ECHR. More precisely, this Art. stipulates that ''collective expulsion of aliens is prohibited''. In 2011, migrants from Somalia and Eritrea were intercepted at sea by the Italian naval authorities and sent back to Libya, while they were from Libya to Italy. The ECtHR found that Italy violated the prohibition of collective expulsion and also held that the migrants had no effective remedy in Italy in that respect and for the first time Art. 4 of the Protocol 4 applies extraterritorially (Hirsi Jamaa v. the United Kingdom, 2012, [GC]. No. 27765/09, ECHR).

In particular, in *Hirsii Jamaa and Others v. Italy*, the ECtHR denoted that:

'the transfer of the applicants to Libya was carried out without any form of examination of each applicant's individual situation. It has not been disputed that the applicants were not subjected to any identification procedure by the Italian authorities, which restricted themselves to embarking all the intercepted migrants onto military ships and disembarking them on Libyan soil. Moreover, the Court notes that the personnel aboard the military ships were not trained to conduct individual interviews and were not assisted by interpreters or legal advisers (Hirsi Jamaa v. the United Kingdom, 2012: para. 185).

However, it was not the first time that the ECtHR highlighted the States Parties' failure to ensure that asylum claims are examined before the applicant's expulsion to their home country. Ten years earlier, in *Čonka v. Belgium*, the ECtHR argued that:

...at no stage in the period between the service of the notice on the aliens to attend the police station and their expulsion did the procedure afford sufficient guarantees demonstrating that the personal circumstances of each of those concerned had been genuinely and individually taken into account'' (Čonka v. Belgium, 2002: para. 63).

EXAMPLES OF NATIONAL POLICIES IN RELATION TO ASYLUM SEEKERS AND REFUGEES

Towards the approach of CoE regarding the protection of the refugees and the asylum seekers, this chapter goes further by pointing out some interesting national practices. On this part, each Member State decided and enforced different aspects of law on the same issue, the refugees and asylum seekers. However, these aspects have two main directions; first, they are strictly addressed on the refugees while entering in a country and, secondly, they focus on a more over-welcoming behavior from citizens and national authorities. The latest direction seems to be met less that the first one, as the European countries try to cope with the huge migration flows in a way that could make them less and deter potential immigrants from entering the European region.

In most of the times, the national borders are guarded by the police or the national army. This phenomenon is very common at the countries of Eastern Europe (Schweitzer, 2012, October 22). For instance, FYROM, Bulgaria, Hungary, Czech Republic and Austria have the leading role on a "coup" against the common EU and CoE policy (How is the migrant crisis dividing EU countries?, 2016, March 4), insisting in closing their borders and improve their security by using the army to protect their national territory from the massive immigration flows (Christides, Amalia, Mayr, Müller, Neukirch, Neumann, Pfister, Puhl, von Rohr and Scheuermann, 2016). It is substantial to underline the fact that the closure of the borders happens via the construction of tall, thick and unapproachable hedges.

At the same time, not only the Eastern European countries built such hedges, but also the United Kingdom - in the aftermath of the worldwide known "Brexit"- built a 13-foot wall on the British – French borders to prevent the immigrants' flows in the country (Britton, 2016, September 7). Another example, could be the 12-foot tall (taller than the famous wall that divided Berlin in the 20th century) wall that is being constructed in Munich and divides the city to protect the local citizens from refugees who will be housed in a camp there (Hall and Holmes, 2016, November 6).

Furthermore, an other one negative feature in relation to the national practices with regards to refugees is the example of Denmark. In January 2016, the Danish parliament adopted a new law that permits police units to investigate the spaces whereas asylum seekers living for any valuable items that worth more than £1.000 ($1.240) and do not have any sentimental value for their owners. According to the Danish authorities, this is a measure that might cover the State's costs for the asylum seekers' treatment (Crouch and Kingsley, 2016, January 26). Moreover, as a response to the above mentioned measure, the Danish government pointed out that nationals are obliged to sell valuable assets that worth more than £1.000 ($1.240) in order to receive state benefits; as a consequence, the new law comes to demonstrate the total equality between Danish people and refugees (Dearden, 2016, January 26).

However, all coins are double-sides; so some other countries such as Sweden give great importance to the quick process of procedures regarding the asylum seekers, to their entrance into the labor market, their family reunification and generally their good quality of life (Becker, 2015, November 3). In parallel, Germany and UK, despite their controversial behavior, try to make the asylum seeking procedures as quick as possible and the thereafter refugees' quality of life in their territory as high as possible (Harding, Oltermann, and Watt, 2016, September 2).

In the next pages, this chapter presents and analyses the Greek approach to the refugee crisis. As we mentioned before, Greece is the first country through which refugees pass while entering to the European territory. So it seems to be the only European country with the most problems to deal with on the refugee matter. However, the same difficult path should be followed by Turkey and Italy because they constitute the 'Mediterranean road to the European paradise' for the refugees as well.

THE GREEK RESPONSE TO THE REFUGEE CRISIS

It was mentioned previously that Greece is always the central point for a large number of migrants who are attempting to enter the EU. The unprecedented flow of migrants the last two years tested Greek asylum system and revealed Greece's inability to control and monitor the massive number of migrants. In 2015, for supporting Greece, the EU adopted two decisions (EU. Council Decision 2015/1601: 80) in order to relocate at least 66,400 persons from Greece to other EU Member States over a period of two years (EU. Council Decision 2015/1523: 146). However, due to resistance from other EU Member States, only 218 people had been relocated from Greece and 279 from Italy. So, the process of the relocation plan is moving so slowly.

It is worthy a mention that in the aftermath of the issuing of two crucial judgements –one by the ECtHR and the other by the Court of Justice of the EU- the Greek asylum system has been identified as having "systemic deficiencies". Thus, Greece had to make significant efforts to comprehensively reform its asylum system. The cornerstone of this reform was the establishment of new reception centers, in order to improve the reception conditions, the fingerprint of irregular migrants and asylum seekers, the improvement of the treatment of unaccompanied minors, and the providing of access to effective remedy in case of any negative decision.

To that extent, the Greek progress is supervised by regional institutions; such as the EU and the CoE. First of all, the European Commission has already issued proceedings against Greece for failing to implement effectively the two abovementioned directives and for not having appropriate and adequate reception conditions (EU. Commission Recommendation: 871). Moreover, the EU Commission - in order to enforce its recommendations -in 2016- published the *Schengen Evaluation Report on Greece* which made significant suggestions regarding the improvement of the external border management and control (European Commission, 2016).

Apart from the functions of the EU Commission, the Committee of Ministers of the CoE has a very important role; the supervision of the implementation of the ECtHR's judgments and the monitoring of Greece's compliance with the ECHR (M.S.S. and Rahimi Groups v. Greece, 2015). At the same time, the regional office of the UN High Commissioner for Refugees (UNHCR) reviews the implementation of Greece's obligations derived by the 1949 Geneva Conventions (UNHCR, 2015; UNHCR, 2014).

The Procedure for Granting International Protection

In 2013, Greece introduced a new procedure in relation to the application process for international protection. The Presidential Decree 113/2013 states that every foreigner and/or stateless person has the right to submit an application for international protection, provided that he or she meets the criteria of the Geneva Conventions and applicable national law or qualifies for subsidiary protection (Art. 4)[1]. After the application made, the national authorities of first reception are obliged to inform the applicants of their rights. The Asylum Service Authority makes decisions on these applications on a case-by-case basis.

Asylum seekers or –much better- all those claiming asylum have the right to stay into the territory of Greece until the application process is completed. And they should not be detained only for the reason that they have applied for international protection.

Moreover, in cases regarding unaccompanied minors, the Asylum Service Authority has to appoint a guardian, in accordance with Presidential Decree 220/2007 (art. 19, para. 1, Nov. 13, 2007). However, minors who are separated from their families or unaccompanied minors are kept in detention centers until their relatives are located and/or until they are housed in appropriate facilities (Presidential Decree No. 113/2013, art. 12).

Once the application process is completed, all the decisions with regards to granting or withdrawing international protection are forwarded to the local office of the UNHCR (Presidential Decree No. 113/2013, art. 14). That happens because the UNHCR has the right to ask for further information on a particular decision.

Furthermore, according to the Presidential Decree 113/2013, the applications for international protection are made at the borders. In these instances, Greek authorities provide the applicants with all the relevant information about for their rights and provide them also with a lawyer and/or an interpreter. The decision with regards to their application should be taken within twenty-eight days from the day of their application. Otherwise, they can enter to Greece in order to ask the authorities to review their case (Presidential Decree 113/2013, art. 24).

Likewise, the Presidential Decree 113/2013 emphasizes under which circumstances the applicants should be kept in detention centers (Presidential Decree 113/2013, art. 12, para. 1). In particular, it notes that a person should be kept in detention until the national authorities confirm his/her documentation and/or in cases that this person constitutes a threat to the public order or to national security (Presidential Decree 113/2013, art. 12, para. 2). However, the detention period should not be longer than three months (Presidential Decree 113/2013, art. 12, para. 6).

In cases that the final decision denies the international protection to an applicant, this applicant has the right to appeal (Presidential Decree 113/2013, art. 25, para. 1). Initially, all the appeals were examined by the Appeals Authority (a body established by Law 3907/2011). Since the mandate of the Appeals Committees expired in 2015, to date there is no appeal process. For this reason, the EU Commission denoted that "the lack of an appeal undermines the effective implementation of the relocation procedure, in which an applicant submits an appeal against a relocation or transfer decision" (EU. Commission Recommendation: 871: para. 18).

Additionally, in 2015, Greece enriched with the obligation to expand its reception capacity for 30,000 people, by providing rent subsidies to the asylum seekers who could not be accommodated in reception centers, and also to host more than 20,000 families with the assistance of the UNHCR.

In 2016, the EU Commission acknowledged that improvements have been made concerning the increase in capacity of reception centers, but stated that reception capacity is still "insufficient". Thus, the EU Commission encouraged Greece to ensure that the reception conditions and access to health care are comparable to the standards derived by Directive 2013/33/EU. It also recommended that Greece ensure that the reception facilities have sufficient staff to handle refugees and that the general maintenance of the reception conditions should be funded by EU funds, if possible.

Greek Failure to Comply With the European Standards

Despite the efforts to improve the reception conditions and/or the detention conditions of the refugees, Greece has several times been found to violate the ECHR in relation to the treatment of refugees. Prior to the enactment of the above mentioned legal framework, an important number of cases were examined by the ECtHR and indicated that Greece has systematically violated the rights of the asylum seekers and/or refugees secured by Art. 3 and Art. 5 of the ECHR.

For instance, in *A.A. v. Greece,* the ECtHR considered the applicant's detention conditions in Samos combined with the duration of three months as a matter of treatment are contrary to the guarantees of Art. 3 (A.A. v. Greece, 2010: para. 62.). At the same time, the ECtHR highlighted that the living conditions of the applicant and his health situation in the detention center of Samos caused by the delay of the Greek authorities to react to the applicant's demands in requesting a doctor. Thus, it had vital consequences up to the level of severity required by Art. 3 of the ECHR.

Similarly, in *Mahmundi and Others v. Greece,* the ECtHR emphasized that the foreign nationals who were detained in the Greek center of Fylakio were held in conditions amounting to inhuman and degrading treatment (Mahmundi and others v. Greece, 2012: para. 66). Yet, the detention center was in a state of serious and continued overpopulation, leading to a large number of detainees having to sleep on the floor. In other words, the ECtHR noted that the large shared dormitories as well as the beds and facilities were not of an acceptable level of cleanliness. All the above amounting to a violation of Art. 3 of the ECHR.

Undouptfully, one of the most important cases raised against Greece –prior to the enactments of the new procedures of granting international protection- is the *M.S.S. v. Belgium and Greece* (2011, [GC], No. 30696/09, ECHR). It is the first case of the ECtHR which considered the compatibility of the Dublin II Regulation with the ECHR. In particular, the ECtHR found that Greece violated Art. 3 because of the applicant's conditions of detention and his living conditions (S.D. v. Greece, 2008: Tabesh v Greece, 2008). Moreover, it is found a violation of Art. 13 of ECHR because of the deficiencies in the asylum procedure followed in the applicant's case and the risk of his expulsion to Afghanistan without any serious examination of the merits of his asylum application and without any access to an effective remedy. However, the ECtHR recognized that by sending the applicant back to Greece and exposing him to risks linked to the deficiencies in the asylum procedure in that State, Belgium also violated its obligations under Art. 3.

However, following the adoption of the Presidential Decree 113/2013, Greece still fails to fulfill its obligations under the ECHR in relation to the treatment of asylum seekers. In 2016, in *R.T. v. Greece* (2016, No. 5124/11, ECHR), the ECtHR found that the applicant did not have sufficient living space at the detention centre; that means a clear violation of Art. 3. Furthermore, his return to Turkey without checking whether his asylum claim was still pending or not, amounts an obvious violation of Art. 13 ECHR.

In addition, in *Mahammad and Others v. Greece*, the ECtHR focused once more on the conditions at the detention centers (Mahammad and Others v. Greece, 2015, No. 48352/12, 15 April 2015, ECHR). The ECtHR denoted that all the applicants reported the serious and permanent overcrowding of the center, forcing many of the detainees to sleep on the floor. Moreover, the dormitories and washing facilities were in serious disrepair; it was also impossible for the applicants to leave the building only under exceptional circumstances.

Finally, the ECtHR held that the detention of an unaccompanied minor at Soufli borders for more than 5 months constitutes a breach of Art. 3 and also a violation of the rights to effective remedy and the right to liberty and security.

CONCLUSION

Following the analysis of the contribution of the CoE and its organs to the protection of rights of the asylum seekers and the refugees, the examination of the regulatory framework on the matter of asylum seekers and refugees, and the inefficiencies of the national measures in order to respond to the massive flows; by giving particular emphasis on the Greek example, the present chapter could conclude whether all these measures are enough with regards to the refugees and asylum seekers' treatment.

The disappearance of more than 10.000 unaccompanied refugee children within the European territory for possible sexual abuse and slavery (Townsend, 2016, January 30), the force to human trafficking for many children, women and men who travel as asylum seekers (Rankin, 2016, May 19), the raise of hate speech and hate crimes by nationals against refugees (Organization for Security and Cooperation in Europe, 2015) as well a number of other facts come to show that both European Union and Council of Europe still have not covered the whole gap on the safeguard of asylum seekers and refugees' rights. As the immigrants' flows arise, the impacts of economic and social crisis still take place in the European households and the European citizens' patience and tolerance reduce, the risks for asylum seekers become more.

The fact that Europe was unprepared for the massive immigrants' entrance in combination with the EU's failure to handle with the issue, which led to extreme national policies by some EU member states, have resulted to the question of the EU capabilities and the up rise of the power and the influence of Council of Europe to substantial decision making procedures.

For the first time is clearly shown the weakness of a specific EU legislation, the Dublin framework on the refugee matter, and the attention turns to another systematic player which is the Council of Europe. As the total and main results of the today's immigration crisis have not been disclosed yet, the future of the two regional organizations, the European Union and the Council of Europe and their role on the regional and international matters is still under the microscope. As for the refugees, as the lawmakers still have pen and paper, their rights will continue to be under improvements.

REFERENCES

Abdulmassih Bulus v. Sweden. (1984). No. 9330/81, Council of Europe: European Commission on Human Rights, 8 December 1984, para. 75.

Addo, K. M., & Grief, N. (1998). Does Article 3 of The European Convention on Human Rights Enshrine Absolute Rights? *European Journal of International Law*, *9*(3), 510–524. doi:10.1093/ejil/9.3.510

Aksar v. the United Kingdom. (1995). [GC] No. 26373/95. ECHR.

Ali v Switzerland (1999) 28 E.H.R.R. 304, ECHR.

Becker, E. (2015, November 3). The Four "Best" Countries for Refugee Resettlement. *UN Dispatch*. Retrieved from http://www.undispatch.com/the-four-best-countries-for-refugee-resettlement/

Berrehab v. the Netherlands (1988). Series A no. 138, p. 14, para. 7.

Bocek, T. (2016). *Statement on the occasion of the European Day on the Protection of Children against Sexual Exploitation and Sexual Abuse*. Retrieved from http://www.coe.int/en/web/portal/resources-special-representative-migration-refugees-tomas-bocek

Bond, M. (2012). *The Council of Europe: Structure, History and Issues in European Politics*. London: Routledge.

Bozano v France, Merits, App No 9990/82, A/111, (1991) 9 EHRR 29. para. 8.

Brems, E., & Gerards, J. (2013). *Shaping Rights in the ECHR: The Role of the European Court of Human Rights in Determining the Scope of Human Rights*. Cambridge, UK: Cambridge University Press. doi:10.1017/CBO9781107337923

Britton, B. (2016, September 7). UK to Build 'Big New Wall' in Calais to Stop Migrants. *CNN*. Retrieved from http://edition.cnn.com/2016/09/07/europe/calais-wall-migrants/

Caprino v. U.K. (1978) No. 6871/75, 4 E.H.R.R. 97.

Chahal v. United Kingdom. (1997) 23 EHRR 413, para. 122.

Chetail, V. (2014). Are Refugee Rights Human Rights? An Unorthodox Questioning of the Relations between Refugee Law and Human Rights Law. In R. Rubio-Maríned (Ed.), *Human Right and Immigration* (p. 17). Oxford, UK: Oxford University Press. doi:10.1093/acprof:oso/9780198701170.003.0002

Christides, G., Amalia, J., Mayr, W., Müller, P., Neukirch, R., Neumann, C., . . . Scheuermann, C. (2016). *Refugee Crisis Pushes Europe to the Brick*. Retrieved from http://www.spiegel.de/international/europe/border-closures-spell-refugee-back-up-in-greece-a-1080643.html

Commissioner for Human Rights. (2016). *Human Rights of Refugee and Migrant Women and Girls Need to be Better Protected: Human Right Comment*. Strasbourg: Council of Europe.

Commissioner for Human Rights. (2016). *Time for Europe to Get Migrant Integration Right: Issue Papers*. Strasbourg: Council of Europe.

Čonka v. Belgium. (2002) No. 51564/99. ECHR. para. 63.

Council of Europe. (1999). *International Law – Conventions of the Council of Europe*. Strasbourg: Council of Europe Publishing.

Council of Europe. (2016). *Commissioner for Human Rights – Country Monitoring*. Strasbourg: Council of Europe Publishers. Retrieved from http://www.coe.int/en/web/commissioner/country-monitoring

Council of Europe. (2016). *The Mandate of the Special Representative on Migration and Refugees*. Strasbourg: Council of Europe.

Council of Europe. (2016). *Special Representative on Migration and Refugees, Report of the fact-finding mission by Ambassador Tomáš Boček Special Representative of the Secretary General on Migration and Refugees to Greece and the Former Yugoslav Republic of Macedonia: Information Documents*. Strasbourg: Council of Europe Publishers.

Council of Europe. (2016). *Special Representative on Migration and Refugees, Report of the fact-finding mission to Turkey by Ambassador Tomáš Boček Special Representative of the Secretary General on Migration and Refugees: Information Documents*. Strasbourg: Council of Europe Publishers.

Council of Europe. (2016). *Special Representative on Migration and Refugees, Report of the fact-finding mission on the situation of migrants and refugees in Calais and Grande-Synthe, France by Ambassador Tomáš Boček: Information Documents*. Strasbourg: Council of Europe Publishers.

Crouch, D., & Kingsley, P. (2016, January 26). Danish Parliament approves plan to seize assets from refugees. *The Guardian*. Retrieved from https://www.theguardian.com/world/2016/jan/26/danish-parliament-approves-plan-to-seize-assets-from-refugees

Cruz Varas v. Sweden. (1991) [GC] No. 15576/89, ECHR; D. v. United Kingdom (1997) 24 EHRR 42.

de Wet, E. (2004). The Prohibition of Torture as an International Norm of *Jus Cogens* and Its Implications for National and Customary Law. *European Journal of International Law*, *15*(1), 97–121. doi:10.1093/ejil/15.1.97

Dearden, L. (2016, January 26). Denmark Approves Controversial Refugee Bill Allowing Police to Seize Asylum Seekers' Cash and Valuables. *Independent.* Retrieved from http://www.independent.co.uk/news/world/europe/denmark-approves-controversial-refugee-bill-allowing-police-to-seize-asylum-seekers-cash-and-a6834581.html

Dearden, L. (2016, February 10). Refugee crisis: Welfare cuts and anti-migration policies 'will not stop' asylum seekers coming to Europe – Report. *Independent.* Retrieved from http://www.independent.co.uk/news/world/europe/refugee-crisis-welfare-cuts-and-anti-migration-policies-will-not-stop-asylum-seekers-coming-to-a6865246.html

East African Asians v. United Kingdom. (1979). (DEC.) [GC] No. 4626/70, ECHR.

Edwards, A. (2014). International Refugee Law. In *International Human Rights Law* (2nd ed.). Oxford, UK: Oxford University Press.

EU. Council Decision 2015/1601 of 22 September 2015 Establishing Provisional Measures in the Area of International Protection for the Benefit of Italy and Greece, 2015 O.J. (L 248) 80.

EU. Council Decision 2015/1523 of 14 September 2015 Establishing Provisional Measures in the Area of International Protection for the Benefit of Italy and of Greece, 2015 O.J. (L 239) 146.

EU. Commission Recommendation of 2/10/2016 Addressed to the Hellenic Republic on the Urgent Measures to Be Taken by Greece in View of the Resumption of Transfers Under Regulation 604/2013, C(2016) 871 final (Feb. 10, 2016).

European Agreement on the Abolition of Visas for Refugees, Strasbourg, 20/04/1959, ETS No.031.

European Agreement on Transfer of Responsibility for Refugees, Strasbourg 16/10/1980, ETS No.107.

European Commission. (2016). *Press Release IP/16/211. Commission Adopts Schengen Evaluation Report on Greece and Proposes Recommendations to Address Deficiencies in External Border Management.* Author.

European Convention for the Protection of Human Rights and Fundamental Freedoms, as amended by Protocols Nos. 11 and 14, 4 November 1950, ETS 5.

European Convention on Extradition, Paris, 13/12/1957, ETS No.024.

European Convention on Nationality. Strasbourg, 6.XI.1997, ETS. No. 166.

European Convention on Social Security, Strasbourg 14/12/1972, ETS. 078.

European Social Charter (revised), Strasbourg, 03/05/1996, ETS No.163.

European Union Agency for Fundamental Rights. (2014). *Handbook on European Law relating to Asylum, Borders and Immigration*. Luxembourg: Publications Office of the European Union.

A.A. v. Greece. (2010). [GC] No. 12186/08, ECHR, para. 62.

Greece, R. U. v. (2011). *No. 2237/08*. ECHR. [GC]

Greece, S. D. v. (2008). *No. 53541/07*. ECHR. [GC]

Gul v. Switzerland (1994). 22 E.H.R.R. 93, para. 42.

Hall, A., & Holmes, S. (2016, November 6). Germany's New Wall: 12ft-High Barrier - Taller than the Infamous Fortification that Once Divided Berlin - is Constructed in Munich to Protect Locals From a Migrant Camp. *Daily Mail*. Retrieved from http://www.dailymail.co.uk/news/article-3909922/A-12ft-high-Munich-Wall-built-protect-locals-German-city-camp-young-migrants-living-community.html#ixzz4RsRVjK8o

Harding, L., Oltermann, P., & Watt, N. (2016, September 2). Refugees Welcome? How UK and Germany Compare on Migration. *The Guardian*. Retrieved from https://www.theguardian.com/world/2015/sep/02/refugees-welcome-uk-germany-compare-migration

Hirsi Jamaa v. the United Kingdom. (2012). [GC]. No. 27765/09, ECHR.

How is the migrant crisis dividing EU countries?. (2016). Retrieved from http://www.bbc.com/news/world-europe-34278886

Human Rights Commissioner Cancels Russia Visit. (2016, October 11). Retrieved from https://themoscowtimes.com/news/human-rights-commissioner-cancels-russia-visit-55684

International Organization for Migration. (2015). World Migration Report 2015: Migrants and Cities – New Partnerships to Manage Mobility. Author.

International Organization of Migration Report for the First Semester of 2016. (n.d.). Retrieved from http://dtmodk.iom.int/docs/Q2_Flows_Compilation_Report.pdf

Jaichand, V., & Suksi, M. (Eds.). (2009). *60 Years of the Universal Declaration of Human Rights in Europe*. Antwerp, Belgium: Intersentia.

Kolompar v. Belgium. (1994). [GC] No. 11613/85, ECHR. para. 123.

Louled Massoud v. Malta. (2010). [GC] No. 24340/08, ECHR.

Mahammad and Others v. Greece (2015) [GC] No. 48352/12, 15 April 2015, ECHR

Mahmundi and others v. Greece (2012) [GC] No 14902/10, ECHR, para. 66.

Mole, N., & Meredith, C. (2010). *Asylum and the European Convention on Human Rights*. Strasbourg: Council of Europe Publishing.

M.S.S. and Rahimi Groups v. Greece. (2015) Nos. 30696/09, 8687/08. Supervision of the Execution of the Court's Judgments.

Muminov v. Russia. (2008) (First Section) No. 42502/06, ECHR

Murdoch, J., & Roche, R. (2016). *The European Convention on Human Rights and Policing*. Strasbourg: Council of Europe Publishing.

O'Flaherty, M., Kędzia, Z., Müller, A., & Ulrich, G. (2011). *Human Rights Diplomacy: Contemporary Perspectives* (pp. 101–124). Leiden: Brill Nijhoff.

Obokata, T., & OConnell, R. (2010). Ambition, achievement and potential: The UK and the Universal Declaration of Human Rights at Sixty. *International Journal of Human Rights*, *14*(3), 394–406. doi:10.1080/13642980802611178

Organization for Security and Cooperation in Europe (OSCE). (2015). *Repost of the Office for Democratic Institutions and human Rights (ODIHR) on hate crime*. Retrieved from http://hatecrime.osce.org/what-hate-crime/racism-and-xenophobia#bm-reports

Presidential Decree No. 220/2007, art. 19, para. 1, Nov. 13, 2007.

Presidential Decree No. 113/2013 on the Establishment of a Common Procedure for Identifying the Refugee Status of Foreigners and Stateless Persons or Subsidiary Protection in Compliance with Directive 2005/85/EC and Other Provisions, June 13, 2013.

Rankin, J. (2016, May 19). Human Traffickers 'Using Migration Crisis' to Force More People into Slavery. *The Guardian*. Retrieved from https://www.theguardian.com/world/2016/may/19/human-traffickers-using-migration-crisis-to-force-more-people-into-slavery

Royer, A. (2010). *The Council of Europe*. Strasbourg, France: Council of Europe Publishing.

Schabas, A. W. (2013). *The Universal Declaration on Human Rights: The Travaux Preparatoire*. Cambridge, UK: Cambridge University Press. doi:10.1017/CBO9781139600491

Schweitzer, A. (2012, October 22). Eastern Europe's Hard Attitude to Refugees is born out of Trauma. *The Guardian*. Retrieved from https://www.theguardian.com/world/commentisfree/2015/oct/22/refugee-eastern-europe-trauma-governments-bigotry

Soering v. United Kingdom (1989) 11 EHRR 439

Statute of the Council of Europe, 87 U.N.T.S. 103, E.T.S. 1.

Tabesh v Greece (2008). No. 8256/07, ECHR.

Townsend, M. (2016, January 30). 10.000 Refugee Children are missing, says Europol. *The Guardian*. Retrieved from https://www.theguardian.com/world/2016/jan/30/fears-for-missing-child-refugees

UNHCR. (2014). *Greece as a Country of Asylum: UNHCR Observations on the Current Asylum System in Greece*. Geneva: UNHCR.

UNHCR. (2015). *Greece as a Country of Asylum: UNHCR's Recommendations*. Geneva: UNHCR.

United Nations Convention relating to the Status of Refugees, 189 U.N.T.S. 150, entered into force April 22, 1954.

v Greece, R. T. (2016). *No. 5124/11*. ECHR.

Vilvarakah and Others v. the United Kingdom. (1991). [GC] Nos. 13163/87; 13164/87; 13165/87; 13447/87; 13448/87, ECHR. para. 102.

Wassenberg, B. (2013). *History of the Council of Europe* (pp. 13–15). Strasbourg: Council of Europe Publishing.

ENDNOTES

1 *Id.* art. 4.

Chapter 5
Supporter, Activist, Rebel, Terrorist:
Children in Syria

Bulut Gurpinar
Gebze Technical University, Turkey

ABSTRACT

Children have always been a part of the war for millennia but child soldiering is often portrayed as something rather new, as a side product of the Post-Cold War in most of the fragile states in the world. Underdevelopment is a feature of the fragile state and especially political violence is a common figure in such states. This paper argues that, children's role changes in fragile states, and further focuses on children in Syrian war and their changing role in the society. While the conflict was turning into a war the role of the children both in the society and in the conflict of which increasing tension was turning it into a war. And when the country, one of the fragile states in the world, collapsed, the government lost control and the children took the sides as terrorists. Given the brief information about the changing roles of Syrian children in this dynamically violent environment, this article will examine the transformation of the role of the children in the fragile state Syria.

INTRODUCTION

Interestingly, despite their significant impact as actors, children are rather neglected in the international relations (IR) studies, hence there are not many studies in the literature addressing the very issue of children in war throughoutly. Child soldiers have been around for millennia, looking at the history, the Spartans of ancient

DOI: 10.4018/978-1-5225-2817-3.ch005

Greece, for example, relied heavily on boys who were around seven years old. Later, the British Navy recruited young boys to serve as cabin boys and cannon prepping throughout the 18th and 19th centuries. Also, substantial numbers of children fought on both sides in the U.S. Civil War, from 1861 to 1865 (Gates and Reich, 2009). Nowadays, more and more children are becoming a part of the conflicts. Of the thirty one countries where there were armed conflicts in 1998, 87 per cent used child soldiers below the age of 18 years while 71 per cent used children under the age of 15 (Global Report, 2008).

State failure is always associated with intrastate violence, the rise of non-state actors, an increased lethality of the weapons employed in offensive and defensive combat, a shady trade in small arms, and a reciprocal commerce in illegally mined and exported minerals, timber, narcotics, and women and children--indeed, in anything that will pay for the desired guns and ammunition. Tensions can deteriorate into conflict through a variety of circumstances, such as predatory or fractured leadership, corruption, or unresolved group grievances. Although the reasons for state weakness and failure are complex, underdevelopment is a feature of a fragile state. Especially political violence is a common figure in such states which are incapable of delivering basic public services to their citizens. When tension and violence exists between groups, the state's ability to provide security and social contract are undermined and further violence may ensue. When the states become "fragile", human rights can be violated or unevenly protected and children may be a part of conflicts due to the lack of governence. States can do more to end child soldier use via policies and practices on arms transfers and military assistance, and in the design of security sector reform programs but when states become "fragile" what can be done to prevent child soldiers?

This paper will try to develop a comprehensive understanding for the relation/correlation between fragile state and the children in conflicts. More and more children are becoming a part of the conflicts, could this trend be driven by the fact that they live in a fragile state? This article attempts to demonstrate the situation of the children in a fragile state, and as an example Syrian war will be examined. First, the definitions of a fragile state and the fragile state index will be given and Syria's position in the fragile state index will be discussed. Then the situation of children in conflicts and in war is demonstrated. Finally, a descriptive picture of children in Syrian war will be presented to see their changing role in war and the link between fragile state index and children suffering will be questioned.

From Failed to Fragile: "Fragile State"

"Failed state" is used by, two retired American burocrats, Gerald B. Helman and Steven R. Ratner in their article called "Saving Failed States" in 1992 and according to Helman and Ratner by the end of the cold war "a disturbing new phenomenon is emerging: the failed nation-state, utterly incapable of sustaining itself as a member of the international community (Helman and Ratner, 1992). Helman and Ratner divide the states into three groups as the failed states (like Bosnia, Cambodia, Liberia, and Somalia, a small group whose governmental structures have been overwhelmed by circumstances), the failing states (Ethiopia, Georgia, and Zaire, where collapse is not imminent but could occur within several years), and the newly independent states in the territories formerly known as Yugoslavia and the Soviet Union, whose viability is difficult to assess (Helman and Ratner, 1992). After this article, *collapsed/failed/ failing states* entered as concepts in the international legal and political discourse (Kaplan, 1994; Pfaff, 1995; Widner, 1995; Mazrui, 1994; Mutharika, 1995; Tyagi, 1995). Since 1992, academics have used the term to describe the absence of the effective government and as early as 1990, "failed state" used by former secretaries Butros-Butros Ghali and Kofi Annan but never by the General Assembly or Security Council (Akpınarlı, 2010). Scholars allege two types of disintegration: the breakup of nation-states into smaller notion-states like Soviet Union of Yugoslavia and the implosion of states (Vale, 1995).

The concept of "the state" is complex and controversial in and of itself, and scholars have long sought to distinguish between varieties of states and varieties of sovereignty (Migdal, 1988; Brooks, 2005; Rotberg, 2003,2004; Stewart, 2006; Lambach, 2007). The state constitute to fulfil a dual function for political order, organise and guarantee public order domestically within a defined territory and second, all states together constitute the global order. As Ulrich Schneckener (2006) argues, "Ineffective, weak, failing or failed states – which can be subsumed under the rubric of fragile statehood – tend to undermine both functions and cause problems at the national, regional and global level."

- Concern over the possibility of state failure thus often has as much to do with dashed expectations about
- Concern over the possibility of state failure thus often has as much to do with dashed expectations about
- Concern over the possibility of state failure thus often has as much to do with dashed expectations about

Fragile states are not like other states, they function according to a different set of sociopolitical dynamics. As such, they harbor uniquely formidable obstacles to stability, development, and democracy. Because of these problems, all transitions are not created equal, and the underlying strength or fragility of societies undergoing those transitions helps determine their success and, more broadly, the prospects for political and economic development. In regions dominated by these countries, borders are more stable, state structures are stronger, institutions are more robust, and growth is faster than elsewhere because populations are more cohesive (Kaplan, 2008). As William Easterly (2000), a well-respected development economist, explains,

Ethnic diversity has a more adverse effect on economic policy and growth when institutions are poor. To put it another way, poor institutions have an even more adverse effect on growth and policy when ethnic diversity is high. Conversely, in countries with sufficiently good institutions, ethnic diversity does not lower growth or worsen economic policies.

In these fragile states, individuals are more likely to feel allegiance to a tribe, religious leader, or clan with which they and their forefathers have been closely connected than to a state with which they have few ties. Groups compete to use the formal institutions for their own selfish objectives (Kaplan, 2008). These conditions provide a suitable situation for the child abuse and there is a link between fragile state and child soldiers.

State failure is always associated with intrastate violence, the rise of non-state actors, an increased lethality of the weapons employed in offensive and defensive combat, a shady trade in small arms, and a reciprocal commerce in illegally mined and exported minerals, timber, narcotics, and women and children--indeed, in anything that will pay for the desired guns and ammunition. There is a tipping point, as Kasfir suggests when nonstate leaders recruit followers and supply them with arms, the arms having been procured from smugglers, on a black market, or by theft or purchase from soldiers or official armories. Until this decisive moment, weak states may appear to be failing. But insurgent attacks fueled by newly obtained arms or provoked by governmental errors or refusals to act, plunge a failing state into a crisis from which it may never recover. When an internal arms race has begun, time for peace is fast running out and failure is probable (Rotberg, 2003).

After the 9/11, the doctrine of pre-emptive military action and the accelerating changes in democracy stated and the national security doctrine authorizing pre-emptive war and the current rapid deterioration of democracy are directly related. If a fragile state can be seen as a threat to other nations, it can be argued that it will be a ligestative point for the war and for the first strike. Fragile state can be seen as a risk for not only itself, but for its neighbours and all around the world and a war based on "fragile" state can be argumentative and questionable.

Quantitative measurement of state failure means the creation of indexes and rankings underlying certain indicators. The *Fragile States Index* (FSI), formerly called *Failed States Index*, the *Fragility Index* (FI) and the *State Fragility Index* (SFI) are particularly important to measure state failure. The Fund for Peace (FFP), The

World Bank, The United Kingdom Department of International Development, and State Failure Task Force are interested in fragile states and they use these indexes for ranking. FFP (2014) defines failed states that:

...state is failing when its government is losing physical control of its territory or lacks a monopoly on the legitimate use of force. Other symptoms of state failure include the erosion of authority to make collective decisions, and inability to provide reasonable public services, and the loss of capacity to interact in formal relations with other states as a full member of the international community.

The Fragile State Index, for 10 years now, created by FFP and published by Foreign Policy, has put countries into perspective by providing an annual snapshot of their vitality and stability and ranking them accordingly (FP, 2014a). FFP created Failed States Index in 2005, then changed the name, and from 2014 to now the index called *"Fragile States Index"* (FSI). Krista Hendry, Executive Director of FFP explains this change; "We decided that instead of talking about whether a state is failed, it made more sense to talk about fragility, because that puts the emphasis on the human beings who are suffering in many of these states."

FSI uses a list of 12 indicators to evaluate state stability; these indicators include demographic pressures, refugees and displaced persons, group grievance, human fight, uneven development, economic decline, delegitimization of state, public services, human rights, security apparatus, factionalized elites, and external intervention (FFP, n.d.). FSI uses the term *"social contract"* to measure the state legitimacy, security apparatus, uneven development, and it defines fragile state with Weberian thinking. Weber's emphasis on the monopoly of violence highlights the state's sovereign authority, and lack of sovereignty is the key element for the fragile state.

FSI measures 177 countries and ranks them from *"worst"* to *"best"* states by combining the 12 different indicators into a single score. The worst states are in danger of or have already virtually collapsed—they are unable to enforce law and order, provide basic social services, or face insurgencies and civil war. The best states are those that have a high quality of life and strong, legitimate states that keep their citizens safe. FSI is based on the FFP proprietary Conflict Assessment Software Tool (CAST) analytical platform (FSI, 2010). Programme divides the world into four regional groupings encompassing twelve smaller regional sub-groupings in order to better analyze and understand the implications of the FSI for every country relative to their *"neighborhood."* (FSI, 2010). After ranking the regions and countries, FSI lists from alert, warning, moderate to sustainable.

After the definition of fragile state and FSI, we can look closer to the Syria's ranking in the FSI as can be seen from Table 1 below.

Table 1. FSI Ranking of Syria, 2005-2015

BDE(178)	Syria	
Years	Rank	Point
2015	9	107,9
2014	15	101,6
2013	21	97,4
2012	23	94,5
2011	48	85,9
2010	48	87,9
2009	39	89,8
2008	35	90,1
2007	40	88,6
2006	33	88,6
2005	29	91,5

Source: FSI 2015

In the FSI 2015 (FSI Syria, 2015) annual ranking, Syria is in the *"high alert"* section with 107,9 total score and has 9 ranking point in 177 countries. As Syria's overall trend from 2006 to 2015 can be seen from the above table, Syria is getting worse and worse by the day. The Uprising in 2011 reflects as a small decline in the score but as the war continues, the fragile index of Syria deteriorates. What can we say about the children of Syria by looking atthe changes in the table? What is happening to children around the country since the beginning of the Arab Uprisings? With a significant decline in controlling power over the states all around the country, armed groups and terrorists took control and children of Syria have been getting victimized and abused. Is it possible to link the use of children in conflicts with the fragile state and collapsed administration?

What we mean by *"state failure"* is perhaps best captured by recalling what we have come to expect from the modern, functioning state. The state is a political entity that successfully exercises a monopoly on the legitimate use of physical force within a given territory and over a given population. A *"normal"* state also commands the loyalty of its citizens and provides core public goods—above all, security and the rule of law, but also markets, transport infrastructure, health, and education. Failed states are those that fall short of these minimal criteria, in that their performance is lacking in terms of security, legitimacy, and/or the capacity to deliver basic welfare-enhancing public goods. State failure is thus a gradational concept, where under-performing states range on a continuum from fragility, to failing and, in extremis, to fully collapsed states (Rotberg, 2003). Viewed through this prism, conditions across much of North Africa and the Middle East appear ominous (Magen, 2012).

Successful states exercise a monopoly on the legitimate use of force within their territory, but they also have the loyalty of their citizens and provide security, the rule of law, markets, infrastructure, markets, health and education. The State Failure Taskforce at George Mason University identified ethnic and revolutionary wars, adverse regime change, and genocide as the four main causes of state failure. All of these are in evidence in today's Arab core states (Teitelbaum, 2012).

Child soldiers can be used not in regular national armies, but in armed groups, guerillas, paramilitary or military forces organized by dissident or secessionist movements, by terrorist organizations or organized crime (Rosenblatt, 1983). "*Child soldier*" issue is an illegal matter, so it can be seen in such criminal areas mostly. For instance, rather than regular/national military forces, paramilitary or rebel groups are more frequently resort to the use of child soldiers, especially active against authoritarian regimes. Children belonging to minorities, mobile or displaced populations

...may be at greater risk of recruitment or use by armed forces or armed groups due to reduced social protection and coping mechanisms, discrimination on the basis of their displaced status or their perceived allegiance with a belligerent (Paris Principles, 2007).

Developing States, having to come to terms with poverty, lack of governance issues, can be a resort to the use of child soldiers. The lack of state sovereignty is the cornerstone of the child soldier issue. Internal or international law and regulation can only yield limited solutions, and when government collapses, in parallel their force and binding will be weaken as well. The child soldiers are mainly an issue in poor, marginalized, or disputed countries, where state sovereignty is challenged. The majority of child soldiers are members of irregular armed groups (Vautravers, 2008). These assumptions can be seen in Syria nowadays.

Children in Conflicts

There is no single or agreed definition of childhood but there is a common idea about the age limit, children are people under 18 years old. Childhood has also become associated with both legal protection and engagement with a sequential attainment of various rights. In terms of national and international law, age is the main criteria for distinguishing an adult from a child (Brocklehurst, 2006). In defining the parameters of childhood, there are various descriptions between national law, international humanitarian law, and regional human rights instruments (Goodwin-Gill and Cohn, 1994).

The earliest documented use of children in warfare begins with the mythologized Children's Crusade in 1212 and throughout the history children of soldiers have joined their parents as soon as they are physically capable (Brocklehurst, 2006). By the end of the eighteenth century in certain regions of France, up to a third of children were killed or abandoned, in particular in towns and in times of famine or hardship (Vautravers, 2008). In the late twentieth century, the use of children in conflicts has increased due to the changing character of warfare. Total war has mobilized citizens including women and children and streets have become battlegrounds. Besides the *"total war"* concept, lighter weaponry contributed to use of children and young fighters in conflicts.

The escalation of warfare brought about by the industrial revolution, the conscription system of the national armed forces of the nineteenth and twentieth centuries, the advent of nuclear weapons and the move towards professionalized armies in the late twentieth century have managed to limit war to a *"symmetric"* confrontation between national actors (Creveld, 1991).

Youth labor and soldier (both issues are linked in a way with the perceptions of the society and the government towards children) can be seen as less costly and children are eager to participate in political activity and war. Gregarious instinct and being a hero attracts children, and they want to become a part of the activity, in this case the activity is war. It can be seen rather pragmatic to use child soldiers as they are easier to lead and command. Historical examples show continuously usage of fanaticized youth groups in times of war, despite their little military value (Creveld, 1982).

In the Second World War, as the war lasted unexpectedly, the drafting age was lowered repeatedly to sustain the armies. Nazi youth organization *"Hitler Jugend"* can be seen as an example of child use in war. Hitler Jugend was a youth movement, officially enrolled in the armed forces from the age of 16 years upwards. It should be noted that allied countries also resorted to the mobilization of their population for the war, women and children served in the forces. During the cold war, children usage in conflicts continued; they were also powerful tools for propaganda war together with the media. For example during the Palestinian intifada children were the catalysts of violent strife against Israeli troops and they were a military art object with specific roles assigned to them, in addition, a stone throwing child was used as a figure and a military art object with specific roles assigned to children of all ages (Cairns, 1996). The use of child soldiers in armed forces and groups has many reasons; such as the mobilization of population for war. For example, in Myanmar 70,000 or more of the Burma army's estimated 350,000 soldiers may be children (HRW, 2002), in Nepal 6,000–9,000 of the Maoist armed forces are believed to be children (HRW, 2007), or in North Korea. It can be argued that international sanctions and pressures can be used as causes and/or pretexts by these countries to militarize and draft their youth.

Increasing use of child soldiers came with the end of the Cold War, especially intra-state wars in the 1990's. The end of the cold war created a new environment in terms of security. It is characterized by the increasingly narrower distinction between peace and war, the increasing numbers of internal conflicts versus the traditional interstate wars and the increasing numbers of failed states, the implications of local and internal conflicts on the regional and international levels. By the end of the cold war extreme changes have occurred, such as the multiplication of actors (including insurgent and irregular groups, foreign and international military contingents, and private military companies), the increased use of irregular and *"asymmetric"* warfare (such as ambushes, terrorism, kidnapping, blackmailing, and torture) and insurgent tactics (such as symbolic action, propaganda and deception, exploitation of the media, targeting representatives of institutions, or the civilian population). New international system made significant changes in child soldiering, both in using them and creating a child image all over the world as icons.

Children can do the things that adults hesitate and "the result is that when children are present in a conflict, experience has shown that they are among the most vicious combatants in the war; indeed, the younger child soldiers are, the more vicious they tend to be" (Frankel, 1995). They could be more obedience and as Nkhonjera (1996) says "they always did what they were told to do, they were fiercely loyal and brave in battle." They are the best soldiers that a commander want, easy to organize and lack of query, total submission. Children are "playing the war game" in Sierre Leone, Mozambique, South Africa and nowadays in Syria, and as can be seen, in these countries the basic protector of children, "government" are collapsed and states are "fragile".

Children in Syria

States can do more to end child soldier use via policies and practices on arms transfers and military assistance, and in the design of security sector reform programs but when states become "fragile" what can be done to prevent child soldiers? Failed State index does not give any information about children but we want to demonstrate what happens to children in failed states and as an example Syria will be taken while the Syrian war will be examined from the view of children of Syria and their changing role in the society. Two million children in Syria are facing malnutrition, disease, early marriage and severe traumas; they are becoming innocent victims of a conflict that has already claimed 70,000 lives (Holmes, 2013).

The role of Syrian children in Syrian war can be seen as victimization which is first caused by the regime, then by the rebels. Later as the war continues children have become constantly suffering from the everlastingviolence. The role of the youth and children is remarkable; however, that of Syrian is especially unusual. Syria's population is perilously young: 50 percent were under 19 years of age, and 57 percent of people under 25 are unemployed (Ajami, 2012). Syrian Uprising affects children the most, for instance, by September 2011, "six months into what was still a peaceful uprising against the Assad regime, and 72 children had been killed" (Saleh,2013).

Children have been the most disadvantageous groups due to their physical and mental capacities. In both cases, children have instrumentalized to perform others/their imagined communities. Children have been used without even understanding the meaning of the war and their abuse has increased with their success. Instead of participating in policy-making and peace building, torture, rape, death and violation of child rights were the issues for the children in the Arab uprising, especially in Syria which is the most fragile state in the region. Militarizing of the children and childhood and identity-affirming acts at the individual and group level also pointed to the importance of everyday symbolic and ideational factors (Weeden, 1999). When the uprising began, the children were ready to take part in it because of politicization.

Children's participation in the Syria war can be divided into three steps: i) unwittingly sparked the revolution, then were targeted by the regime in response, ii) as a result of the regime brutality along with adults spurred to further anti-Assad action, rather than silence and submission, iii) staying in the country and victimization by the terrorists or leaving the country and being a refugee.

Politicizing Syrian childhood and occupying their school time with creating a cult around Assad happened before the revolution, subjective school books, political ideology education classes, singing praises during the morning salute to the flag, and being forced to march chanting for the regime on national holidays, the cult of personality was everywhere (Starr, 2012).

In the early demonstrations, children were the most of those killed, according to Yazbek one doctor says:

There were about 80 dead bodies and approximately 250 patients… 90% of the dead were young men and the killing was done with regular bullets. I was impressed by all the young boys between 15 and 16 years old... Their moustaches were just starting to grow; it was like fuzz. They were just children and they were shot in the head or in the chest (Yazbek, 2012).

Uprising and demonstrations are escalated when the regime victimize children and divide them into two groups assupporters and rebellions, like the first Syrian demonstration against the regime's cruel incarceration of those schoolchildren and the torturing of many of them to death, as in the case of Hamza Ali al-Khateeb (Blanford & Hider, 2011). At the 10th week of the demonstrations, Hamza, a boy from the southern town of Deraa, with the accusation of drawing anti-regime graffiti on town walls, had been subjected to death by getting horrifically tortured. A month later his tortured dead body had been given to his family by the security forces and Hamza's death has given protesters a figurehead for their anger (alexander, 2011). The murder of Hamza is a prime example of the regime's actual targeting of children (Sangeeta et al. 2013). This sparked a conflict of children between Deraa and Damascus and a war inbetween war, war of children, has just started at the beginning.

The regime has sent schoolchildren to a pro-Assad demonstration in Damascus holding up pictures of him and posters that read, *"All of us are with you, Bashar."* This action is evidence of the shift in the power structure that the schoolchildren of Deraa have brought into existence and affirms the power of their voices and graffiti that mark the birth of a new generation that refuses obliquity and subordination. The regime's recruitment of Damascus schoolchildren to lead a pro-Assad demonstration evokes primarily the fragility of the regime and evinces the power of the Syrian children (al- Natour, 2013). Assad's regime has abused those schoolchildren and exploited their childhood by using them as its defenders and young soldiers. "Commanders of armed groups prefer child soldiers because young children, especially the girls, are more obedient, vulnerable, and malleable, and their moral codes are unformed and readily manipulated." (Morales, 2008).

The uncertainty of their destiny and unpredictability of the outcome of going to school during this troubling time have changed schoolchildren's perspectives. Many children refuse to go to school, as the trip to school is becoming more risky every day; either they come into range of a sniper and get killed, or they go home traumatized from the anxiety of being at risk. After the eruption of the revolution, Assad transformed many schools into prisons, where people are executed (Yazbek, 2012, 253). Schools, which are supposed to be the emblem of enlightenment and freedom of speech and thinking, are becoming the darkest places in people's lives, where they lose not only their lives but also everything related to their humanity. The regime shifts the mission of institutions of education from education to the production of a generation of illiterate Syrians that is not only disfigured physically but probably also more damaged psychologically. Militarizing and politicizing institutions of education and directing the malaise towards the future generations' intellectual maturity and critical thinking is a war crime that Assad has committed against his people, especially children. Without showing any respect for children's rights, both the regime and its opponents have circulated images of dead children, dramatizing the loss of their lives and inspiring resistance (Ziter, 2013, 116). In these circumstances as Miriam Cooke noted, "The thin line between what is considered normal behavior and what is considered abnormal is never drawn." (Cooke, 1988,

52). Machiavellian way of thinking is used to normalize everything for the defendence of the regime/power.

As a result of the regime brutality children along with adults spurred to further anti-Assad action, rather than silence and submission. Especially the most important protest came against barrel bomb attacks. People across the Arab world have been expressing solidarity with child victims of barrel bomb attacks in Syria - and opposing President Assad - with the hashtag *"We are the child, you are the barrel"*. The use of barrel bombs has escalated in Aleppo, according to the UN (2013). Pictures claiming to show what the weapons did to child victims (which we could not verify - and which are mostly rather too graphic to show or link to) have started spreading on social media networks and with this protest, victimization of children became a world issue (BBC, 2015).

After the Isis and other terrorist groups' invasion, children abuse escalated. The most horrifying protest against this situation was children in *"death cage"* as pretending like Isis hostages. Anti-government activists in Syria have dressed young children up as Isis hostages and put them in a cage next to a flaming torch in a protest mimicking the death of Jordanian pilot. The children, wearing orange jumpsuits like those frequently seen in the group's execution videos, were holding banners with slogans condemning President Bashar al-Assad. One complained of the international attention given to Isis. It said in Arabic: "We saw your media about the burning Jordanian pilot but we didn't see it when children were burnt." (Dearden, 2015).

In Syria there are tens of thousands of children now living under the control of ISIS and children are actively recruiting as next generation of ISIS fighters, namely as "cubs of the caliphate" (Williams, 2015). The main aim is to create a new army of unquestioning, ideologically pure fighters, ready to become a *"hero"*.

Children were between a rock and a hard place after the Isis, staying in the country and victimization by the terrorists or leaving the country and being a refugee. Several different forms of violence may be referred for refugees after leaving the country: early marriage, sexual slavery, the threat from the local community and the fear of violence (Charles and Denman, 2013, 96). In children's eye, displacement has drastically shifted their sense of belonging. The displaced children compensate for their sense of estrangement and displacement by clinging to the belongings they used to own before their displacement. The children's sense of belonging is inextricably intertwined with their reshaping of the national identity. When children left Syria, they left all their belongings, including their childhood pictures and school and birth certificates (al-Natour, 2013).

Another serious problem which Syrian people faced is fear of sexual violence. According to the *"Save the Children"* charity report, one of the main reasons for families fleeing their homes are sexual violence, the report also touches the very topic of early marriage of young girls forced by their families who are trying to reduce the numbers of mouths they have to feed or hoping that a husband will be able to provide greater security for the threat of sexual violence (Holmes, 2013). Besides from the dangers during the journey to another country women are in much danger because of sexual violence. Since the very beginning of the uprising, children have been suffering. However now with a great detoriation of their sad position in war; they are facing the death while trying to survive. This has been the principal factor behind the almost biblical exodus of desperate migrants in Europe in 2015 (Independent, 2016), which has slowed down slightly but certainly is not going to stop any soon.

CONCLUSION

A brutal civil war in Syria has brought anarchy to the country. Syria's children are the greatest victims of their country's conflict; *the most fragile part of a fragile state*. Syrian children have been shot at, tortured and raped during the unrest and civil war period, suffering from layers and layers of emotional trauma. Children have been participating in all aspects of the revolution, including demonstrations and funeral processions. In this study, we try to demonstrate the victimized children in Syria through the frame of *"fragile state"* term. The data clearly shows that Syria is getting worse in FSI, and in the FSI 2015 annual ranking, Syria is in the *"high alert"* section and has ranked ninth among 177 countries.

Children's position in Syrian war has dramatically differed from the previous conflicts. They have become political figure from the beginning and their role has changed in the society afterwards. Being a most fragile part of the society, they achieved to spark a revolution and made protest against the regime, although their strong voices are not enough for a peace. Without showing any respect for children's rights, both the regime and its opponents have circulated images of dead children, dramatizing the loss of their lives and inspiring resistance. Children have been victimized and their human rights have been violated.

The situation of the Syrian children in war can be analyzed through a chain of a "iconic child pictures". They have first started their involvement as supporters, yet they later have become rebels, then they have ended up either tortured or dead. From the beginning of the uprising till today, child photos made remarkable attention in the world, pictures of dead or suffering children do become iconic, in ways that both hurt and help. Alan Kurdi's photo, the three-year-old Syrian boy who drowned in the Mediterranean Sea is another iconic figure of Syrian war and refugee problem during the Syrian refugee crisis. Alan's lying lifeless body on the beach became a symbol of dying humanity, like Napalm girl photo, quickly spread around the world, prompting international responses and caused grave international outrage. This study is not about imaging of children in war, but maybe it could be a cornerstone for further studies.

Lack of sovereignty is the key element for the fragile state but in Syria the children's situation cannot be solely explained with this factor. The biggest challenge of all in ending the child soldiering lies in the types of conflicts that employ the young. Children tend to be recruited in brutal, long-running civil wars, the kind that simmers for years or even decades. Unfortunately, these wars constitute the main form of armed conflict today. A new approach is urgently needed, an approach which recognizes the vital importance of social cohesion to the development process. Thus, to rebuild *"failed states"*, perhaps we should start at the bottom rather than the top by focusing on people, especially on children, who are our future. Perhaps it should only suggest, rather than insist on, a new formulation, a new fragile state definitions which can include children and their happiness, their rights to be considered. Rather than focusing on "state", maybe we can focuse on "people/children" and begin to think what lies beyond the numbers of indexes. This solution entails reconceptualizing international institutions that are presently based on the nation-state as the representational unit.

Perhaps it is time to contemplate new social formations that are more in line with the wishes of the people our present institutions purport to serve and represent. Whatever the new emergent formations, international law should make every effort to make space for them.

ACKNOWLEDGMENT

I would like to thank my colleague Gokben Aydilek for her patience, understanding, guidance, and most of all the encouragement she has given me during my study.

REFERENCES

Ajami, F. (2012). *The Syrian Rebellion*. Stanford, CA: Hoover Institution Press.

Akpınarlı, N. (2010). *The Fragility of the 'Failed State' Paradigm*. Leiden, Germany: Brill Academic Publishers.

al-Natour, M. (2013). Nation, Gender, and Identity: Children in the Syrian Revolution 2011. *Journal of International Women's Studies*, *14*(5), 28–49.

Alexander, H. (2011). How A 13-Year-Old Boy Became The Face Of The Syrian Uprising. *The Telegraph*. Retrieved from http://www.telegraph.co.uk/news/worldnews/middleeast/syria/8556619/How-a-13-year-old-boy-became-the-face-of-the-Syrian-uprising.html

BBC. (2015). 'We are the child': The anti-Assad Slogan Spreading across the Middle East. *BBC Trending*. Retrieved from http://www.bbc.com/news/blogs-trending-33066361

Blanford, N., & Hider, J. (2011). Regime Sends Children and Conscripts Out On Streets to Hold Back Arab Spring. *The Times*. Retrieved from http://www.thetimes.co.uk/tto/news/world/middleeast/article2965581.ece

Brocklehurst, H. (2006). *Who's Afraid of Children? Children, Conflict and International Relations*. Ashgate Publishing Limited.

Brooks, R. E. (2005). Failed States, or the State as Failure?. *The University of Chicago Law Review. University of Chicago. Law School*, *72*(4), 1160.

Cairns, E. (1996). *Children and Political Violence*. London: Blackwell.

Charles, L., & Denman, K. (2013). Syrian and Palestinian Syrian Refugees in Lebanon: The Plight of Women and Children. *Journal of International Women's Studies*, *14*(5), 96–111.

Cooke, M. (1988). *War's Other Voices: Women Writers on the Lebanese Civil War*. New York: Cambridge University Press.

Dearden, L. (2015). *Syrian Children Dressed Up As Isis Hostages in Death Cage For Anti-Assad Protest*. Academic Press.

Easterly, W. (2000). *Can Institutions Resolve Ethnic Conflict?*. Policy Research Working Paper Series 2482, World Bank.

FFP. (2014). *Fragile State Index*. Retrieved from http://www.fundforpeace.org/programs/fsi/fsindex.php

FFP. (n.d.). *Fragile State Index*. Retrieved from http://fsi.fundforpeace.org/indicators

FP. (2014a). *Fragile States Index*. Retrieved from http://foreignpolicy.com/fragile-states-2014/

FP. (2014b). *From Failed to Fragile*. Retrieved from http://foreignpolicy.com/fragile-states-2014/#postcards

Frankel, M. (1995, August 14). Boy Soldiers. *Newsweek*, 45.

FSI. (2010). *The Failed States Index*. Retrieved from http://www.fundforpeace.org/global/library/cr-10-99-fs-failedstatesindex2010-1103g.pdf

FSI. (2015). *Fragile State Index 2015*. Retrieved from http://library.fundforpeace.org/library/fragilestatesindex-2015.pdf

FSI Syria. (2015). Retrieved from http://fsi.fundforpeace.org/2015-syria

Gates, S., & Reich, S. (2009). Think Again: Child Soldiers. *Foreign Policy*, *22*(May).

Guy, G.-G., & Cohn, I. (1994). *Child Soldiers*. Clarendon Press.

Helman, G. B. & Ratner, S. R. (1992). Saving Failed States. *Foreign Policy*, *89*, 3-20. Retrieved from http://foreignpolicy.com/2010/06/15/saving-failed-states

Holmes, O. (2013). *Syria's children shot at, tortured, raped - charity report*. Retrieved from http://uk.reuters.com/article/uk-syria-crisis-children-idUKBRE92C00R20130313

HRW. (2002). *My Gun was as Tall as Me: Child Soldiers in Burma*. Retrieved from http://www.hrw.org/legacy/reports/2002/burma/

HRW. (2007). *Maoists Should Release Child Soldiers Today*. Retrieved from http://www.hrw.org/en/news/2007/05/06/nepal-maoists-should-release-child-soldiers-now

Kaplan, R. D. (1994, February). The Coming Anarchy. *Atlantic Monthly*, 44.

Kaplan, S. (2008). Fixing Fragile States. Policy Review, 152, 63-77.

Lambach, D. (2007). Close Encounters in the Third Dimension: The Regional Effects of State Failure. In State Failure Revisited I, Globalization of Security and Neighborhood Effects. Institute for Development and Peace, University of Duisburg-Essen (INEF Report, 87/2007).

Magen, A. (2012). On Political Order and the Arab Spring. *Israel Journal of Foreign Affairs VI*, *1*(1), 9–21. doi:10.1080/23739770.2012.11446483

Mazrui, A. (1994, Fall). The Message of Rwanda: Recolonize Africa? *New Perspectives Quarterly*, 18.

Migdal, J. (1988). Strong Societies and Weak States: StateSociety Relations and State Capabilities in the Third World. Academic Press.

Morales, W. Q. (2008). *Girl Child Soldiers: The Other Face of Sexual Exploitation and Gender Violence*. Air & Space Power Journal.

Mutharika, P. (1995). The Role of International Law in the Twenty-First Century: An African Perspective. *Fordham International Law Journal*, 17.

Nkhonjera, P. (1996, January). Children in Bondage. *World Press Review*, *43*, 10.

Paris Principles. (2007). Retrieved from http://www.unicef.org/emerg/files/ParisPrinciples310107English.pdf

Patrick, S. (2006). *Weak States and Global Threats: Assessing Evidence of 'Spillovers'*. Center for Global Development, Working Paper No: 73.

Pfaff, W. (1995). A New Colonialism?. Academic Press.

Report, G. (2008). *Coalition to Stop the Use of Child Soldiers.* Child Soldiers Global Report. Retrieved from https://www.hrw.org/legacy/pub/2008/children/Child_Soldiers_Global_Report_Summary.pdf

Rosenblatt, R. (1983). *Children of War.* London: New English Library.

Rotberg, R. I. (Ed.). (2003). *State Failure and State Weakness in a Time of Terror.* Washington, DC: Academic Press.

Rotberg, R. I. (2004). *When States Fail: Causes and Consequences.* Princeton University Press. doi:10.1515/9781400835799

Saleh, L. (2013). "We Thought We Were Playing": Children's Participation in the Syrian Revolution. *Journal of International Women's Studies*, *14*, 87.

Sangeeta, S., Garofalo, E., & Olimat, M. (2013). Introduction: Children and Arab Spring. *Journal of International Women's Studies*, *14*(5), 1–3.

Schneckener, U. (2006). Fragile Statehood, Armed Non-State Actors and Security Governance. In *Private Actors and Security Governance* (pp. 23–41). Geneva, Switzerland: DCAF.

Starr, S. (2012). *Revolt in Syria: Eye-witness to the Uprising*. Hurst Publishers.

Sylvester, J. H. (1994). *Sub-Saharan Africa: Economic Stagnation, Political Disintegration and the Specter of Recolonization*. 27 LoY. L.A. L. REv. 1299.

Teitelbaum, J. (2012). Failing States: The Real Meaning of the Arab Uprisings. In *Advancing a Free Society*. Hoover Institution, Stanford.

Tyagi, Y. K. (1995). *The Concept of Humanitarian Intervention Revisited*. Michigan Journal of International Law.

UN. (2013). Retrieved from http://www.un.org/apps/news/story.asp?NewsID=46834#.V2E9nLuLTIU

Vale, P. (1995). Engaging the World's Marginalized and Promoting Global Change: Challenges for the United Nations at Fifty. *HARV. INT'L L.J., 36*(283).

Van Creveld, M. (1982). *Fighting Power: German and US Army Performance, 1939–1945*. Westport, CT: Greenwood.

Van Creveld, M. (1991). *Technology and War from 2000 BC to the Present*. London: Brassey's.

Vautravers, A. J. (2008). Why Child Soldiers are such a Complex Issue. *Refugee Survey Quarterly*, *27*(4), 96–107. doi:10.1093/rsq/hdp002

Wedeen, L. (1999). *Ambiguities of Domination: Politics, Rhetoric, and Symbols in Contemporary Syria*. Chicago: University of Chicago Press.

Widner, J. (1995). States and Statelessness in Late Twentieth Century Africa. *Daedalus*, *124*(3), 129-153.

Williams, E. (2015). *Children of ISIS*. Retrieved from http://www.pbs.org/wgbh/frontline/film/children-of-isis/transcript/

Yazbek, S. (2012). A Woman. In *The Crossfire: Diaries of the Syrian Revolution* (p. 113). London: Haus Publishing Ltd.

Ziter, E. (2013). The Image of the Martyr in Syrian Performance and Web Activism. *The Drama Review, 57*(1), 116-136.

Chapter 6
The Syrian Refugee Crisis and the Role of the Organization of Islamic Cooperation (OIC)

Zahid Shahab Ahmed
Deakin University, Australia

ABSTRACT

Following the Arab Spring, the Middle East is in chaos with ongoing wars in Yemen and Syria. There are millions of Syrians seeking refuge in neighboring countries like Turkey and Lebanon, and in European countries like Greece, Hungary, and Germany. Nonetheless, the largest proportion of Syrian refugees in hosted by neighboring countries needing continuous support of the international community. As the issue of Syrian refugees is transnational, there is a need to look for multilateral options for dealing with the crisis. Thus, the role of the Organization of Islamic Cooperation (OIC) becomes crucial. Irrespective of being labelled as a 'talk fest', there is no denying of the fact that OIC has significant potential for tackling grave challenges facing the Muslim world. The problems range from extremism and radicalization to poverty and illiteracy. Now there is the emergent challenge of refugees from the Middle Eastern crisis. This paper evaluates the role of OIC with reference to the Syrian refugee crisis in the Middle East and beyond.

DOI: 10.4018/978-1-5225-2817-3.ch006

INTRODUCTION

The present situation of the Middle East can be best understood in the context of the Arab Spring. In 2010, a Tunisian street vendor, Mohammed Bouazizi, self-immolated himself as a protest against the Tunisian authorities. This personal act triggered a mass movement ultimately leading to the resignation of Tunisian President Zine El Abidine Ben Ali. From Tunisia, this generated spill over effects in other parts of the Muslim world. This phenomenon of resistance against authoritarianism has already toppled regimes in Yemen and Egypt. In addition, popular uprisings have been seen in Syria and Bahrain. Some small scale troubles were also witnessed in Jordan and the UAE (Notten, 2014).

With the Arab Spring stretching to the Middle East, the sectarian nature of conflicts has been very visible. In Bahrain, Shia majority protested against the Sunni government, but the Sunni-dominated GCC helped to crush the resistance. There is a strong sectarian dimension in the Syrian conflict where Iran and Hezbollah are aiding the minority Shia regime of Assad while Qatar and Saudi Arabia are backing the Sunni opposition (rebels) (Notten, 2014). Yemen has become another regional conflict hotspot after removal of President Abdrabbuh Mansour Hadi due to the fight between the Zaidi Shia rebels (Houthis) and the government forces. Saudi Arabia and Iran support different factions in the civil wars in Syria and Yemen. Thus, civil wars have become proxy battlegrounds for Saudi Arabia and Iran's power struggle in the Middle East (Soloway, 2016).

OIC was established as a response to a common external threat – Israel. In the aftermath of the attack on Al-Aqsa Mosque in Jerusalem in 1969, Muslim leaders from around the world united to launch a struggle for the control of the Muslim holy sites in Jerusalem. However, the Organization has fallen short of playing its essential role via-a-vis issues of peace and security in the Muslim world. Irrespective of being labelled as a 'talk fest', there is no denying of the fact that OIC has significant potential for tackling grave challenges facing the Muslim world. The problems range from extremism and radicalization to poverty and illiteracy. Now there is the emergent challenge of refugees from the Middle Eastern crisis. This paper evaluates the role of OIC with reference to the Syrian refugee crisis in the Middle East and beyond. However, before we do that, it is important to be aware of the OIC's role with reference to the issue of refugees.

THE SYRIAN REFUGEES

The Syrian Civil War is a multi-party armed conflict that was triggered by the turmoil of the 2011 Arab Spring. In this multi-party conflict, Iran, Russia, and Lebanon's

Hezbollah support the government of Bashar al-Assad. On the other side, Turkey, Saudi Arabia, France, Qatar, and the US support the opposition to the government. With the involvement of multiple stakeholders, it is natural for a conflict to grow out of proportion. This has been the case of the Syrian Civil War because, by the end of 2014, around 7.6 million Syrians were internally displaced and additional 3.7 million took refuge in other countries (Ostrand, 2015, p. 255). In October 2016, UNHCR reported more than 4.7 million Syrian refugees, including 2.9 million in neighbouring Muslim countries (UNHCR, 2016). This is in addition to a massive loss of human lives that keep on rising due to the increasing intensity of war. According to an estimate, 470,000 Syrians had died by February 2016 (Barnard, 2016). The sudden influx of Syrian refugees has placed enormous stress of resources in neighbouring Lebanon, Jordan, Iraq, Egypt, and Turkey. Since 2013, there has been a rapid escalation in number of Syrians refugees, especially in neighbouring countries (See Table 1).

Since the beginning of the crisis in Syria in 2011, Syrian refugees have been opting for a dangerous journey across the Mediterranean Sea for refuge in Europe. In 2015, 3,770 migrants died crossing the Mediterranean into Europe (BBC, 2016). There are a range of reasons for moving beyond initial ports of entries, for instance secure and sustainable livelihood in Europe. Initial ports of entries are Turkey, Greece and Italy with Turkey being home to the world's largest refugee population – over 2.7 million (UNHCR, 2016). From Turkey, Syrians refugees have been trying to get to Europe, especially Germany, Sweden, and the UK. During 2012-14, asylum was granted by Germany to 39,965, Sweden to 31,771, and the UK to 3,548 Syrians (Ostrand, 2015, p. 270). According to estimate, more than one million refugees, mainly Syrians, reached Europe in 2015 creating a crisis and fissures within the EU. In 2015, 292,540 asylum applications were approved within the EU to applicants from Syria, Eritrea, Iraq, Afghanistan, and Iran (BBC, 2016).

Other than the cultural differences, often refugees have been seen through a traditional security lens. Specifically, with regard to Syrian refugees, concerns

Table 1. Syrian refugees in neighbouring countries

Country	No. of Refugees
Turkey	2,733,655
Lebanon	1,033,513
Iraq	225,455
Jordan	656,400
Egypt	116,175

Source: (UNHCR, 2016)

have been expressed by host countries about the possible infiltration of 'terrorists' or 'armed persons' under the guise of refugees. A study done in Turkey found that, members of hosting communities "have stated that most of the Syrians are not innocent refugees or victims of war, but rather they are Islamic militants and Jihadists" (Ozden, 2013, p. 11). In a survey conducted by Pew Research Centre, half of the population in eight out of ten countries stated, "incoming refugees increase the likelihood of terrorism in our country" (Wike, Stokes, & Simmons, 2016). The opinion of the public in Europe is not any different from their leaders. Recently, German Chancellor Angela Merkel said, "in part, the refugee flow was even used to smuggle terrorists" (Barkin & Carrel, 2016). There is some evidence suggesting that attackers of Paris attacks in November 2015 had entered Europe "posing as refugees" using fake Syrian documents (Gordon, 2016). However, there is still no credible evidence that would justify blanket ban on all refugees seeking protection.

While refugees are increasingly seen as threats to cultures and security of host countries, local communities view refugees as taking their jobs and social benefits. A study conducted in Europe found that people associate the risk of fewer jobs with refugees (Wike et al., 2016). The bigger challenges of hosting refugees are more social and political than economic as "the impact on the economy as a whole is usually not very large" (Cassidy, 2015). There is lack of research on economic consequences, both positive and negative, on host countries.

The above-mentioned factors in the EU and Turkey paved the way for a controversial deal between the two parties in 2016. The main idea of the agreement is to discourage refugees from reaching Europe with Turkey being the key actor. As per the deal, "one Syrian refugee on the Greek islands will be returned to Turkey and, in exchange, a Syrian asylum seeker in Turkey will" be settled in Europe (Kingsley, 2016). Turkey is promised aid of $6.6 billion for dealing with refugees in addition to visa relaxations for its citizens into the EU region (Kanter, 2016). There continues to be a criticism of the EU's this deal because it contradicts its institutional values and the 1951 Refugee Convention. There is another challenge of many Syrian refugees joining their families already settled in Europe, and the EU regulations have provisions for additional valid family members (Collett, 2016). So far, the deal is in serious crisis because it because only 3,000 Syrian refugees were settled by September 2016 – far short of the target of 160,000. Also following the failed coup attempt in Turkey, Ankara pulled back its officers in Greece (Somaskanda, 2016). This further slowed the process that had led to the return of less than 500 Syrian refugees to Turkey from Greece (Somaskanda, 2016). This policy of 'one in, one out' is not only time consuming but is not sustainable because it just focuses on diverting problem, in this case refugees, elsewhere.

THE ROLE OF OIC

Issues of peace and security within the Muslim world are among the top areas of cooperation for the OIC. In 2011, the organization's name was changed from Organization of Islamic Conference to "Organization of Islamic Cooperation". The Organization was established as a response to a common external threat – Israel. Prior to this juncture, the desire for a unified voice of the Muslim *ummah* was represented in localized pan-Islamic political movements, for example the Muslim Brotherhood of Egypt. With 57 member states representing 1.6 billion Muslims, OIC is the second largest multilateral/inter-governmental organization after the UN – well placed to play a much-needed role in dealing with issues of peace and security (Sharqieh, 2012, 162). However, due to differences among its member states, mainly between Iran and Saudi Arabia, the OIC is failing to deal with the ongoing crises in the Middle East. Similar is the criticism on the UN and the EU for failing to deal with the Syrian refugee crisis (MacEoin, 2015).

The OIC, as the umbrella organization of the Muslim world, has been monitoring and reacting to situations affecting Muslims in Muslim majority and non-Muslim countries. Ever since its creation, the issues of Palestine and Kashmir have been central to its work. The Organization has also been able to expand its agenda to deal with emergent challenges to Muslims in the world, for example Muslim refugees, and Islamophobia in the West. It in the post 9/11 context that the OIC decided to address the issue of Islamophobia and regularly publishes in this area. In the aftermath of the ongoing Syrian refugee crisis, the OIC has also observed a rise in Islamophobia in Europe and aims to address it (OIC, 2015b, p. 38). In Europe, cultural differences between the host communities and Muslim refugees have been referred to as reasons for Europe resistance to Muslim migrants. In 2015, the Hungarian Prime Minister, Viktor Orban, was criticized for refusing to host Muslim refugees for keeping "Europe Christian" (Mackey, 2015).

This reaction in Europe is also influenced by erstwhile experience of some states finding it difficult to assimilate migrants from Muslim countries like Turkey, Pakistan, Bangladesh, and Somalia (MacEoin, 2015). However, similar has been the case of Muslim countries hosting Syrian refugees, for example in Turkey, "many accused Syrians of not having manners, speaking and laughing very loudly, being uneducated, having too many children, and harassing women in streets" (Ozden, 2013, p. 10). While, there is evidence to a sudden influx of refugees escalating Islamophobia in Europe, it is important for the OIC is to also address challenges faced by Muslim refugees in Muslim countries. So far, the Organization's work has been limited to statements, for example in *OIC Journal*, it was states that, "the mass migration has, along with Hungary's closing its borders with Croatia, caused many challenges in recent times on account of the failure of the European leaders to reach as agreement limiting the flow of asylum seekers" (OIC, 2015b, p. 38).

Although largely ineffective, the OIC is an important institution for tackling the refugee crises. Being the umbrella organization of the Muslim majority countries, the OIC role in tackling issues of peace and security is crucial because most of the refugees are from Muslim states and hosted by Muslim states. The issue of refugees has been on the OIC agenda for nearly a decade and there has been a direct cooperation between the OIC and the UN. It was in 2006 when the issue of refugees was discussed in an OIC ministerial conference. At the meeting, it was emphasized that OIC members hosting large numbers of refugees need more support from the international community. In addition, it was report that, "there is a growing perception among OIC Member States that refugees burdens are disproportionately spread ... They [members] believe that the international community is not supportive enough in helping them cope with the burden resulting from the presence of refugees and not active enough in seeking political settlements to resolve the refugee-producing crises" (OIC, 2006, p. 13). Similarly, a report mentioned that ten countries accounting for 2.5 percent of the world's GDP are hosting 56 percent of the world's refugees (*Daily Mail*, 4 October 2016); therefore, the sharing of the burden of the refugees is disproportionately spread across the world.

The issue of cooperation with UN agencies, like UNHCR, was the key point of the OIC ministerial meeting held in Turkmenistan in 2012. It was time when OIC members were hosting nearly 11 million refugees – around 50 percent of the world's total (AI, 2015; OIC, 2012, p. 2). At a 2014 meeting between the OIC and the UN, the OIC side emphasized on 'conflict prevention' being a priority area for the Organization. Earlier in 2013, the UN Department of Political Affairs (DPA) had helped in establishing the OIC's Peace, Security and Mediation Unit (Shaikh, 2013). The Unit has operational for nearly three years but its presence is invisible because, so far, the progress has been limited to regular political consultation between the Unit and the UN's DPA in New York (OIC, 2014a). For greater cooperation on tackling refugee crises, the OIC has held coordinating meetings with the United Nations Office of Coordination of Humanitarian Affairs (UNOCHA). The first of such meetings took place in Jeddah in 2006 (OIC, 2007, p. 7), but since then there is no visible evidence of this any meaningful cooperation.

There has been a criticism of rich Gulf countries not taking Syrian refugees, but there is a need to examine this matter carefully. Firstly, Gulf countries are party to the conflict as they are supporting the Opposition against Assad in Syria. Within GCC countries there is a strong opposition to taking Syrian refugee, for instance, a Kuwaiti official said, "They [Lebanon and Turkey] are better suited for the Syrian refugees .... It is not right for us to accept a people that are difference from us. We don't want people that suffer from internal stress and trauma in our country"

Table 2. Top six refugee hosting countries, 2016

Country	Number of Refugees
Turkey	2 million
Pakistan	1.5 million
Lebanon	1.15 million
Iran	950,000
Ethiopia	659,524
Jordan	654,141

Source: (AI, 2015)

(MacEoin, 2015). However, the opposition to Syrian refugees is not an exclusive case because the GCC members are not signatory to the International Convention on Refugee Rights and Statelessness. At the OIC Ministerial Conference on Refugees in 2012, António Guterres (2012) (United Nations High Commissioner for Refugees) had pointed to the need of OIC members signing the Refugee Convection. But still thousands of Syrians refugees have been accommodated on temporary visas in the Gulf states, but refugees move in search of permanent settlement elsewhere, for example in Europe (Kinninmont, 2015). In addition, refugees find it is cheaper to live in Lebanon and Turkey than in Kuwait (MacEoin, 2015). Secondly, there is commitment to humanitarian support is reflected through their continuous monetary support for Syrian refugees. Finally, GCC countries have a long history of generous humanitarian support. For GCC countries, especially Saudi Arabia, aid is used as a tool to maintain leading role in the Muslim world; thus, most of foreign assistance has gone to Muslim countries in Asia and Africa. During 1974 to 1994, Arab countries contributed 13.5 percent towards foreign aid (Villanger, 2007, p. 223). Among the GCC states, Kuwait is a leading contributor of foreign aid for Syrian refugees - $800 million during 2012-2015 – followed by the UAE's contribution of $364 million during the same period (Kinninmont, 2015). The contributions of the Gulf States are far lower than $1 billion from the UK and $3 billion from the US because these are still small economies (Kinninmont, 2015). Internally, there is shortage of funding towards humanitarian crises like the Syrian refugees. The UN reported a shortage of 77 percent ($3.47 billion) of at the end of May 2015 (*Jordan Times*, 25 June 2015). Due to shortage of funds, the World Food Program around 30 percent of Syrian refugees from its food voucher program in 2015 (Kinninmont, 2015). This also meant the host countries have been left to deal with refugees through their own resources.

While many rich Muslim countries are providing direct funding to UN agencies, there is also ongoing work of the OIC that has received less attention. The OIC has the Islamic Development Bank (IDB) with its headquarters in Jeddah. IDB aims to enhance economic cooperation in OIC member states and in 2008 had US$2 billion in capital (Zuhur, 2011, p. 169). In 2006, the Saudi government provided $1 billion to IDB's poverty alleviation program, which is operational in Africa and Asia (Johnson, 2010). The head of the IDB, Dr Ahmad Mohamed Ali, announced at the international donors' conference in London to increase the Group's support to $9 billion during 2016-18 to support countries hosting Syrian refugees (OIC, 2016, p. 15). This is a step in the right direction because host countries need help to counter economic costs of hosting refugees. This response is linked to an increasing demand from host communities for more support from the international community. Countries that host the largest proportion of Syrian refugees receive little international support. To ease the burden of Syrian refugees on Jordan and Lebanon, Japan announced aid of $970 million in April 2016 (The Japan Times, 16 April 2016). Despite international support, host countries are facing consequences of hosting an increasing number of Syrian refugees, for instance clashes between the refugees and the host communities.

There is a realization at the OIC level about the mistreatment of Syria refugees. Thus, the Organization has been trying to pressurize the international community to do more. Looking at Europe, it is also clear that Syrian refugees are just not seen as refugees, but as Muslim refugees. Therefore, the OIC has been calling on international community for considering the crisis as international and not just exclusive to the Middle East or Muslims (OIC, 2015a). at an emergency meeting at the OIC Secretariat in Jeddah, it Secretary General Iyad Ameen Madani said the following:

The Syrian refugees who downed in the Mediterranean, or suffocated in a human trafficker's truck in Austria, none of them are responsible for starting the Syrian crisis or for the failure to stop it. Yet, they are and continue to be the direct victims of both that crisis as well as the failure of the international community, particularly the Members of the UN Security Council, and the countries of the region, to find a solution to it. This must not, and cannot continue to be so (OIC, 2015c).

In the case of the Syrian refugees, the OIC role has also been limited because its donors – rich GCC states – have been preferring regional solutions to regional problems (Kinninmont, 2015). In addition, GCC members have preferred direct coordination with UN agencies instead of using the OIC route. Thus, the forum of OIC has not been used beyond certain statements on the situation in Syria and the plight of Syrians. In addition, the OIC was used as a political tool by the powerful and rich GCC states for their agenda against the Assad regime in Syria. Saudi Arabia for pushing ahead its strict agenda against Bashar al Assad's government in

Syria hosted the OIC's fourth extraordinary summit in Mecca in August 2016. The meeting was attended by 15 heads of states – all Sunni majority states except for Iran with most dependent on heavy Saudi funding – and the decision was made to suspend Syria's membership (OIC, 2014b).[1] Similar to what appears to be a norm at OIC and otherwise, only Iranian President Mahmoud Ahmedinejad objected to the decision of OIC (Alsharif, 2012). If the idea was to isolate and pressurize Assad's regime by suspending Syria's OIC membership, then it did not work. Syria views it as a violation of the OIC's Charter. Through this decision, a big door for playing an effective role in conflict resolution was shut for the OIC. Since them, the OIC has been supportive of external efforts for conflict resolution in Syria, for example through the UN Special Envoy, and the UN Security Council. Ideally, forums like the International Syria Support Group, in which the OIC participates,should have been formulated by the OIC.[2]This also points to the lack of significance of the OIC in the eyes of the leadership of its member states. In addition, the Organization lacks mechanisms to tap on opportunities.

CONCLUSION

The Syrian refugee crisis is on the rise as evident from the response of the international community. There is a lack of political will to deal with the crisis, which is not specific to Muslim countries as evident through the shortage of funding and refusal from many countries, especially in Europe, to accommodate Syrian refugees. In Europe, Syrian refugees are not just refugees, but Muslims with possible connections to armed groups and terrorist. In host communities, especially in Turkey and Europe, Syrian refugees are seen also a threat to local cultures. Then, host communities have been complaining about lack of support for them for bearing the economic burden of hosting thousands of refugees. With reference to Syrian refugees, the huge bulk is still hosted by neighbouring Muslim majority states like Turkey and Jordan. As the country of origin and many host countries are OIC member, the significance of the Organization in tackling with the crisis needs no further justification. However, the role of the OIC has been limited to reactionary statement demanding international community to do more and pledging funding through IDB. The OIC needs to mechanisms in places for effectively and collectively, on behalf of its members, dealing with causes and consequences of humanitarian crises. This would help in mainstreaming coordination with the UN and the EU, and other relevant organizations. While, the OIC has some coordination with the UN, it needs to initiate cooperation with the EU to handle issues of refugees and challenging emerging from the Syrian refugee crisis, such as Islamophobia in Europe. Lastly, it is very important for the OIC to develop mechanism for addressing the root causes of conflicts.

REFERENCES

AI. (2015, October 12). *Global refugee crisis - by the numbers*. Retrieved from https://www.amnesty.org/en/latest/news/2015/10/global-refugee-crisis-by-the-numbers/

Alsharif, A. (2012, August 14). *Organisation of Islamic Cooperation suspends Syria*. Retrieved from http://www.reuters.com/article/us-syria-crisis-islamic-summit-idUSBRE87E19F20120815

Barkin, N., & Carrel, P. (2016, July 11). *'Terrorists' smuggled into Europe with refugees, Merkel says*. Retrieved from http://www.reuters.com/article/us-europe-migrants-extremists-merkel-idUSKCN0ZR1AH

Barnard, A. (2016, February 11). Death toll from war in Syria now 470,000, group finds. *The New York Times*.

BBC. (2016, March 4). *Migrant crisis: Migration to Europe explained in seven charts*. Retrieved from http://www.bbc.com/news/world-europe-34131911

Cassidy, J. (2015, November 18). The economics of Syrian refugees. *The New Yorker*.

Collett, E. (2016, March 1). *The paradox of the EU-Turkey refugee deal*. Retrieved from http://www.migrationpolicy.org/news/paradox-eu-turkey-refugee-deal

Gordon, A. (2016, October 10). Seven of the nine jihadis involved in the Paris terror attacks entered Europe through Hungary by pretending to be refugees. *Daily Mail*.

Guterres, A. (2012, May 11). *OIC Ministerial Conference on Refugees in the Muslim world; opening remarks by Mr António Guterres, United Nations High Commissioners for Refugees*. Retrieved from http://www.unhcr.org/admin/hcspeeches/4fb270979/oic-ministerial-conference-refugees-muslim-world-opening-remarks-mr-antonio.html

Johnson, T. (2010, June 29). *The Organization of the Islamic Conference*. Retrieved from http://www.cfr.org/religion/organization-islamic-conference/p22563

Kanter, J. (2016, March 18). European Union reaches deal with Turkey to return new asylum seekers. *The New York Times*.

Kingsley, P. (2016, March 9). EU-Turkey refugee deal - Q&A. *The Guardian*.

Kinninmont, J. (2015, September 8). *Why aren't Gulf countries taking in Syrian refugees?*. Retrieved from https://www.chathamhouse.org/expert/comment/why-aren-t-gulf-countries-taking-syrian-refugees

MacEoin, D. (2015, September 16). *The Arab states and the refugees*. Retrieved from https://www.gatestoneinstitute.org/6502/refugees-arab-states

Mackey, R. (2015, September 3). Hungarian leader rebuked for saying Muslim migrants must be blocked 'to keep Europe Christian'. *The New York Times*.

Notten, P. W. F. V. (2014). After the Arab Spring: An opportunity for scenarios. *European Journal of Future Research*, *15*(28), 1–6.

OIC. (2006). *OIC ministerial conference on the problems of refugees in the Muslim world*. OIC.

OIC. (2007). *Follow-up report on cooperation between the Organization of the Islamic Conference (OIC) and the United Nations*. Jeddah: Organization of Islamic Cooperation (OIC).

OIC. (2012). *Ashgabat Declaration of the International Ministerial Conference of the Organization of Islamic Cooperation on refugees in the Muslim world*. Jeddah: Organization of Islamic Cooperation (OIC).

OIC. (2014a). *Final document of the general meeting on cooperation between the United Nations and the Organization of Islamic Cooperation*. Jeddah: Organization of Islamic Cooperation (OIC).

OIC. (2014b). *Statement of the Secretary General of the Organization of Islamic Cooperation, Iyad Ameen Madani, at the the Opening Session of the Geneva-II Peace Conference on Syria, Montreux - Switzerland*. Retrieved from http://www.oic-oci.org/oicv2/m/en/topic/?t_id=8846&t_ref=3547&lan=

OIC. (2015a). *Appeal to the international community by the OIC Secretary General to counter the Syrian refugee crisis*. Retrieved from http://www.oic-oci.org/oicv3/topic/?t_id=10404&t_ref=4107&lan=en

OIC. (2015b). Growth in Islamophobia with influx of refugees into Europe. *OIC Journal*, 38-41.

OIC. (2015c). *OIC convenes an emergency meeting to mobilize efforts to address Syrian refugee crisis*. Retrieved from http://www.oic-oci.org/oicv3/topic/?t_id=10430&t_ref=4117&lan=en

OIC. (2016). IDB Group allocates US$9 billion to support countries hosting Syrian refugees. *OIC Journal*, 15.

Ostrand, N. (2015). The Syrian refugees crisis: A comparison of responses by Germany, Sweden, the United Kingdom, and the United States. *Journal on Migration and Human Security*, *3*(3), 255–279. doi:10.14240/jmhs.v3i3.51

Ozden, S. (2013). *Syrian refugees in Turkey*. Retrieved from http://www.migrationpolicycentre.eu/docs/MPC-RR-2013-05.pdf

Shaikh, H. (2013, September 8). OIC's new mediation unit now in operation. *Arab News*.

Sharqieh, I. (2012). Can the Organization of Islamic Cooperation (OIC) resolve conflicts? *Peace and Conflict Studies*, *19*(2), 162–179.

Soloway, B. (2016). *Hajj closed to Iranians after year of discord*. Retrieved from http://foreignpolicy.com/2016/05/12/hajj-closed-to-iranians-after-year-of-discord/?utm_content=buffer6fdee&utm_medium=social&utm_source=facebook.com&utm_campaign=buffer

Somaskanda, S. (2016, September 9). Can this man save the Europe-Turkey migrant deal? *Foreign Policy*.

UNHCR. (2016). *Stories from Syrian refugees*. Retrieved from http://data.unhcr.org/syrianrefugees/syria.php

Villanger, E. (2007). Arab foreign aid: Disbursement patterns, and policies and motives. *Forum for Development Studies*, *34*(2), 223–256. doi:10.1080/08039410.2007.9666378

Wike, R., Stokes, B., & Simmons, K. (2016). *Europeans fear wave of refugees will mean more terrorism, fewer jobs*. Retrieved from http://www.pewglobal.org/2016/07/11/europeans-fear-wave-of-refugees-will-mean-more-terrorism-fewer-jobs/

Zuhur, S. (2011). *Saudi Arabia*. Santa Barbara, CA: ABC-CLIO.

ENDNOTES

1. The Kings of Bahrain and Jordan, Presidents of Egypt, Iran, Yemen, Pakistan, Tunis, Nigeria, Chad, Gabon, Sudan, Bangladesh, Uganda and Turkey attended the summit.
2. The OIC Secretary General, Iyad Madani, had participated in meeting of the International Syria Support Group in Munich in February 2016.

Chapter 7
Hate Speech Towards Syrian Refugees in Turkish Online Reader Comments

Nurhan Kavaklı
Uskudar University, Turkey

ABSTRACT

The aim of this study is to examine the hate speech in the reader comments towards Syrian refugee s in Turkey. Within the framework of this purpose, the reader comments made on the news about the violence towards a Syrian child, which took place on the web page of national newspaper Hürriyet, are analysed. It is hoped that, this study will help reveal the concerns or motives which lie behind the negative point of views and opinions towards Syrian refugees. Thus, it may make a contribution to determining the counter-strategies against the intolerance and hostility towards the refugees.

INTRODUCTION

From the beginning of the civil war in Syria, Turkey draws attention as a country to which Syrians escape to from war by either taking refuge in or using as a bridge on their way to Europe. A majority of the Syrian refugees, whose population is more than 2.5 million (UNHRC, 2016), are living in difficult conditions inside or outside refugee camps. Among the many difficulties that the refugees face are being a target group for intolerance, hostility and hate speech. New media allows the users to participate in media content and therefore, contributes to the democratization of social communication. This is also one of the places where Syrian Refugees could be a target group for hate speech.

DOI: 10.4018/978-1-5225-2817-3.ch007

The benefits of new media technologies and forms contrast traditional media. Such as being digital, interactive, hypersexual, visual, easily shared, and having a multimedia form. These could also pave a new way for production, dissemination and accession of hate speech. Alongside the different new media applications that let the user-derived contents (Facebook, Twitter, YouTube etc.) get into circulation, there are also practises in which the online newspapers give place to reader comments. Owing to the reader comments, the passive position of the readers in traditional journalism that only allow the readers consume news content, has turned into an active one. News readers, herein after, have the chance to transfer their own point of views and opinions of the subject of the news to a public sphere more easily. This situation is positive in terms of building up democratic participation. However, on the other hand, as already mentioned above, it could be a new communication platform where all kinds of hate speech can either be produced or popularized. In other words, the reader comments could degrade into a vehicle for hate speech when readers post malicious comments and direct hatred toward a particular group in the society.

However, to what extent the opinions expressed in the online reader comments are their own opinions is questionable. If we follow in the footsteps of Stuart Hall and Teun van Dijk, we can see that these comments are not formed by themselves independently from dominant ideologies; in other words, power relations in society. According to Hall, "A discourse is a way of talking about or representing something. It produces knowledge that shapes perceptions and practice. It is part of the way in which power operates. Therefore, it has consequences for both, those who employ it and those subjected to it." (1992: 318). Hall (1979: 340) also indicates that the media, which is a powerful source of discourses, constructs for us a definition of 'other'. The media which has become a part of social structure cannot be conceptualized apart from social structure and practice. According to Hall, the media has a dominating power in political, cultural and economical domains: Media legitimates the power relations in a society via its representational practices, which are constructed constantly in the superiority relations of society and, are presented to the society by being repeatedly reproduced. Power relations have to be legitimized continuously by the media as a result of the fact that media is a place in which opposing discourses can flow and struggle to become dominant (1979: 341-346). Van Dijk (1991: 35, 226) regards news as a discourse; however, how the dominant ideologies direct public discourse via media in society is realized by their formation of social cognition on individual level. The dominant ideologies transferred to society by the discourses in media affect the social representations that shape the attitudes, opinions and beliefs of individuals towards a certain social group. The social representations which are re-interpreted by the interaction of individuals in a public sphere are used in the reconstruction of the dominant ideologies in the end. Therefore, the answers of such questions e.g.

"who is a refugee?", "what kind of a person s/he is?", which are already introduced in the media texts, are influential on an individual's interpretation practices and they function in the construction of social "reality" about refugees. In conclusion, this constructed social "reality" can determine the formation of emotions, opinions and behaviours of individuals towards refugees. In this context, it should be taken into consideration that hate speech emerged in the reader comments about Syrian refugees, whom this study is focused on, is formed within the dominant ideologies of society. It also should be taken into consideration that, reader comments show a tendency to be in the same ideological and political position of the newspaper in which they take place. The studies done on reader comments in internet newspapers discovered that the newspaper and audience in society are in accordance with each other in reproduction of dominant discourses– with respect to the tendencies of the mentioned newspaper. (E.g. Cantek Şenol, 2007: 75; Özdemir: 2009).

In this study, within the framework of the points mentioned above, the discursive tendencies towards Syrian refugees in reader comments will be investigated. In the section entitled Main Focus of the Chapter, we will evaluate whether or not the reader comments include hate speech towards Syrian refugees; if so, what beliefs and intentions motivate hate speech directed to Syrians refugees. In order to do so 200 reader comments under the category of "Prominent" among the coverage titled "A Shop Owner Beat a Syrian Child" which took place on the web page of *Hürriyet* newspaper on 21st July 2015, will be analysed by the critical discourse analysis method. If we think of *Hürriyet*'s ideological position, the paper is somewhere in the middle of the political spectrum. It is not an opponent to the political power. However, it has a distanced attitude towards it. It is also a mass newspaper with a high circulation (see Alexa, 2015). Therefore, it is assumed that the reader comments given place in the newspaper will show more successful results in regards to representing the majority of society.

In the news, it is mentioned that a child refugee trying to sell tissue paper in a restaurant in İzmir (a seaside city in western extremity of Anatolia and the third most populous city in Turkey) is hit by someone in-charge. The news is chosen because of its properties, such as- it embodies a violent response and reaction that occurs towards the refugees and similar violence directed towards a small and defenceless child which made it difficult to legitimize the violence.

Before moving onto the next part of the article, an explanation should be made regarding the legal status of Syrians living in Turkey. The status of people who have to leave their countries and move across to other countries are described as asylum seekers, refugees or migrants, depending on the laws or the international agreements the hosting countries adopted. In order to define the legal status of Syrians in Turkey, Turkey applies the 1951 Refugee Convention that it was one of the original signatories of. Since then, it has adopted the Convention with a "geographical limitation" which means that Turkey does not assume full responsibility for refugees coming from countries that are not members of the Council of Europe. Under the Convention, Syrians may be granted a limited protection by Turkey, such as staying for a certain time of period (http://www.refugeesolidaritynetwork.org/learn-more/turkey-asylum-basics/). In the face of difficulties that Syrians are experiencing in Turkey, the Turkish Parliament passed a new law, that went into effect in 2014, in order to ease the legal and bureaucratic conditions for Syrians. However, Turkey's "temporary protection" policy for Syrians remains the same (Kap, 2014). In this study, the word "refugee" is used for Syrians in all kinds of legal statuses in Turkey.

BACKGROUND

Although there isn't a conventional agreement on the definition of hate speech, we will rely on the definition offered by the advisory decision of Committee of Ministers of the Council of Europe in 1997. In the mentioned decision, which is accepted widely as a reference point, Hate speech is defined as:

The term "hate speech" shall be understood as covering all forms of expression which spread, incite, promote or justify racial hatred, xenophobia, anti-Semitism or other forms of hatred based on intolerance, including: intolerance expressed by aggressive nationalism and ethnocentrism, discrimination and hostility against minorities, migrants and people of immigrant origin. (Council of Europe, 1997)

It can also be said that hate speech can be defined as praising the people or groups that a person identifies themselves with, and insulting the other or the others (Weber, 2009:3). According to Raphael Cohen-Almagor (2011), hate speech aims at a group of people and includes hostility and malicious intentions based upon prejudice because of their inherited or existing properties. There is a purpose of encouraging, offending, dehumanising, mobbing, intimidating, victimizing, insensitivity and brutality against the groups in the target of hate speech. The emergence of hate speech happens on the basis of lexical praxis. This lexical praxis covers rude, provocative, insulting, slang, cynical, marginal, aggressive, discriminatory, furious, and labelling usages of words, which serves the praxis of "othering". By labelling "us" and "the other", the one that is not one of "us" is defined. While producing hate speech prejudice, discrimination and stereotypes are widely used. Although all these instruments can be used together, it is also possible to use only some of them. The one that is prominent among these is especially the stigma mechanism. Stigma can be summarized as negative labels tagged on a racial, ethnic, sexist or religious group. According to Erving Goffman (1963), stigma what may be described as a label makes a person feel as someone who is not wanted, liked and approved of. Stigmatization, with regard to prejudices, is society's attitudes towards certain groups and even all behaviours that cast these groups out of the society. All the positive properties of the person or the group which is othered are ignored by stigmatization. Nothing can help to change the negative image of the other.

As there isn't a common definition of hate speech that has been agreed on and also the risk of intermingling the borders between freedom of expression and hate speech, it has proven to be a difficult to study area. However, since hate speech constitutes the mental maps of crime and has the danger of evolving easily to violence, these kind of studies become more important and necessary for the battle against hate speech.

Hate speech, which mostly feeds on provoking prejudices, can make the target groups enemies and thus, can encourage violence against these groups. As it is seen in many modern countries today, hate speech can fuel intolerance and violence towards some groups, especially disempowered groups such as refugees, in society.

Considering the existing studies on the relation between Syrian refugees and media in Turkey, it is seen that almost all of them focus on the national media coverage of the issue. In important parts of the studies, the focus is on racist, exclusionary or other forms of hate speeches. Among these, the ones that are studied by discourse analysis are more important for this study as they indicate the relationship between the dominant ideologies put into circulation of public sphere by media and the formation of social perception towards Syrian refugees.

In these studies, which generally follow in the footsteps of Van Dijk who sees news as a discourse, it is determined that the media produces negative prejudices towards refugees and the refugees are represented with contents not reflecting the reality. As it is also mentioned in the introduction part of this study, Van Dijk points out that "social cognition" is the "minds" of people that are shaped by media in the constitution period of social power. According to Van Dijk when people comment on refugees or various ethnic groups or events about them they don't totally use their own ideological framework (2005: 317, 361). Instead, they use the ideological framework which the power shapes via discourses on media in order to affect the information and beliefs towards various social groups in society (Van Dijk, 1991: 238). To analyse the structure of racist, discriminatory discourses formed on media, however, Van Dijk tends towards linguistic factors such as headlines, news scheme or word choice. It is seen that there are also findings supporting Van Dijk in the studies which analyse discriminatory discourses towards Syrian refugees in Turkey. For instance, the study by Çoban Keneş (2016) in which the author analysed the role of metaphors about refugees in newspaper reports on the construction of discriminatory hegemony/discourses finds that "the refugees are positioned as negative actors of discriminatory, racist discourses implicitly and indirectly". In the article, a similar event to the *Hürriyet* newspaper mentioned in this study, took place in the sample. It is put forward that the refugees are referred to using metaphors such as "inflow", "wave", "explosion", "bill", "cost", "burden", and "fugitive" that have connotations of economy or social threat.

In another study that discusses news discourses, similar findings are also found which mention "how the discriminatory opinions and judgements about refugees are legitimized, and how and by which words the refugees are defined" (Doğanay, Ü. and Çoban Keneş, H: 2016). In the aforementioned study, it is revealed that the Syrian refugees are presented as a "threat", an "economic burden" and a "security problem". As for another finding which draws attention in the studies is the detection of the usage of some positive metaphors or words in the news causing perception confusion in public opinion. For instance, Çoban Keneş (2016:276) points out that on one hand the refugees are presented negatively for being "the cause of unemployment" or "economic burden" and on the other hand they are presented as "low-cost labour" that will lighten the employer's load and consequently provide economic support. Similar perception confusion also emerges in the study of Mesut Yücebaş (2015) which focuses on the new provincialism concept that developed into a Syrian refugee image in Gaziantep's local press.

Yücebaş draws attention to the paradox caused by the discourse of hospitality in which Syrian refugees seen as "the guests" to "us" Turkish people, who are hospitable and charitable, there is a discourse of threat in which the refugees are mentioned as "the guests" who pose a threat to "us" the host. A similar paradox is also seen in "opportunity" and "burden" discourses towards refugees. Yücebaş determines that this paradox which emerges on a discourse level corresponds to the social dynamics (development, will to grow, hesitancy made by profit urges and the wish to provide stability that the system and the traditions promise) of Gaziantep and also in every part of Turkey (The emphases belong to the author of this chapter). In another study, however, it is pointed out that although the refugees are shown as war victims in news media, Turkey is also shown as a victim of refugee "inflow" (Göker and Keskin, 2015).

MAIN FOCUS OF THE CHAPTER

The main focus of the chapter is on the discursive tendencies towards Syrian refugees in the reader comments, especially those containing hate speech. Within the context of the study, the first 200 readers' comments which took place under the category of "prominent" of the reader comments made on the 21st July-24th July are analysed by critical discourse analysis method. Although the method of critical discourse analysis of Van Dijk, which is used widely in analysing media texts, is used as a base, the method is applied according to the aim and scope of the study. While analysing the comments, it is tried to reveal whether the comments that reached the level of hate speech are present. In order to do that the comments are put into categories according to the qualities and characteristics they have. For the analysis, the categories, which were developed based on international scientific studies and used by Hrant Dink Foundation for its monthly reports called "The Examination of Hate Speech in the Media" are used. (Hrant Dink Foundation is a non-governmental organization named in memory of murdered Turkish-Armenian journalist, Hrant Dink, who was a target of hate-speech.) (Dink, 2013)

The categories are below:

1. **Exaggeration / Distortion:** Speeches including negative generalizations, distortions, exaggerations or attributions that are towards a group on the basis of a person or an event.
2. **Swearing/Insult/Humiliation:** Speeches including direct swearing, insulting or humiliation of a certain group.
3. **Using Natural Identity Element as a Hate-Humiliation Factor/ Symbolization:** Speeches in which natural identity element is used and symbolized as a hate, humiliation factor.
4. **Hostility / War Speech:** Speeches in which there are hostile expressions that recall war about a group.

Findings

Table 1 shows the distribution of comments containing and excluding hate speech.

Table 1. Distribution of comments

Distribution of Comments	
Comments Containing Hate Speech	65
Exaggeration/Distortion	33
Swearing/Insult/Humiliation	12
Using Natural Identity Elements as a Hate-Humiliation Factor/Symbolization	3
Hostilitiy/War Speech	17
Comments not Including Hate Speech	135
Total	200

Exaggeration / Distortion

In the comments of this category, it is seen that there are a lot of prejudices and stigmatization carried with it towards Syrian refugees and even all Arabs. Being a Syrian or Arab is presented as a cause of negation by making generalizations, distortions and insulting epithets for all Syrians and Arabs in the comments. The comments, in which there are emotions fuelling violence such as "boredom", "intolerance", "annoyance" and "anger", approach to refugees as "an economic threat", "economic burden", " a security problem" and "a cultural threat". In the discourses, which are basically developed with the opposition of Syrians/Arabs (Other) – Turks (Us), metaphors such as "sticky creatures", "cruddy", "freak", "imposter", "harasser", "thief", "prostitute" and "drifter" are made for Syrians/Arabs. On the other hand Turks are referred with praising statements such as "honest", "hard-working", "civilized", "honourable" or "responsible". For instance, a reader nicknamed "Foremost Motherland" associates all the Syrian refugees with crime by exaggeration:

If anyone wants the Syrians let him/her look after them at his/her home... When these Syrians go hungry and commit a theft or attack our own people I'll see you then ... Let the oil-rich Arabs do a favour. We are not the world's fools. The country is filled with Syrians who have all kinds of diseases"

In another comment, it is implied that the main purpose of the Syrian refugees is to settle down in Turkey under a pretense of war. It is even exaggeratedly claimed that Syrians who came to Turkey are Kurds that want to change the demographic structure of Turkey in favour of Kurds:

Özgür Gencer: *The solution is simple. His mother and his other cognates will pick up their marbles and go to Middle Eastern territories where they belong (...) Don't they come to İzmir and say "we escaped from war" without shame? Most of those you call Syrian are actually El Kurdo. Their aim is to ruin Turkey's demographic structure completely.*

When taking into consideration the Justice and Development Party's (AKP) open door policy for Syrian refugees, it seems possible to make a relation between the reactions at AKP politics in society and this kind of discourse in the readers' comments which totally miss out the extent of the humanitarian plight and the political and economic injustices the refugees face. As it can be seen in the two comments quoted below, political power is named as "Arab lover" and the reactions towards political power and reactions towards Syrian refugees are intertwined:

Aydan Gorben: *You Arab lovers, all of you deserve to go to Arabia. Just as you put the culture of Arabs in our country, you are losers living in ignorance, defending freakiness. God damn all of you.*

Boramir Faramir: *As if a Muslim should help another Muslim. Whatever happens to us is because of this inferior Arabic culture and religion. The country is burning furiously because of this Arab love.*

It can be said that, the fear or reaction caused by the religion-based ideological structure, which AKP aims to adopt for the society is reinforced to perceive Syrian refugees as a threat. This situation will especially make sense when the marks left on the collective memory of society by the ideological preferences of the Turkish Republic, founded in 1923, (a nation state which does not prioritize religious references, which is rational and facing the West while turning its back to the East) are taken into consideration.

In the comments mentioned above, it is stated that the "open door" policy of AKP is a product of its own political benefits and preferences rather than humanistic concerns. The anxieties about the concerns that Turkey would be removed from its modern and secular national identity feed negative emotions towards refugees. On the other hand, Europe's (the West's) reluctance in opening its doors to refugees is also shown as an evidence for Turkey's false refugee politics. This attitude of Europe's towards refugees is used to justify the negative approaches in the comments.

Uğur Öznem: *Don't ever take offense, these will raise all kinds of issues with us after years, why don't Germany, France or other countries accept them because they are not stupid if they accept them both their cultures and their race will be in danger and they will start to be corrupted they know it very well and they do the right thing.*

As it is seen in the quoted comments, all of them fail to notice and even legitimize some facts such as; the reality of the war in Syria, the distinctive cyclical and geopolitical dynamics of this war, the struggle of the refugees to survive in a foreign country and more importantly, a small child's exposure to physical violence.

Swearing / Insult / Humiliation

In the comments of this category, which consist of direct swearing, humiliation and insult, refugees are referred to with negative words such as "god damned freaks", "rubbish", "bigots", "cockroach", "miserable", "cavemen", "inferior". An angry, irritated and aggressive language is used towards refugees, which works up intolerance and hatred. The negativities that Syrian refugees face in Turkey are reflected as the result of their own cultural, political and social character or backgrounds, and thus, there is an indirect implication that they deserve the things they experience. Another distortion and exaggeration made based on the event in the news, however, is the negative generalizations made about the social and family structure of Syrians and also their culture. Considering the fact that the child in the news is selling tissue papers alone, Syrians/Arabs are seen as a society having poor family ties and values and they are blamed for it.

Aydan Gorben: *Arab lovers, this kid's family is thoughtless like you, they neither wear a condom nor think about the future of their child, all Arabs are like this, throw the child in the street. Buddy you are all like this which of you know civilization and which of you have provided benefit to humanity?*

Abdullah Barış: *First the government accepts the refugees, and then releases them in the streets thinking the public will somehow look after them as they do to the dogs. If it weren't, it would make the municipalities pick up them. That's why I don't pity them at all. Besides, if they were an honest family, the mother and the father would work and the kids would play in parks".*

Hasan Cimsir: *If the most literate, the most beautiful city let in immigrants consisted of cavemen like this that's just the way it goes.*

Aydan Gorben: *Buddy, you Arab addicted thieves.... Just to spite we will chase away all the Arabs from this country... Go away to Arabia... You wicked tortoises.*

Ataseven Citizen: *These are the freaks mostly coming from Arabic Muslim countries who do not respect children and women, who do not use birth protection, and breed rapidly.*

In the comments such as those mentioned above, Arabic identity and culture of Syrians draw attention as the major axis where the negativity is set. By making a hierarchical order between Turkish and Arabic cultures, Arabic culture is described as an inferior culture. In other words, Arabic culture is seen as a counter-culture to Turkish culture that can spoil Turkish culture. Humiliating or excluding different groups by focusing on the cultural differences rather than biological differences as it is seen in those readers' comments reminds us of "cultural racism" Cultural racism could be defined as a refined replacement of earlier biological racism. The cultural racism that originated in Europe and defined by Barker (1981) as "a theory of human nature where humans are considered equal but where cultural differences make it natural for nation states to form closed communities, as relations between cultures are essentially hostile. (Wren: 2001:143). Relying on the assumption that all important cultural innovations emote from Europe, it switches the focus from race to culture in explaining why Europeans are superior than non-Europeans. (Wren, 2001: 144). The new cultural racism, which is categorizing culture hierarchically, is based on looking down on the properties of the group described as "unworthy" or "lowlife" such as; work ethic, self-confidence, the ability to discipline oneself and individual success. The American version of this cultural racism frame was originally labelled as the "culture of poverty" in the 1960s in the United States. According to this frame, the victim (minorities) is the one to blame for their position which is the result of "their lack of effort", "loose family organization" and "inappropriate values" (Silva, 2006:40). In the comments, there is a contrast of Arab Islam and Turkish Islam, which supports the theme of threat to social-cultural structure. On the one hand, Arabic Islam is matched with bigotry, backwardness and fanaticism. On the other hand, it is emphasized that Turks have a modern Islamic understanding including their own cultural values and this understanding is praised. In this context, it is referred in the comments that Syrian refugees will change the religious understanding in Turkey negatively and this will pull the country backwards.

Using Natural Identity Element as a Hate-Humiliation Factor/ Symbolization

Discourses that only use nationalistic, religious, racial or similar identity elements as hate factors are the least among the other discourse categories. At the same time, it is seen that more than one category can take place in the same comment and it is so common to use natural identity elements as a humiliation factor in other categories. This situation is more valid for the swearing / insult / humiliation category analysed above. However, while evaluating the categories, the classification is done by looking at the most dominant property. For this reason, in this category, only the comments in which natural identity elements are predominately used as a hate–humiliation factor are taken into consideration. In the aforementioned comments, speeches humiliating Arabs are seen to be formed on the emphasis of the Arabic identity of the Syrians. In the comments, it is seen that not only Arabic identity but also other identities such as "Kurd" or "Easterners" are used as an element of humiliation. In one of these comments which is made by Gül Güler it is said that: "I think it is baseless to refer to the people of İzmir about this subject, that waiter is most probably an easterner, too".

Thus, while disapproving the behaviour towards the Syrian refugee child, it is implied that this sort of primitive behaviour can only come from an easterner. Another theme in which Arabic identity is used as an insulting factor is the Turkish War of Independence. By making a parallel between the Turkish War of Independence and the war in Syria, it is expressed that Turks fought for their country at the risk of their lives and died for the "motherland". Syrians, however, are highlighted to be scared and running away from their "motherland". The Turkish War of Independence and motherland are turned into a myth and Turks are being hailed as heroic. It is mentioned that it is the general character of Syrians (Arabs) to be a "coward" and "not being capable of protecting their motherland". In this case, a connotation emerges that Syrians, who are humiliated for being "dishonourable and cowards", do not deserve tolerance. For instance, a comment by "Aegean Doctor", mentions that the refugees do not deserve to live in Turkey by saying "…when it serves their purpose these creatures are good at playing on people's heartstrings. Why didn't they stay in their own country, fight for independence and be martyred if necessary…? Since my grandfathers died in the Independence War, I had never seen a grandfather... But I'm sure both of their grandfathers are alive". In another comment, a reader named Erol Birbey accuses and humiliates all Arabs for being cowards and dishonourable people, who take the easy way out, by saying "If they were men, they would stay in their country and struggle, but not if they are Arabs. They lack honour and courage!

Hostility / War Speech

In the comments analysed under this category, it is seen that Syrian refugees are presented as a threat to Turkey's internal and external security and economy. While making a connection between threat to internal security and ordinary crimes and terror in general, external security terror is indicated once again. In the comments, the refugees, who are mentioned with negative epithets such as "Arabic drifters", "disgusting", "nuisance", "suicide bomb", "thief", "rapist", are defined as potential "criminals" or "terrorists" that can turn into "enemies". For example, as seen in the comment quoted below, a kind of perception is created that the Syrian refugee child is a potential internal security threat to Turkey.

> ***Adnan Avni:*** *"Buddy, if there is such an internal disturbance that Arabic kid will shoot you or be a suicide bomb, as well. Turkey is for Turkish citizens, if our country is lost, nobody will help us." a kind of perception is created that the Syrian refugee kid is a potential internal security threat to Turkey.*

Another point that draws attention in the comments having hostility speech is that these comments are like an answer to the readers that are pro-refugees who are reminded of the hard conditions refugees are in. They argue that the refugees are guests and call for the others to be fair. For instance, a comment by Adnan Avni reads "If the Syrians break into your house and kill you, if they rape you or steal your money, then may that silly child conscious literature do you no good". Thus by creating a contrast between "conscious" and "logic" it is emphasized to be "logical" in order to prevent the threat. Some comments which are quoted below, go as far as to claim that the verbal or physical violence against refugees are a right response from the citizen and legitimize the violence against the Syrian child. It is also referred that the child probably deserved the beating as he "bullied" or "annoyed" the shop owner, otherwise he wouldn't have beaten him:

Burak Gel: *Let no one throw mud at the shop owner, we all know how these beggars cling on to people in İstanbul and after disturbing people how they try to grab with their "little Turkish" in the end"*

Timuçin Batur: *The main reason why the Syrian kid was hit there is his RESISTANCE; bullying the shop owner without listening to the warnings regardless of his stature.*

Mahlas Mahlasoğlu: *All right, it is a kid but... The man already warned him. Moreover, thousands of shop owners feel very dejected because of Syrians. If you annoy the man's customer what can they do? (...) For many years, we dealt with eastern people who clung onto our legs. And now these ones. I pity the kid, but people have a tolerance limit, too. Who knows how many times he's been there?"*

Even in some of the comments the violence against the Syrian refugee kid is praised and glorified directly without any sign of holding back. For instance, in a comment by a reader named Orhan Köse, it says that "May God bless the one who hit the kid. Thank you."

Overall, in those comments quoted it is also possible to see the marks of the traditional Turkish Middle East policy developed after the foundation of the Turkish Republic which sided with the West and had a cold, distant and cautious point of view, while even looking down on the Middle East. In addition to that, in the comments which express the feeling of insecurity strengthened by the Middle East based terrorist actions in recent years with exaggerated and aggressive language, it is possible to say that Syrian refugees are perceived as forced guests and seen with a potential which could turn into an enemy at any time.

CONCLUSION

Online reader comments, which have become a new element of the news in online journalism, now enable the audience, who were in a consuming position in traditional media, to become an active one to some degree in the production process of news. Through the reader comments, the readers get a chance to have an affect on news editors and journalists and so that they may change both the content of the news and the perception of the news stories. That also means that the readers could also play a role in the formation of public opinion on various topics at a national or international scale. Although this situation is positive with regards to its contribution to the democratic quality and functioning of the public sphere, it may also create some unfavourable situations in the sense of producing and popularizing hate speech.

The findings of this study which focus on the discourses produced about Syrian refugees in reader comments, confirm that the reader comments is an important component for producing and spreading hate speech. After the analysis of the reader comments of the news titled "A Shop Owner beat a Syrian Child" on *Hürriyet* newspaper's web page, it is seen that 65 comments out of 200 in total are at a level of hate speech. This number draws attention as a considerable amount. Among the categories of hate speech, the comments that take place under Exaggeration / Distortion (33) are the most in number. There are 17 reader comments under the category of Hostility / War Speech, 12 reader comments under the category Swearing / Insult / Humiliation, and 3 reader comments under the category of using natural identity elements as a hate-humiliation factor. Overall, it is found that instead of having a logical level that is necessary for a qualified discussion, these comments contain negative emotions and aggression. Stigmatization based on prejudices and stereotypes towards Syrian refugees are highly common in these comments that lack a consideration for questioning based upon facts.

Syrian refugees are perceived as "the other" in terms of a discrimination of us/ them or an opposition of Turks-Turkey-homeland / Syrians-Arabs-Kurds-enemies. The theme that is used mainly in the various forms of hate speech towards refugees in the comments is the theme of "threat". The theme of threat varies in itself as a threat to internal and external security of the country, a threat to Turkish economy and a threat to the social, cultural and religious structure of Turkey. The Syrians are negated as a group who should be excluded or unwelcomed by definitions such as "criminal", "terrorist", "enemy", "having low morality", "bigot" and "reactionist". In the discourses that are developed upon humiliating or othering cultural and religious identities of Syrians resulted in cultural racism and discrimination. It indicates that the refugees will ruin the modern Islamic understanding in Turkey, Turkey's cultural development and its modern structure.

With the references about the Turkish War for Independence, the discourse of the holy homeland is made by emphasizing the price the Turks paid for their "motherland", and it is stressed that the Turks saved the homeland at the expense of their souls and life. Within this discourse Syrians are presented as "coward" and "dishonourable" people who do not have the guts to fight for their own country and it is meant that they should be expelled from Turkey. It is also seen that the reaction and anxiety to the political and social preferences of AKP, which are perceived as religiously strong and imprudently close to the Ottoman rather than the Republic, is projected onto the refugees in the comments directly or indirectly. AKP's open door policy applied to Syrian refugees and its Middle East policy, which is radically different from Turkey's previous policy, are also evaluated and criticised in this context. In addition, the reluctance of Europe to open its door to Syrian refugees is also used to humiliate the refugees and shown as a proof that not accepting the refugees is wise and best for Turkey. In the comments that are all formed in the framework of this thematic structure, it is totally ignored that the fact that Syrian refugees are in Turkey in order to save their lives from the war along with the political, economic, social and psychological hardship conditions under which the refugees try to survive. Therefore, discourses that fuel hatred and prevent empathy towards Syrian refugees in the society are carried to the public sphere by reader comments. Even, instead of criticizing the violence against the Syrian child in the news, there are some comments which legitimize or approve the usage of violence. On the basis of the refugee child who was exposed to violence, all Syrian refugees are portrayed as a target and are shown to be "guilty and responsible" instead of being "victims" of the negative events that they experienced. When it is taken into consideration that hate speech can easily turn into hate crime, this situation seems problematic with regards to the emergence of more violence towards Syrian refugees.

ACKNOWLEDGMENT

I would like to thank Kash Prateek for a professional proof-reading this book chapter.

REFERENCES

Alexa. (2015). *Top cites in Turkey*. Retrieved from http://www.alexa.com/topsites/countries/TR

Barker, M. (1981). *The new racism: Conservatives and the ideology of the tribe*. London: Junction Books.

Çoban Keneş, H. (2016). Metaforun ayrımcı hegemonyanın inşasındaki rolü: Suriyelilerin haberleştirilmesindeki metafor kullanımı. *Gaziantep University Journal of Social Sciences*, *15*(2), 253–280. doi:10.21547/jss.256727

Cohen-Almagor, R. (2011). Fighting hate and bigotry on the Internet. *Policy & Internet*, *3*(3), 1–26. doi:10.2202/1944-2866.1059

Doğanay, Ü., & Çoban Keneş, H. (2016). Yazılı basında suriyeli 'mülteciler': Ayrımcı söylemlerin rasyonel ve duygusal gerekçelerinin inşası. *Mülkiye Dergisi*, *40*(1), 143–184.

Goffman, E. (1963). *Stigma*. London: Penguin.

Göker, G. & Keskin, S. (2015). Haber medyası ve mülteciler: Suriyeli mültecilerin Türk yazılı basınındaki temsili. *İletişim Kuram ve Araştırma Dergisi*, *41*, 229-256.

Hall, S. (1979). Culture, the media and the 'ideological effect. In J. Curan, M. Gurevitch, & J. Woollacott (Eds.), *Mass communication and society* (pp. 315–348). London: Edward Arnold.

Hall, S. (1992). The west and the rest: Discourse and power. In S. Hall & B. Gieben (Eds.), *Formations of modernity* (pp. 275–333). Polity Press and Blackwell Pub.

Hrant Dink Foundation. (2013). *Medyada nefret söylemi ve ayrımcı dil eylül - aralık 2013 raporu*. Retrieved from http://nefretsoylemi.org/rapor/Eylul-Aralik2013_nefretsoylemi_ayrimcisoylem_raporu.pdf

Hürriyet. (2015, July 21). *Suriyeli çocuğa esnaftan dayak*. Retrieved from http://www.hurriyet.com.tr/suriyeli-cocuga-esnaftan-dayak-29603820

Kap, D. (2014). Suriyeli mülteciler: Türkiye'nin müstakbel vatandaşları. *Akademik Perspektif*, *1*(3), 30–35.

Refugee Solidarity Network. (2016). *Refugees & asylum in Turkey: Legal overview*. Retrieved from http://www.refugeesolidaritynetwork.org/learn-more/turkey-asylum-basics/

Silva, E. B. (2006). *Racism without racist: Color bind racism and persistance of racial inequality in the United States*. New York: Rowman & Littlefield Publishers.

UNHCR, Syria Regional Refugee Response, Inter-agency Information Sharing Portal. (n.d.). Retrieved from http://data.unhcr.org/syrianrefugees/country.php?id=224

Van Dijk, T. (2001). *Critical discourse analysis. In The handbook of discourse analysis*. Oxford, UK: Blackwell Publishing.

Van Dijk, T. (2005). *Racism and discourse in Spain and Latin America*. Amsterdam: John Benjamins Publishing Co. doi:10.1075/dapsac.14

Weber, A. (2009). *Manuel on hate speech*. Strasbourg: Council of Europe Publishing.

Wren, K. (2001). Cultural racism: Something rotten in the state of Denmark? *Social & Cultural Geography*, *2*(2), 141–162. doi:10.1080/14649360120047788

Yücebaş, M. (2015). Gaziantep yerel basınında Suriyeli İmgesi: Yeni taşranın yeni suskunları: Suriyeliler. *Birikim Dergisi*, *311*, 38–47.

Chapter 8
LGBT Right Activism and the Risk of Christianophobia in Nigeria

Endong Floribert Patrick Calvain
University of Calabar, Nigeria

ABSTRACT

Nigerian conservatism and doctrinaire religion have been cardinal forces behind the adoption of a homophobic legislation in Nigeria. This scenario has spurred many (pro)-gay activists into anchoring their advocacy on a "Christianophobic" rhetoric which labels Christianity and religious fanaticism as two forms of bigotry, barbarism and Nazism, as well as facets of an anti-progressive movement. Such an aggressive advocacy tactic has been making a case for the systematic "de-Christianization" and "de-Islamization" of Nigerians' minds. Using empirical understandings, this chapter argues that, Nigerian LGBT activists shape their advocacy strategies according to some Western atheistic models; models which have progressively given rise to gay totalitarianism and "Christianophobia" in a number of western countries. The paper highlights indexes pointing to a future "Christianophobia" in Nigeria, driven by a "Christianophobic" gay activism and finally argues that any pro-gay advocacy rooted in the de-Christianization of Nigerians unarguably proffers the disrespect of religious freedom.

DOI: 10.4018/978-1-5225-2817-3.ch008

INTRODUCTION

Atheistic schools of thought and other detractors of religion tend to associate Christian doctrines and religious fanaticism with backwardness, absurdity and anti-progressivism. In line with this, socio-philosophical forces such as modernism, individualism, secularism and more especially human rights have systematically militated against religion (religious dogmas) and members of religious denominations across the world. These socio-philosophical forces have somehow led to the progressive phobia and demise of religion. They have equally worked towards discrediting religion and reducing its influence in the public life. The concept of human rights in particular has, to a great extent, caused many religious dogmas and rituals/traditions to be relegated to the status of barbaric, repugnant and immoral traditions. This is more evidenced by the fact that issues like gender and racial equality, as well as pro-gay proselytism are today successfully discrediting and overshadowing most of the religious dogmas that hitherto stigmatized and oppressed particular minority groups (Crabtree, 2011; Zimrak, 2015). The phenomenal proliferation of the human right idiom in the world has, in this respect, functioned as a solid arsenal and a catalyst of the global movement in favor of gay rights. No doubt, Scott cited by Ray (2016) pointedly concedes that the human right philosophy has enabled the global gay community to gain socio-political power and to move from a socially vulnerable or weak bloc to a powerful minority. As he succinctly contends, "In the space of just half a century this tiny 1-3% of the population have made themselves a global political power with greater influence in the courtrooms and legislatures of the world than the Church of Jesus Christ. This astonishing transformation surpasses that of Darwinism, Marxism, and even Islam in its speed and breadth of reach".

The human rights philosophy strongly advocates the legitimization or decriminalization of homosexuality not only in secular circles but equally – though recently – in religious communities. Such tenets of the human rights concept have been in total disregard of religious injunctions and conservative/traditionalist cultural models still prevailing in some countries, particularly black African and Arab countries. With this, human right activists and pro-gay schools of thought have, in their complex approaches to defending the rights of homosexuals, considered Christianity – or religion in general – coupled with conservatism as the principal "wild wheat" to off root from people's mentalities. In tandem with this, LGBTI rights activists in Nigeria have virtually made it their cardinal prerogative to tentatively de-Christianize and de-Islamize the minds of Nigerians. Such de-Christianization and de-Islamization of the minds of Nigerians are regarded by these activists as a bi-dimensional strategy to create conditions favorable for the decriminalization of homosexuality and enable social tolerance in favor of LGBT communities in the Nigerian Federation. Such a strategy has often incorporated strongly worded reflections and more or less "aggressive" discourses against Christian doctrines and Islamic traditions, particularly those firmly in favor of anti-gay proselytism. The reflections and discourses formulated by the radical gay right activists often describe Christians' anti-gay positions and campaigns as forms of "bigotry", "Nazism", "Fascism" and barbarism among other negative connotations.

Using critical observations and literary sources, this paper seeks, primarily to show how the LGBT Right movement is progressively encouraging or preparing the ground for a predictable "Christianophobia" (the acute persecution of Christian faithful) in Nigeria. Secondarily, the paper seeks to examine the extent to which such a "Christianophobia" is inimical to the civilities of freedom of religion and freedom of expression, thereby constituting an anti-human right enterprise. In other words, the chapter seeks to show how Nigerian human right activists partly participate in the very "felony" they claim to criticize: the violation of some of the human rights, namely those of freedom of religion and freedom of thought and expression. The chapter is divided into four main sections. The first section provides a theoretical framework composed of atheism and modernization. The second section shows how Nigerian-based gay activists tend to anchor their advocacy on a de-Christianization or de-Islamization of the minds of "homophobic" Nigerians. The third section examines the extent to which atheistic and aggressive models of gay-activism (borrowed from the West) may engender Christianphobia in Nigeria. And the last main section deals with the LGBT right movement in Nigeria and the freedom of religion.

THEORETICAL FRAMEWORK

This chapter is anchored on two theories namely atheism and modernization. Given their broad nature, it will be expedient to highlight the specific keystones of these theories that will drive analysis in this study.

The Atheism/Atheistic Theory

Atheism is construed as a socio-philosophical movement which negates the existence of God or gods. It is often viewed as synonymous with non-theism given the fact that it is antithetical to theism – which is the belief in one or more gods. Thinkers such as Karl Max are believed by many critics to be among the intellectual forces which gave a philosophical dimension to atheism. In effect, Karl Marx reasons that in a world of reason, the existence of God has no meaning or is just so exotic. According to him, advocating religion – in an incredulous world as ours – is like pushing an extra terrestrial concept on earth. It is, for instance, like taking paper money to a country where people trade by batter. As he succinctly puts it,

Take paper money to a country in which this use of paper money is not known, and everyone will laugh at your subjective representation. Go with your gods to a country in which other gods are worshipped, and you will be shown that you are the victim of fancies and abstractions. And rightly, anyone who had brought a migrant god to the ancient Greeks, would have found the proof of the non-existence of this god, because it did not exist for the Greeks. What is the case in a certain country for certain foreign gods, takes place for god in general in the country of reason: it is an area in which his existence ceases. (Marx, 1962, p.415)

The atheists do not only strongly reject the belief in a specific god (notably the Christian God), but most often oppose the thesis that humanity should depend on such a god, religious models/precepts or other spiritual arbiters to design moral codes to live by; as well as to adopt suitable behavioral patterns. Moral codes and laws should rather be designed according to the cannons of humanism, naturalism and science. Such humanistic cannons regard man as the summit of the cosmos; that is, the "Supreme Being" and not God or gods. It is in tandem with this that O'Hair defines atheism as the "mental attitude which unreservedly accepts the supremacy of reason and aims at establishing a lifestyle and ethical outlook verifiable by experience and scientific method, independent of all arbitrary assumptions of authority and creeds" (cited by Mastin 2011, para 2). Based on this rejection or skepticism regarding the claim that God is an infallible source of inspiration for any human endeavor, atheistic advocates of the LGBT right movement have attacked homophobic laws and sentiments which are rooted in religious beliefs. They have mainly associated religious argumentations on gay sexual ethics with nonsense. A good example is *Gay Humanist Quarterly*'s editor, Brett Lock who refers to anti-gay religious fundamentalists as "the forces of evil" (Brett, 2007, p. 2)

In Nigeria, the most vocal advocates of the LGBT right movement have openly embraced atheism, humanism or have clearly manifested sentiments that are in line with these two movements. Apart from rare initiatives or voices such as Rev Jide Marculay – who, with his creation of a gay-only church (House of Rainbow) has based his advocacy on a postmodern form of Christianity – virtually all Nigerian-based advocates of the LGBT right movement have directly or indirectly proffered adhesion to atheism and humanism. One of the iconic figures of the LGBT right advocacy in the country Yemisi Ilesanmi explicates how atheism affects her pro-gay activism. She asserts that "my atheism has helped me to stand up against religious bullies, who use the Bible and the Quran to justify their hate for gays, lesbians, transsexual and bisexuals" (Para 4). She further laments the fact that religion carries a lot of unwarranted weight in Nigeria in particular and Africa in general. This, she says, is highly responsible for the state of backwardness and "obscurity" in which the continent has been.

Modernization Theory

The modernization theory is a developmental theory which has often been considered to analyze economic and political growth in Third world countries. The theory is however broad as it can also be used to explain social progress in these Third World countries. Generally speaking, the modernization theory states that the highly developed or industrialized countries (essentially the US-led west) should – or are bound to – be seen by the less developed countries as constituting an infallible developmental model. In tandem with this, the act of following the developmental footsteps of these western countries, should be the ultimate purpose of Third Worlds in all spheres: economical, political and social. According to the modernist theorists, industrialization and scientific development (research) constitute two liberalizing and progressive forces that the more industrialized (western) countries have been able to harness. Their serious advances in these two domains makes them infallible models for African states and other Third World countries. The theory indirectly brings to the fore two major understandings. The first is that the traditional societies of Third World countries (including Back Africa) are not only *under*developed. Rather, they are *un*developed as they still await the impact of industrial transformation (Giddens, 1982). The second understanding is that African countries (including Nigeria) have to thread paths that are similar to those followed by the industrialized west. In concord with this line of argumentation, Karl Marx enthuses that "the country that is more developed industrially only shows to the less developed, the image of its own future" (cited in Tunde 2008, p.34).

Since independence, most African countries have, in one way or the other, been following the footsteps of Europe and America (Endong, 2016). This has been to the extent that skeptical futurists have been speculating that it will be hard for most African states not to be a replica of the west in the years to come. Sachs somehow alludes to this scenario when he notes that:

Like a towering lighthouse guiding sailors towards the coast, development stood as the idea which oriented emerging nations in their journey through post war history [...] the counties of the South proclaimed modernization as their primary aspiration after they had been freed from colonial domination. (cited in Matunhu, 2011, p.66)

In the same line of argument, Tunde (2005) notes that western developmental models have been so flamboyant, attractive and irresistible to other peoples or civilizations of the world. This has been to the extent that, these western developmental outlooks have become widespread, particularly in the Third World countries. He adds that "undoubtedly, [even] without colonization, African societies would still have sought industrialization and western type [of] modernization, as have peoples in virtually every other region in the world" (p.32). This gives the impression that the westernization of Africa through modernization is a kind of fatalism. And in the course of modernization, African countries will be bound to adopt most, if not all the concepts endorsed in the west as civilities or cultural aphorisms, one of which is the LGBT right concept (Ray 2016).

A number of pro-gay activists have based their advocacy on the modernization theory, arguing that African countries should follow the example of the industrialized west which has largely embraced the LGBT right movement. According to them, shunning religious fundamentalism and tolerating gayness and the LGBT right "wisdom" constitute a sign of modernism and civilization. Such actions are imperatives susceptible to enable a significant African peoples' shift from backwardness and obscurity to light. Gay activist Yemisi makes allusion to this imperative when she laments that: many religious and fundamentalists of African extraction continue to use the 'holy' books such as the Bible to justify the oppression of LGBT communities even when "the original owners of this religion [the West] inform them that the book has been updated and some parts are no longer applicable. Africans still insist that it is must be applicable because it says so in the book they were given. How pathetic!" (para 5).

THE DE-CHRISTIANIZATION OF NIGERIANS' MINDSETS AS LGBT RIGHT ADVOCACY STRATEGY

Before delving in showing how Nigerian gay activist advocate a "de-Christianisation" of Nigerians' mindsets, it will be expedient to do a brief excursion into fundamental religion's position on the LGBT right movement in Nigeria. And as earlier alluded to, the Church has, to an extent, regarded the concept of human right as a spiritual evil in disguise. This is thanks to the fact that this modern legalist parlance or idiom has largely questioned a number religious doctrines pertaining to issues like gender relations, children rights and sexual ethics – particularly gay sexual ethics. Nigerian clergyman Akintola describes recent developments in human rights frameworks as devilish schemes or ploys by western legislators aimed at making laws that "upturn the natural order and throw God away from the public domain". He decries the fact that the human right concept – as we see it in contemporary times – advocates injunctions and precepts that undeniably run counter to Christian principles and tend to glaringly overthrow the "natural order of things". As he enthuses,

Marriage and family life as we know them in the word of God have been jettisoned. People of the same sex are legally permitted to marry. Parents' right to discipline their children is legally denied, the age of discretion that used to be 21 has been

lowered to 18 and there are efforts at reducing it to 16 if not 14. (Cited in Duke 2014, para 3).

Fundamental Christianity, like many other religious vitalities, has therefore vigorously and dogmatically resisted a number of human rights through adhesion to patriarchal (gender insensitive) doctrines and religious fixations that violate children's rights. It is not an overstatement to enthuse that, in today's world, religious groups represent one of the principal detractors of most of the basic human rights (Karaim, 2011; Van den Berg, Bos, Derks, Ganzevoort, Jovanovic, Korte & Sremac, 2014). Taking into account all these indexes, it has pertinently been argued that, "by far, the loudest anti-gay rights voice is Christian and Muslim" (Crabtree, 2011). Homosexuality and the LGBT right proselytism – as a human right issue – are today envisaged by Christian observers not only as a vector of the adulteration of Christian ethics but equally as a major threat to the corporate existence of some churches. As Crabtree (2011) opines, "slave liberation and many other equal rights frequently caused splits to occur within organized religions, as gay rights are threatening to do now to the Church of England". The gay right idiom is therefore often considered a kind of abomination, an apostasy, a heresy and an anathema in Christian/religious circles. According to highly fundamentalist observers, the concept is to be eternally demonized and strongly combated by the Church (the various Christian denominations).

Doctrinaire Christianity has thus been a serious obstacle to the LGBT right activism in Nigeria. It has somehow represented a death threat to Nigerian gays and lesbians. Christianity – or rather overzealous religiosity – is thus believed to motivate the lynching, blackmailing, stigmatization, disowning, intimidation and other forms of violence inflicted by a number of social forces to members of LGBT communities in Nigeria. Many of the Nigerian advocates of the homophobic legal tools and violent repressions against homosexuality and gay proselytism firmly believe to work for an evangelic, salvific, prophetic, "sanctification" and patriotic cause or purpose. However, this claim has been problematized on many grounds.

To surmount or "curtail" the staunch Christian resistance to the inter-related phenomena of homosexuality, same-sex marriage and the LGBTI right movement, some Nigerian human right activists and LGBT people have resorted to multiple aggressive paradigms and more or less "original" strategies. Some of these human right activists have systematically "queered" the church or "Christianized" homosexuality through the creation of gay-only churches. An egregious example is Rowland Olajide's House of Rainbow (otherwise called Nigerian LGBTI Church). Contrary to these advocates of a "queered African Christianity", other pro-gay activists – and perhaps those belonging to the mainstream advocacy school – have resorted to the tentative de-Christianization or de-Islamization of the mindsets of

Nigerians. This de-Christianization and de-islamization have consisted in proffering an activism which is anchored on a very aggressive pro-gay rhetoric, one which severely cracks down on religious dogmatism and which tends to randomly demonize religion. In his article titled "Religious Fanatics Blamed for Nigeria's Draconic Anti-Gay Bill", Duke (2014) slams religious fundamentalists, derogatorily referring to them as the principal architects of the "draconian and fundamentally stupid piece of legislation" – the *Same-Sex Prohibition Act*. In the course of elaborating his acerb criticism, he particularly cracks down on ecclesiastic figures such as Akinola (Head of the Nigerian Anglican Church) who, in addition to their cardinal role in the promulgation of the anti-gay legislation, have in one way or the other somehow supported homophobia in Nigeria. To buttress his points, he quotes LGBT right activist Ugwu Damian who situates the LGBT right question in Nigerian within the context of the rise of religious fundamentalism in the country and its tremendous influence in various vital sectors of the country. Ugwu, (quoted by Duke 2014), underscores the role both indigenous and exogenous religious fundamentalists and legislators have played – and are continuously playing – to stultify pro gay activism in Nigeria. He laments that: "supporters of the bill [the *Same Sex Prohibition Act*] were given ample time to organize and mobilize their supporters, while LGBT activists and civil society organizations opposed to the bill were refused permission to attend the public hearing. Those who managed to scale the security barriers to attend the hearing were constantly jeered at and booed by religious fundamentalists while being intimidated by legislators".

Like Duke and Damian (cited above), a number of Nigerian pro-gay activists and critics view de-Christianization and de-Islamization of the spirit of Nigerians as (the most) strategic action and a *sine qua non* for gay-right activism in Nigeria to bear plenty fruits. In the thinking of these anti-religion activists, the de-Christianization and de-Islamization of the Nigerian socio-cultural ecology pass through the elaboration of an aggressive discourse profoundly based on fighting words. Such a discourse systematically associates religion with backwardness, barbarism, Nazism, absurdity, obscurantism and other repugnant schools of thought. Gay right activist Yemisi (2016) succinctly echoes such a theory when she urges that "we [Nigerians] must rid ourselves of mental slavery, self-righteousness and religious stupidity before we can truly empathize with another human being or other earthlings. We must break the need to justify our actions with quotes from some imported 'holy books'" (p.17).

In their anti-religion arguments, some Nigerian gay activists have even dismissed Christianity and Islam as irrelevant frameworks for determining morality on Nigerian soil. This is, in part, connectable to the fact that the principle of secularity of the state remains a constitutional prescription in Nigeria, even though this has only been on paper. Other gay right activists (notably Yemisi quoted above) dismiss the two religions (Christianity and Islam) on ground of their presumed un-Africaness.

This has principally been to counter anti-gay postulations and theories (by the Nigerian political class and other conservative social arbiters) which insinuate that homosexuality and the LGBTI right movement are western in nature. And on such basis, they are clearly incompatible with core African cultural values. In effect, to some Nigerian atheists, humanists and non-religious observers, Christianity and Islam are "imported" religions. On this basis, if homosexuality is to be criminalized and repressed on ground of its un-Africaness, so too should Islam and Christianity.

Similarly to their western counterparts, most Nigerian (pro-) gay activists imagine and enthuse that the world will be a heaven for LGBT persons if religion is totally absent from it. They often reason like the Gay and Lesbian Humanist Association (2007) which, in a strongly worded advertisement captioned "Imagine No Religion", visibly attempts to instigate its readership to develop a complex phobia for religion. In a highly assertive tone, the queer association actually states that:

Are'nt you sick and tired of the homophobia spouted by religious leaders? It is true to say that almost all antigay groups today are religion-based. When they're not issuing proclamations, fatwas and edicts, they're campaigning against our human rights, peddling their bigotry, telling us we're sick, diseased, perverted and destined for hellfire, or promoting quack therapies to "cure" us. Join GALHA [Gay and Lesbian Humanist Association] in its fight to curb the influence of religious homophobia. Stand up to the homophobes who preach hatred, intolerance and discrimination in the name of faith and ancient texts. (Gay and Lesbian Association, 2007, p.32)

It is observable that, according to many Nigerian pro-gay activists, the act of denouncing homophobia entails the virulent censuring of religion. Gay right activism is therefore tantamount to a frontal attack and hard verbalization against religious dogmas, (particularly those of Christian and Islamic origins) as well their faithful adepts. It is important here to underscore the fact that, the anti-religious strategies adopted by Nigerian gay-right activists are in line with – or are simply inspired by – those of their counterparts from Europe and America. As has been observed by a number of studies, pro-gay proselytism has progressively planted the seeds of Christianophobia in countries like the US and Britain (Alliance Defending Freedom, 2015; Bielefedt, 2012; Turek, 2010; Veith, 2011; Zimrak 2015). Pro-gay movements have embarked on more sophisticated advocacy schemes to discredit religion in general and Christianity in particular – in such countries as the US – as a way of popularizing their "ideals". In his online article titled "Gay Totalitarianism and the Coming Persecution of Christians" Zmirak (2015) corroborates this observation as he notes that in most pro-gay Western countries, the various demands by pro-gay activists have spectacularly gone "from libertarian ('Don't arrest us for sodomy') to totalitarian ('Take part in our weddings or we'll destroy your livelihoods')".

Taking the specific case of the American society, he further observes that gay activists and their allies have spewed immense hate at Christians, on account of the latter's persisting opposition to the LGBT right movement. Gay activists tend to brand Christians as "'bigots", 'Neanderthals' and 'haters', whose views must be ritually rejected by anyone hoping to keep a job in today's America — even in a Catholic high school". Major ideological state apparatuses such as the media, the law and other elite institutions have succeeded "in lumping Christian sexual morals in with white racism", and it is just a matter of time before Catholics, Protestants, Orthodox (and many religious minorities) find themselves "labeled as members of 'extremist sects', no more to be trusted with the care of their own children than the Branch Davidians were?"

In the same line of argument, Voshel (2016) describes LGBT right activism as a ploy that has progressively taken a worrisome dimension and which has become highly destructive to Christianity in America and some other parts of the west. She notes that:

Over a period of a few decades, activists for the LGBT movement transitioned steadily from their initial demands for equal protection under the law to demands for gay marriage, to denaturing the very construct of humanity by insisting on a gender free society, to promoting the right to force society at large to accept as infallible an individual's ability to discern and to declare one's self to be whatever sex one chooses. (p.14)

The LGBT right movement in Africa as a whole and Nigeria in particular has "not yet" mutated and grown to the dimension it has attained in the US-led west. Pro-gay activists operating in Nigeria can be said to barely be at the level of pushing liberalism. They merely advocate the decriminalization of homosexuality and have not yet proffered totalitarian approaches for their survival and political ascension in the country. However, as shall be discussed in subsequent sections of this discourse, this gay liberalism already augurs a number of dramatic developments that may not be favorable to puritanical Christian liturgies and religious conservative institutions. Already, there is a proliferating hate spewed at Christianity and Islam that can be perceived and be problematized. This hate may, to an extent be read as LGBT right activists' calculated response to the visibly cruel treatment some social institutions accord LGBT people, in guise of upholding a "holy war" or spiritual-cultural cleansing.

One must recognize that the religiously motivated cruelty and "repressions" of homosexuality and related sexualities by Nigerian anti-gay institutions are unarguably inconsistent with the ideals and precepts of the Christian faith. For instance, it is inconceivable to justify the killing/lynching of gays in public and in a barbaric way – as it is often the case in Nigeria – with the need to keep Christian doctrines or precepts. It is fair to argue that social imaginations that support the killing or brutalization of LGBT community have nothing to do with "genuine" Christianity as the Bible does not encourage the killing or harming of a ("presumed") sinner (Mathew 5:1-10). Homosexuality may be despised and condemned by the Bible but homophobia is not Christian. This is in line with the aphorism stating that God hates sin but loves sinners. On this premise, hating homosexuals on grounds that they are sinners is to be problematized. This notwithstanding, it is likewise objectionable to justify hate campaigns against Christians – especially in a random manner – on the basis that they opposed gay proselytism or view homosexuality as an aberration and bane to religious precepts. As we shall discuss in subsequent sections of this discourse, it is part of their right to freedom of thought and religion.

PRO-GAY GOVERNMENTS AND THE PERSECUTION OF CHRISTIANS IN NIGERIA ARE FORESEEABLE.

For the moment, Christian vitalities' anti-gay ploys have been colossal and far reaching, though utterly asphyxiating for the LGBT communities in Black Africa in general and Nigeria in particular. A number of critics have even used both futurist and optimist languages to predict the eternal anti-gay stance of African Christian circles and Black African nations (Ajayi 2011; Chika 2015; Mark 2014; Schumacher 2010). However, it remains pertinent to explore the extent to which the Christian churches' resistance to the LGBT right movement will be given credence by subsequent Nigerian governments. From a wide range of thought-provoking indicators or indexes, one may enthuse that the LGBT rights idiom has the potential to thrive in most African states (notably Nigeria), perhaps in a very remote future. One of these indexes is the fact that, Africa has most often followed the same path to human, economic and political development as the US-led West which, today, seems to prioritize LGBT rights over religious rights. We may, at this juncture borrow Karl Max's dictum that all under-developed or developing societies are destined to be like Europe and the rest of the developed West.

According to Marx, "the country that is more developed industrially only shows to the less developed, the image of its own future" (cited in Tunde 2005). Though this dictum may, to an extent, be associated with ethnocentrism and be deemed highly speculative, it remains clear that, since independence, it has been difficult for most African states to design a path to development which clearly, radically and fruitfully departs from western models and outlooks. The so-called indigenization model and African renaissance paradigm adopted by African states to resist Western imperialism particularly at the socio-cultural realm have shown glaring weaknesses and evidences of impracticability (Endong, 2015a,b; Endong, 2016; Tunde 2005).

Meanwhile, through colonialism, neo-colonization and cultural homogenization/ globalization, African states have been compelled to copy the West in many ways. The western systems of administration, economic development and educational models are in vogue in most African states, so much so that there is a popular dictum or myths in the Black continent stipulating that contemporary Africa is dominantly westernized. It is the absence of an authentic African model of human, economic and political development which has motivated most development scholars to see –with a great degree of pertinence – the West as a development pathfinder which has set the pace of civilization and development for other nations (notably Nigeria) to follow. Only a "miracle" will bring about a paradigm shift with respect to Black Africa's position on the LGBT rights issue. This is to say that only a miracle will cause Africa as a whole not to follow the pace set by the West concerning the LGBT right concept. Already, countries like South Africa have legalized homosexuality and are presently using such muscled tactics as the severe repressions to curb endogenous homophobic feelings from conservative and religious forces (Karaim, 2011; Tamale, 2011; Yasu, 2010).

In line with Max's reflection and the modernization theory, it may be enthused that, the present situation of "persecution" and attempted cowing of vocal anti-gay Christians (the gay-totalitarianism) in most pro-LGBT right countries (which happen to be much of the US-led West) are just the image of what may – or will – happen to African Christians inclined to the same anti-gay paradigms, perhaps in a remote future. A great number of colossal socio-cultural and religious barriers will certainly need to be broken for this to happen; however, our observation is that it shall – unfortunately for Christian and conservative Nigerians – come to pass. Fundamental and scriptural Christianity and conservative forces will hardly give way to gay proselytism in the Black African socio-cultural context. A number of indexes show that these forces will vigorously and perhaps, eternally resist the LGBT right movement. As Chika pungently argues,

What is certain is that Africa will continue to remain a very hostile continent to the gay community. There is not only the fact that Africa considers homosexual acts unnatural and a bane to African culture, the continent sees it as an example of the West again trying to impose their will on a continent whose member-countries are dependent on handouts from the West. (p.32)

With the same amount of pride, certitude and intransigency, Senate President David Mark, (one of the main architects of the Nigerian legislation on homosexuality [the Same Sex (Prohibition) Act], describes the present muscled tactics employed by the west to pressure African to accept the decriminalization of homosexuality as a futile project. To him, the tactics are not sufficient to mold Nigerian politics. As he succinctly posits,

If there is any country that wants to stop giving us aid because we want to pass the bill on same sex, that country can go ahead. We are a sovereign nation and we have the rights to decide for ourselves because no country can interfere in the way we run our country. Same sex marriage is against our own culture and tradition and against our beliefs. (cited in Ajayi, 2014, p.34)

In spite of all these assertive statements by African politicians and ideologues, the proliferation of the LGBT right movement and the persecution of any voice that is antithetical to it, are just a matter of time. In effect, if Africa in general and Nigeria in particular has to see the west as its *future* in terms development (in the political, economic and social realms), the decriminalization of homosexuality and eventual/subsequent persecution of anti-gay Christian forces are policies which are very much predictable or at least, to be envisaged. Already, a number of concrete and perceivable harbingers point to such a pro-gay development. According to a 2015 poll conducted by NOI (cited in Endong 2016), the level of support of Nigerian homophobic laws by the populace has been dropping. In comparison with earlier polls on the issue, it has been illustrated that Nigerians' support of the Same Sex Marriage Prohibition Act dropped from 98% in 2010 to 93% in 2013 and to 89% in 2015. It has equally been found that among young Nigerian within the age brackets of 16 to 25, the acceptance rate of LGBT people is at an all-time high of 30% (Bisi, 2015, Endong & Vareba, 2015; The Initiative for Equal Rights [TIERs], 2014).

Another index of a reversal of the situation in favor of the LGBT right movement is the fact that, some of the political figures that strongly masterminded or saluted the harsh laws passed against homosexuality in Nigeria are beginning to reverse themselves on the question. A good number of them are now advocating a revision of present bills on gay ethics (the *Same-Sex Marriage Prohibition Act*). This could be illustrated by ex-Nigerian President Goodluck Johnathan who, in a recent interview granted the London based Bloomerg TV, succinctly said:

When it comes to equality, we must all have the same rights as Nigerian citizens. [...] In the light of deepening debates for all Nigerians and other citizens of the world to be treated equally and without discrimination, and with the clear knowledge that the issue of sexual orientation is still evolving, the nation may at the appropriate time revisit the law. (Cited in Ebuzor 2016, para 5)

A number of similar developments in the Nigerian Christiano-spiritual sphere had already started pointing to these pro-gay mutations. An egregious illustration of this fact is the emergence of liberal, postmodern, secular-humanist and alternative religious forces which, professing profound adhesion to Christian theologies, are systematically Christianizing homosexuality, according to models observed in the West. Reverend Jide Macaulay's House of Rainbow (LGBT-only church) should be mentioned here. The emergence of this movement – which fruitfully works in concert with other pro-gay forces in Nigeria – is, to an extent, reminiscent of the ploys undertaken by LGBT people in the West and which later enabled them to move from grass to grace. As succinctly put by Ray (2016), pro-gay activism in the West just needed half a century for LGBT people (constituting virtually 1-3% of the world population) to become a global political power with influence greater than that of the religious forces in the courtrooms and legislatures of the world. Ray thus describes the success of the LGBT right movement in the West and its supremacy over religion as an "astonishing transformation [which] surpasses that of Darwinism, Marxism, and even Islam in its speed and breadth of reach". Conscious of this potential of the LGBT right activism in Nigeria, gay-apostle Rev. Jide Macaulay (2008) proudly underscores that "they [the anti-gay people] are afraid of our growing influence as we gather allies not just from the West, a people that are not afraid but powerful and resilient".

The progressive change of minds in favor of the LGBT right movement in Nigeria is a welcomed index and development, particularly for the humanist, the LGBT communities and the pro-gay activists. It is not in itself, a menace for (fundamental) Christianity. What is problematic is the kind of aggressive advocacy which accompanies or perpetrates this change. Gay activists tend to sow seeds of a future Christianophobia by anchoring their advocacy on Christianophobic rhetoric. They tend to sell the message that Christianity is just a stupidity, an oddity and a form of obscurantism in a world that cherishes a western model of development and "progress". Following the advocacy tactics proffered by their western counterparts, Nigerian gay activists tend to propagate the belief that, for homosexuality and other "queer" sexual identities to thrive in this modern and globalizing world, Christianity must be sidelined or "strangulated". In other word, religion – notably Christianity – is obsolete and a menace to healthy thinking and progress.

LGBT ADVOCACY STRATEGIES AND THE RESPECT OF FREEDOM OF RELIGION AND THOUGHT

In a world that is more and more buying the LGBT right concept and which seems to be giving an immeasurable credence to the human right aphorism, it may appear odd, backward, pertinacious and very offensive to be the an advocate of Christian churches and other religious bodies which abhor and proscribe homosexuality. In such a socio-political context, it appears retrograding to make a case for homophobic liturgies. It is like being an advocate of the devil. The dominant humanistic thinking is that efforts must be crystallized towards debunking religious "fundamentalism" which many see as a serious bane of the promulgation of gay rights in African countries. One even notices that any voice which, as a free thinker, expresses opposition to homosexuality is intolerantly labeled fundamentalist or bigot, and as we know, these labels carry with them a negative baggage or a host of awful connotations. However, without wanting to be "the advocate of the devil", it must be highlighted that such a dominant tendency among (Nigerian) LGBT right activists of randomly profiling and labeling Christianity on account of its opposition to homosexuality is an attack on freedom of religion and thought.

Actually, there is urgent need to differentiate "normal" manifestation of hostility towards homosexuality (the act) from homophobia (the hate of human beings) manifested through the stigmatization, wanton lynching of LGBT people and the criminalization of homosexuality. As we have earlier underlined, these forms of aggressions are questionable, problematic and contradictory to the religious precepts which preach the divine love of mankind. In order word, it is doubtful that the motivation of homophobic fundamentalists be Christian. Manifesting hostility to homosexuality (the act) is a normal expression and manifestation of one's thought and religion. Such a manifestation is endorsed by Article 18 of the Universal Declaration of Human Right which clearly states that Christians and other religious vitalities should be allowed to manifest their belief in all circumstances. As the Declaration puts it,

Everyone has the right to freedom of thought, conscience and religion; this right includes freedom to change his religion or belief, and freedom, either alone or in community with others and in public or private, to manifest his religion or belief in teaching, practice, worship and observance.

The same Article further explicates that freedom of thought and religion should be allowed on all matters, including homosexuality.

The right to freedom of thought, conscience and religion (which includes the freedom to hold beliefs) in article 18.1 is far-reaching and profound; it encompasses freedom of thought on all matters, personal conviction and the commitment to religion or belief, whether manifested individually or in community with others [...]

These provisions of the Universal Declaration of Human Right indirectly call on anti-religious activists to review or nuance their views and reaction to Nigerian Christians' hostility to homosexuality. If one voices his/her belief that homosexuality is a sin based on the latter's reading of the Bible, he or she is simply manifesting his/her religion. It is surely regrettable that the Nigerian state is not fully secularized (as demanded by the country's constitution). It is also to be decried that political forces will prefer to be officiously inspired by religion instead of allying with secularist forces on the matter of homosexuality and LGBT right movement. However, it will not be fair to see such a development as a serious felony committed by Christians.

Christianity – like other puritanical religions – will always want to defend what it believes to be sound and virtuous according to its code of morals and according to the Holy Scriptures. The principle of freedom of religion and thought allows for, and perfectly rationalizes such an act. It is left on the state or government to design methods to secularize the state. It is equally the state's responsibility to make sure that religion does not drive or inform its policies and legislations. Attempts at stigmatizing, labeling, cowing and intimidating Christians on account of their faith is clearly questionable – and is here problematized – as it represents a violation of the Christians' right to freedom of religion and freedom of belief and conscience. As Turek (2010) puts it, it is a form of intolerance, which is equal to the presumed intolerance the pro-gay activists claim to be combating. Tukek further argues that gay activists claim to be fighting for tolerance and diversity by labeling Christianity as a movement close to Nazism and fascism meanwhile they are the most intolerant and least diverse people one can find. According to them, it is only people who have favorable views on homosexuality that should be lauded. "They [thus] advocate a form of totalitarianism by shutting out different viewpoints and insisting that everyone must agree with them on such a controversial issue".

A critical and honest look at the situation reveals that the LGBT right movement has raised a serious dilemma in the realm of human rights framing, promotion and protection in most countries of the world. This dilemma is illustrated by the fact that two types of human rights (namely LGBT rights *versus* the right of religion or the freedom of religion) seem to be competing for supremacy. Scholars and institutions such as Cochrane (2004) and the International Network of Civil Liberties Organizations (2015) have defended the compatibility of these two categories of human rights. However, scratching beneath the surface reveals that the situation (that is the LGBT right-religious freedom divide) is more complex than envisaged.

The visible conflict between these two categories of rights seems to have even attained the level of an impasse. Advocates of the respective categories of rights mutually denounce their moves. Advocates from both sides view activism by the adverse camp as an effort to undermine their rights. In tandem with this, pro-LGBT or gay advocates mainly interpret Christians' resistance to gay proselytism as an attempt by the latter to impose their views on sexuality and morality, even in states constitutionally driven by the secularist doctrine. The International Network of Civil Liberties Organizations (2015) notes for instance that: "religious freedom means the right to our beliefs. That right is fundamental and must be vigorously defended. But religious freedom does not give us the right to impose our views on others, including by discriminating against or otherwise harming them" (p. 4). In tandem with this, endogenous human right activists in Nigeria interpret Christian opposition to homosexuality as a ploy to silence the voice of LGBT people and undermine their views on sexuality and their potential atheist orientation.

This reading of Christianity as a social force bent on forcing its views on sexuality has been faulty on various grounds; one of which is the fact that LGBT right activists most often consider the aggressive and inhuman acts of "so-called" Christians to generally brand Christianity as homophobic. Since the debut of this thorny debate on homosexuality, hardly has a religious leader (openly) called for the killing or brutalization of homosexuals in Nigeria. Religious leaders have expressed their position (their antipathy) on the issue and populist politicians have capitalized on popular imaginations about the issue (the LGBT right concept). The killing, stigmatizing, ostracism, brutalization of the LGBT people and the criminalization of homosexuality are more the regrettable consequences of Nigerian conservatism – which considers gayness as cultural pollution and a social pathology imported from the west. Religion's part has mainly been in denouncing homosexuality as a sin according to the Bible – which, to this author, is no offence, if one is to be mindful of the Universal Declaration of Human Rights which guarantees freedom of religion and freedom of thought.

CONCLUSION

Conservative social arbiters and religious opinion leaders have been cardinal forces behind the adoption of a homophobic legislation in Nigeria. This scenario has spurred many (pro)-gay activists to "impulsively" anchor their LGBT right advocacy on a visibly *Christianophobic* rhetoric which derogatorily brands or frames Christianity and religious fanaticism as two forms of bigotry, barbarism, obscurantism and Nazism, as well as a backward or anti-progressive movements. Such an aggressive advocacy tactic has been making a case for the systematic "de-Christianization" and "de-Islamization" of Nigerians' minds. The dominant tendency among LGBT right activists has been to bash Christianity and puritanical liturgies as they see these phenomena as unrepentant enemies of gays. The impression some of their campaigns give is that, religion is no longer relevant in today's world, particularly as it presumably represents a threat to the human right idiom.

Using critical observations and secondary sources, this chapter has critically illustrated the theory that Nigerian LGBT activists tend to shape their advocacy strategies according to the models adopted by their western counterparts. These aggressive models of advocacy have successfully given rise to a relative degree of gay totalitarianism and Christianophobia in a number of western countries including the US and Britain. The chapter highlighted a number of indexes that are pointing to the fact that the anti-Christian rhetoric adopted by most gay activists is planting the seed of a future Christianophobia in Nigeria. The paper ended up by strongly arguing that any pro-gay advocacy rooted in the de-Christianization of Nigerians unarguably proffers the disrespect of the right to religious freedom, to the advantage of LGBT rights.

REFERENCES

Ajayi, F. (2011). Legalizing same sex marriage in Nigeria is against African deities. *Nigeria World Magazine*, *18*, 30–36.

Alliance Defending Freedom. (2015). The Obama administration's attacks on religious freedom, sanctity of life, and marriage and family. Washington: DC: Alliance Defending Freedom.

Beirich, H. (2016). Religious liberty and the anti-LGBT right. The hardline groups promoting "religious freedom restoration acts" to justify anti-gay discrimination. Washington, DC: Southern Poverty Law Centre.

Bielefeldt, H. (2012). Freedom of religion or belief – A human right pressure. *Oxford Journal of Law and Religion*, *11*, 1–21.

Bisi, A. (2015). *Nigeria: We may be free but homophobic hatred remains our nation's shame. World Press*. Retrieved October 18, 2016, from http://www.nigeria-we-may-be-free-bu-homophobic-hatred-remains-our-nations-shame/bisi/alimi/com

Brett, L. (2007). Faith, homophobia and human rights. Gay Humanist Quarterly, 2(1), 7-8.

Brett, L. (2007). From the editor. *Gay Humanist Quarterly*, *7*, 2.

Chapman, K. C. (2012). Gay rights, the Bible and public accommodations: An empirical approach to religious exemptions for holdout state. *The Georgetown Law Journal*, *100*, 1783–1827.

Cochrane, D. B. (2004). Christian opposition to homosexuality. In J. McNinch & M. Cronin (Eds.), *I could not speak my heart: Education and social justice for LGBT youth*. Regina: Canadian Plains Research Centre.

Crabtree, V. (2011). Anti religious forces: Specific factors fuelling secularization. *Academic Studies of Religion*, *4*(3), 56–78.

Duke, B. (2014). Religious fanatics blamed for Nigeria's draconian anti-gay bill, approved this week. *The Free Thinker*. Retrieved February 2, 2016, from http://www.religious-fanatics-blamed-for-nigerias-draconian-antigay-bill-approved-this-week/thefreethinker.com

Ebuzor, C. (2016). Ex President says gay marriage law might be revisited. *Pulse*. Retrieved June 19, 2016, from http://pulse.ng/local/goodluck-jonathan-ex-president-says-gay-marriage-law-might-be-revisited-id5119539.html

Endong, F. P. C. (2015a). Christian resistance to gay-proselytism in a secular Nigeria: Anathema or social heroism?. *ERAS: European Review of Applied Sociology*, *8*(11), 5–13.

Endong, F. P. C. (2015b). Framing the queers and the LGBT right movement in Africa: A study of Nigerian bloggers and web journalists. *Journal of Global Research in Education and Social Sciences*, *6*(4), 50–60.

Endong, F. P. C. (2016). The LGBT right movement in Africa and the myth of the Whiteman's superiority. *Journal of Globalization Studies*, *7*(1), 3–15.

Endong, F. P. C., & Vareba, A. L. (2015). Resisting anti-gay laws through media advocacy and online communities of meaning: A study of Nigerian homosexuals. *Journal for Studies in Management and Planning*, *10*(2), 94–106.

Epprecht, M. (2010). Understanding homophobia in Africa today. *Perspectives. Political Analysis and Commentary from Africa*, *4*(10), 10–15.

Gay and Lesbian Humanist Association. (2007). Imagine no religion. *Gay Humanist Quarterly*, *7*, 31–31.

Gay and Lesbian Humanist Association. (2007). Nigeria: Humanist jeered for supporting gay rights. *Gay Humanist Quarterly*, *7*, 23–24.

Giddens, A. (1982). *Sociology. A brief but critical introduction*. Washington, DC: Harcourt Brace, Jovanovich Publishers.

International Humanist and Ethical Union. (2012). *Freedom of thought 2012. A global report on discrimination against humanists, atheists and the nonreligious*. New York: IHEU.

International Network of Civil Liberties Organizations. (2015). *Drawing the line: Tackling tensions between religious freedom and equality*. London: INCLO.

Jerusalem Institute of Justice. (2015). *Freedom of religion. A human rights-based approach to discrimination against religious minorities in the Palestinian Authority*. Jerusalem: Jerusalem Institute of Justice.

Kaoma, J. K. (2015). *Colonizing African Values – How the US Christian right is transforming sexual politics in Africa*. Somerville: Political Research Associates.

Karaim, R. (2011). Gay Rights. Has the movement's success sparked a backlash?. *CQ Global Researcher*, *5*(5), 107–132.

Koama, K. (2010). The US Christian right and the attack on gay in Africa. *The Public Eye Magazine*, *9*(10), 37–68.

Macaulay, J. R. (2008). *What the Bible says about homosexuality to Nigerian*. Retrieved April 4, 2016, from http://www.rowland-jide-macaulay/what-the-bible-says-about-homosexuality-to-nigerians.htm

Marx, K. (1962). Frammento dell'appendice della dissertazione dottorale. In A. Sabetti (Ed.), *Sulla fondazione del materialism storico* (pp. 398–217). Florence, Italy: Observatore Romano.

Mastin, L. (2011). *Arguments for atheism*. Retrieved October 16, 2016, from http://www.argument-for-atheism-mastin-luke.com

Matunhu, J. (2011). A critique of modernization and dependency theories in Africa: Critical assessment. *African Journal of History and Culture*, *3*(5), 65–72.

Nabagesera, K. J. (2014). Exploring the intersection of religious freedom and human right. *Bombastic Magazine*, *1*, 34–35.

NAIJ. (2013). *Being gay is natural – Yemisi Ilesanmi, coordinator of the Nigerian lesbian, gay, bisexual and transsexual, LGBT community*. Retrieved October 16, 2016, from http://www.being-gay-is-natural/yemisi-ilesanmi/naij.com

Ndashe, S. (2010). The battle for the recognition of LGBTI rights as human rights. *Perspectives. Political Analysis and Commentary from Africa*, *4*(10), 4–9.

Ray, C. (2016). Homosexuality – a Sign of the End of the Age?. *Living Waters*, *16*, 23–48.

Sanderson, T. (2007). Secularism holds the key to justice for all. Gay Humanist Quarterly, 2(1), 7-8.

Schumacher, W. (2010). African churches and homosexuality. *Concordia Theology*, *36*, 77–89.

Tamale, S. (2011). Researching and theorizing sexualities in Africa. In S. Tamale (Ed.), *African sexualities: A reader* (pp. 1–47). Kampala: Pambazuka.

The Initiative for Equal Rights. (2014). *Survey on homosexuality perception in Nigeria*. Lagos: The Initiative for Equal Rights.

Tunde, O. (2005). The Myth of Neo-Colonialism. *Africa Economic Analysis*, *23*, 30–49.

Turek, K. (2010). *Gay totalitarianism vs Christian liberty*. Retrieved October 18, 2016, from http://crossexamined.org/gay-totalitarianism-vs-christian-liberty/

Van de Berg, M., Bos, D. J., Derks, M., Ganzevoort, R., Jovanovic, M., Korte, A. M., & Sremac, S. (2014). Religion, Homosexuality and Contested Social Orders in the Netherlands, the Western Balkans and Sweden. In *Religion in Times of Crisis* (pp. 116–134). Boston: Brill. doi:10.1163/9789004277793_008

Veith, G. (2011). *Gay marriage & totalitarianism*. Retrieved October 18, 2016, from http://www.patheos.com/blogs/geneveith/2011/07/gay-marriage-totalitarianism/

Yasu, R. (2010). Identity, law, justice. Thinking about sexual rights and citizenship in post-apartheid South Africa. *Perspectives, Political Analysis and Commentary from Africa*, *4*(10), 18–23.

Zmirak, J. (2015). Gay totalitarianism and the upcoming persecution of Christians. *The Stream*, *19*, 43–67.

KEY TERMS AND DEFINITIONS

Atheism: Derived from the Greek word "Atheos" (which means without God), atheism is the lack of belief in the existence of God or gods, thus the rejection of theism. According to atheists, there is no such thing as God or gods. Atheism equally entails the belief that the universe can be explained without the help of a divine power and that, moral and ethical codes can be designed without getting inspiration from God or spiritual sources. It lauds scientific reasoning and humanism over religion.

Christianophobia: This is a neologism conceived to refer to any irrational fear or hatred manifested against Christians or Christianity.

De-Christianization: De-Christianization is used as the contrary of Christianization which entails the process through which something is made to have a Christian nature or be plausible within Christian circles. De-Christianization consists in causing someone to reject Christian values or Biblical precepts.

De-Islamization: De-Islamization is a process whereby efforts are produced to cause something to lose its Islamic nature. It is also a process whereby someone (a Muslim) is made to reject Islamic precepts.

Gay Totalitarianism: In principle, totalitarianism refers to a system of government in which all powers are in the hands of the state. In a totalitarian state, the government asserts its sovereignty over everything; both the public and the private sectors are controlled by the government. Gay totalitarianism is used by some authors who are critical of the "excessive" growth of the influence of pro-gay activists in the world. These authors often use the term to mean the tendency by most western governments to alter social institutions and pass pro-gay legislations which show no tolerance for Christian views and tend to undemocratically discriminate against voices that plead in disfavor of homosexuality.

Homophobia: A term used to refer to any irrational fear or hatred of homosexual feelings, behaviors, thoughts, or people. It equally means a bias evaluation of homosexual identities which may – or always – leads to discrimination against homosexual individuals.

Homosexuality: A term invented by nineteenth century German sexologists to describe an attraction between two individuals of the same sex at the physical, sexual, emotional, intellectual, and spiritual levels.

Human Rights: The human rights framework actually protects civil, political, socio-cultural and economic rights. It is guided by the principles of universality, people's participation, indivisibility, transparency, accountability, and non-discrimination.

LGBT Rights Movement: The abbreviation "LGBT" stands for Lesbian, Gay, Bisexual and Transgender. Some authors prefer to employ a longer abbreviation which includes Intersexual and Queers, thus LGBTIQ. The LGBT right movement is a complex form of program aimed at advocating the rights of non-heterosexuals rights. LGBT rights include but are not limited to (1) recognition of same-sex relationships (through same-sex marriage or similar unions), (2) right to adopt children, (3) right to donate blood, (4) recognition of LGBT parenting, (5) immigration equality rights, (6) right for protection against discrimination in employment and housing procedures, (7) protection against bullying of any sort, (8) equal access to assisted reproductive technology, and (9) access to sex reassignment surgery and hormone, among others.

Same-Sex Prohibition Act: Name given to a 2013 Nigerian legislation dealing with gayness and same sex marriage. The law prescribes a 14-year jail sentence for any person convicted of homosexuality, and up to 12-year jail sentence for any party which assists same sex unions.

Related References

To continue our tradition of advancing academic research, we have compiled a list of recommended IGI Global readings. These references will provide additional information and guidance to further enrich your knowledge and assist you with your own research and future publications.

Adeyemo, O. (2013). The nationwide health information network: A biometric approach to prevent medical identity theft. In *User-driven healthcare: Concepts, methodologies, tools, and applications* (pp. 1636–1649). Hershey, PA: IGI Global. doi:10.4018/978-1-4666-2770-3.ch081

Adler, M., & Henman, P. (2009). Justice beyond the courts: The implications of computerisation for procedural justice in social security. In A. Martínez & P. Abat (Eds.), *E-justice: Using information communication technologies in the court system* (pp. 65–86). Hershey, PA: IGI Global. doi:10.4018/978-1-59904-998-4.ch005

Aflalo, E., & Gabay, E. (2013). An information system for coping with student dropout. In L. Tomei (Ed.), *Learning tools and teaching approaches through ICT advancements* (pp. 176–187). Hershey, PA: IGI Global. doi:10.4018/978-1-4666-2017-9.ch016

Ahmed, M. A., Janssen, M., & van den Hoven, J. (2012). Value sensitive transfer (VST) of systems among countries: Towards a framework. *International Journal of Electronic Government Research, 8*(1), 26–42. doi:10.4018/jegr.2012010102

Aikins, S. K. (2008). Issues and trends in internet-based citizen participation. In G. Garson & M. Khosrow-Pour (Eds.), *Handbook of research on public information technology* (pp. 31–40). Hershey, PA: IGI Global. doi:10.4018/978-1-59904-857-4.ch004

Aikins, S. K. (2009). A comparative study of municipal adoption of internet-based citizen participation. In C. Reddick (Ed.), *Handbook of research on strategies for local e-government adoption and implementation: Comparative studies* (pp. 206–230). Hershey, PA: IGI Global. doi:10.4018/978-1-60566-282-4.ch011

Aikins, S. K. (2012). Improving e-government project management: Best practices and critical success factors. In *Digital democracy: Concepts, methodologies, tools, and applications* (pp. 1314–1332). Hershey, PA: IGI Global. doi:10.4018/978-1-4666-1740-7.ch065

Akabawi, M. S. (2011). Ghabbour group ERP deployment: Learning from past technology failures. In E. Business Research and Case Center (Ed.), Cases on business and management in the MENA region: New trends and opportunities (pp. 177-203). Hershey, PA: IGI Global. doi:10.4018/978-1-60960-583-4.ch012

Akabawi, M. S. (2013). Ghabbour group ERP deployment: Learning from past technology failures. In *Industrial engineering: Concepts, methodologies, tools, and applications* (pp. 933–958). Hershey, PA: IGI Global. doi:10.4018/978-1-4666-1945-6.ch051

Akbulut, A. Y., & Motwani, J. (2008). Integration and information sharing in e-government. In G. Putnik & M. Cruz-Cunha (Eds.), *Encyclopedia of networked and virtual organizations* (pp. 729–734). Hershey, PA: IGI Global. doi:10.4018/978-1-59904-885-7.ch096

Akers, E. J. (2008). Technology diffusion in public administration. In G. Garson & M. Khosrow-Pour (Eds.), *Handbook of research on public information technology* (pp. 339–348). Hershey, PA: IGI Global. doi:10.4018/978-1-59904-857-4.ch033

Al-Shafi, S. (2008). Free wireless internet park services: An investigation of technology adoption in Qatar from a citizens perspective. *Journal of Cases on Information Technology*, *10*(3), 21–34. doi:10.4018/jcit.2008070103

Al-Shafi, S., & Weerakkody, V. (2009). Implementing free wi-fi in public parks: An empirical study in Qatar. *International Journal of Electronic Government Research*, *5*(3), 21–35. doi:10.4018/jegr.2009070102

Aladwani, A. M. (2002). Organizational actions, computer attitudes and end-user satisfaction in public organizations: An empirical study. In C. Snodgrass & E. Szewczak (Eds.), *Human factors in information systems* (pp. 153–168). Hershey, PA: IGI Global. doi:10.4018/978-1-931777-10-0.ch012

Aladwani, A. M. (2002). Organizational actions, computer attitudes, and end-user satisfaction in public organizations: An empirical study. *Journal of Organizational and End User Computing*, *14*(1), 42–49. doi:10.4018/joeuc.2002010104

Allen, B., Juillet, L., Paquet, G., & Roy, J. (2005). E-government and private-public partnerships: Relational challenges and strategic directions. In M. Khosrow-Pour (Ed.), *Practicing e-government: A global perspective* (pp. 364–382). Hershey, PA: IGI Global. doi:10.4018/978-1-59140-637-2.ch016

Alshawaf, A., & Knalil, O. E. (2008). IS success factors and IS organizational impact: Does ownership type matter in Kuwait? *International Journal of Enterprise Information Systems*, *4*(2), 13–33. doi:10.4018/jeis.2008040102

Ambali, A. R. (2009). Digital divide and its implication on Malaysian e-government: Policy initiatives. In H. Rahman (Ed.), *Social and political implications of data mining: Knowledge management in e-government* (pp. 267–287). Hershey, PA: IGI Global. doi:10.4018/978-1-60566-230-5.ch016

Amoretti, F. (2007). Digital international governance. In A. Anttiroiko & M. Malkia (Eds.), *Encyclopedia of digital government* (pp. 365–370). Hershey, PA: IGI Global. doi:10.4018/978-1-59140-789-8.ch056

Amoretti, F. (2008). Digital international governance. In A. Anttiroiko (Ed.), *Electronic government: Concepts, methodologies, tools, and applications* (pp. 688–696). Hershey, PA: IGI Global. doi:10.4018/978-1-59904-947-2.ch058

Amoretti, F. (2008). E-government at supranational level in the European Union. In A. Anttiroiko (Ed.), *Electronic government: Concepts, methodologies, tools, and applications* (pp. 1047–1055). Hershey, PA: IGI Global. doi:10.4018/978-1-59904-947-2.ch079

Amoretti, F. (2008). E-government regimes. In A. Anttiroiko (Ed.), *Electronic government: Concepts, methodologies, tools, and applications* (pp. 3846–3856). Hershey, PA: IGI Global. doi:10.4018/978-1-59904-947-2.ch280

Amoretti, F. (2009). Electronic constitution: A Braudelian perspective. In F. Amoretti (Ed.), *Electronic constitution: Social, cultural, and political implications* (pp. 1–19). Hershey, PA: IGI Global. doi:10.4018/978-1-60566-254-1.ch001

Amoretti, F., & Musella, F. (2009). Institutional isomorphism and new technologies. In M. Khosrow-Pour (Ed.), *Encyclopedia of information science and technology* (2nd ed.; pp. 2066–2071). Hershey, PA: IGI Global. doi:10.4018/978-1-60566-026-4.ch325

Andersen, K. V., & Henriksen, H. Z. (2007). E-government research: Capabilities, interaction, orientation, and values. In D. Norris (Ed.), *Current issues and trends in e-government research* (pp. 269–288). Hershey, PA: IGI Global. doi:10.4018/978-1-59904-283-1.ch013

Anderson, K. V., & Henriksen, H. Z. (2005). The first leg of e-government research: Domains and application areas 19982003. *International Journal of Electronic Government Research, 1*(4), 26–44. doi:10.4018/jegr.2005100102

Anttiroiko, A. (2009). Democratic e-governance. In M. Khosrow-Pour (Ed.), *Encyclopedia of information science and technology* (2nd ed.; pp. 990–995). Hershey, PA: IGI Global. doi:10.4018/978-1-60566-026-4.ch158

Baker, P. M., Bell, A., & Moon, N. W. (2009). Accessibility issues in municipal wireless networks. In C. Reddick (Ed.), *Handbook of research on strategies for local e-government adoption and implementation: Comparative studies* (pp. 569–588). Hershey, PA: IGI Global. doi:10.4018/978-1-60566-282-4.ch030

Becker, S. A., Keimer, R., & Muth, T. (2010). A case on university and community collaboration: The sci-tech entrepreneurial training services (ETS) program. In S. Becker & R. Niebuhr (Eds.), *Cases on technology innovation: Entrepreneurial successes and pitfalls* (pp. 68–90). Hershey, PA: IGI Global. doi:10.4018/978-1-61520-609-4.ch003

Becker, S. A., Keimer, R., & Muth, T. (2012). A case on university and community collaboration: The sci-tech entrepreneurial training services (ETS) program. In Regional development: Concepts, methodologies, tools, and applications (pp. 947-969). Hershey, PA: IGI Global. doi:10.4018/978-1-4666-0882-5.ch507

Bernardi, R. (2012). Information technology and resistance to public sector reforms: A case study in Kenya. In T. Papadopoulos & P. Kanellis (Eds.), *Public sector reform using information technologies: Transforming policy into practice* (pp. 59–78). Hershey, PA: IGI Global. doi:10.4018/978-1-60960-839-2.ch004

Bernardi, R. (2013). Information technology and resistance to public sector reforms: A case study in Kenya. In *User-driven healthcare: Concepts, methodologies, tools, and applications* (pp. 14–33). Hershey, PA: IGI Global. doi:10.4018/978-1-4666-2770-3.ch002

Bolívar, M. P., Pérez, M. D., & Hernández, A. M. (2012). Municipal e-government services in emerging economies: The Latin-American and Caribbean experiences. In Y. Chen & P. Chu (Eds.), *Electronic governance and cross-boundary collaboration: Innovations and advancing tools* (pp. 198–226). Hershey, PA: IGI Global. doi:10.4018/978-1-60960-753-1.ch011

Borycki, E. M., & Kushniruk, A. W. (2010). Use of clinical simulations to evaluate the impact of health information systems and ubiquitous computing devices upon health professional work. In S. Mohammed & J. Fiaidhi (Eds.), *Ubiquitous health and medical informatics: The ubiquity 2.0 trend and beyond* (pp. 552–573). Hershey, PA: IGI Global. doi:10.4018/978-1-61520-777-0.ch026

Borycki, E. M., & Kushniruk, A. W. (2011). Use of clinical simulations to evaluate the impact of health information systems and ubiquitous computing devices upon health professional work. In *Clinical technologies: Concepts, methodologies, tools and applications* (pp. 532–553). Hershey, PA: IGI Global. doi:10.4018/978-1-60960-561-2.ch220

Buchan, J. (2011). Developing a dynamic and responsive online learning environment: A case study of a large Australian university. In B. Czerkawski (Ed.), *Free and open source software for e-learning: Issues, successes and challenges* (pp. 92–109). Hershey, PA: IGI Global. doi:10.4018/978-1-61520-917-0.ch006

Buenger, A. W. (2008). Digital convergence and cybersecurity policy. In G. Garson & M. Khosrow-Pour (Eds.), *Handbook of research on public information technology* (pp. 395–405). Hershey, PA: IGI Global. doi:10.4018/978-1-59904-857-4.ch038

Burn, J. M., & Loch, K. D. (2002). The societal impact of world wide web - Key challenges for the 21st century. In A. Salehnia (Ed.), *Ethical issues of information systems* (pp. 88–106). Hershey, PA: IGI Global. doi:10.4018/978-1-931777-15-5.ch007

Burn, J. M., & Loch, K. D. (2003). The societal impact of the world wide web-Key challenges for the 21st century. In M. Khosrow-Pour (Ed.), *Advanced topics in information resources management* (Vol. 2, pp. 32–51). Hershey, PA: IGI Global. doi:10.4018/978-1-59140-062-2.ch002

Bwalya, K. J., Du Plessis, T., & Rensleigh, C. (2012). The "quicksilver initiatives" as a framework for e-government strategy design in developing economies. In K. Bwalya & S. Zulu (Eds.), *Handbook of research on e-government in emerging economies: Adoption, e-participation, and legal frameworks* (pp. 605–623). Hershey, PA: IGI Global. doi:10.4018/978-1-4666-0324-0.ch031

Cabotaje, C. E., & Alampay, E. A. (2013). Social media and citizen engagement: Two cases from the Philippines. In S. Saeed & C. Reddick (Eds.), *Human-centered system design for electronic governance* (pp. 225–238). Hershey, PA: IGI Global. doi:10.4018/978-1-4666-3640-8.ch013

Camillo, A., Di Pietro, L., Di Virgilio, F., & Franco, M. (2013). Work-groups conflict at PetroTech-Italy, S.R.L.: The influence of culture on conflict dynamics. In B. Christiansen, E. Turkina, & N. Williams (Eds.), *Cultural and technological influences on global business* (pp. 272–289). Hershey, PA: IGI Global. doi:10.4018/978-1-4666-3966-9.ch015

Capra, E., Francalanci, C., & Marinoni, C. (2008). Soft success factors for m-government. In A. Anttiroiko (Ed.), *Electronic government: Concepts, methodologies, tools, and applications* (pp. 1213–1233). Hershey, PA: IGI Global. doi:10.4018/978-1-59904-947-2.ch089

Cartelli, A. (2009). The implementation of practices with ICT as a new teaching-learning paradigm. In A. Cartelli & M. Palma (Eds.), *Encyclopedia of information communication technology* (pp. 413–417). Hershey, PA: IGI Global. doi:10.4018/978-1-59904-845-1.ch055

Charalabidis, Y., Lampathaki, F., & Askounis, D. (2010). Investigating the landscape in national interoperability frameworks. *International Journal of E-Services and Mobile Applications*, *2*(4), 28–41. doi:10.4018/jesma.2010100103

Charalabidis, Y., Lampathaki, F., & Askounis, D. (2012). Investigating the landscape in national interoperability frameworks. In A. Scupola (Ed.), *Innovative mobile platform developments for electronic services design and delivery* (pp. 218–231). Hershey, PA: IGI Global. doi:10.4018/978-1-4666-1568-7.ch013

Chen, I. (2005). Distance education associations. In C. Howard, J. Boettcher, L. Justice, K. Schenk, P. Rogers, & G. Berg (Eds.), *Encyclopedia of distance learning* (pp. 599–612). Hershey, PA: IGI Global. doi:10.4018/978-1-59140-555-9.ch087

Chen, I. (2008). Distance education associations. In L. Tomei (Ed.), *Online and distance learning: Concepts, methodologies, tools, and applications* (pp. 562–579). Hershey, PA: IGI Global. doi:10.4018/978-1-59904-935-9.ch048

Chen, Y. (2008). Managing IT outsourcing for digital government. In A. Anttiroiko (Ed.), *Electronic government: Concepts, methodologies, tools, and applications* (pp. 3107–3114). Hershey, PA: IGI Global. doi:10.4018/978-1-59904-947-2.ch229

Chen, Y., & Dimitrova, D. V. (2006). Electronic government and online engagement: Citizen interaction with government via web portals. *International Journal of Electronic Government Research*, *2*(1), 54–76. doi:10.4018/jegr.2006010104

Chen, Y., & Knepper, R. (2005). Digital government development strategies: Lessons for policy makers from a comparative perspective. In W. Huang, K. Siau, & K. Wei (Eds.), *Electronic government strategies and implementation* (pp. 394–420). Hershey, PA: IGI Global. doi:10.4018/978-1-59140-348-7.ch017

Chen, Y., & Knepper, R. (2008). Digital government development strategies: Lessons for policy makers from a comparative perspective. In H. Rahman (Ed.), *Developing successful ICT strategies: Competitive advantages in a global knowledge-driven society* (pp. 334–356). Hershey, PA: IGI Global. doi:10.4018/978-1-59904-654-9.ch017

Cherian, E. J., & Ryan, T. W. (2014). Incongruent needs: Why differences in the iron-triangle of priorities make health information technology adoption and use difficult. In C. El Morr (Ed.), *Research perspectives on the role of informatics in health policy and management* (pp. 209–221). Hershey, PA: IGI Global. doi:10.4018/978-1-4666-4321-5.ch012

Cho, H. J., & Hwang, S. (2010). Government 2.0 in Korea: Focusing on e-participation services. In C. Reddick (Ed.), *Politics, democracy and e-government: Participation and service delivery* (pp. 94–114). Hershey, PA: IGI Global. doi:10.4018/978-1-61520-933-0.ch006

Chorus, C., & Timmermans, H. (2010). Ubiquitous travel environments and travel control strategies: Prospects and challenges. In M. Wachowicz (Ed.), *Movement-aware applications for sustainable mobility: Technologies and approaches* (pp. 30–51). Hershey, PA: IGI Global. doi:10.4018/978-1-61520-769-5.ch003

Chuanshen, R. (2007). E-government construction and China's administrative litigation act. In A. Anttiroiko & M. Malkia (Eds.), *Encyclopedia of digital government* (pp. 507–510). Hershey, PA: IGI Global. doi:10.4018/978-1-59140-789-8.ch077

Ciaghi, A., & Villafiorita, A. (2012). Law modeling and BPR for public administration improvement. In K. Bwalya & S. Zulu (Eds.), *Handbook of research on e-government in emerging economies: Adoption, e-participation, and legal frameworks* (pp. 391–410). Hershey, PA: IGI Global. doi:10.4018/978-1-4666-0324-0.ch019

Ciaramitaro, B. L., & Skrocki, M. (2012). mHealth: Mobile healthcare. In B. Ciaramitaro (Ed.), Mobile technology consumption: Opportunities and challenges (pp. 99-109). Hershey, PA: IGI Global. doi:10.4018/978-1-61350-150-4.ch007

Comite, U. (2012). Innovative processes and managerial effectiveness of e-procurement in healthcare. In A. Manoharan & M. Holzer (Eds.), *Active citizen participation in e-government: A global perspective* (pp. 206–229). Hershey, PA: IGI Global. doi:10.4018/978-1-4666-0116-1.ch011

Cordella, A. (2013). E-government success: How to account for ICT, administrative rationalization, and institutional change. In J. Gil-Garcia (Ed.), *E-government success factors and measures: Theories, concepts, and methodologies* (pp. 40–51). Hershey, PA: IGI Global. doi:10.4018/978-1-4666-4058-0.ch003

Cropf, R. A. (2009). ICT and e-democracy. In M. Khosrow-Pour (Ed.), *Encyclopedia of information science and technology* (2nd ed.; pp. 1789–1793). Hershey, PA: IGI Global. doi:10.4018/978-1-60566-026-4.ch281

Cropf, R. A. (2009). The virtual public sphere. In M. Pagani (Ed.), *Encyclopedia of multimedia technology and networking* (2nd ed.; pp. 1525–1530). Hershey, PA: IGI Global. doi:10.4018/978-1-60566-014-1.ch206

D'Abundo, M. L. (2013). Electronic health record implementation in the United States healthcare industry: Making the process of change manageable. In V. Wang (Ed.), *Handbook of research on technologies for improving the 21st century workforce: Tools for lifelong learning* (pp. 272–286). Hershey, PA: IGI Global. doi:10.4018/978-1-4666-2181-7.ch018

Damurski, L. (2012). E-participation in urban planning: Online tools for citizen engagement in Poland and in Germany. *International Journal of E-Planning Research, 1*(3), 40–67. doi:10.4018/ijepr.2012070103

de Almeida, M. O. (2007). E-government strategy in Brazil: Increasing transparency and efficiency through e-government procurement. In M. Gascó-Hernandez (Ed.), *Latin America online: Cases, successes and pitfalls* (pp. 34–82). Hershey, PA: IGI Global. doi:10.4018/978-1-59140-974-8.ch002

de Juana Espinosa, S. (2008). Empirical study of the municipalitites' motivations for adopting online presence. In A. Anttiroiko (Ed.), *Electronic government: Concepts, methodologies, tools, and applications* (pp. 3593–3608). Hershey, PA: IGI Global. doi:10.4018/978-1-59904-947-2.ch262

de Souza Dias, D. (2002). Motivation for using information technology. In C. Snodgrass & E. Szewczak (Eds.), *Human factors in information systems* (pp. 55–60). Hershey, PA: IGI Global. doi:10.4018/978-1-931777-10-0.ch005

Demediuk, P. (2006). Government procurement ICT's impact on the sustainability of SMEs and regional communities. In S. Marshall, W. Taylor, & X. Yu (Eds.), *Encyclopedia of developing regional communities with information and communication technology* (pp. 321–324). Hershey, PA: IGI Global. doi:10.4018/978-1-59140-575-7.ch056

Devonshire, E., Forsyth, H., Reid, S., & Simpson, J. M. (2013). The challenges and opportunities of online postgraduate coursework programs in a traditional university context. In B. Tynan, J. Willems, & R. James (Eds.), *Outlooks and opportunities in blended and distance learning* (pp. 353–368). Hershey, PA: IGI Global. doi:10.4018/978-1-4666-4205-8.ch026

Di Cerbo, F., Scotto, M., Sillitti, A., Succi, G., & Vernazza, T. (2007). Toward a GNU/Linux distribution for corporate environments. In S. Sowe, I. Stamelos, & I. Samoladas (Eds.), *Emerging free and open source software practices* (pp. 215–236). Hershey, PA: IGI Global. doi:10.4018/978-1-59904-210-7.ch010

Diesner, J., & Carley, K. M. (2005). Revealing social structure from texts: Meta-matrix text analysis as a novel method for network text analysis. In V. Narayanan & D. Armstrong (Eds.), *Causal mapping for research in information technology* (pp. 81–108). Hershey, PA: IGI Global. doi:10.4018/978-1-59140-396-8.ch004

Dologite, D. G., Mockler, R. J., Bai, Q., & Viszhanyo, P. F. (2006). IS change agents in practice in a US-Chinese joint venture. In M. Hunter & F. Tan (Eds.), *Advanced topics in global information management* (Vol. 5, pp. 331–352). Hershey, PA: IGI Global. doi:10.4018/978-1-59140-923-6.ch015

Drnevich, P., Brush, T. H., & Luckock, G. T. (2011). Process and structural implications for IT-enabled outsourcing. *International Journal of Strategic Information Technology and Applications*, *2*(4), 30–43. doi:10.4018/jsita.2011100103

Dwivedi, A. N. (2009). Handbook of research on information technology management and clinical data administration in healthcare (Vols. 1–2). Hershey, PA: IGI Global. doi:10.4018/978-1-60566-356-2

Elbeltagi, I., McBride, N., & Hardaker, G. (2006). Evaluating the factors affecting DSS usage by senior managers in local authorities in Egypt. In M. Hunter & F. Tan (Eds.), *Advanced topics in global information management* (Vol. 5, pp. 283–307). Hershey, PA: IGI Global. doi:10.4018/978-1-59140-923-6.ch013

Eom, S., & Fountain, J. E. (2013). Enhancing information services through public-private partnerships: Information technology knowledge transfer underlying structures to develop shared services in the U.S. and Korea. In J. Gil-Garcia (Ed.), *E-government success around the world: Cases, empirical studies, and practical recommendations* (pp. 15–40). Hershey, PA: IGI Global. doi:10.4018/978-1-4666-4173-0.ch002

Esteves, T., Leuenberger, D., & Van Leuven, N. (2012). Reaching citizen 2.0: How government uses social media to send public messages during times of calm and times of crisis. In K. Kloby & M. D'Agostino (Eds.), *Citizen 2.0: Public and governmental interaction through web 2.0 technologies* (pp. 250–268). Hershey, PA: IGI Global. doi:10.4018/978-1-4666-0318-9.ch013

Estevez, E., Fillottrani, P., Janowski, T., & Ojo, A. (2012). Government information sharing: A framework for policy formulation. In Y. Chen & P. Chu (Eds.), *Electronic governance and cross-boundary collaboration: Innovations and advancing tools* (pp. 23–55). Hershey, PA: IGI Global. doi:10.4018/978-1-60960-753-1.ch002

Ezz, I. E. (2008). E-governement emerging trends: Organizational challenges. In A. Anttiroiko (Ed.), *Electronic government: Concepts, methodologies, tools, and applications* (pp. 3721–3737). Hershey, PA: IGI Global. doi:10.4018/978-1-59904-947-2.ch269

Fabri, M. (2009). The Italian style of e-justice in a comparative perspective. In A. Martínez & P. Abat (Eds.), *E-justice: Using information communication technologies in the court system* (pp. 1–19). Hershey, PA: IGI Global. doi:10.4018/978-1-59904-998-4.ch001

Fagbe, T., & Adekola, O. D. (2010). Workplace safety and personnel well-being: The impact of information technology. *International Journal of Green Computing, 1*(1), 28–33. doi:10.4018/jgc.2010010103

Fagbe, T., & Adekola, O. D. (2011). Workplace safety and personnel well-being: The impact of information technology. In *Global business: Concepts, methodologies, tools and applications* (pp. 1438–1444). Hershey, PA: IGI Global. doi:10.4018/978-1-60960-587-2.ch509

Farmer, L. (2008). Affective collaborative instruction with librarians. In S. Kelsey & K. St.Amant (Eds.), *Handbook of research on computer mediated communication* (pp. 15–24). Hershey, PA: IGI Global. doi:10.4018/978-1-59904-863-5.ch002

Favier, L., & Mekhantar, J. (2007). Use of OSS by local e-administration: The French situation. In K. St.Amant & B. Still (Eds.), *Handbook of research on open source software: Technological, economic, and social perspectives* (pp. 428–444). Hershey, PA: IGI Global. doi:10.4018/978-1-59140-999-1.ch033

Fernando, S. (2009). Issues of e-learning in third world countries. In M. Khosrow-Pour (Ed.), *Encyclopedia of information science and technology* (2nd ed.; pp. 2273–2277). Hershey, PA: IGI Global. doi:10.4018/978-1-60566-026-4.ch360

Filho, J. R., & dos Santos Junior, J. R. (2009). Local e-government in Brazil: Poor interaction and local politics as usual. In C. Reddick (Ed.), *Handbook of research on strategies for local e-government adoption and implementation: Comparative studies* (pp. 863–878). Hershey, PA: IGI Global. doi:10.4018/978-1-60566-282-4.ch045

Fletcher, P. D. (2004). Portals and policy: Implications of electronic access to U.S. federal government information services. In A. Pavlichev & G. Garson (Eds.), *Digital government: Principles and best practices* (pp. 52–62). Hershey, PA: IGI Global. doi:10.4018/978-1-59140-122-3.ch004

Fletcher, P. D. (2008). Portals and policy: Implications of electronic access to U.S. federal government information services. In A. Anttiroiko (Ed.), *Electronic government: Concepts, methodologies, tools, and applications* (pp. 3970–3979). Hershey, PA: IGI Global. doi:10.4018/978-1-59904-947-2.ch289

Forlano, L. (2004). The emergence of digital government: International perspectives. In A. Pavlichev & G. Garson (Eds.), *Digital government: Principles and best practices* (pp. 34–51). Hershey, PA: IGI Global. doi:10.4018/978-1-59140-122-3.ch003

Franzel, J. M., & Coursey, D. H. (2004). Government web portals: Management issues and the approaches of five states. In A. Pavlichev & G. Garson (Eds.), *Digital government: Principles and best practices* (pp. 63–77). Hershey, PA: IGI Global. doi:10.4018/978-1-59140-122-3.ch005

Gaivéo, J. M. (2013). Security of ICTs supporting healthcare activities. In M. Cruz-Cunha, I. Miranda, & P. Gonçalves (Eds.), *Handbook of research on ICTs for human-centered healthcare and social care services* (pp. 208–228). Hershey, PA: IGI Global. doi:10.4018/978-1-4666-3986-7.ch011

Garson, G. D. (1999). *Information technology and computer applications in public administration: Issues and trends*. Hershey, PA: IGI Global. doi:10.4018/978-1-87828-952-0

Garson, G. D. (2003). Toward an information technology research agenda for public administration. In G. Garson (Ed.), *Public information technology: Policy and management issues* (pp. 331–357). Hershey, PA: IGI Global. doi:10.4018/978-1-59140-060-8.ch014

Garson, G. D. (2004). The promise of digital government. In A. Pavlichev & G. Garson (Eds.), *Digital government: Principles and best practices* (pp. 2–15). Hershey, PA: IGI Global. doi:10.4018/978-1-59140-122-3.ch001

Garson, G. D. (2007). An information technology research agenda for public administration. In G. Garson (Ed.), *Modern public information technology systems: Issues and challenges* (pp. 365–392). Hershey, PA: IGI Global. doi:10.4018/978-1-59904-051-6.ch018

Gasco, M. (2007). Civil servants' resistance towards e-government development. In A. Anttiroiko & M. Malkia (Eds.), *Encyclopedia of digital government* (pp. 190–195). Hershey, PA: IGI Global. doi:10.4018/978-1-59140-789-8.ch028

Gasco, M. (2008). Civil servants' resistance towards e-government development. In A. Anttiroiko (Ed.), *Electronic government: Concepts, methodologies, tools, and applications* (pp. 2580–2588). Hershey, PA: IGI Global. doi:10.4018/978-1-59904-947-2.ch190

Ghere, R. K. (2010). Accountability and information technology enactment: Implications for social empowerment. In E. Ferro, Y. Dwivedi, J. Gil-Garcia, & M. Williams (Eds.), *Handbook of research on overcoming digital divides: Constructing an equitable and competitive information society* (pp. 515–532). Hershey, PA: IGI Global. doi:10.4018/978-1-60566-699-0.ch028

Gibson, I. W. (2012). Simulation modeling of healthcare delivery. In A. Kolker & P. Story (Eds.), *Management engineering for effective healthcare delivery: Principles and applications* (pp. 69–89). Hershey, PA: IGI Global. doi:10.4018/978-1-60960-872-9.ch003

Gil-Garcia, J. R. (2007). Exploring e-government benefits and success factors. In A. Anttiroiko & M. Malkia (Eds.), *Encyclopedia of digital government* (pp. 803–811). Hershey, PA: IGI Global. doi:10.4018/978-1-59140-789-8.ch122

Gil-Garcia, J. R., & González Miranda, F. (2010). E-government and opportunities for participation: The case of the Mexican state web portals. In C. Reddick (Ed.), *Politics, democracy and e-government: Participation and service delivery* (pp. 56–74). Hershey, PA: IGI Global. doi:10.4018/978-1-61520-933-0.ch004

Goldfinch, S. (2012). Public trust in government, trust in e-government, and use of e-government. In Z. Yan (Ed.), *Encyclopedia of cyber behavior* (pp. 987–995). Hershey, PA: IGI Global. doi:10.4018/978-1-4666-0315-8.ch081

Goodyear, M. (2012). Organizational change contributions to e-government project transitions. In S. Aikins (Ed.), *Managing e-government projects: Concepts, issues, and best practices* (pp. 1–21). Hershey, PA: IGI Global. doi:10.4018/978-1-4666-0086-7.ch001

Gordon, S., & Mulligan, P. (2003). Strategic models for the delivery of personal financial services: The role of infocracy. In S. Gordon (Ed.), *Computing information technology: The human side* (pp. 220–232). Hershey, PA: IGI Global. doi:10.4018/978-1-93177-752-0.ch014

Gordon, T. F. (2007). Legal knowledge systems. In A. Anttiroiko & M. Malkia (Eds.), *Encyclopedia of digital government* (pp. 1161–1166). Hershey, PA: IGI Global. doi:10.4018/978-1-59140-789-8.ch175

Graham, J. E., & Semich, G. W. (2008). Integrating technology to transform pedagogy: Revisiting the progress of the three phase TUI model for faculty development. In L. Tomei (Ed.), *Adapting information and communication technologies for effective education* (pp. 1–12). Hershey, PA: IGI Global. doi:10.4018/978-1-59904-922-9.ch001

Grandinetti, L., & Pisacane, O. (2012). Web services for healthcare management. In D. Prakash Vidyarthi (Ed.), *Technologies and protocols for the future of internet design: Reinventing the web* (pp. 60–94). Hershey, PA: IGI Global. doi:10.4018/978-1-4666-0203-8.ch004

Groenewegen, P., & Wagenaar, F. P. (2008). VO as an alternative to hierarchy in the Dutch police sector. In G. Putnik & M. Cruz-Cunha (Eds.), *Encyclopedia of networked and virtual organizations* (pp. 1851–1857). Hershey, PA: IGI Global. doi:10.4018/978-1-59904-885-7.ch245

Gronlund, A. (2001). Building an infrastructure to manage electronic services. In S. Dasgupta (Ed.), *Managing internet and intranet technologies in organizations: Challenges and opportunities* (pp. 71–103). Hershey, PA: IGI Global. doi:10.4018/978-1-878289-95-7.ch006

Gronlund, A. (2002). Introduction to electronic government: Design, applications and management. In Å. Grönlund (Ed.), *Electronic government: Design, applications and management* (pp. 1–21). Hershey, PA: IGI Global. doi:10.4018/978-1-930708-19-8.ch001

Gupta, A., Woosley, R., Crk, I., & Sarnikar, S. (2009). An information technology architecture for drug effectiveness reporting and post-marketing surveillance. In J. Tan (Ed.), *Medical informatics: Concepts, methodologies, tools, and applications* (pp. 631–646). Hershey, PA: IGI Global. doi:10.4018/978-1-60566-050-9.ch047

Hallin, A., & Lundevall, K. (2007). mCity: User focused development of mobile services within the city of Stockholm. In I. Kushchu (Ed.), Mobile government: An emerging direction in e-government (pp. 12-29). Hershey, PA: IGI Global. doi:10.4018/978-1-59140-884-0.ch002

Hallin, A., & Lundevall, K. (2009). mCity: User focused development of mobile services within the city of Stockholm. In S. Clarke (Ed.), Evolutionary concepts in end user productivity and performance: Applications for organizational progress (pp. 268-280). Hershey, PA: IGI Global. doi:10.4018/978-1-60566-136-0.ch017

Hallin, A., & Lundevall, K. (2009). mCity: User focused development of mobile services within the city of Stockholm. In D. Taniar (Ed.), Mobile computing: Concepts, methodologies, tools, and applications (pp. 3455-3467). Hershey, PA: IGI Global. doi:10.4018/978-1-60566-054-7.ch253

Hanson, A. (2005). Overcoming barriers in the planning of a virtual library. In M. Khosrow-Pour (Ed.), *Encyclopedia of information science and technology* (pp. 2255–2259). Hershey, PA: IGI Global. doi:10.4018/978-1-59140-553-5.ch397

Haque, A. (2008). Information technology and surveillance: Implications for public administration in a new word order. In T. Loendorf & G. Garson (Eds.), *Patriotic information systems* (pp. 177–185). Hershey, PA: IGI Global. doi:10.4018/978-1-59904-594-8.ch008

Hauck, R. V., Thatcher, S. M., & Weisband, S. P. (2012). Temporal aspects of information technology use: Increasing shift work effectiveness. In J. Wang (Ed.), *Advancing the service sector with evolving technologies: Techniques and principles* (pp. 87–104). Hershey, PA: IGI Global. doi:10.4018/978-1-4666-0044-7.ch006

Hawk, S., & Witt, T. (2006). Telecommunications courses in information systems programs. *International Journal of Information and Communication Technology Education*, *2*(1), 79–92. doi:10.4018/jicte.2006010107

Helms, M. M., Moore, R., & Ahmadi, M. (2009). Information technology (IT) and the healthcare industry: A SWOT analysis. In J. Tan (Ed.), *Medical informatics: Concepts, methodologies, tools, and applications* (pp. 134–152). Hershey, PA: IGI Global. doi:10.4018/978-1-60566-050-9.ch012

Hendrickson, S. M., & Young, M. E. (2014). Electronic records management at a federally funded research and development center. In J. Krueger (Ed.), *Cases on electronic records and resource management implementation in diverse environments* (pp. 334–350). Hershey, PA: IGI Global. doi:10.4018/978-1-4666-4466-3.ch020

Henman, P. (2010). Social policy and information communication technologies. In J. Martin & L. Hawkins (Eds.), *Information communication technologies for human services education and delivery: Concepts and cases* (pp. 215–229). Hershey, PA: IGI Global. doi:10.4018/978-1-60566-735-5.ch014

Hismanoglu, M. (2011). Important issues in online education: E-pedagogy and marketing. In U. Demiray & S. Sever (Eds.), *Marketing online education programs: Frameworks for promotion and communication* (pp. 184–209). Hershey, PA: IGI Global. doi:10.4018/978-1-60960-074-7.ch012

Ho, K. K. (2008). The e-government development, IT strategies, and portals of the Hong Kong SAR government. In A. Anttiroiko (Ed.), *Electronic government: Concepts, methodologies, tools, and applications* (pp. 715–733). Hershey, PA: IGI Global. doi:10.4018/978-1-59904-947-2.ch060

Holden, S. H. (2003). The evolution of information technology management at the federal level: Implications for public administration. In G. Garson (Ed.), *Public information technology: Policy and management issues* (pp. 53–73). Hershey, PA: IGI Global. doi:10.4018/978-1-59140-060-8.ch003

Holden, S. H. (2007). The evolution of federal information technology management literature: Does IT finally matter? In G. Garson (Ed.), *Modern public information technology systems: Issues and challenges* (pp. 17–34). Hershey, PA: IGI Global. doi:10.4018/978-1-59904-051-6.ch002

Holland, J. W. (2009). Automation of American criminal justice. In M. Khosrow-Pour (Ed.), *Encyclopedia of information science and technology* (2nd ed.; pp. 300–302). Hershey, PA: IGI Global. doi:10.4018/978-1-60566-026-4.ch051

Holloway, K. (2013). Fair use, copyright, and academic integrity in an online academic environment. In *Digital rights management: Concepts, methodologies, tools, and applications* (pp. 917–928). Hershey, PA: IGI Global. doi:10.4018/978-1-4666-2136-7.ch044

Horiuchi, C. (2005). E-government databases. In L. Rivero, J. Doorn, & V. Ferraggine (Eds.), *Encyclopedia of database technologies and applications* (pp. 206–210). Hershey, PA: IGI Global. doi:10.4018/978-1-59140-560-3.ch035

Horiuchi, C. (2006). Creating IS quality in government settings. In E. Duggan & J. Reichgelt (Eds.), *Measuring information systems delivery quality* (pp. 311–327). Hershey, PA: IGI Global. doi:10.4018/978-1-59140-857-4.ch014

Hsiao, N., Chu, P., & Lee, C. (2012). Impact of e-governance on businesses: Model development and case study. In *Digital democracy: Concepts, methodologies, tools, and applications* (pp. 1407–1425). Hershey, PA: IGI Global. doi:10.4018/978-1-4666-1740-7.ch070

Huang, T., & Lee, C. (2010). Evaluating the impact of e-government on citizens: Cost-benefit analysis. In C. Reddick (Ed.), *Citizens and e-government: Evaluating policy and management* (pp. 37–52). Hershey, PA: IGI Global. doi:10.4018/978-1-61520-931-6.ch003

Hunter, M. G., Diochon, M., Pugsley, D., & Wright, B. (2002). Unique challenges for small business adoption of information technology: The case of the Nova Scotia ten. In S. Burgess (Ed.), *Managing information technology in small business: Challenges and solutions* (pp. 98–117). Hershey, PA: IGI Global. doi:10.4018/978-1-930708-35-8.ch006

Hurskainen, J. (2003). Integration of business systems and applications in merger and alliance: Case metso automation. In T. Reponen (Ed.), *Information technology enabled global customer service* (pp. 207–225). Hershey, PA: IGI Global. doi:10.4018/978-1-59140-048-6.ch012

Iazzolino, G., & Pietrantonio, R. (2011). The soveria.it project: A best practice of e-government in southern Italy. In D. Piaggesi, K. Sund, & W. Castelnovo (Eds.), *Global strategy and practice of e-governance: Examples from around the world* (pp. 34–56). Hershey, PA: IGI Global. doi:10.4018/978-1-60960-489-9.ch003

Imran, A., & Gregor, S. (2012). A process model for successful e-government adoption in the least developed countries: A case of Bangladesh. In F. Tan (Ed.), *International comparisons of information communication technologies: Advancing applications* (pp. 321–350). Hershey, PA: IGI Global. doi:10.4018/978-1-61350-480-2.ch014

Inoue, Y., & Bell, S. T. (2005). Electronic/digital government innovation, and publishing trends with IT. In M. Khosrow-Pour (Ed.), *Encyclopedia of information science and technology* (pp. 1018–1023). Hershey, PA: IGI Global. doi:10.4018/978-1-59140-553-5.ch180

Islam, M. M., & Ehsan, M. (2013). Understanding e-governance: A theoretical approach. In M. Islam & M. Ehsan (Eds.), *From government to e-governance: Public administration in the digital age* (pp. 38–49). Hershey, PA: IGI Global. doi:10.4018/978-1-4666-1909-8.ch003

Jaeger, B. (2009). E-government and e-democracy in the making. In M. Khosrow-Pour (Ed.), *Encyclopedia of information science and technology* (2nd ed.; pp. 1318–1322). Hershey, PA: IGI Global. doi:10.4018/978-1-60566-026-4.ch208

Jain, R. B. (2007). Revamping the administrative structure and processes in India for online diplomacy. In A. Anttiroiko & M. Malkia (Eds.), *Encyclopedia of digital government* (pp. 1418–1423). Hershey, PA: IGI Global. doi:10.4018/978-1-59140-789-8.ch217

Jain, R. B. (2008). Revamping the administrative structure and processes in India for online diplomacy. In A. Anttiroiko (Ed.), *Electronic government: Concepts, methodologies, tools, and applications* (pp. 3142–3149). Hershey, PA: IGI Global. doi:10.4018/978-1-59904-947-2.ch233

Jauhiainen, J. S., & Inkinen, T. (2009). E-governance and the information society in periphery. In C. Reddick (Ed.), *Handbook of research on strategies for local e-government adoption and implementation: Comparative studies* (pp. 497–514). Hershey, PA: IGI Global. doi:10.4018/978-1-60566-282-4.ch026

Jensen, M. J. (2009). Electronic democracy and citizen influence in government. In C. Reddick (Ed.), *Handbook of research on strategies for local e-government adoption and implementation: Comparative studies* (pp. 288–305). Hershey, PA: IGI Global. doi:10.4018/978-1-60566-282-4.ch015

Jiao, Y., Hurson, A. R., Potok, T. E., & Beckerman, B. G. (2009). Integrating mobile-based systems with healthcare databases. In J. Erickson (Ed.), *Database technologies: Concepts, methodologies, tools, and applications* (pp. 484–504). Hershey, PA: IGI Global. doi:10.4018/978-1-60566-058-5.ch031

Joia, L. A. (2002). A systematic model to integrate information technology into metabusinesses: A case study in the engineering realms. In F. Tan (Ed.), *Advanced topics in global information management* (Vol. 1, pp. 250–267). Hershey, PA: IGI Global. doi:10.4018/978-1-930708-43-3.ch016

Jones, T. H., & Song, I. (2000). Binary equivalents of ternary relationships in entity-relationship modeling: A logical decomposition approach. *Journal of Database Management, 11*(2), 12–19. doi:10.4018/jdm.2000040102

Juana-Espinosa, S. D. (2007). Empirical study of the municipalitites' motivations for adopting online presence. In L. Al-Hakim (Ed.), *Global e-government: Theory, applications and benchmarking* (pp. 261–279). Hershey, PA: IGI Global. doi:10.4018/978-1-59904-027-1.ch015

Jun, K., & Weare, C. (2012). Bridging from e-government practice to e-government research: Past trends and future directions. In K. Bwalya & S. Zulu (Eds.), *Handbook of research on e-government in emerging economies: Adoption, e-participation, and legal frameworks* (pp. 263–289). Hershey, PA: IGI Global. doi:10.4018/978-1-4666-0324-0.ch013

Junqueira, A., Diniz, E. H., & Fernandez, M. (2010). Electronic government implementation projects with multiple agencies: Analysis of the electronic invoice project under PMBOK framework. In J. Cordoba-Pachon & A. Ochoa-Arias (Eds.), *Systems thinking and e-participation: ICT in the governance of society* (pp. 135–153). Hershey, PA: IGI Global. doi:10.4018/978-1-60566-860-4.ch009

Juntunen, A. (2009). Joint service development with the local authorities. In C. Reddick (Ed.), *Handbook of research on strategies for local e-government adoption and implementation: Comparative studies* (pp. 902–920). Hershey, PA: IGI Global. doi:10.4018/978-1-60566-282-4.ch047

Kamel, S. (2001). *Using DSS for crisis management.* Hershey, PA: IGI Global. doi:10.4018/978-1-87828-961-2.ch020

Kamel, S. (2006). DSS for strategic decision making. In M. Khosrow-Pour (Ed.), *Cases on information technology and organizational politics & culture* (pp. 230–246). Hershey, PA: IGI Global. doi:10.4018/978-1-59904-411-8.ch015

Kamel, S. (2009). The software industry in Egypt as a potential contributor to economic growth. In M. Khosrow-Pour (Ed.), *Encyclopedia of information science and technology* (2nd ed.; pp. 3531–3537). Hershey, PA: IGI Global. doi:10.4018/978-1-60566-026-4.ch562

Kamel, S., & Hussein, M. (2008). Xceed: Pioneering the contact center industry in Egypt. *Journal of Cases on Information Technology, 10*(1), 67–91. doi:10.4018/jcit.2008010105

Kamel, S., & Wahba, K. (2003). The use of a hybrid model in web-based education: "The Global campus project. In A. Aggarwal (Ed.), *Web-based education: Learning from experience* (pp. 331–346). Hershey, PA: IGI Global. doi:10.4018/978-1-59140-102-5.ch020

Kardaras, D. K., & Papathanassiou, E. A. (2008). An exploratory study of the e-government services in Greece. In G. Garson & M. Khosrow-Pour (Eds.), *Handbook of research on public information technology* (pp. 162–174). Hershey, PA: IGI Global. doi:10.4018/978-1-59904-857-4.ch016

Kassahun, A. E., Molla, A., & Sarkar, P. (2012). Government process reengineering: What we know and what we need to know. In *Digital democracy: Concepts, methodologies, tools, and applications* (pp. 1730–1752). Hershey, PA: IGI Global. doi:10.4018/978-1-4666-1740-7.ch086

Khan, B. (2005). Technological issues. In B. Khan (Ed.), *Managing e-learning strategies: Design, delivery, implementation and evaluation* (pp. 154–180). Hershey, PA: IGI Global. doi:10.4018/978-1-59140-634-1.ch004

Khasawneh, A., Bsoul, M., Obeidat, I., & Al Azzam, I. (2012). Technology fears: A study of e-commerce loyalty perception by Jordanian customers. In J. Wang (Ed.), *Advancing the service sector with evolving technologies: Techniques and principles* (pp. 158–165). Hershey, PA: IGI Global. doi:10.4018/978-1-4666-0044-7.ch010

Khatibi, V., & Montazer, G. A. (2012). E-research methodology. In A. Juan, T. Daradoumis, M. Roca, S. Grasman, & J. Faulin (Eds.), *Collaborative and distributed e-research: Innovations in technologies, strategies and applications* (pp. 62–81). Hershey, PA: IGI Global. doi:10.4018/978-1-4666-0125-3.ch003

Kidd, T. (2011). The dragon in the school's backyard: A review of literature on the uses of technology in urban schools. In L. Tomei (Ed.), *Online courses and ICT in education: Emerging practices and applications* (pp. 242–257). Hershey, PA: IGI Global. doi:10.4018/978-1-60960-150-8.ch019

Kidd, T. T. (2010). My experience tells the story: Exploring technology adoption from a qualitative perspective - A pilot study. In H. Song & T. Kidd (Eds.), *Handbook of research on human performance and instructional technology* (pp. 247–262). Hershey, PA: IGI Global. doi:10.4018/978-1-60566-782-9.ch015

Kieley, B., Lane, G., Paquet, G., & Roy, J. (2002). e-Government in Canada: Services online or public service renewal? In Å. Grönlund (Ed.), Electronic government: Design, applications and management (pp. 340-355). Hershey, PA: IGI Global. doi:10.4018/978-1-930708-19-8.ch016

Kim, P. (2012). "Stay out of the way! My kid is video blogging through a phone!": A lesson learned from math tutoring social media for children in underserved communities. In *Wireless technologies: Concepts, methodologies, tools and applications* (pp. 1415–1428). Hershey, PA: IGI Global. doi:10.4018/978-1-61350-101-6.ch517

Kirlidog, M. (2010). Financial aspects of national ICT strategies. In S. Kamel (Ed.), *E-strategies for technological diffusion and adoption: National ICT approaches for socioeconomic development* (pp. 277–292). Hershey, PA: IGI Global. doi:10.4018/978-1-60566-388-3.ch016

Kisielnicki, J. (2006). Transfer of information and knowledge in the project management. In E. Coakes & S. Clarke (Eds.), *Encyclopedia of communities of practice in information and knowledge management* (pp. 544–551). Hershey, PA: IGI Global. doi:10.4018/978-1-59140-556-6.ch091

Kittner, M., & Van Slyke, C. (2006). Reorganizing information technology services in an academic environment. In M. Khosrow-Pour (Ed.), *Cases on the human side of information technology* (pp. 49–66). Hershey, PA: IGI Global. doi:10.4018/978-1-59904-405-7.ch004

Knoell, H. D. (2008). Semi virtual workplaces in German financial service enterprises. In P. Zemliansky & K. St.Amant (Eds.), *Handbook of research on virtual workplaces and the new nature of business practices* (pp. 570–581). Hershey, PA: IGI Global. doi:10.4018/978-1-59904-893-2.ch041

Koh, S. L., & Maguire, S. (2009). Competing in the age of information technology in a developing economy: Experiences of an Indian bank. In S. Koh & S. Maguire (Eds.), *Information and communication technologies management in turbulent business environments* (pp. 326–350). Hershey, PA: IGI Global. doi:10.4018/978-1-60566-424-8.ch018

Kollmann, T., & Häsel, M. (2009). Competence of information technology professionals in internet-based ventures. In I. Lee (Ed.), *Electronic business: Concepts, methodologies, tools, and applications* (pp. 1905–1919). Hershey, PA: IGI Global. doi:10.4018/978-1-60566-056-1.ch118

Kollmann, T., & Häsel, M. (2009). Competence of information technology professionals in internet-based ventures. In A. Cater-Steel (Ed.), *Information technology governance and service management: Frameworks and adaptations* (pp. 239–253). Hershey, PA: IGI Global. doi:10.4018/978-1-60566-008-0.ch013

Kollmann, T., & Häsel, M. (2010). Competence of information technology professionals in internet-based ventures. In *Electronic services: Concepts, methodologies, tools and applications* (pp. 1551–1565). Hershey, PA: IGI Global. doi:10.4018/978-1-61520-967-5.ch094

Kraemer, K., & King, J. L. (2006). Information technology and administrative reform: Will e-government be different? *International Journal of Electronic Government Research, 2*(1), 1–20. doi:10.4018/jegr.2006010101

Kraemer, K., & King, J. L. (2008). Information technology and administrative reform: Will e-government be different? In D. Norris (Ed.), *E-government research: Policy and management* (pp. 1–20). Hershey, PA: IGI Global. doi:10.4018/978-1-59904-913-7.ch001

Lampathaki, F., Tsiakaliaris, C., Stasis, A., & Charalabidis, Y. (2011). National interoperability frameworks: The way forward. In Y. Charalabidis (Ed.), *Interoperability in digital public services and administration: Bridging e-government and e-business* (pp. 1–24). Hershey, PA: IGI Global. doi:10.4018/978-1-61520-887-6.ch001

Lan, Z., & Scott, C. R. (1996). The relative importance of computer-mediated information versus conventional non-computer-mediated information in public managerial decision making. *Information Resources Management Journal*, *9*(1), 27–0. doi:10.4018/irmj.1996010103

Law, W. (2004). *Public sector data management in a developing economy*. Hershey, PA: IGI Global. doi:10.4018/978-1-59140-259-6.ch034

Law, W. K. (2005). Information resources development challenges in a cross-cultural environment. In M. Khosrow-Pour (Ed.), *Encyclopedia of information science and technology* (pp. 1476–1481). Hershey, PA: IGI Global. doi:10.4018/978-1-59140-553-5.ch259

Law, W. K. (2009). Cross-cultural challenges for information resources management. In M. Khosrow-Pour (Ed.), *Encyclopedia of information science and technology* (2nd ed.; pp. 840–846). Hershey, PA: IGI Global. doi:10.4018/978-1-60566-026-4.ch136

Law, W. K. (2011). Cross-cultural challenges for information resources management. In *Global business: Concepts, methodologies, tools and applications* (pp. 1924–1932). Hershey, PA: IGI Global. doi:10.4018/978-1-60960-587-2.ch704

Malkia, M., & Savolainen, R. (2004). eTransformation in government, politics and society: Conceptual framework and introduction. In M. Malkia, A. Anttiroiko, & R. Savolainen (Eds.), eTransformation in governance: New directions in government and politics (pp. 1-21). Hershey, PA: IGI Global. doi:10.4018/978-1-59140-130-8.ch001

Mandujano, S. (2011). Network manageability security. In D. Kar & M. Syed (Eds.), *Network security, administration and management: Advancing technology and practice* (pp. 158–181). Hershey, PA: IGI Global. doi:10.4018/978-1-60960-777-7.ch009

Marich, M. J., Schooley, B. L., & Horan, T. A. (2012). A normative enterprise architecture for guiding end-to-end emergency response decision support. In M. Jennex (Ed.), *Managing crises and disasters with emerging technologies: Advancements* (pp. 71–87). Hershey, PA: IGI Global. doi:10.4018/978-1-4666-0167-3.ch006

Markov, R., & Okujava, S. (2008). Costs, benefits, and risks of e-government portals. In G. Putnik & M. Cruz-Cunha (Eds.), *Encyclopedia of networked and virtual organizations* (pp. 354–363). Hershey, PA: IGI Global. doi:10.4018/978-1-59904-885-7.ch047

Martin, N., & Rice, J. (2013). Evaluating and designing electronic government for the future: Observations and insights from Australia. In V. Weerakkody (Ed.), *E-government services design, adoption, and evaluation* (pp. 238–258). Hershey, PA: IGI Global. doi:10.4018/978-1-4666-2458-0.ch014

i. Martinez, A. C. (2008). Accessing administration's information via internet in Spain. In F. Tan (Ed.), *Global information technologies: Concepts, methodologies, tools, and applications* (pp. 2558–2573). Hershey, PA: IGI Global. doi:10.4018/978-1-59904-939-7.ch186

Mbarika, V. W., Meso, P. N., & Musa, P. F. (2006). A disconnect in stakeholders' perceptions from emerging realities of teledensity growth in Africa's least developed countries. In M. Hunter & F. Tan (Eds.), *Advanced topics in global information management* (Vol. 5, pp. 263–282). Hershey, PA: IGI Global. doi:10.4018/978-1-59140-923-6.ch012

Mbarika, V. W., Meso, P. N., & Musa, P. F. (2008). A disconnect in stakeholders' perceptions from emerging realities of teledensity growth in Africa's least developed countries. In F. Tan (Ed.), *Global information technologies: Concepts, methodologies, tools, and applications* (pp. 2948–2962). Hershey, PA: IGI Global. doi:10.4018/978-1-59904-939-7.ch209

Means, T., Olson, E., & Spooner, J. (2013). Discovering ways that don't work on the road to success: Strengths and weaknesses revealed by an active learning studio classroom project. In A. Benson, J. Moore, & S. Williams van Rooij (Eds.), *Cases on educational technology planning, design, and implementation: A project management perspective* (pp. 94–113). Hershey, PA: IGI Global. doi:10.4018/978-1-4666-4237-9.ch006

Melitski, J., Holzer, M., Kim, S., Kim, C., & Rho, S. (2008). Digital government worldwide: An e-government assessment of municipal web sites. In G. Garson & M. Khosrow-Pour (Eds.), *Handbook of research on public information technology* (pp. 790–804). Hershey, PA: IGI Global. doi:10.4018/978-1-59904-857-4.ch069

Memmola, M., Palumbo, G., & Rossini, M. (2009). Web & RFID technology: New frontiers in costing and process management for rehabilitation medicine. In L. Al-Hakim & M. Memmola (Eds.), *Business web strategy: Design, alignment, and application* (pp. 145–169). Hershey, PA: IGI Global. doi:10.4018/978-1-60566-024-0.ch008

Meng, Z., Fahong, Z., & Lei, L. (2008). Information technology and environment. In Y. Kurihara, S. Takaya, H. Harui, & H. Kamae (Eds.), *Information technology and economic development* (pp. 201–212). Hershey, PA: IGI Global. doi:10.4018/978-1-59904-579-5.ch014

Mentzingen de Moraes, A. J., Ferneda, E., Costa, I., & Spinola, M. D. (2011). Practical approach for implementation of governance process in IT: Information technology areas. In N. Shi & G. Silvius (Eds.), *Enterprise IT governance, business value and performance measurement* (pp. 19–40). Hershey, PA: IGI Global. doi:10.4018/978-1-60566-346-3.ch002

Merwin, G. A. Jr, McDonald, J. S., & Odera, L. C. (2008). Economic development: Government's cutting edge in IT. In M. Raisinghani (Ed.), *Handbook of research on global information technology management in the digital economy* (pp. 1–37). Hershey, PA: IGI Global. doi:10.4018/978-1-59904-875-8.ch001

Meso, P., & Duncan, N. (2002). Can national information infrastructures enhance social development in the least developed countries? An empirical investigation. In M. Dadashzadeh (Ed.), *Information technology management in developing countries* (pp. 23–51). Hershey, PA: IGI Global. doi:10.4018/978-1-931777-03-2.ch002

Meso, P. N., & Duncan, N. B. (2002). Can national information infrastructures enhance social development in the least developed countries? In F. Tan (Ed.), *Advanced topics in global information management* (Vol. 1, pp. 207–226). Hershey, PA: IGI Global. doi:10.4018/978-1-930708-43-3.ch014

Middleton, M. (2008). Evaluation of e-government web sites. In G. Garson & M. Khosrow-Pour (Eds.), *Handbook of research on public information technology* (pp. 699–710). Hershey, PA: IGI Global. doi:10.4018/978-1-59904-857-4.ch063

Mingers, J. (2010). Pluralism, realism, and truth: The keys to knowledge in information systems research. In D. Paradice (Ed.), *Emerging systems approaches in information technologies: Concepts, theories, and applications* (pp. 86–98). Hershey, PA: IGI Global. doi:10.4018/978-1-60566-976-2.ch006

Mital, K. M. (2012). ICT, unique identity and inclusive growth: An Indian perspective. In A. Manoharan & M. Holzer (Eds.), *E-governance and civic engagement: Factors and determinants of e-democracy* (pp. 584–612). Hershey, PA: IGI Global. doi:10.4018/978-1-61350-083-5.ch029

Mizell, A. P. (2008). Helping close the digital divide for financially disadvantaged seniors. In F. Tan (Ed.), *Global information technologies: Concepts, methodologies, tools, and applications* (pp. 2396–2402). Hershey, PA: IGI Global. doi:10.4018/978-1-59904-939-7.ch173

Molinari, F., Wills, C., Koumpis, A., & Moumtzi, V. (2011). A citizen-centric platform to support networking in the area of e-democracy. In H. Rahman (Ed.), *Cases on adoption, diffusion and evaluation of global e-governance systems: Impact at the grass roots* (pp. 282–302). Hershey, PA: IGI Global. doi:10.4018/978-1-61692-814-8.ch014

Molinari, F., Wills, C., Koumpis, A., & Moumtzi, V. (2013). A citizen-centric platform to support networking in the area of e-democracy. In H. Rahman (Ed.), *Cases on progressions and challenges in ICT utilization for citizen-centric governance* (pp. 265–297). Hershey, PA: IGI Global. doi:10.4018/978-1-4666-2071-1.ch013

Monteverde, F. (2010). The process of e-government public policy inclusion in the governmental agenda: A framework for assessment and case study. In J. Cordoba-Pachon & A. Ochoa-Arias (Eds.), *Systems thinking and e-participation: ICT in the governance of society* (pp. 233–245). Hershey, PA: IGI Global. doi:10.4018/978-1-60566-860-4.ch015

Moodley, S. (2008). Deconstructing the South African government's ICT for development discourse. In A. Anttiroiko (Ed.), *Electronic government: Concepts, methodologies, tools, and applications* (pp. 622–631). Hershey, PA: IGI Global. doi:10.4018/978-1-59904-947-2.ch053

Moodley, S. (2008). Deconstructing the South African government's ICT for development discourse. In C. Van Slyke (Ed.), *Information communication technologies: Concepts, methodologies, tools, and applications* (pp. 816–825). Hershey, PA: IGI Global. doi:10.4018/978-1-59904-949-6.ch052

Mora, M., Cervantes-Perez, F., Gelman-Muravchik, O., Forgionne, G. A., & Mejia-Olvera, M. (2003). DMSS implementation research: A conceptual analysis of the contributions and limitations of the factor-based and stage-based streams. In G. Forgionne, J. Gupta, & M. Mora (Eds.), *Decision-making support systems: Achievements and challenges for the new decade* (pp. 331–356). Hershey, PA: IGI Global. doi:10.4018/978-1-59140-045-5.ch020

Mörtberg, C., & Elovaara, P. (2010). Attaching people and technology: Between e and government. In S. Booth, S. Goodman, & G. Kirkup (Eds.), *Gender issues in learning and working with information technology: Social constructs and cultural contexts* (pp. 83–98). Hershey, PA: IGI Global. doi:10.4018/978-1-61520-813-5.ch005

Murphy, J., Harper, E., Devine, E. C., Burke, L. J., & Hook, M. L. (2011). Case study: Lessons learned when embedding evidence-based knowledge in a nurse care planning and documentation system. In A. Cashin & R. Cook (Eds.), *Evidence-based practice in nursing informatics: Concepts and applications* (pp. 174–190). Hershey, PA: IGI Global. doi:10.4018/978-1-60960-034-1.ch014

Mutula, S. M. (2013). E-government's role in poverty alleviation: Case study of South Africa. In H. Rahman (Ed.), *Cases on progressions and challenges in ICT utilization for citizen-centric governance* (pp. 44–68). Hershey, PA: IGI Global. doi:10.4018/978-1-4666-2071-1.ch003

Nath, R., & Angeles, R. (2005). Relationships between supply characteristics and buyer-supplier coupling in e-procurement: An empirical analysis. *International Journal of E-Business Research, 1*(2), 40–55. doi:10.4018/jebr.2005040103

Nissen, M. E. (2006). Application cases in government. In M. Nissen (Ed.), *Harnessing knowledge dynamics: Principled organizational knowing & learning* (pp. 152–181). Hershey, PA: IGI Global. doi:10.4018/978-1-59140-773-7.ch008

Norris, D. F. (2003). Leading-edge information technologies and American local governments. In G. Garson (Ed.), *Public information technology: Policy and management issues* (pp. 139–169). Hershey, PA: IGI Global. doi:10.4018/978-1-59140-060-8.ch007

Norris, D. F. (2008). Information technology among U.S. local governments. In G. Garson & M. Khosrow-Pour (Eds.), *Handbook of research on public information technology* (pp. 132–144). Hershey, PA: IGI Global. doi:10.4018/978-1-59904-857-4.ch013

Northrop, A. (1999). The challenge of teaching information technology in public administration graduate programs. In G. Garson (Ed.), *Information technology and computer applications in public administration: Issues and trends* (pp. 1–22). Hershey, PA: IGI Global. doi:10.4018/978-1-87828-952-0.ch001

Northrop, A. (2003). Information technology and public administration: The view from the profession. In G. Garson (Ed.), *Public information technology: Policy and management issues* (pp. 1–19). Hershey, PA: IGI Global. doi:10.4018/978-1-59140-060-8.ch001

Northrop, A. (2007). Lip service? How PA journals and textbooks view information technology. In G. Garson (Ed.), *Modern public information technology systems: Issues and challenges* (pp. 1–16). Hershey, PA: IGI Global. doi:10.4018/978-1-59904-051-6.ch001

Null, E. (2013). Legal and political barriers to municipal networks in the United States. In A. Abdelaal (Ed.), *Social and economic effects of community wireless networks and infrastructures* (pp. 27–56). Hershey, PA: IGI Global. doi:10.4018/978-1-4666-2997-4.ch003

Okunoye, A., Frolick, M., & Crable, E. (2006). ERP implementation in higher education: An account of pre-implementation and implementation phases. *Journal of Cases on Information Technology*, *8*(2), 110–132. doi:10.4018/jcit.2006040106

Olasina, G. (2012). A review of egovernment services in Nigeria. In A. Tella & A. Issa (Eds.), *Library and information science in developing countries: Contemporary issues* (pp. 205–221). Hershey, PA: IGI Global. doi:10.4018/978-1-61350-335-5.ch015

Orgeron, C. P. (2008). A model for reengineering IT job classes in state government. In G. Garson & M. Khosrow-Pour (Eds.), *Handbook of research on public information technology* (pp. 735–746). Hershey, PA: IGI Global. doi:10.4018/978-1-59904-857-4.ch066

Owsinski, J. W., & Pielak, A. M. (2011). Local authority websites in rural areas: Measuring quality and functionality, and assessing the role. In Z. Andreopoulou, B. Manos, N. Polman, & D. Viaggi (Eds.), *Agricultural and environmental informatics, governance and management: Emerging research applications* (pp. 39–60). Hershey, PA: IGI Global. doi:10.4018/978-1-60960-621-3.ch003

Owsiński, J. W., Pielak, A. M., Sęp, K., & Stańczak, J. (2014). Local web-based networks in rural municipalities: Extension, density, and meaning. In Z. Andreopoulou, V. Samathrakis, S. Louca, & M. Vlachopoulou (Eds.), *E-innovation for sustainable development of rural resources during global economic crisis* (pp. 126–151). Hershey, PA: IGI Global. doi:10.4018/978-1-4666-4550-9.ch011

Pagani, M., & Pasinetti, C. (2008). Technical and functional quality in the development of t-government services. In A. Anttiroiko (Ed.), *Electronic government: Concepts, methodologies, tools, and applications* (pp. 2943–2965). Hershey, PA: IGI Global. doi:10.4018/978-1-59904-947-2.ch220

Pani, A. K., & Agrahari, A. (2005). On e-markets in emerging economy: An Indian experience. In M. Khosrow-Pour (Ed.), *Advanced topics in electronic commerce* (Vol. 1, pp. 287–299). Hershey, PA: IGI Global. doi:10.4018/978-1-59140-819-2.ch015

Papadopoulos, T., Angelopoulos, S., & Kitsios, F. (2011). A strategic approach to e-health interoperability using e-government frameworks. In A. Lazakidou, K. Siassiakos, & K. Ioannou (Eds.), *Wireless technologies for ambient assisted living and healthcare: Systems and applications* (pp. 213–229). Hershey, PA: IGI Global. doi:10.4018/978-1-61520-805-0.ch012

Papadopoulos, T., Angelopoulos, S., & Kitsios, F. (2013). A strategic approach to e-health interoperability using e-government frameworks. In *User-driven healthcare: Concepts, methodologies, tools, and applications* (pp. 791–807). Hershey, PA: IGI Global. doi:10.4018/978-1-4666-2770-3.ch039

Papaleo, G., Chiarella, D., Aiello, M., & Caviglione, L. (2012). Analysis, development and deployment of statistical anomaly detection techniques for real e-mail traffic. In T. Chou (Ed.), *Information assurance and security technologies for risk assessment and threat management: Advances* (pp. 47–71). Hershey, PA: IGI Global. doi:10.4018/978-1-61350-507-6.ch003

Papp, R. (2003). Information technology & FDA compliance in the pharmaceutical industry. In M. Khosrow-Pour (Ed.), *Annals of cases on information technology* (Vol. 5, pp. 262–273). Hershey, PA: IGI Global. doi:10.4018/978-1-59140-061-5.ch017

Parsons, T. W. (2007). Developing a knowledge management portal. In A. Tatnall (Ed.), *Encyclopedia of portal technologies and applications* (pp. 223–227). Hershey, PA: IGI Global. doi:10.4018/978-1-59140-989-2.ch039

Passaris, C. E. (2007). Immigration and digital government. In A. Anttiroiko & M. Malkia (Eds.), *Encyclopedia of digital government* (pp. 988–994). Hershey, PA: IGI Global. doi:10.4018/978-1-59140-789-8.ch148

Pavlichev, A. (2004). The e-government challenge for public administration. In A. Pavlichev & G. Garson (Eds.), *Digital government: Principles and best practices* (pp. 276–290). Hershey, PA: IGI Global. doi:10.4018/978-1-59140-122-3.ch018

Penrod, J. I., & Harbor, A. F. (2000). Designing and implementing a learning organization-oriented information technology planning and management process. In L. Petrides (Ed.), *Case studies on information technology in higher education: Implications for policy and practice* (pp. 7–19). Hershey, PA: IGI Global. doi:10.4018/978-1-878289-74-2.ch001

Planas-Silva, M. D., & Joseph, R. C. (2011). Perspectives on the adoption of electronic resources for use in clinical trials. In M. Guah (Ed.), *Healthcare delivery reform and new technologies: Organizational initiatives* (pp. 19–28). Hershey, PA: IGI Global. doi:10.4018/978-1-60960-183-6.ch002

Pomazalová, N., & Rejman, S. (2013). The rationale behind implementation of new electronic tools for electronic public procurement. In N. Pomazalová (Ed.), *Public sector transformation processes and internet public procurement: Decision support systems* (pp. 85–117). Hershey, PA: IGI Global. doi:10.4018/978-1-4666-2665-2.ch006

Postorino, M. N. (2012). City competitiveness and airport: Information science perspective. In M. Bulu (Ed.), *City competitiveness and improving urban subsystems: Technologies and applications* (pp. 61–83). Hershey, PA: IGI Global. doi:10.4018/978-1-61350-174-0.ch004

Poupa, C. (2002). Electronic government in Switzerland: Priorities for 2001-2005 - Electronic voting and federal portal. In Å. Grönlund (Ed.), *Electronic government: Design, applications and management* (pp. 356–369). Hershey, PA: IGI Global. doi:10.4018/978-1-930708-19-8.ch017

Powell, S. R. (2010). Interdisciplinarity in telecommunications and networking. In *Networking and telecommunications: Concepts, methodologies, tools and applications* (pp. 33–40). Hershey, PA: IGI Global. doi:10.4018/978-1-60566-986-1.ch004

Priya, P. S., & Mathiyalagan, N. (2011). A study of the implementation status of two e-governance projects in land revenue administration in India. In M. Shareef, V. Kumar, U. Kumar, & Y. Dwivedi (Eds.), *Stakeholder adoption of e-government services: Driving and resisting factors* (pp. 214–230). Hershey, PA: IGI Global. doi:10.4018/978-1-60960-601-5.ch011

Prysby, C., & Prysby, N. (2000). Electronic mail, employee privacy and the workplace. In L. Janczewski (Ed.), *Internet and intranet security management: Risks and solutions* (pp. 251–270). Hershey, PA: IGI Global. doi:10.4018/978-1-878289-71-1.ch009

Prysby, C. L., & Prysby, N. D. (2003). Electronic mail in the public workplace: Issues of privacy and public disclosure. In G. Garson (Ed.), *Public information technology: Policy and management issues* (pp. 271–298). Hershey, PA: IGI Global. doi:10.4018/978-1-59140-060-8.ch012

Prysby, C. L., & Prysby, N. D. (2007). You have mail, but who is reading it? Issues of e-mail in the public workplace. In G. Garson (Ed.), *Modern public information technology systems: Issues and challenges* (pp. 312–336). Hershey, PA: IGI Global. doi:10.4018/978-1-59904-051-6.ch016

Radl, A., & Chen, Y. (2005). Computer security in electronic government: A state-local education information system. *International Journal of Electronic Government Research, 1*(1), 79–99. doi:10.4018/jegr.2005010105

Rahman, H. (2008). Information dynamics in developing countries. In C. Van Slyke (Ed.), *Information communication technologies: Concepts, methodologies, tools, and applications* (pp. 104–114). Hershey, PA: IGI Global. doi:10.4018/978-1-59904-949-6.ch008

Ramanathan, J. (2009). Adaptive IT architecture as a catalyst for network capability in government. In P. Saha (Ed.), *Advances in government enterprise architecture* (pp. 149–172). Hershey, PA: IGI Global. doi:10.4018/978-1-60566-068-4.ch007

Ramos, I., & Berry, D. M. (2006). Social construction of information technology supporting work. In M. Khosrow-Pour (Ed.), *Cases on information technology: Lessons learned* (Vol. 7, pp. 36–52). Hershey, PA: IGI Global. doi:10.4018/978-1-59140-673-0.ch003

Ray, D., Gulla, U., Gupta, M. P., & Dash, S. S. (2009). Interoperability and constituents of interoperable systems in public sector. In V. Weerakkody, M. Janssen, & Y. Dwivedi (Eds.), *Handbook of research on ICT-enabled transformational government: A global perspective* (pp. 175–195). Hershey, PA: IGI Global. doi:10.4018/978-1-60566-390-6.ch010

Reddick, C. G. (2007). E-government and creating a citizen-centric government: A study of federal government CIOs. In G. Garson (Ed.), *Modern public information technology systems: Issues and challenges* (pp. 143–165). Hershey, PA: IGI Global. doi:10.4018/978-1-59904-051-6.ch008

Reddick, C. G. (2010). Citizen-centric e-government. In C. Reddick (Ed.), *Homeland security preparedness and information systems: Strategies for managing public policy* (pp. 45–75). Hershey, PA: IGI Global. doi:10.4018/978-1-60566-834-5.ch002

Reddick, C. G. (2010). E-government and creating a citizen-centric government: A study of federal government CIOs. In C. Reddick (Ed.), *Homeland security preparedness and information systems: Strategies for managing public policy* (pp. 230–250). Hershey, PA: IGI Global. doi:10.4018/978-1-60566-834-5.ch012

Reddick, C. G. (2010). Perceived effectiveness of e-government and its usage in city governments: Survey evidence from information technology directors. In C. Reddick (Ed.), *Homeland security preparedness and information systems: Strategies for managing public policy* (pp. 213–229). Hershey, PA: IGI Global. doi:10.4018/978-1-60566-834-5.ch011

Reddick, C. G. (2012). Customer relationship management adoption in local governments in the United States. In S. Chhabra & M. Kumar (Eds.), *Strategic enterprise resource planning models for e-government: Applications and methodologies* (pp. 111–124). Hershey, PA: IGI Global. doi:10.4018/978-1-60960-863-7.ch008

Reeder, F. S., & Pandy, S. M. (2008). Identifying effective funding models for e-government. In A. Anttiroiko (Ed.), *Electronic government: Concepts, methodologies, tools, and applications* (pp. 1108–1138). Hershey, PA: IGI Global. doi:10.4018/978-1-59904-947-2.ch083

Riesco, D., Acosta, E., & Montejano, G. (2003). An extension to a UML activity graph from workflow. In L. Favre (Ed.), *UML and the unified process* (pp. 294–314). Hershey, PA: IGI Global. doi:10.4018/978-1-93177-744-5.ch015

Ritzhaupt, A. D., & Gill, T. G. (2008). A hybrid and novel approach to teaching computer programming in MIS curriculum. In S. Negash, M. Whitman, A. Woszczynski, K. Hoganson, & H. Mattord (Eds.), *Handbook of distance learning for real-time and asynchronous information technology education* (pp. 259–281). Hershey, PA: IGI Global. doi:10.4018/978-1-59904-964-9.ch014

Roche, E. M. (1993). International computing and the international regime. *Journal of Global Information Management, 1*(2), 33–44. doi:10.4018/jgim.1993040103

Rocheleau, B. (2007). Politics, accountability, and information management. In G. Garson (Ed.), *Modern public information technology systems: Issues and challenges* (pp. 35–71). Hershey, PA: IGI Global. doi:10.4018/978-1-59904-051-6.ch003

Rodrigues Filho, J. (2010). E-government in Brazil: Reinforcing dominant institutions or reducing citizenship? In C. Reddick (Ed.), *Politics, democracy and e-government: Participation and service delivery* (pp. 347–362). Hershey, PA: IGI Global. doi:10.4018/978-1-61520-933-0.ch021

Rodriguez, S. R., & Thorp, D. A. (2013). eLearning for industry: A case study of the project management process. In A. Benson, J. Moore, & S. Williams van Rooij (Eds.), Cases on educational technology planning, design, and implementation: A project management perspective (pp. 319-342). Hershey, PA: IGI Global. doi:10.4018/978-1-4666-4237-9.ch017

Roman, A. V. (2013). Delineating three dimensions of e-government success: Security, functionality, and transformation. In J. Gil-Garcia (Ed.), *E-government success factors and measures: Theories, concepts, and methodologies* (pp. 171–192). Hershey, PA: IGI Global. doi:10.4018/978-1-4666-4058-0.ch010

Ross, S. C., Tyran, C. K., & Auer, D. J. (2008). Up in smoke: Rebuilding after an IT disaster. In H. Nemati (Ed.), *Information security and ethics: Concepts, methodologies, tools, and applications* (pp. 3659–3675). Hershey, PA: IGI Global. doi:10.4018/978-1-59904-937-3.ch248

Ross, S. C., Tyran, C. K., Auer, D. J., Junell, J. M., & Williams, T. G. (2005). Up in smoke: Rebuilding after an IT disaster. *Journal of Cases on Information Technology*, *7*(2), 31–49. doi:10.4018/jcit.2005040103

Roy, J. (2008). Security, sovereignty, and continental interoperability: Canada's elusive balance. In T. Loendorf & G. Garson (Eds.), *Patriotic information systems* (pp. 153–176). Hershey, PA: IGI Global. doi:10.4018/978-1-59904-594-8.ch007

Rubeck, R. F., & Miller, G. A. (2009). vGOV: Remote video access to government services. In A. Scupola (Ed.), Cases on managing e-services (pp. 253-268). Hershey, PA: IGI Global. doi:10.4018/978-1-60566-064-6.ch017

Saekow, A., & Boonmee, C. (2011). The challenges of implementing e-government interoperability in Thailand: Case of official electronic correspondence letters exchange across government departments. In Y. Charalabidis (Ed.), *Interoperability in digital public services and administration: Bridging e-government and e-business* (pp. 40–61). Hershey, PA: IGI Global. doi:10.4018/978-1-61520-887-6.ch003

Saekow, A., & Boonmee, C. (2012). The challenges of implementing e-government interoperability in Thailand: Case of official electronic correspondence letters exchange across government departments. In *Digital democracy: Concepts, methodologies, tools, and applications* (pp. 1883–1905). Hershey, PA: IGI Global. doi:10.4018/978-1-4666-1740-7.ch094

Sagsan, M., & Medeni, T. (2012). Understanding "knowledge management (KM) paradigms" from social media perspective: An empirical study on discussion group for KM at professional networking site. In M. Cruz-Cunha, P. Gonçalves, N. Lopes, E. Miranda, & G. Putnik (Eds.), *Handbook of research on business social networking: Organizational, managerial, and technological dimensions* (pp. 738–755). Hershey, PA: IGI Global. doi:10.4018/978-1-61350-168-9.ch039

Sahi, G., & Madan, S. (2013). Information security threats in ERP enabled e-governance: Challenges and solutions. In *Enterprise resource planning: Concepts, methodologies, tools, and applications* (pp. 825–837). Hershey, PA: IGI Global. doi:10.4018/978-1-4666-4153-2.ch048

Sanford, C., & Bhattacherjee, A. (2008). IT implementation in a developing country municipality: A sociocognitive analysis. *International Journal of Technology and Human Interaction*, *4*(3), 68–93. doi:10.4018/jthi.2008070104

Schelin, S. H. (2003). E-government: An overview. In G. Garson (Ed.), *Public information technology: Policy and management issues* (pp. 120–138). Hershey, PA: IGI Global. doi:10.4018/978-1-59140-060-8.ch006

Schelin, S. H. (2004). Training for digital government. In A. Pavlichev & G. Garson (Eds.), *Digital government: Principles and best practices* (pp. 263–275). Hershey, PA: IGI Global. doi:10.4018/978-1-59140-122-3.ch017

Schelin, S. H. (2007). E-government: An overview. In G. Garson (Ed.), *Modern public information technology systems: Issues and challenges* (pp. 110–126). Hershey, PA: IGI Global. doi:10.4018/978-1-59904-051-6.ch006

Schelin, S. H., & Garson, G. (2004). Theoretical justification of critical success factors. In G. Garson & S. Schelin (Eds.), *IT solutions series: Humanizing information technology: Advice from experts* (pp. 4–15). Hershey, PA: IGI Global. doi:10.4018/978-1-59140-245-9.ch002

Scime, A. (2002). Information systems and computer science model curricula: A comparative look. In M. Dadashzadeh, A. Saber, & S. Saber (Eds.), *Information technology education in the new millennium* (pp. 146–158). Hershey, PA: IGI Global. doi:10.4018/978-1-931777-05-6.ch018

Scime, A. (2009). Computing curriculum analysis and development. In M. Khosrow-Pour (Ed.), *Encyclopedia of information science and technology* (2nd ed.; pp. 667–671). Hershey, PA: IGI Global. doi:10.4018/978-1-60566-026-4.ch108

Scime, A., & Wania, C. (2008). Computing curricula: A comparison of models. In C. Van Slyke (Ed.), *Information communication technologies: Concepts, methodologies, tools, and applications* (pp. 1270–1283). Hershey, PA: IGI Global. doi:10.4018/978-1-59904-949-6.ch088

Seidman, S. B. (2009). An international perspective on professional software engineering credentials. In H. Ellis, S. Demurjian, & J. Naveda (Eds.), *Software engineering: Effective teaching and learning approaches and practices* (pp. 351–361). Hershey, PA: IGI Global. doi:10.4018/978-1-60566-102-5.ch018

Seifert, J. W. (2007). E-government act of 2002 in the United States. In A. Anttiroiko & M. Malkia (Eds.), *Encyclopedia of digital government* (pp. 476–481). Hershey, PA: IGI Global. doi:10.4018/978-1-59140-789-8.ch072

Seifert, J. W., & Relyea, H. C. (2008). E-government act of 2002 in the United States. In A. Anttiroiko (Ed.), *Electronic government: Concepts, methodologies, tools, and applications* (pp. 154–161). Hershey, PA: IGI Global. doi:10.4018/978-1-59904-947-2.ch013

Seufert, S. (2002). E-learning business models: Framework and best practice examples. In M. Raisinghani (Ed.), *Cases on worldwide e-commerce: Theory in action* (pp. 70–94). Hershey, PA: IGI Global. doi:10.4018/978-1-930708-27-3.ch004

Shareef, M. A., & Archer, N. (2012). E-government service development. In M. Shareef, N. Archer, & S. Dutta (Eds.), *E-government service maturity and development: Cultural, organizational and technological perspectives* (pp. 1–14). Hershey, PA: IGI Global. doi:10.4018/978-1-60960-848-4.ch001

Shareef, M. A., & Archer, N. (2012). E-government initiatives: Review studies on different countries. In M. Shareef, N. Archer, & S. Dutta (Eds.), *E-government service maturity and development: Cultural, organizational and technological perspectives* (pp. 40–76). Hershey, PA: IGI Global. doi:10.4018/978-1-60960-848-4.ch003

Shareef, M. A., Kumar, U., & Kumar, V. (2011). E-government development: Performance evaluation parameters. In M. Shareef, V. Kumar, U. Kumar, & Y. Dwivedi (Eds.), *Stakeholder adoption of e-government services: Driving and resisting factors* (pp. 197–213). Hershey, PA: IGI Global. doi:10.4018/978-1-60960-601-5.ch010

Shareef, M. A., Kumar, U., Kumar, V., & Niktash, M. (2012). Electronic-government vision: Case studies for objectives, strategies, and initiatives. In M. Shareef, N. Archer, & S. Dutta (Eds.), *E-government service maturity and development: Cultural, organizational and technological perspectives* (pp. 15–39). Hershey, PA: IGI Global. doi:10.4018/978-1-60960-848-4.ch002

Shukla, P., Kumar, A., & Anu Kumar, P. B. (2013). Impact of national culture on business continuity management system implementation. *International Journal of Risk and Contingency Management, 2*(3), 23–36. doi:10.4018/ijrcm.2013070102

Shulman, S. W. (2007). The federal docket management system and the prospect for digital democracy in U S rulemaking. In G. Garson (Ed.), *Modern public information technology systems: Issues and challenges* (pp. 166–184). Hershey, PA: IGI Global. doi:10.4018/978-1-59904-051-6.ch009

Simonovic, S. (2007). Problems of offline government in e-Serbia. In A. Anttiroiko & M. Malkia (Eds.), *Encyclopedia of digital government* (pp. 1342–1351). Hershey, PA: IGI Global. doi:10.4018/978-1-59140-789-8.ch205

Simonovic, S. (2008). Problems of offline government in e-Serbia. In A. Anttiroiko (Ed.), *Electronic government: Concepts, methodologies, tools, and applications* (pp. 2929–2942). Hershey, PA: IGI Global. doi:10.4018/978-1-59904-947-2.ch219

Singh, A. M. (2005). Information systems and technology in South Africa. In M. Khosrow-Pour (Ed.), *Encyclopedia of information science and technology* (pp. 1497–1502). Hershey, PA: IGI Global. doi:10.4018/978-1-59140-553-5.ch263

Singh, S., & Naidoo, G. (2005). Towards an e-government solution: A South African perspective. In W. Huang, K. Siau, & K. Wei (Eds.), *Electronic government strategies and implementation* (pp. 325–353). Hershey, PA: IGI Global. doi:10.4018/978-1-59140-348-7.ch014

Snoke, R., & Underwood, A. (2002). Generic attributes of IS graduates: An analysis of Australian views. In F. Tan (Ed.), *Advanced topics in global information management* (Vol. 1, pp. 370–384). Hershey, PA: IGI Global. doi:10.4018/978-1-930708-43-3.ch023

Sommer, L. (2006). Revealing unseen organizations in higher education: A study framework and application example. In A. Metcalfe (Ed.), *Knowledge management and higher education: A critical analysis* (pp. 115–146). Hershey, PA: IGI Global. doi:10.4018/978-1-59140-509-2.ch007

Song, H., Kidd, T., & Owens, E. (2011). Examining technological disparities and instructional practices in English language arts classroom: Implications for school leadership and teacher training. In L. Tomei (Ed.), *Online courses and ICT in education: Emerging practices and applications* (pp. 258–274). Hershey, PA: IGI Global. doi:10.4018/978-1-60960-150-8.ch020

Speaker, P. J., & Kleist, V. F. (2003). Using information technology to meet electronic commerce and MIS education demands. In A. Aggarwal (Ed.), *Web-based education: Learning from experience* (pp. 280–291). Hershey, PA: IGI Global. doi:10.4018/978-1-59140-102-5.ch017

Spitler, V. K. (2007). Learning to use IT in the workplace: Mechanisms and masters. In M. Mahmood (Ed.), *Contemporary issues in end user computing* (pp. 292–323). Hershey, PA: IGI Global. doi:10.4018/978-1-59140-926-7.ch013

Stellefson, M. (2011). Considerations for marketing distance education courses in health education: Five important questions to examine before development. In U. Demiray & S. Sever (Eds.), *Marketing online education programs: Frameworks for promotion and communication* (pp. 222–234). Hershey, PA: IGI Global. doi:10.4018/978-1-60960-074-7.ch014

Straub, D. W., & Loch, K. D. (2006). Creating and developing a program of global research. *Journal of Global Information Management*, *14*(2), 1–28. doi:10.4018/jgim.2006040101

Straub, D. W., Loch, K. D., & Hill, C. E. (2002). Transfer of information technology to the Arab world: A test of cultural influence modeling. In M. Dadashzadeh (Ed.), *Information technology management in developing countries* (pp. 92–134). Hershey, PA: IGI Global. doi:10.4018/978-1-931777-03-2.ch005

Straub, D. W., Loch, K. D., & Hill, C. E. (2003). Transfer of information technology to the Arab world: A test of cultural influence modeling. In F. Tan (Ed.), *Advanced topics in global information management* (Vol. 2, pp. 141–172). Hershey, PA: IGI Global. doi:10.4018/978-1-59140-064-6.ch009

Suki, N. M., Ramayah, T., Ming, M. K., & Suki, N. M. (2013). Factors enhancing employed job seekers intentions to use social networking sites as a job search tool. In A. Mesquita (Ed.), *User perception and influencing factors of technology in everyday life* (pp. 265–281). Hershey, PA: IGI Global. doi:10.4018/978-1-4666-1954-8.ch018

Suomi, R. (2006). Introducing electronic patient records to hospitals: Innovation adoption paths. In T. Spil & R. Schuring (Eds.), *E-health systems diffusion and use: The innovation, the user and the use IT model* (pp. 128–146). Hershey, PA: IGI Global. doi:10.4018/978-1-59140-423-1.ch008

Swim, J., & Barker, L. (2012). Pathways into a gendered occupation: Brazilian women in IT. *International Journal of Social and Organizational Dynamics in IT*, *2*(4), 34–51. doi:10.4018/ijsodit.2012100103

Tarafdar, M., & Vaidya, S. D. (2006). Adoption and implementation of IT in developing nations: Experiences from two public sector enterprises in India. In M. Khosrow-Pour (Ed.), *Cases on information technology planning, design and implementation* (pp. 208–233). Hershey, PA: IGI Global. doi:10.4018/978-1-59904-408-8.ch013

Tarafdar, M., & Vaidya, S. D. (2008). Adoption and implementation of IT in developing nations: Experiences from two public sector enterprises in India. In G. Garson & M. Khosrow-Pour (Eds.), *Handbook of research on public information technology* (pp. 905–924). Hershey, PA: IGI Global. doi:10.4018/978-1-59904-857-4.ch076

Thesing, Z. (2007). Zarina thesing, pumpkin patch. In M. Hunter (Ed.), *Contemporary chief information officers: Management experiences* (pp. 83–94). Hershey, PA: IGI Global. doi:10.4018/978-1-59904-078-3.ch007

Thomas, J. C. (2004). Public involvement in public administration in the information age: Speculations on the effects of technology. In M. Malkia, A. Anttiroiko, & R. Savolainen (Eds.), *eTransformation in governance: New directions in government and politics* (pp. 67–84). Hershey, PA: IGI Global. doi:10.4018/978-1-59140-130-8.ch004

Treiblmaier, H., & Chong, S. (2013). Trust and perceived risk of personal information as antecedents of online information disclosure: Results from three countries. In F. Tan (Ed.), *Global diffusion and adoption of technologies for knowledge and information sharing* (pp. 341–361). Hershey, PA: IGI Global. doi:10.4018/978-1-4666-2142-8.ch015

van Grembergen, W., & de Haes, S. (2008). IT governance in practice: Six case studies. In W. van Grembergen & S. De Haes (Eds.), *Implementing information technology governance: Models, practices and cases* (pp. 125–237). Hershey, PA: IGI Global. doi:10.4018/978-1-59904-924-3.ch004

van Os, G., Homburg, V., & Bekkers, V. (2013). Contingencies and convergence in European social security: ICT coordination in the back office of the welfare state. In M. Cruz-Cunha, I. Miranda, & P. Gonçalves (Eds.), *Handbook of research on ICTs and management systems for improving efficiency in healthcare and social care* (pp. 268–287). Hershey, PA: IGI Global. doi:10.4018/978-1-4666-3990-4.ch013

Velloso, A. B., Gassenferth, W., & Machado, M. A. (2012). Evaluating IBMEC-RJ's intranet usability using fuzzy logic. In M. Cruz-Cunha, P. Gonçalves, N. Lopes, E. Miranda, & G. Putnik (Eds.), *Handbook of research on business social networking: Organizational, managerial, and technological dimensions* (pp. 185–205). Hershey, PA: IGI Global. doi:10.4018/978-1-61350-168-9.ch010

Villablanca, A. C., Baxi, H., & Anderson, K. (2009). Novel data interface for evaluating cardiovascular outcomes in women. In A. Dwivedi (Ed.), *Handbook of research on information technology management and clinical data administration in healthcare* (pp. 34–53). Hershey, PA: IGI Global. doi:10.4018/978-1-60566-356-2.ch003

Villablanca, A. C., Baxi, H., & Anderson, K. (2011). Novel data interface for evaluating cardiovascular outcomes in women. In *Clinical technologies: Concepts, methodologies, tools and applications* (pp. 2094–2113). Hershey, PA: IGI Global. doi:10.4018/978-1-60960-561-2.ch806

Virkar, S. (2011). Information and communication technologies in administrative reform for development: Exploring the case of property tax systems in Karnataka, India. In J. Steyn, J. Van Belle, & E. Mansilla (Eds.), *ICTs for global development and sustainability: Practice and applications* (pp. 127–149). Hershey, PA: IGI Global. doi:10.4018/978-1-61520-997-2.ch006

Virkar, S. (2013). Designing and implementing e-government projects: Actors, influences, and fields of play. In S. Saeed & C. Reddick (Eds.), *Human-centered system design for electronic governance* (pp. 88–110). Hershey, PA: IGI Global. doi:10.4018/978-1-4666-3640-8.ch007

Wallace, A. (2009). E-justice: An Australian perspective. In A. Martínez & P. Abat (Eds.), *E-justice: Using information communication technologies in the court system* (pp. 204–228). Hershey, PA: IGI Global. doi:10.4018/978-1-59904-998-4.ch014

Wang, G. (2012). E-democratic administration and bureaucratic responsiveness: A primary study of bureaucrats' perceptions of the civil service e-mail box in Taiwan. In K. Kloby & M. D'Agostino (Eds.), *Citizen 2.0: Public and governmental interaction through web 2.0 technologies* (pp. 146–173). Hershey, PA: IGI Global. doi:10.4018/978-1-4666-0318-9.ch009

Wangpipatwong, S., Chutimaskul, W., & Papasratorn, B. (2011). Quality enhancing the continued use of e-government web sites: Evidence from e-citizens of Thailand. In V. Weerakkody (Ed.), *Applied technology integration in governmental organizations: New e-government research* (pp. 20–36). Hershey, PA: IGI Global. doi:10.4018/978-1-60960-162-1.ch002

Wedemeijer, L. (2006). Long-term evolution of a conceptual schema at a life insurance company. In M. Khosrow-Pour (Ed.), *Cases on database technologies and applications* (pp. 202–226). Hershey, PA: IGI Global. doi:10.4018/978-1-59904-399-9.ch012

Whybrow, E. (2008). Digital access, ICT fluency, and the economically disadvantages: Approaches to minimize the digital divide. In F. Tan (Ed.), *Global information technologies: Concepts, methodologies, tools, and applications* (pp. 1409–1422). Hershey, PA: IGI Global. doi:10.4018/978-1-59904-939-7.ch102

Whybrow, E. (2008). Digital access, ICT fluency, and the economically disadvantages: Approaches to minimize the digital divide. In C. Van Slyke (Ed.), *Information communication technologies: Concepts, methodologies, tools, and applications* (pp. 764–777). Hershey, PA: IGI Global. doi:10.4018/978-1-59904-949-6.ch049

Wickramasinghe, N., & Geisler, E. (2010). Key considerations for the adoption and implementation of knowledge management in healthcare operations. In M. Saito, N. Wickramasinghe, M. Fuji, & E. Geisler (Eds.), *Redesigning innovative healthcare operation and the role of knowledge management* (pp. 125–142). Hershey, PA: IGI Global. doi:10.4018/978-1-60566-284-8.ch009

Wickramasinghe, N., & Geisler, E. (2012). Key considerations for the adoption and implementation of knowledge management in healthcare operations. In *Organizational learning and knowledge: Concepts, methodologies, tools and applications* (pp. 1316–1328). Hershey, PA: IGI Global. doi:10.4018/978-1-60960-783-8.ch405

Wickramasinghe, N., & Goldberg, S. (2007). A framework for delivering m-health excellence. In L. Al-Hakim (Ed.), *Web mobile-based applications for healthcare management* (pp. 36–61). Hershey, PA: IGI Global. doi:10.4018/978-1-59140-658-7.ch002

Wickramasinghe, N., & Goldberg, S. (2008). Critical success factors for delivering m-health excellence. In N. Wickramasinghe & E. Geisler (Eds.), *Encyclopedia of healthcare information systems* (pp. 339–351). Hershey, PA: IGI Global. doi:10.4018/978-1-59904-889-5.ch045

Wyld, D. (2009). Radio frequency identification (RFID) technology. In J. Symonds, J. Ayoade, & D. Parry (Eds.), *Auto-identification and ubiquitous computing applications* (pp. 279–293). Hershey, PA: IGI Global. doi:10.4018/978-1-60566-298-5.ch017

Yaghmaei, F. (2010). Understanding computerised information systems usage in community health. In J. Rodrigues (Ed.), *Health information systems: Concepts, methodologies, tools, and applications* (pp. 1388–1399). Hershey, PA: IGI Global. doi:10.4018/978-1-60566-988-5.ch088

Yee, G., El-Khatib, K., Korba, L., Patrick, A. S., Song, R., & Xu, Y. (2005). Privacy and trust in e-government. In W. Huang, K. Siau, & K. Wei (Eds.), *Electronic government strategies and implementation* (pp. 145–190). Hershey, PA: IGI Global. doi:10.4018/978-1-59140-348-7.ch007

Yeh, S., & Chu, P. (2010). Evaluation of e-government services: A citizen-centric approach to citizen e-complaint services. In C. Reddick (Ed.), *Citizens and e-government: Evaluating policy and management* (pp. 400–417). Hershey, PA: IGI Global. doi:10.4018/978-1-61520-931-6.ch022

Young-Jin, S., & Seang-tae, K. (2008). E-government concepts, measures, and best practices. In A. Anttiroiko (Ed.), *Electronic government: Concepts, methodologies, tools, and applications* (pp. 32–57). Hershey, PA: IGI Global. doi:10.4018/978-1-59904-947-2.ch004

Yun, H. J., & Opheim, C. (2012). New technology communication in American state governments: The impact on citizen participation. In K. Bwalya & S. Zulu (Eds.), *Handbook of research on e-government in emerging economies: Adoption, e-participation, and legal frameworks* (pp. 573–590). Hershey, PA: IGI Global. doi:10.4018/978-1-4666-0324-0.ch029

Zhang, N., Guo, X., Chen, G., & Chau, P. Y. (2011). User evaluation of e-government systems: A Chinese cultural perspective. In F. Tan (Ed.), *International enterprises and global information technologies: Advancing management practices* (pp. 63–84). Hershey, PA: IGI Global. doi:10.4018/978-1-60960-605-3.ch004

Zuo, Y., & Hu, W. (2011). Trust-based information risk management in a supply chain network. In J. Wang (Ed.), *Supply chain optimization, management and integration: Emerging applications* (pp. 181–196). Hershey, PA: IGI Global. doi:10.4018/978-1-60960-135-5.ch013

Compilation of References

A.A. v. Greece. (2010). [GC] No. 12186/08, ECHR, para. 62.

Abdulmassih Bulus v. Sweden. (1984). No. 9330/81, Council of Europe: European Commission on Human Rights, 8 December 1984, para. 75.

Addo, K. M., & Grief, N. (1998). Does Article 3 of The European Convention on Human Rights Enshrine Absolute Rights? *European Journal of International Law*, *9*(3), 510–524. doi:10.1093/ejil/9.3.510

Adeyemo, O. (2013). The nationwide health information network: A biometric approach to prevent medical identity theft. In *User-driven healthcare: Concepts, methodologies, tools, and applications* (pp. 1636–1649). Hershey, PA: IGI Global. doi:10.4018/978-1-4666-2770-3.ch081

Adler, M., & Henman, P. (2009). Justice beyond the courts: The implications of computerisation for procedural justice in social security. In A. Martínez & P. Abat (Eds.), *E-justice: Using information communication technologies in the court system* (pp. 65–86). Hershey, PA: IGI Global. doi:10.4018/978-1-59904-998-4.ch005

Aflalo, E., & Gabay, E. (2013). An information system for coping with student dropout. In L. Tomei (Ed.), *Learning tools and teaching approaches through ICT advancements* (pp. 176–187). Hershey, PA: IGI Global. doi:10.4018/978-1-4666-2017-9.ch016

Agelidis, D. (2015). *Asylum- seeking only through Skype and not always.* Retrieved from http://www.efsyn.gr/h-istoria-tis-efsyn accessed on 14/06/2016

Aggeli, D., Dimitriadi, A., & Triantafilidou, A. (2014). *Evaluating the cost –effectiveness control policies irregular migration in Greece.* Midas Report, ELIAMEP, 10/2014. Retrieved from http://www.eliamep.gr/wp-content/uploads/2014/11/MIDAS-REPORT-GR-1.pdf

Ahmed, M. A., Janssen, M., & van den Hoven, J. (2012). Value sensitive transfer (VST) of systems among countries: Towards a framework. *International Journal of Electronic Government Research*, *8*(1), 26–42. doi:10.4018/jegr.2012010102

AI. (2015, October 12). *Global refugee crisis - by the numbers.* Retrieved from https://www.amnesty.org/en/latest/news/2015/10/global-refugee-crisis-by-the-numbers/

Aikins, S. K. (2008). Issues and trends in internet-based citizen participation. In G. Garson & M. Khosrow-Pour (Eds.), *Handbook of research on public information technology* (pp. 31–40). Hershey, PA: IGI Global. doi:10.4018/978-1-59904-857-4.ch004

Aikins, S. K. (2009). A comparative study of municipal adoption of internet-based citizen participation. In C. Reddick (Ed.), *Handbook of research on strategies for local e-government adoption and implementation: Comparative studies* (pp. 206–230). Hershey, PA: IGI Global. doi:10.4018/978-1-60566-282-4.ch011

Aikins, S. K. (2012). Improving e-government project management: Best practices and critical success factors. In *Digital democracy: Concepts, methodologies, tools, and applications* (pp. 1314–1332). Hershey, PA: IGI Global. doi:10.4018/978-1-4666-1740-7.ch065

Ajami, F. (2012). *The Syrian Rebellion*. Stanford, CA: Hoover Institution Press.

Ajayi, F. (2011). Legalizing same sex marriage in Nigeria is against African deities. *Nigeria World Magazine*, *18*, 30–36.

Akabawi, M. S. (2011). Ghabbour group ERP deployment: Learning from past technology failures. In E. Business Research and Case Center (Ed.), Cases on business and management in the MENA region: New trends and opportunities (pp. 177-203). Hershey, PA: IGI Global. doi:10.4018/978-1-60960-583-4.ch012

Akabawi, M. S. (2013). Ghabbour group ERP deployment: Learning from past technology failures. In *Industrial engineering: Concepts, methodologies, tools, and applications* (pp. 933–958). Hershey, PA: IGI Global. doi:10.4018/978-1-4666-1945-6.ch051

Akbulut, A. Y., & Motwani, J. (2008). Integration and information sharing in e-government. In G. Putnik & M. Cruz-Cunha (Eds.), *Encyclopedia of networked and virtual organizations* (pp. 729–734). Hershey, PA: IGI Global. doi:10.4018/978-1-59904-885-7.ch096

Akers, E. J. (2008). Technology diffusion in public administration. In G. Garson & M. Khosrow-Pour (Eds.), *Handbook of research on public information technology* (pp. 339–348). Hershey, PA: IGI Global. doi:10.4018/978-1-59904-857-4.ch033

Akpınarlı, N. (2010). *The Fragility of the 'Failed State' Paradigm*. Leiden, Germany: Brill Academic Publishers.

Akrivopoulou, C. M. (Ed.). (2012). *Human Rights and Risks in the Digital Era: Globalization and the Effects of Information Technologies: Globalization and the Effects of Information Technologies*. Hershey, PA: IGI Global.

Aksar v. the United Kingdom. (1995). [GC] No. 26373/95. ECHR.

Aladwani, A. M. (2002). Organizational actions, computer attitudes and end-user satisfaction in public organizations: An empirical study. In C. Snodgrass & E. Szewczak (Eds.), *Human factors in information systems* (pp. 153–168). Hershey, PA: IGI Global. doi:10.4018/978-1-931777-10-0.ch012

Aladwani, A. M. (2002). Organizational actions, computer attitudes, and end-user satisfaction in public organizations: An empirical study. *Journal of Organizational and End User Computing*, *14*(1), 42–49. doi:10.4018/joeuc.2002010104

Alexa. (2015). *Top cites in Turkey*. Retrieved from http://www.alexa.com/topsites/countries/TR

Alexander, H. (2011). How A 13-Year-Old Boy Became The Face Of The Syrian Uprising. *The Telegraph*. Retrieved from http://www.telegraph.co.uk/news/worldnews/middleeast/syria/8556619/How-a-13-year-old-boy-became-the-face-of-the-Syrian-uprising.html

Ali v Switzerland (1999) 28 E.H.R.R. 304, ECHR.

Allen, B., Juillet, L., Paquet, G., & Roy, J. (2005). E-government and private-public partnerships: Relational challenges and strategic directions. In M. Khosrow-Pour (Ed.), *Practicing e-government: A global perspective* (pp. 364–382). Hershey, PA: IGI Global. doi:10.4018/978-1-59140-637-2.ch016

Alliance Defending Freedom. (2015). The Obama administration's attacks on religious freedom, sanctity of life, and marriage and family. Washington: DC: Alliance Defending Freedom.

al-Natour, M. (2013). Nation, Gender, and Identity: Children in the Syrian Revolution 2011. *Journal of International Women's Studies*, *14*(5), 28–49.

Al-Shafi, S. (2008). Free wireless internet park services: An investigation of technology adoption in Qatar from a citizens perspective. *Journal of Cases on Information Technology*, *10*(3), 21–34. doi:10.4018/jcit.2008070103

Al-Shafi, S., & Weerakkody, V. (2009). Implementing free wi-fi in public parks: An empirical study in Qatar. *International Journal of Electronic Government Research*, *5*(3), 21–35. doi:10.4018/jegr.2009070102

Alsharif, A. (2012, August 14). *Organisation of Islamic Cooperation suspends Syria*. Retrieved from http://www.reuters.com/article/us-syria-crisis-islamic-summit-idUSBRE87E19F20120815

Alshawaf, A., & Knalil, O. E. (2008). IS success factors and IS organizational impact: Does ownership type matter in Kuwait? *International Journal of Enterprise Information Systems*, *4*(2), 13–33. doi:10.4018/jeis.2008040102

Altheide, D. (2006). *Terrorist and the Politics of Fear*. Oxford, UK: Altamira Press.

Ambali, A. R. (2009). Digital divide and its implication on Malaysian e-government: Policy initiatives. In H. Rahman (Ed.), *Social and political implications of data mining: Knowledge management in e-government* (pp. 267–287). Hershey, PA: IGI Global. doi:10.4018/978-1-60566-230-5.ch016

Amnesty International. (2016). *EU-Turkey refugee deal a historic blow to rights*. Retrieved from https://www.amnesty.org/en/latest/news/2016/03/eu-turkey-refugee-deal-a-historic-blow-to-rights/

Amoretti, F. (2007). Digital international governance. In A. Anttiroiko & M. Malkia (Eds.), *Encyclopedia of digital government* (pp. 365–370). Hershey, PA: IGI Global. doi:10.4018/978-1-59140-789-8.ch056

Amoretti, F. (2008). Digital international governance. In A. Anttiroiko (Ed.), *Electronic government: Concepts, methodologies, tools, and applications* (pp. 688–696). Hershey, PA: IGI Global. doi:10.4018/978-1-59904-947-2.ch058

Amoretti, F. (2008). E-government at supranational level in the European Union. In A. Anttiroiko (Ed.), *Electronic government: Concepts, methodologies, tools, and applications* (pp. 1047–1055). Hershey, PA: IGI Global. doi:10.4018/978-1-59904-947-2.ch079

Amoretti, F. (2008). E-government regimes. In A. Anttiroiko (Ed.), *Electronic government: Concepts, methodologies, tools, and applications* (pp. 3846–3856). Hershey, PA: IGI Global. doi:10.4018/978-1-59904-947-2.ch280

Amoretti, F. (2009). Electronic constitution: A Braudelian perspective. In F. Amoretti (Ed.), *Electronic constitution: Social, cultural, and political implications* (pp. 1–19). Hershey, PA: IGI Global. doi:10.4018/978-1-60566-254-1.ch001

Amoretti, F., & Musella, F. (2009). Institutional isomorphism and new technologies. In M. Khosrow-Pour (Ed.), *Encyclopedia of information science and technology* (2nd ed.; pp. 2066–2071). Hershey, PA: IGI Global. doi:10.4018/978-1-60566-026-4.ch325

Andersen, K. V., & Henriksen, H. Z. (2007). E-government research: Capabilities, interaction, orientation, and values. In D. Norris (Ed.), *Current issues and trends in e-government research* (pp. 269–288). Hershey, PA: IGI Global. doi:10.4018/978-1-59904-283-1.ch013

Anderson, K. V., & Henriksen, H. Z. (2005). The first leg of e-government research: Domains and application areas 19982003. *International Journal of Electronic Government Research*, *1*(4), 26–44. doi:10.4018/jegr.2005100102

Anti-Islam movement PEGIDA stages protests across Europe. (2016). Retrieved from http://www.reuters.com/article/us-europe-migrants-protests-germany-idUSKCN0VF0P4

Anti-Nazi couple's barn burned down in eastern Germany. (2015). Retrieved from http://www.bbc.com/news/world-europe-33928047

Anttiroiko, A. (2009). Democratic e-governance. In M. Khosrow-Pour (Ed.), *Encyclopedia of information science and technology* (2nd ed.; pp. 990–995). Hershey, PA: IGI Global. doi:10.4018/978-1-60566-026-4.ch158

Athens News Agency - Macedonian Press Agency (ANA-MPA). (2016). *Greece calls NATO to remain in the Aegean.* Retrieved from http://www.kathimerini.gr/863741/article/epikairothta/politikh/yper-ths-paramonhs-toy-nato-sto-aigaio-tassetai-h-ellada accessed on 14/06/2016

Augé, M. (2002). *Diario de Guerra: el mundo después del 11 de Septiembre.* Barcelona: Gedisa.

Badiou, A. (2008). The communist hypothesis. *New Left Review, 49*. Retrieved on https://newleftreview.org/II/49/alain-badiou-the-communist-hypothesis

Baker, P. M., Bell, A., & Moon, N. W. (2009). Accessibility issues in municipal wireless networks. In C. Reddick (Ed.), *Handbook of research on strategies for local e-government adoption and implementation: Comparative studies* (pp. 569–588). Hershey, PA: IGI Global. doi:10.4018/978-1-60566-282-4.ch030

Barker, M. (1981). *The new racism: Conservatives and the ideology of the tribe*. London: Junction Books.

Barkin, N., & Carrel, P. (2016, July 11). *'Terrorists' smuggled into Europe with refugees, Merkel says*. Retrieved from http://www.reuters.com/article/us-europe-migrants-extremists-merkel-idUSKCN0ZR1AH

Barnard, A. (2016, February 11). Death toll from war in Syria now 470,000, group finds. *The New York Times*.

Baudrillard, J. (2001). The spirit of terrorism. *Telos*, *121*, 134-142.

Baudrillard, J. (1994). *Simulacra and simulation*. University of Michigan press.

Baudrillard, J. (1995). *The Gulf War did not take place*. Indianapolis, IN: Indiana University Press.

Baudrillard, J. (2006). Virtuality and Events: The hell of power. *Baudrillard Studies*, *3*(2), 1–4.

Baudrillard, J., & Evans, A. B. (1991). Simulacra and Science Fiction (Simulacres et science-fiction). *Science Fiction Studies*, *1*, 309–313.

Bauman, Z. (1998b). On glocalization: Or globalization for some, localization for some others. *Thesis Eleven, 54*(1), 37-49.

Bauman, Z. (1998a). *Globalization: The human consequences*. New York: Columbia University Press.

Bauman, Z. (2001). Consuming life. *Journal of Consumer Culture*, *1*(1), 9–29. doi:10.1177/146954050100100102

Bauman, Z. (2006). *Liquid Fear*. Cambridge, UK: Polity Press.

Bauman, Z., & Lyon, D. (2013). *Liquid surveillance: A conversation*. New York: John Wiley & Sons.

Bayrakli, E., & Hafez, F. (2016). *European Islamophobia Report 2015*. Istanbul: SETA.

BBC. (2015). 'We are the child': The anti-Assad Slogan Spreading across the Middle East. *BBC Trending*. Retrieved from http://www.bbc.com/news/blogs-trending-33066361

BBC. (2016, March 4). *Migrant crisis: Migration to Europe explained in seven charts*. Retrieved from http://www.bbc.com/news/world-europe-34131911

Becker, E. (2015, November 3). The Four "Best" Countries for Refugee Resettlement. *UN Dispatch*. Retrieved from http://www.undispatch.com/the-four-best-countries-for-refugee-resettlement/

Becker, S. A., Keimer, R., & Muth, T. (2012). A case on university and community collaboration: The sci-tech entrepreneurial training services (ETS) program. In Regional development: Concepts, methodologies, tools, and applications (pp. 947-969). Hershey, PA: IGI Global. doi:10.4018/978-1-4666-0882-5.ch507

Becker, S. A., Keimer, R., & Muth, T. (2010). A case on university and community collaboration: The sci-tech entrepreneurial training services (ETS) program. In S. Becker & R. Niebuhr (Eds.), *Cases on technology innovation: Entrepreneurial successes and pitfalls* (pp. 68–90). Hershey, PA: IGI Global. doi:10.4018/978-1-61520-609-4.ch003

Beck, U. (1992). *Risk society: Towards a new modernity* (Vol. 17). London: Sage.

Beck, U. (2002). The terrorist threat world risk society revisited. *Theory, Culture & Society*, *19*(4), 39–55. doi:10.1177/0263276402019004003

Beck, U. (2009). *World at risk*. Cambridge, UK: Polity Press.

Beirich, H. (2016). Religious liberty and the anti-LGBT right. The hardline groups promoting "religious freedom restoration acts" to justify anti-gay discrimination. Washington, DC: Southern Poverty Law Centre.

Benjamin, W. (1986). *Reflections essays, aphorisms, autobiographical writing Walter Benjamin*. New York: Schocken Books.

Bernardi, R. (2012). Information technology and resistance to public sector reforms: A case study in Kenya. In T. Papadopoulos & P. Kanellis (Eds.), *Public sector reform using information technologies: Transforming policy into practice* (pp. 59–78). Hershey, PA: IGI Global. doi:10.4018/978-1-60960-839-2.ch004

Bernardi, R. (2013). Information technology and resistance to public sector reforms: A case study in Kenya. In *User-driven healthcare: Concepts, methodologies, tools, and applications* (pp. 14–33). Hershey, PA: IGI Global. doi:10.4018/978-1-4666-2770-3.ch002

Bernstein, R. J. (2013). *The abuse of evil: The corruption of politics and religion since 9/11*. New York: John Wiley & Sons.

Berrehab v. the Netherlands (1988). Series A no. 138, p. 14, para. 7.

Bielefeldt, H. (2012). Freedom of religion or belief – A human right pressure. *Oxford Journal of Law and Religion*, *11*, 1–21.

Bisi, A. (2015). *Nigeria: We may be free but homophobic hatred remains our nation's shame*. *World Press*. Retrieved October 18, 2016, from http://www.nigeria-we-may-be-free-bu-homophobic-hatred-remains-our-nations-shame/bisi/alimi/com

Blanford, N., & Hider, J. (2011). Regime Sends Children and Conscripts Out On Streets to Hold Back Arab Spring. *The Times*. Retrieved from http://www.thetimes.co.uk/tto/news/world/middleeast/article2965581.ece

Bloch, E. (1977). *Nonsynchronism and the Obligation to Its Dialectics. New German Critique No. 11*. Duke University Press.

Bocek, T. (2016). *Statement on the occasion of the European Day on the Protection of Children against Sexual Exploitation and Sexual Abuse*. Retrieved from http://www.coe.int/en/web/portal/resources-special-representative-migration-refugees-tomas-bocek

Bolívar, M. P., Pérez, M. D., & Hernández, A. M. (2012). Municipal e-government services in emerging economies: The Latin-American and Caribbean experiences. In Y. Chen & P. Chu (Eds.), *Electronic governance and cross-boundary collaboration: Innovations and advancing tools* (pp. 198–226). Hershey, PA: IGI Global. doi:10.4018/978-1-60960-753-1.ch011

Bond, M. (2012). *The Council of Europe: Structure, History and Issues in European Politics*. London: Routledge.

Borycki, E. M., & Kushniruk, A. W. (2010). Use of clinical simulations to evaluate the impact of health information systems and ubiquitous computing devices upon health professional work. In S. Mohammed & J. Fiaidhi (Eds.), *Ubiquitous health and medical informatics: The ubiquity 2.0 trend and beyond* (pp. 552–573). Hershey, PA: IGI Global. doi:10.4018/978-1-61520-777-0.ch026

Borycki, E. M., & Kushniruk, A. W. (2011). Use of clinical simulations to evaluate the impact of health information systems and ubiquitous computing devices upon health professional work. In *Clinical technologies: Concepts, methodologies, tools and applications* (pp. 532–553). Hershey, PA: IGI Global. doi:10.4018/978-1-60960-561-2.ch220

Bourdieu, P., & Wacquant, D. (1992). *An Invitation to reflective Sociology*. Chicago, IL: Chicago University Press.

Bozano v France, Merits, App No 9990/82, A/111, (1991) 9 EHRR 29. para. 8.

Brems, E., & Gerards, J. (2013). *Shaping Rights in the ECHR: The Role of the European Court of Human Rights in Determining the Scope of Human Rights*. Cambridge, UK: Cambridge University Press. doi:10.1017/CBO9781107337923

Brett, L. (2007). Faith, homophobia and human rights. Gay Humanist Quarterly, 2(1), 7-8.

Brett, L. (2007). From the editor. *Gay Humanist Quarterly*, *7*, 2.

Britton, B. (2016, September 7). UK to Build 'Big New Wall' in Calais to Stop Migrants. *CNN*. Retrieved from http://edition.cnn.com/2016/09/07/europe/calais-wall-migrants/

Brocklehurst, H. (2006). *Who's Afraid of Children? Children, Conflict and International Relations*. Ashgate Publishing Limited.

Brooks, R. E. (2005). Failed States, or the State as Failure?. *The University of Chicago Law Review. University of Chicago. Law School*, *72*(4), 1160.

Buchan, J. (2011). Developing a dynamic and responsive online learning environment: A case study of a large Australian university. In B. Czerkawski (Ed.), *Free and open source software for e-learning: Issues, successes and challenges* (pp. 92–109). Hershey, PA: IGI Global. doi:10.4018/978-1-61520-917-0.ch006

Buell, F. (1994). *National Culture and the New Global System*. Baltimore, MD: John Hopkins University Press.

Buenger, A. W. (2008). Digital convergence and cybersecurity policy. In G. Garson & M. Khosrow-Pour (Eds.), *Handbook of research on public information technology* (pp. 395–405). Hershey, PA: IGI Global. doi:10.4018/978-1-59904-857-4.ch038

Burn, J. M., & Loch, K. D. (2002). The societal impact of world wide web - Key challenges for the 21st century. In A. Salehnia (Ed.), *Ethical issues of information systems* (pp. 88–106). Hershey, PA: IGI Global. doi:10.4018/978-1-931777-15-5.ch007

Burn, J. M., & Loch, K. D. (2003). The societal impact of the world wide web-Key challenges for the 21st century. In M. Khosrow-Pour (Ed.), *Advanced topics in information resources management* (Vol. 2, pp. 32–51). Hershey, PA: IGI Global. doi:10.4018/978-1-59140-062-2.ch002

Bwalya, K. J., Du Plessis, T., & Rensleigh, C. (2012). The "quicksilver initiatives" as a framework for e-government strategy design in developing economies. In K. Bwalya & S. Zulu (Eds.), *Handbook of research on e-government in emerging economies: Adoption, e-participation, and legal frameworks* (pp. 605–623). Hershey, PA: IGI Global. doi:10.4018/978-1-4666-0324-0.ch031

Cabotaje, C. E., & Alampay, E. A. (2013). Social media and citizen engagement: Two cases from the Philippines. In S. Saeed & C. Reddick (Eds.), *Human-centered system design for electronic governance* (pp. 225–238). Hershey, PA: IGI Global. doi:10.4018/978-1-4666-3640-8.ch013

Cairns, E. (1996). *Children and Political Violence*. London: Blackwell.

Camillo, A., Di Pietro, L., Di Virgilio, F., & Franco, M. (2013). Work-groups conflict at PetroTech-Italy, S.R.L.: The influence of culture on conflict dynamics. In B. Christiansen, E. Turkina, & N. Williams (Eds.), *Cultural and technological influences on global business* (pp. 272–289). Hershey, PA: IGI Global. doi:10.4018/978-1-4666-3966-9.ch015

Campbell, Z. (2016). *Shoot First. Coast Guard Fired at Migrant Boats, European Boarder Agency Documents Show*. Retrieved from https://theintercept.com/2016/08/22/coast-guard-fired-at-migrant-boats-european-border-agency-documents-show/

Capra, E., Francalanci, C., & Marinoni, C. (2008). Soft success factors for m-government. In A. Anttiroiko (Ed.), *Electronic government: Concepts, methodologies, tools, and applications* (pp. 1213–1233). Hershey, PA: IGI Global. doi:10.4018/978-1-59904-947-2.ch089

Caprino v. U.K. (1978) No. 6871/75, 4 E.H.R.R. 97.

Cartelli, A. (2009). The implementation of practices with ICT as a new teaching-learning paradigm. In A. Cartelli & M. Palma (Eds.), *Encyclopedia of information communication technology* (pp. 413–417). Hershey, PA: IGI Global. doi:10.4018/978-1-59904-845-1.ch055

Case of Dahlab v Switzerland, 15/02/2001, Application no. 42393/98. (n.d.). Retrieved from http://hudoc.echr.coe.int/eng?i=001-22643#{"itemid":["001-22643"]}

Case of Dogru v France, 04/03/2009, Application no. 27058/05. (n.d.). Retrieved from http://hudoc.echr.coe.int/eng?i=001-90039

Case of Islam (A.P.) v. Secretary of State for the Home Department Regina v. Immigration Appeal Tribunal and Another Ex Parte Shah (A.P.), 25/03/1999, House of Lords. (n.d.). Retrieved from www.parliament.uk

Case of Kervanci v France, 04/03/2009, Application no. 31645/04. (n.d.). Retrieved from http://hudoc.echr.coe.int/eng?i=001-90047

Case of M.C. v. Bulgaria, 04/03/2004, Application no. 39272/98. (n.d.). Retrieved from https://www.coe.int/t/dg2/equality/domesticviolencecampaign/resources/M.C.v.BULGARIA_en.asp

Case of Minister for Immigration and Multicultural Affairs v. Haji Ibrahim, 26/08/2000 HCA 55,SI57/1999, Australia: High Court. (n.d.). Retrieved from http://www.refworld.org/docid/3deb737f7.html

Case of R.U. v. Greece, 07/09/2011, Application no. 2237/08. (n.d.). Retrieved from http://www.asylumlawdatabase.eu/en/content/ecthr-ru-v-greece-application-no-223708

Case of Rahimi v. Greece, 05/07/2011, Application No. 8687/08. (n.d.). Retrieved from http://www.asylumlawdatabase.eu/en/content/ecthr-rahimi-v-greece-application-no-868708-1

Case of Saadi v. United Kingdom, 29/01/2008, Application no13229/03, Council of Europe: European Court of Human Rights. (n.d.). Retrieved from http://www.refworld.org/docid/47a074302.html

Case of Sahin v Tutrkey, 10/11/2005, Application no 44774/98. (n.d.). Retrieved from http://www.tjsl.edu/slomansonb/SahinTurk.pdf

Case of Sharifi and Others v. Italy and Greece, 21/10/2014 no 16643l09. (n.d.). Retrieved from http://hudoc.echr.coe.int/eng?i=001-163391

Cassidy, J. (2015, November 18). The economics of Syrian refugees. *The New Yorker*.

Chahal v. United Kingdom. (1997) 23 EHRR 413, para. 122.

Chapman, K. C. (2012). Gay rights, the Bible and public accommodations: An empirical approach to religious exemptions for holdout state. *The Georgetown Law Journal*, *100*, 1783–1827.

Charalabidis, Y., Lampathaki, F., & Askounis, D. (2010). Investigating the landscape in national interoperability frameworks. *International Journal of E-Services and Mobile Applications*, *2*(4), 28–41. doi:10.4018/jesma.2010100103

Charalabidis, Y., Lampathaki, F., & Askounis, D. (2012). Investigating the landscape in national interoperability frameworks. In A. Scupola (Ed.), *Innovative mobile platform developments for electronic services design and delivery* (pp. 218–231). Hershey, PA: IGI Global. doi:10.4018/978-1-4666-1568-7.ch013

Charles, L., & Denman, K. (2013). Syrian and Palestinian Syrian Refugees in Lebanon: The Plight of Women and Children. *Journal of International Women's Studies*, *14*(5), 96–111.

Chen, I. (2005). Distance education associations. In C. Howard, J. Boettcher, L. Justice, K. Schenk, P. Rogers, & G. Berg (Eds.), *Encyclopedia of distance learning* (pp. 599–612). Hershey, PA: IGI Global. doi:10.4018/978-1-59140-555-9.ch087

Chen, I. (2008). Distance education associations. In L. Tomei (Ed.), *Online and distance learning: Concepts, methodologies, tools, and applications* (pp. 562–579). Hershey, PA: IGI Global. doi:10.4018/978-1-59904-935-9.ch048

Chen, Y. (2008). Managing IT outsourcing for digital government. In A. Anttiroiko (Ed.), *Electronic government: Concepts, methodologies, tools, and applications* (pp. 3107–3114). Hershey, PA: IGI Global. doi:10.4018/978-1-59904-947-2.ch229

Chen, Y., & Dimitrova, D. V. (2006). Electronic government and online engagement: Citizen interaction with government via web portals. *International Journal of Electronic Government Research*, *2*(1), 54–76. doi:10.4018/jegr.2006010104

Chen, Y., & Knepper, R. (2005). Digital government development strategies: Lessons for policy makers from a comparative perspective. In W. Huang, K. Siau, & K. Wei (Eds.), *Electronic government strategies and implementation* (pp. 394–420). Hershey, PA: IGI Global. doi:10.4018/978-1-59140-348-7.ch017

Chen, Y., & Knepper, R. (2008). Digital government development strategies: Lessons for policy makers from a comparative perspective. In H. Rahman (Ed.), *Developing successful ICT strategies: Competitive advantages in a global knowledge-driven society* (pp. 334–356). Hershey, PA: IGI Global. doi:10.4018/978-1-59904-654-9.ch017

Cherian, E. J., & Ryan, T. W. (2014). Incongruent needs: Why differences in the iron-triangle of priorities make health information technology adoption and use difficult. In C. El Morr (Ed.), *Research perspectives on the role of informatics in health policy and management* (pp. 209–221). Hershey, PA: IGI Global. doi:10.4018/978-1-4666-4321-5.ch012

Chetail, V. (2014). Are Refugee Rights Human Rights? An Unorthodox Questioning of the Relations between Refugee Law and Human Rights Law. In R. Rubio-Maríned (Ed.), *Human Right and Immigration* (p. 17). Oxford, UK: Oxford University Press. doi:10.1093/acprof:oso/9780198701170.003.0002

Cho, H. J., & Hwang, S. (2010). Government 2.0 in Korea: Focusing on e-participation services. In C. Reddick (Ed.), *Politics, democracy and e-government: Participation and service delivery* (pp. 94–114). Hershey, PA: IGI Global. doi:10.4018/978-1-61520-933-0.ch006

Chorus, C., & Timmermans, H. (2010). Ubiquitous travel environments and travel control strategies: Prospects and challenges. In M. Wachowicz (Ed.), *Movement-aware applications for sustainable mobility: Technologies and approaches* (pp. 30–51). Hershey, PA: IGI Global. doi:10.4018/978-1-61520-769-5.ch003

Christides, G., Amalia, J., Mayr, W., Müller, P., Neukirch, R., Neumann, C., . . . Scheuermann, C. (2016). *Refugee Crisis Pushes Europe to the Brick*. Retrieved from http://www.spiegel.de/international/europe/border-closures-spell-refugee-back-up-in-greece-a-1080643.html

Chuanshen, R. (2007). E-government construction and China's administrative litigation act. In A. Anttiroiko & M. Malkia (Eds.), *Encyclopedia of digital government* (pp. 507–510). Hershey, PA: IGI Global. doi:10.4018/978-1-59140-789-8.ch077

Ciaghi, A., & Villafiorita, A. (2012). Law modeling and BPR for public administration improvement. In K. Bwalya & S. Zulu (Eds.), *Handbook of research on e-government in emerging economies: Adoption, e-participation, and legal frameworks* (pp. 391–410). Hershey, PA: IGI Global. doi:10.4018/978-1-4666-0324-0.ch019

Ciaramitaro, B. L., & Skrocki, M. (2012). mHealth: Mobile healthcare. In B. Ciaramitaro (Ed.), Mobile technology consumption: Opportunities and challenges (pp. 99-109). Hershey, PA: IGI Global. doi:10.4018/978-1-61350-150-4.ch007

Çoban Keneş, H. (2016). Metaforun ayrımcı hegemonyanın inşasındaki rolü: Suriyelilerin haberleştirilmesindeki metafor kullanımı. *Gaziantep University Journal of Social Sciences*, *15*(2), 253–280. doi:10.21547/jss.256727

Cochrane, D. B. (2004). Christian opposition to homosexuality. In J. McNinch & M. Cronin (Eds.), *I could not speak my heart: Education and social justice for LGBT youth*. Regina: Canadian Plains Research Centre.

Cohen-Almagor, R. (2011). Fighting hate and bigotry on the Internet. *Policy & Internet*, *3*(3), 1–26. doi:10.2202/1944-2866.1059

Collett, E. (2016, March 1). *The paradox of the EU-Turkey refugee deal*. Retrieved from http://www.migrationpolicy.org/news/paradox-eu-turkey-refugee-deal

Comite, U. (2012). Innovative processes and managerial effectiveness of e-procurement in healthcare. In A. Manoharan & M. Holzer (Eds.), *Active citizen participation in e-government: A global perspective* (pp. 206–229). Hershey, PA: IGI Global. doi:10.4018/978-1-4666-0116-1.ch011

Commissioner for Human Rights. (2016). *Human Rights of Refugee and Migrant Women and Girls Need to be Better Protected: Human Right Comment*. Strasbourg: Council of Europe.

Commissioner for Human Rights. (2016). *Time for Europe to Get Migrant Integration Right: Issue Papers*. Strasbourg: Council of Europe.

Čonka v. Belgium. (2002) No. 51564/99. ECHR. para. 63.

Connolly, K. (2016). *Tensions rise in Germany over handling of mass sexual assaults in Cologne.* Retrieved from www.theguardian.com/world/2016/jan/06/tensions-rise-ingermany-over-handling-of-mass-sexual-assaults-in-cologne

Constitution of Greece. (1975). *Article 13 §1, 2.* Retrieved from http://www.hri.org/docs/syntagma/artcl25.html#A13

Convention on the Elimination of all Forms of Discrimination against Women (CEDAW Convention). (n.d.). Retrieved from http://www.iwraw-ap.org/cedaw/what-is-cedaw/cedaw-principles/

Cooke, M. (1988). *War's Other Voices: Women Writers on the Lebanese Civil War.* New York: Cambridge University Press.

Cordella, A. (2013). E-government success: How to account for ICT, administrative rationalization, and institutional change. In J. Gil-Garcia (Ed.), *E-government success factors and measures: Theories, concepts, and methodologies* (pp. 40–51). Hershey, PA: IGI Global. doi:10.4018/978-1-4666-4058-0.ch003

Costra-Kostritsky, V. (2012). *France and the veil – the dark side of the law.* Retrieved from https://www.opendemocracy.net/5050/valeria-costa-kostritsky/france-and-veil-%E2%80%93-dark-side-of-law

Council of Europe. (1999). *International Law – Conventions of the Council of Europe.* Strasbourg: Council of Europe Publishing.

Council of Europe. (2016). *Commissioner for Human Rights – Country Monitoring.* Strasbourg: Council of Europe Publishers. Retrieved from http://www.coe.int/en/web/commissioner/country-monitoring

Council of Europe. (2016). *Special Representative on Migration and Refugees, Report of the fact-finding mission by Ambassador Tomáš Boček Special Representative of the Secretary General on Migration and Refugees to Greece and the Former Yugoslav Republic of Macedonia: Information Documents.* Strasbourg: Council of Europe Publishers.

Council of Europe. (2016). *Special Representative on Migration and Refugees, Report of the fact-finding mission on the situation of migrants and refugees in Calais and Grande-Synthe, France by Ambassador Tomáš Boček: Information Documents.* Strasbourg: Council of Europe Publishers.

Council of Europe. (2016). *Special Representative on Migration and Refugees, Report of the fact-finding mission to Turkey by Ambassador Tomáš Boček Special Representative of the Secretary General on Migration and Refugees: Information Documents.* Strasbourg: Council of Europe Publishers.

Council of Europe. (2016). *The Mandate of the Special Representative on Migration and Refugees.* Strasbourg: Council of Europe.

Crabtree, V. (2011). Anti religious forces: Specific factors fuelling secularization. *Academic Studies of Religion, 4*(3), 56–78.

Cresswell, T. (2006). The right to mobility: The production of mobility in the courtroom. *Antipode*, *38*(4), 735–754. doi:10.1111/j.1467-8330.2006.00474.x

Cropf, R. A. (2009). ICT and e-democracy. In M. Khosrow-Pour (Ed.), *Encyclopedia of information science and technology* (2nd ed.; pp. 1789–1793). Hershey, PA: IGI Global. doi:10.4018/978-1-60566-026-4.ch281

Cropf, R. A. (2009). The virtual public sphere. In M. Pagani (Ed.), *Encyclopedia of multimedia technology and networking* (2nd ed.; pp. 1525–1530). Hershey, PA: IGI Global. doi:10.4018/978-1-60566-014-1.ch206

Crouch, D., & Kingsley, P. (2016, January 26). Danish Parliament approves plan to seize assets from refugees. *The Guardian*. Retrieved from https://www.theguardian.com/world/2016/jan/26/danish-parliament-approves-plan-to-seize-assets-from-refugees

Cruz Varas v. Sweden. (1991) [GC] No. 15576/89, ECHR; D. v. United Kingdom (1997) 24 EHRR 42.

D'Abundo, M. L. (2013). Electronic health record implementation in the United States healthcare industry: Making the process of change manageable. In V. Wang (Ed.), *Handbook of research on technologies for improving the 21st century workforce: Tools for lifelong learning* (pp. 272–286). Hershey, PA: IGI Global. doi:10.4018/978-1-4666-2181-7.ch018

Damurski, L. (2012). E-participation in urban planning: Online tools for citizen engagement in Poland and in Germany. *International Journal of E-Planning Research*, *1*(3), 40–67. doi:10.4018/ijepr.2012070103

Dann, G., & Jacobsen, J. (2003). Leading the tourist by the nose. In G. M. S. Dann (Ed.), *The Tourist as a metaphor of the social World*. New York: CABI.

Davis, A. (2014). *Women, Race and Class*. Athens: Arxeio 17 migada.

de Almeida, M. O. (2007). E-government strategy in Brazil: Increasing transparency and efficiency through e-government procurement. In M. Gascó-Hernandez (Ed.), *Latin America online: Cases, successes and pitfalls* (pp. 34–82). Hershey, PA: IGI Global. doi:10.4018/978-1-59140-974-8.ch002

de Juana Espinosa, S. (2008). Empirical study of the municipalitites' motivations for adopting online presence. In A. Anttiroiko (Ed.), *Electronic government: Concepts, methodologies, tools, and applications* (pp. 3593–3608). Hershey, PA: IGI Global. doi:10.4018/978-1-59904-947-2.ch262

De Landa, M. (2006). *A new Philosophy of Society: assembling Theory and social complexity*. London: Bloomsbury.

de Souza Dias, D. (2002). Motivation for using information technology. In C. Snodgrass & E. Szewczak (Eds.), *Human factors in information systems* (pp. 55–60). Hershey, PA: IGI Global. doi:10.4018/978-1-931777-10-0.ch005 de Wet, E. (2004). The Prohibition of Torture as an International Norm of *Jus Cogens* and Its Implications for National and Customary Law. *European Journal of International Law*, *15*(1), 97–121. doi:10.1093/ejil/15.1.97

Dearden, L. (2015). *Syrian Children Dressed Up As Isis Hostages in Death Cage For Anti-Assad Protest*. Academic Press.

Dearden, L. (2016, February 10). Refugee crisis: Welfare cuts and anti-migration policies 'will not stop' asylum seekers coming to Europe – Report. *Independent*. Retrieved from http://www.independent.co.uk/news/world/europe/refugee-crisis-welfare-cuts-and-anti-migration-policies-will-not-stop-asylum-seekers-coming-to-a6865246.html

Dearden, L. (2016, January 26). Denmark Approves Controversial Refugee Bill Allowing Police to Seize Asylum Seekers' Cash and Valuables. *Independent*. Retrieved from http://www.independent.co.uk/news/world/europe/denmark-approves-controversial-refugee-bill-allowing-police-to-seize-asylum-seekers-cash-and-a6834581.html

Debord, G. (1988). *Comments on the Society of the Spectacle*. Athens: Eleutheros Tipos, thesis 9.

Demediuk, P. (2006). Government procurement ICT's impact on the sustainability of SMEs and regional communities. In S. Marshall, W. Taylor, & X. Yu (Eds.), *Encyclopedia of developing regional communities with information and communication technology* (pp. 321–324). Hershey, PA: IGI Global. doi:10.4018/978-1-59140-575-7.ch056

Der I. I. I. Weg beim Imia-Gedenken in Athens, 06/02/2016. (n.d.). Retrieved from http://archive.is/2MMnP#selection-173.0-173.154

Derrida, J. (2000). Of Hospitality: Anne Dufourmantelle Invites Jacques Derrida to Respond (R. Bowlby, Trans.). Stanford, CA: Stanford Univ. Press.

Devonshire, E., Forsyth, H., Reid, S., & Simpson, J. M. (2013). The challenges and opportunities of online postgraduate coursework programs in a traditional university context. In B. Tynan, J. Willems, & R. James (Eds.), *Outlooks and opportunities in blended and distance learning* (pp. 353–368). Hershey, PA: IGI Global. doi:10.4018/978-1-4666-4205-8.ch026

Di Cerbo, F., Scotto, M., Sillitti, A., Succi, G., & Vernazza, T. (2007). Toward a GNU/Linux distribution for corporate environments. In S. Sowe, I. Stamelos, & I. Samoladas (Eds.), *Emerging free and open source software practices* (pp. 215–236). Hershey, PA: IGI Global. doi:10.4018/978-1-59904-210-7.ch010

Diesner, J., & Carley, K. M. (2005). Revealing social structure from texts: Meta-matrix text analysis as a novel method for network text analysis. In V. Narayanan & D. Armstrong (Eds.), *Causal mapping for research in information technology* (pp. 81–108). Hershey, PA: IGI Global. doi:10.4018/978-1-59140-396-8.ch004

Diken, B. (2001). Immigration, multiculturalism and post politics after nine eleven. *Third Text*, *15*(57), 3–12. doi:10.1080/09528820108576937

Directorate General For Internal Policies Policy Department C. Citizens' Rights And Constitutional Affairs & Gender Equality. (2013). *Overview of the worldwide best practices for rape prevention and for assisting women victims of rape*. European Parliament. Retrieved from http://www.europarl.europa.eu/RegData/etudes/etudes/join/2013/493025/IPOL-FEMM_ET(2013)493025_EN.pdf

Doğanay, Ü., & Çoban Keneş, H. (2016). Yazılı basında suriyeli 'mülteciler': Ayrımcı söylemlerin rasyonel ve duygusal gerekçelerinin inşası. *Mülkiye Dergisi*, *40*(1), 143–184.

Dologite, D. G., Mockler, R. J., Bai, Q., & Viszhanyo, P. F. (2006). IS change agents in practice in a US-Chinese joint venture. In M. Hunter & F. Tan (Eds.), *Advanced topics in global information management* (Vol. 5, pp. 331–352). Hershey, PA: IGI Global. doi:10.4018/978-1-59140-923-6.ch015

Drnevich, P., Brush, T. H., & Luckock, G. T. (2011). Process and structural implications for IT-enabled outsourcing. *International Journal of Strategic Information Technology and Applications*, *2*(4), 30–43. doi:10.4018/jsita.2011100103

Duke, B. (2014). Religious fanatics blamed for Nigeria's draconian anti-gay bill, approved this week. *The Free Thinker*. Retrieved February 2, 2016, from http://www.religious-fanatics-blamed-for-nigerias-draconian-antigay-bill-approved-this-week/thefreethinker.com

Durkheim, E. (2014). *The rules of sociological method: and selected texts on sociology and its method*. New York, NY: Simon and Schuster.

Dwivedi, A. N. (2009). Handbook of research on information technology management and clinical data administration in healthcare (Vols. 1–2). Hershey, PA: IGI Global. doi:10.4018/978-1-60566-356-2

East African Asians v. United Kingdom. (1979). (DEC.) [GC] No. 4626/70, ECHR.

Easterly, W. (2000). *Can Institutions Resolve Ethnic Conflict?*. Policy Research Working Paper Series 2482, World Bank.

Ebuzor, C. (2016). Ex President says gay marriage law might be revisited. *Pulse*. Retrieved June 19, 2016, from http://pulse.ng/local/goodluck-jonathan-ex-president-says-gay-marriage-law-might-be-revisited-id5119539.html

ecre. (2016). *Joint Statement: European leaders should keep the borders open and allow access to asylum*. Retrieved from http://www.ecre.org/joint-statement-european-leaders-keep-the-borders-open-and-allow-access-to-asylum/?option=com_downloads&id=1078

Edwards, A. (2014). International Refugee Law. In *International Human Rights Law* (2nd ed.). Oxford, UK: Oxford University Press.

Elbeltagi, I., McBride, N., & Hardaker, G. (2006). Evaluating the factors affecting DSS usage by senior managers in local authorities in Egypt. In M. Hunter & F. Tan (Eds.), *Advanced topics in global information management* (Vol. 5, pp. 283–307). Hershey, PA: IGI Global. doi:10.4018/978-1-59140-923-6.ch013

Enders, W., & Hoover, G. A. (2012). The nonlinear relationship between terrorism and poverty. *The American Economic Review*, *102*(3), 267–272. doi:10.1257/aer.102.3.267

Enders, W., & Sandler, T. (2011). *The political economy of terrorism*. Cambridge, UK: Cambridge University Press. doi:10.1017/CBO9780511791451

Endong, F. P. C. (2015a). Christian resistance to gay-proselytism in a secular Nigeria: Anathema or social heroism?. *ERAS: European Review of Applied Sociology*, *8*(11), 5–13.

Endong, F. P. C. (2015b). Framing the queers and the LGBT right movement in Africa: A study of Nigerian bloggers and web journalists. *Journal of Global Research in Education and Social Sciences*, *6*(4), 50–60.

Endong, F. P. C. (2016). The LGBT right movement in Africa and the myth of the Whiteman's superiority. *Journal of Globalization Studies*, *7*(1), 3–15.

Endong, F. P. C., & Vareba, A. L. (2015). Resisting anti-gay laws through media advocacy and online communities of meaning: A study of Nigerian homosexuals. *Journal for Studies in Management and Planning*, *10*(2), 94–106.

Eom, S., & Fountain, J. E. (2013). Enhancing information services through public-private partnerships: Information technology knowledge transfer underlying structures to develop shared services in the U.S. and Korea. In J. Gil-Garcia (Ed.), *E-government success around the world: Cases, empirical studies, and practical recommendations* (pp. 15–40). Hershey, PA: IGI Global. doi:10.4018/978-1-4666-4173-0.ch002

Epprecht, M. (2010). Understanding homophobia in Africa today. *Perspectives. Political Analysis and Commentary from Africa*, *4*(10), 10–15.

Esteves, O. (2015). *Islamophobia in France, National Report 2015* (E. Bayrakli & F. Hafez, Eds.). Istanbul: SETA.

Esteves, T., Leuenberger, D., & Van Leuven, N. (2012). Reaching citizen 2.0: How government uses social media to send public messages during times of calm and times of crisis. In K. Kloby & M. D'Agostino (Eds.), *Citizen 2.0: Public and governmental interaction through web 2.0 technologies* (pp. 250–268). Hershey, PA: IGI Global. doi:10.4018/978-1-4666-0318-9.ch013

Estevez, E., Fillottrani, P., Janowski, T., & Ojo, A. (2012). Government information sharing: A framework for policy formulation. In Y. Chen & P. Chu (Eds.), *Electronic governance and cross-boundary collaboration: Innovations and advancing tools* (pp. 23–55). Hershey, PA: IGI Global. doi:10.4018/978-1-60960-753-1.ch002

EU refuses to fund Greek border fence with Turkey. (2012). *Daily News*. Retrieved from http://www.hurriyetdailynews.com/eu-refuses-to-fund-greek-border-fence-with-turkey.aspx?pagrlID=238&nID=13346&NewsCatlID=338

EU. Commission Recommendation of 2/10/2016 Addressed to the Hellenic Republic on the Urgent Measures to Be Taken by Greece in View of the Resumption of Transfers Under Regulation 604/2013, C(2016) 871 final (Feb. 10, 2016).

EU. Council Decision 2015/1523 of 14 September 2015 Establishing Provisional Measures in the Area of International Protection for the Benefit of Italy and of Greece, 2015 O.J. (L 239) 146.

EU. Council Decision 2015/1601 of 22 September 2015 Establishing Provisional Measures in the Area of International Protection for the Benefit of Italy and Greece, 2015 O.J. (L 248) 80.

European Agreement on the Abolition of Visas for Refugees, Strasbourg, 20/04/1959, ETS No.031.

European Agreement on Transfer of Responsibility for Refugees, Strasbourg 16/10/1980, ETS No.107.

European Commission. (2016). *Press Release IP/16/211. Commission Adopts Schengen Evaluation Report on Greece and Proposes Recommendations to Address Deficiencies in External Border Management*. Author.

European Commission. Factsheet on the EU-Turkey Agreement. (2016). Retrieved from http://europa.eu/rapid/press-release_MEMO-16-963_en.htm

European Committee for the Prevention of Torture and Inhuman or Degrading Treatment or Punishment (CPT). (2011). *Public statement concerning Greece*. Retrieved from http://www.cpt.coe.int/documents/grc/2011-10-inf-eng.htm

European Convention for the Protection of Human Rights and Fundamental Freedoms, as amended by Protocols Nos. 11 and 14, 4 November 1950, ETS 5.

European Convention on Extradition, Paris, 13/12/1957, ETS No.024.

European Convention on Nationality. Strasbourg, 6.XI.1997, ETS. No. 166.

European Convention on Social Security, Strasbourg 14/12/1972, ETS. 078.

European Council. Foreign Affairs & International Relations. (2016). Retrieved from http://www.consilium.europa.eu/en/press/press-releases/2016/03/18-eu-turkey-statement/

European Court of Human Rights & Council of Europe. (n.d.). *European Convention of Human Rights*. Retrieved from http://www.echr.coe.int/Documents/Convention_ENG.pdf

European Social Charter (revised), Strasbourg, 03/05/1996, ETS No.163.

European Union Agency for Fundamental Rights. (2014). *Handbook on European Law relating to Asylum, Borders and Immigration*. Luxembourg: Publications Office of the European Union.

European Union: Council of the European Union. (2001). *Council Directive 20 01/55/EC of 20 July 2001 on Minimum Standards for Giving Temporary Protection in the Event of a Mass Influx of Displaced Persons and on Measures Promoting a Balance of Efforts Between Member States in Receiving such Persons and Bearing the Consequences Thereof, 7/08/2001, OJ L.212/12-212/23; 7.8.2001, 2001/55/EC*. Retrieved from http://www.refworld.org/docid/3ddcee2e4.html

European Women's Lobby (EWL). (2013). *EWL Barometer on Rape in the EU 2013*. Retrieved from file:///C:/Users/spiros/Downloads/ewl_barometre_final_11092013.pdf

Ezz, I. E. (2008). E-governement emerging trends: Organizational challenges. In A. Anttiroiko (Ed.), *Electronic government: Concepts, methodologies, tools, and applications* (pp. 3721–3737). Hershey, PA: IGI Global. doi:10.4018/978-1-59904-947-2.ch269

Fabri, M. (2009). The Italian style of e-justice in a comparative perspective. In A. Martínez & P. Abat (Eds.), *E-justice: Using information communication technologies in the court system* (pp. 1–19). Hershey, PA: IGI Global. doi:10.4018/978-1-59904-998-4.ch001

Fagbe, T., & Adekola, O. D. (2010). Workplace safety and personnel well-being: The impact of information technology. *International Journal of Green Computing*, *1*(1), 28–33. doi:10.4018/jgc.2010010103

Fagbe, T., & Adekola, O. D. (2011). Workplace safety and personnel well-being: The impact of information technology. In *Global business: Concepts, methodologies, tools and applications* (pp. 1438–1444). Hershey, PA: IGI Global. doi:10.4018/978-1-60960-587-2.ch509

Fanon, F. (2004). *The Wretched of the Earth.* New York: Grove Press.

Farmer, L. (2008). Affective collaborative instruction with librarians. In S. Kelsey & K. St.Amant (Eds.), *Handbook of research on computer mediated communication* (pp. 15–24). Hershey, PA: IGI Global. doi:10.4018/978-1-59904-863-5.ch002

Farrington, J. H. (2007). The new narrative of accessibility: Its potential contribution to discourses in (transport) geography. *Journal of Transport Geography*, *15*(5), 319–330. doi:10.1016/j.jtrangeo.2006.11.007

Favier, L., & Mekhantar, J. (2007). Use of OSS by local e-administration: The French situation. In K. St.Amant & B. Still (Eds.), *Handbook of research on open source software: Technological, economic, and social perspectives* (pp. 428–444). Hershey, PA: IGI Global. doi:10.4018/978-1-59140-999-1.ch033

Fernando, S. (2009). Issues of e-learning in third world countries. In M. Khosrow-Pour (Ed.), *Encyclopedia of information science and technology* (2nd ed.; pp. 2273–2277). Hershey, PA: IGI Global. doi:10.4018/978-1-60566-026-4.ch360

FFP. (2014). *Fragile State Index.* Retrieved from http://www.fundforpeace.org/programs/fsi/fsindex.php

FFP. (n.d.). *Fragile State Index.* Retrieved from http://fsi.fundforpeace.org/indicators

Filho, J. R., & dos Santos Junior, J. R. (2009). Local e-government in Brazil: Poor interaction and local politics as usual. In C. Reddick (Ed.), *Handbook of research on strategies for local e-government adoption and implementation: Comparative studies* (pp. 863–878). Hershey, PA: IGI Global. doi:10.4018/978-1-60566-282-4.ch045

Fletcher, P. D. (2004). Portals and policy: Implications of electronic access to U.S. federal government information services. In A. Pavlichev & G. Garson (Eds.), *Digital government: Principles and best practices* (pp. 52–62). Hershey, PA: IGI Global. doi:10.4018/978-1-59140-122-3.ch004

Fletcher, P. D. (2008). Portals and policy: Implications of electronic access to U.S. federal government information services. In A. Anttiroiko (Ed.), *Electronic government: Concepts, methodologies, tools, and applications* (pp. 3970–3979). Hershey, PA: IGI Global. doi:10.4018/978-1-59904-947-2.ch289

Forlano, L. (2004). The emergence of digital government: International perspectives. In A. Pavlichev & G. Garson (Eds.), *Digital government: Principles and best practices* (pp. 34–51). Hershey, PA: IGI Global. doi:10.4018/978-1-59140-122-3.ch003

Fotiadis, A. (2015). *Border Merchants*. Athens: Potamos.

Foucault, M. (2009). *Security, Territory, Population. Lectures at the College de France 1977-1978*. New York: Picador- Palgrave Macmillan.

FP. (2014a). *Fragile States Index*. Retrieved from http://foreignpolicy.com/fragile-states-2014/

FP. (2014b). *From Failed to Fragile*. Retrieved from http://foreignpolicy.com/fragile-states-2014/#postcards

Fragkoulis, F. (2016). *The gradual Islamisation of Greece*. Retrieved from http://www.kathimerini.gr/850302/opinion/epikairothta/politikh/h-proioysa-islamopoihsh-ths-elladas

Frankel, M. (1995, August 14). Boy Soldiers. *Newsweek*, 45.

Franzel, J. M., & Coursey, D. H. (2004). Government web portals: Management issues and the approaches of five states. In A. Pavlichev & G. Garson (Eds.), *Digital government: Principles and best practices* (pp. 63–77). Hershey, PA: IGI Global. doi:10.4018/978-1-59140-122-3.ch005

FSI Syria. (2015). Retrieved from http://fsi.fundforpeace.org/2015-syria

FSI. (2010). *The Failed States Index*. Retrieved from http://www.fundforpeace.org/global/library/cr-10-99-fs-failedstatesindex2010-1103g.pdf

FSI. (2015). *Fragile State Index 2015*. Retrieved from http://library.fundforpeace.org/library/fragilestatesindex-2015.pdf

Gaivéo, J. M. (2013). Security of ICTs supporting healthcare activities. In M. Cruz-Cunha, I. Miranda, & P. Gonçalves (Eds.), *Handbook of research on ICTs for human-centered healthcare and social care services* (pp. 208–228). Hershey, PA: IGI Global. doi:10.4018/978-1-4666-3986-7.ch011

Garson, G. D. (1999). *Information technology and computer applications in public administration: Issues and trends*. Hershey, PA: IGI Global. doi:10.4018/978-1-87828-952-0

Garson, G. D. (2003). Toward an information technology research agenda for public administration. In G. Garson (Ed.), *Public information technology: Policy and management issues* (pp. 331–357). Hershey, PA: IGI Global. doi:10.4018/978-1-59140-060-8.ch014

Garson, G. D. (2004). The promise of digital government. In A. Pavlichev & G. Garson (Eds.), *Digital government: Principles and best practices* (pp. 2–15). Hershey, PA: IGI Global. doi:10.4018/978-1-59140-122-3.ch001

Garson, G. D. (2007). An information technology research agenda for public administration. In G. Garson (Ed.), *Modern public information technology systems: Issues and challenges* (pp. 365–392). Hershey, PA: IGI Global. doi:10.4018/978-1-59904-051-6.ch018

Gasco, M. (2007). Civil servants' resistance towards e-government development. In A. Anttiroiko & M. Malkia (Eds.), *Encyclopedia of digital government* (pp. 190–195). Hershey, PA: IGI Global. doi:10.4018/978-1-59140-789-8.ch028

Gasco, M. (2008). Civil servants' resistance towards e-government development. In A. Anttiroiko (Ed.), *Electronic government: Concepts, methodologies, tools, and applications* (pp. 2580–2588). Hershey, PA: IGI Global. doi:10.4018/978-1-59904-947-2.ch190

Gates, S., & Reich, S. (2009). Think Again: Child Soldiers. *Foreign Policy*, *22*(May).

Gay and Lesbian Humanist Association. (2007). Imagine no religion. *Gay Humanist Quarterly*, *7*, 31–31.

Gay and Lesbian Humanist Association. (2007). Nigeria: Humanist jeered for supporting gay rights. *Gay Humanist Quarterly*, *7*, 23–24.

German neo-Nazis raised the flag of the Third Reich in Acropolis. (2016). Retrieved from http://www.skai.gr/news/greece/article/306395/germanoi-neonazi-sikosan-simaia-tou-g-raih-stin-akropoli/

Germann Molz, J. (2014). *Travel Connection: tourism. Technology and togetherness in a mobile World*. New York: Routledge.

Germany rape law: "No means No" law passed. (2016). Retrieved from http://www.bbc.com/news/world-europe-36726095

Ghere, R. K. (2010). Accountability and information technology enactment: Implications for social empowerment. In E. Ferro, Y. Dwivedi, J. Gil-Garcia, & M. Williams (Eds.), *Handbook of research on overcoming digital divides: Constructing an equitable and competitive information society* (pp. 515–532). Hershey, PA: IGI Global. doi:10.4018/978-1-60566-699-0.ch028

Gibson, I. W. (2012). Simulation modeling of healthcare delivery. In A. Kolker & P. Story (Eds.), *Management engineering for effective healthcare delivery: Principles and applications* (pp. 69–89). Hershey, PA: IGI Global. doi:10.4018/978-1-60960-872-9.ch003

Giddens, A. (1982). *Sociology. A brief but critical introduction*. Washington, DC: Harcourt Brace, Jovanovich Publishers.

Giddens, A. (1991). *Modernity and self-identity: Self and society in the late modern age*. Stanford, CA: Stanford University Press.

Giddens, A. (1999). Risk and responsibility. *The Modern Law Review*, *62*(1), 1–10. doi:10.1111/1468-2230.00188

Giddens, A. (2009). *The politics of climate change*. Cambridge, UK: Polity Press.

Gil-Garcia, J. R. (2007). Exploring e-government benefits and success factors. In A. Anttiroiko & M. Malkia (Eds.), *Encyclopedia of digital government* (pp. 803–811). Hershey, PA: IGI Global. doi:10.4018/978-1-59140-789-8.ch122

Gil-Garcia, J. R., & González Miranda, F. (2010). E-government and opportunities for participation: The case of the Mexican state web portals. In C. Reddick (Ed.), *Politics, democracy and e-government: Participation and service delivery* (pp. 56–74). Hershey, PA: IGI Global. doi:10.4018/978-1-61520-933-0.ch004

Gillespie, A. (2006). tourist photography and the reverse gaze. *Ethos (Berkeley, Calif.)*, *34*(3), 343–346. doi:10.1525/eth.2006.34.3.343

Goffman, E. (1963). *Stigma*. London: Penguin.

Göker, G. & Keskin, S. (2015). Haber medyası ve mülteciler: Suriyeli mültecilerin Türk yazılı basınındaki temsili. *İletişim Kuram ve Araştırma Dergisi*, *41*, 229-256.

Goldfinch, S. (2012). Public trust in government, trust in e-government, and use of e-government. In Z. Yan (Ed.), *Encyclopedia of cyber behavior* (pp. 987–995). Hershey, PA: IGI Global. doi:10.4018/978-1-4666-0315-8.ch081

Goodyear, M. (2012). Organizational change contributions to e-government project transitions. In S. Aikins (Ed.), *Managing e-government projects: Concepts, issues, and best practices* (pp. 1–21). Hershey, PA: IGI Global. doi:10.4018/978-1-4666-0086-7.ch001

Gordon, A. (2016, October 10). Seven of the nine jihadis involved in the Paris terror attacks entered Europe through Hungary by pretending to be refugees. *Daily Mail*.

Gordon, S., & Mulligan, P. (2003). Strategic models for the delivery of personal financial services: The role of infocracy. In S. Gordon (Ed.), *Computing information technology: The human side* (pp. 220–232). Hershey, PA: IGI Global. doi:10.4018/978-1-93177-752-0.ch014

Gordon, T. F. (2007). Legal knowledge systems. In A. Anttiroiko & M. Malkia (Eds.), *Encyclopedia of digital government* (pp. 1161–1166). Hershey, PA: IGI Global. doi:10.4018/978-1-59140-789-8.ch175

Graham, J. E., & Semich, G. W. (2008). Integrating technology to transform pedagogy: Revisiting the progress of the three phase TUI model for faculty development. In L. Tomei (Ed.), *Adapting information and communication technologies for effective education* (pp. 1–12). Hershey, PA: IGI Global. doi:10.4018/978-1-59904-922-9.ch001

Grandinetti, L., & Pisacane, O. (2012). Web services for healthcare management. In D. Prakash Vidyarthi (Ed.), *Technologies and protocols for the future of internet design: Reinventing the web* (pp. 60–94). Hershey, PA: IGI Global. doi:10.4018/978-1-4666-0203-8.ch004

Greece, R. U. v. (2011). *No. 2237/08*. ECHR. [GC]

Greece, S. D. v. (2008). *No. 53541/07*. ECHR. [GC]

Groenewegen, P., & Wagenaar, F. P. (2008). VO as an alternative to hierarchy in the Dutch police sector. In G. Putnik & M. Cruz-Cunha (Eds.), *Encyclopedia of networked and virtual organizations* (pp. 1851–1857). Hershey, PA: IGI Global. doi:10.4018/978-1-59904-885-7.ch245

Gronlund, A. (2001). Building an infrastructure to manage electronic services. In S. Dasgupta (Ed.), *Managing internet and intranet technologies in organizations: Challenges and opportunities* (pp. 71–103). Hershey, PA: IGI Global. doi:10.4018/978-1-878289-95-7.ch006

Gronlund, A. (2002). Introduction to electronic government: Design, applications and management. In Å. Grönlund (Ed.), *Electronic government: Design, applications and management* (pp. 1–21). Hershey, PA: IGI Global. doi:10.4018/978-1-930708-19-8.ch001

Gul v. Switzerland (1994). 22 E.H.R.R. 93, para. 42.

Gupta, A., Woosley, R., Crk, I., & Sarnikar, S. (2009). An information technology architecture for drug effectiveness reporting and post-marketing surveillance. In J. Tan (Ed.), *Medical informatics: Concepts, methodologies, tools, and applications* (pp. 631–646). Hershey, PA: IGI Global. doi:10.4018/978-1-60566-050-9.ch047

Guterres, A. (2012, May 11). *OIC Ministerial Conference on Refugees in the Muslim world; opening remarks by Mr António Guterres, United Nations High Commissioners for Refugees*. Retrieved from http://www.unhcr.org/admin/hcspeeches/4fb270979/oic-ministerial-conference-refugees-muslim-world-opening-remarks-mr-antonio.html

Guy, G.-G., & Cohn, I. (1994). *Child Soldiers*. Clarendon Press.

Hague, B. (2016). *Athens Muslims worship underground in absence of official mosque*. Retrieved from http://www.abc.net.au/news/2016-06-11/muslims-forced-to-worship-in-underground-mosque-in-athens/7501488

Hall, A., & Holmes, S. (2016, November 6). Germany's New Wall: 12ft-High Barrier - Taller than the Infamous Fortification that Once Divided Berlin - is Constructed in Munich to Protect Locals From a Migrant Camp. *Daily Mail*. Retrieved from http://www.dailymail.co.uk/news/article-3909922/A-12ft-high-Munich-Wall-built-protect-locals-German-city-camp-young-migrants-living-community.html#ixzz4RsRVjK8o

Hallin, A., & Lundevall, K. (2007). mCity: User focused development of mobile services within the city of Stockholm. In I. Kushchu (Ed.), Mobile government: An emerging direction in e-government (pp. 12-29). Hershey, PA: IGI Global. doi:10.4018/978-1-59140-884-0.ch002

Hallin, A., & Lundevall, K. (2009). mCity: User focused development of mobile services within the city of Stockholm. In D. Taniar (Ed.), Mobile computing: Concepts, methodologies, tools, and applications (pp. 3455-3467). Hershey, PA: IGI Global. doi:10.4018/978-1-60566-054-7.ch253

Hallin, A., & Lundevall, K. (2009). mCity: User focused development of mobile services within the city of Stockholm. In S. Clarke (Ed.), Evolutionary concepts in end user productivity and performance: Applications for organizational progress (pp. 268-280). Hershey, PA: IGI Global. doi:10.4018/978-1-60566-136-0.ch017

Hall, S. (1979). Culture, the media and the 'ideological effect. In J. Curan, M. Gurevitch, & J. Woollacott (Eds.), *Mass communication and society* (pp. 315–348). London: Edward Arnold.

Hall, S. (1992). The west and the rest: Discourse and power. In S. Hall & B. Gieben (Eds.), *Formations of modernity* (pp. 275–333). Polity Press and Blackwell Pub.

Hannam, K., Sheller, M., & Urry, J. (2006). Editorial: Mobilities, immobilities and moorings. *Mobilities*, *1*(1), 1–22. doi:10.1080/17450100500489189

Hanson, A. (2005). Overcoming barriers in the planning of a virtual library. In M. Khosrow-Pour (Ed.), *Encyclopedia of information science and technology* (pp. 2255–2259). Hershey, PA: IGI Global. doi:10.4018/978-1-59140-553-5.ch397

Haque, A. (2008). Information technology and surveillance: Implications for public administration in a new word order. In T. Loendorf & G. Garson (Eds.), *Patriotic information systems* (pp. 177–185). Hershey, PA: IGI Global. doi:10.4018/978-1-59904-594-8.ch008

Harding, L., Oltermann, P., & Watt, N. (2016, September 2). Refugees Welcome? How UK and Germany Compare on Migration. *The Guardian*. Retrieved from https://www.theguardian.com/world/2015/sep/02/refugees-welcome-uk-germany-compare-migration

Hardt, M., & Negri, A. (2001). *Empire*. Harvard University Press.

Harvey, D. (1989). *The postmodern condition: An enquiry into the origins of cultural change*. Oxford, UK: Blackwell.

Harvey, D. (1999). Time-space compression and the postmodern condition. *Modernity: Critical Concepts*, *4*, 98–118.

Hauck, R. V., Thatcher, S. M., & Weisband, S. P. (2012). Temporal aspects of information technology use: Increasing shift work effectiveness. In J. Wang (Ed.), *Advancing the service sector with evolving technologies: Techniques and principles* (pp. 87–104). Hershey, PA: IGI Global. doi:10.4018/978-1-4666-0044-7.ch006

Hawk, S., & Witt, T. (2006). Telecommunications courses in information systems programs. *International Journal of Information and Communication Technology Education*, *2*(1), 79–92. doi:10.4018/jicte.2006010107

Hellenic Republic Citizen Protection Ministry. (2012). *Statement by the Minister for Citizen Protection and former Commissioner, Mr. Christos Papoutsis, about the fence in Evros, following the statements made today by the Spokesman for the European Commission, Mr. Michele Cercone.* Retrieved from http://www.minocp.gov.gr/index.php?option=ozo_content&lang=perform=view&id=4080&Itemid=529?option=ozo_search&lang=EN accessed on 03/06/2016

Helman, G. B. & Ratner, S. R. (1992). Saving Failed States. *Foreign Policy*, *89*, 3-20. Retrieved from http://foreignpolicy.com/2010/06/15/saving-failed-states

Helms, M. M., Moore, R., & Ahmadi, M. (2009). Information technology (IT) and the healthcare industry: A SWOT analysis. In J. Tan (Ed.), *Medical informatics: Concepts, methodologies, tools, and applications* (pp. 134–152). Hershey, PA: IGI Global. doi:10.4018/978-1-60566-050-9.ch012

Hendrickson, S. M., & Young, M. E. (2014). Electronic records management at a federally funded research and development center. In J. Krueger (Ed.), *Cases on electronic records and resource management implementation in diverse environments* (pp. 334–350). Hershey, PA: IGI Global. doi:10.4018/978-1-4666-4466-3.ch020

Henman, P. (2010). Social policy and information communication technologies. In J. Martin & L. Hawkins (Eds.), *Information communication technologies for human services education and delivery: Concepts and cases* (pp. 215–229). Hershey, PA: IGI Global. doi:10.4018/978-1-60566-735-5.ch014

Hirsi Jamaa v. the United Kingdom. (2012). [GC]. No. 27765/09, ECHR.

Hismanoglu, M. (2011). Important issues in online education: E-pedagogy and marketing. In U. Demiray & S. Sever (Eds.), *Marketing online education programs: Frameworks for promotion and communication* (pp. 184–209). Hershey, PA: IGI Global. doi:10.4018/978-1-60960-074-7.ch012

Hobbes, T. (2006). *Leviathan*. London: A&C Black.

Hobbes, T. (2013). *Elements of law, natural and political*. Abingdon, UK: Routledge.

Ho, K. K. (2008). The e-government development, IT strategies, and portals of the Hong Kong SAR government. In A. Anttiroiko (Ed.), *Electronic government: Concepts, methodologies, tools, and applications* (pp. 715–733). Hershey, PA: IGI Global. doi:10.4018/978-1-59904-947-2.ch060

Holden, S. H. (2003). The evolution of information technology management at the federal level: Implications for public administration. In G. Garson (Ed.), *Public information technology: Policy and management issues* (pp. 53–73). Hershey, PA: IGI Global. doi:10.4018/978-1-59140-060-8.ch003

Holden, S. H. (2007). The evolution of federal information technology management literature: Does IT finally matter? In G. Garson (Ed.), *Modern public information technology systems: Issues and challenges* (pp. 17–34). Hershey, PA: IGI Global. doi:10.4018/978-1-59904-051-6.ch002

Holland, J. W. (2009). Automation of American criminal justice. In M. Khosrow-Pour (Ed.), *Encyclopedia of information science and technology* (2nd ed.; pp. 300–302). Hershey, PA: IGI Global. doi:10.4018/978-1-60566-026-4.ch051

Holloway, K. (2013). Fair use, copyright, and academic integrity in an online academic environment. In *Digital rights management: Concepts, methodologies, tools, and applications* (pp. 917–928). Hershey, PA: IGI Global. doi:10.4018/978-1-4666-2136-7.ch044

Holmes, O. (2013). *Syria's children shot at, tortured, raped - charity report*. Retrieved from http://uk.reuters.com/article/uk-syria-crisis-children-idUKBRE92C00R20130313

Horiuchi, C. (2005). E-government databases. In L. Rivero, J. Doorn, & V. Ferraggine (Eds.), *Encyclopedia of database technologies and applications* (pp. 206–210). Hershey, PA: IGI Global. doi:10.4018/978-1-59140-560-3.ch035

Horiuchi, C. (2006). Creating IS quality in government settings. In E. Duggan & J. Reichgelt (Eds.), *Measuring information systems delivery quality* (pp. 311–327). Hershey, PA: IGI Global. doi:10.4018/978-1-59140-857-4.ch014

How is the migrant crisis dividing EU countries?. (2016). Retrieved from http://www.bbc.com/news/world-europe-34278886

Howie, L. (2010). *Terror on the Screen Witnesses and the Re-animation of 9/11 as Image-event, Popular Culture and Pornography*. Washington, DC: New Academia Publishing.

Howie, L. (2010). *Terror on the Screen*. Washington, DC: New Academia Publishing.

Howie, L. (2011). The were created by Man… and they have a plan: Subjective and objective violence in Battlestar Gallactica and the War on terror. *International Zizek Studies.*, *5*(2), 1–19.

Howie, L. (2012). *Witnesses to Terror: Understanding the Meanings and Consequences of Terrorism*. Hampshire, UK: Palgrave Macmillan. doi:10.1057/9781137271761

Hrant Dink Foundation. (2013). *Medyada nefret söylemi ve ayrımcı dil eylül - aralık 2013 raporu*. Retrieved from http://nefretsoylemi.org/rapor/Eylul-Aralik2013_nefretsoylemi_ayrimcisoylem_raporu.pdf

HRW. (2002). *My Gun was as Tall as Me: Child Soldiers in Burma*. Retrieved from http://www.hrw.org/legacy/reports/2002/burma/

HRW. (2007). *Maoists Should Release Child Soldiers Today*. Retrieved from http:// www.hrw.org/en/news/2007/05/06/nepal-maoists-should-release-child-soldiers-now

Hsiao, N., Chu, P., & Lee, C. (2012). Impact of e-governance on businesses: Model development and case study. In *Digital democracy: Concepts, methodologies, tools, and applications* (pp. 1407–1425). Hershey, PA: IGI Global. doi:10.4018/978-1-4666-1740-7.ch070

Huang, T., & Lee, C. (2010). Evaluating the impact of e-government on citizens: Cost-benefit analysis. In C. Reddick (Ed.), *Citizens and e-government: Evaluating policy and management* (pp. 37–52). Hershey, PA: IGI Global. doi:10.4018/978-1-61520-931-6.ch003

Hubert, P. (2016). *Frontex -Greece- unredacted Original Documents*. Retrieved from https://www.documentcloud.org/documents/3013909-Frontex-Greece-unredacted.html

Hufton, O. (2003). *History of Women in Europe 1500-1800*. Athens: Nefeli.

Huggler, J. (2016). *Germany passes 'no means no' rape law*. Retrieved from http://www.telegraph.co.uk/news/2016/07/07/germany-passes-no-means-no-rape-law/

Human Rights Commissioner Cancels Russia Visit. (2016, October 11). Retrieved from https://themoscowtimes.com/news/human-rights-commissioner-cancels-russia-visit-55684

Hunter, M. G., Diochon, M., Pugsley, D., & Wright, B. (2002). Unique challenges for small business adoption of information technology: The case of the Nova Scotia ten. In S. Burgess (Ed.), *Managing information technology in small business: Challenges and solutions* (pp. 98–117). Hershey, PA: IGI Global. doi:10.4018/978-1-930708-35-8.ch006

Hürriyet. (2015, July 21). *Suriyeli çocuğa esnaftan dayak*. Retrieved from http://www.hurriyet.com.tr/suriyeli-cocuga-esnaftan-dayak-29603820

Hurskainen, J. (2003). Integration of business systems and applications in merger and alliance: Case metso automation. In T. Reponen (Ed.), *Information technology enabled global customer service* (pp. 207–225). Hershey, PA: IGI Global. doi:10.4018/978-1-59140-048-6.ch012

Iazzolino, G., & Pietrantonio, R. (2011). The soveria.it project: A best practice of e-government in southern Italy. In D. Piaggesi, K. Sund, & W. Castelnovo (Eds.), *Global strategy and practice of e-governance: Examples from around the world* (pp. 34–56). Hershey, PA: IGI Global. doi:10.4018/978-1-60960-489-9.ch003

Ignatieff, M. (2013). *The lesser evil: Political ethics in an age of terror*. Princeton, NJ: Princeton University Press.

i. Martinez, A. C. (2008). Accessing administration's information via internet in Spain. In F. Tan (Ed.), *Global information technologies: Concepts, methodologies, tools, and applications* (pp. 2558–2573). Hershey, PA: IGI Global. doi:10.4018/978-1-59904-939-7.ch186

Imran, A., & Gregor, S. (2012). A process model for successful e-government adoption in the least developed countries: A case of Bangladesh. In F. Tan (Ed.), *International comparisons of information communication technologies: Advancing applications* (pp. 321–350). Hershey, PA: IGI Global. doi:10.4018/978-1-61350-480-2.ch014

Innerarity, D. (2013). Power and knowledge: The politics of the knowledge society. *European Journal of Social Theory*, *16*(1), 3–16. doi:10.1177/1368431012468801

Inoue, Y., & Bell, S. T. (2005). Electronic/digital government innovation, and publishing trends with IT. In M. Khosrow-Pour (Ed.), *Encyclopedia of information science and technology* (pp. 1018–1023). Hershey, PA: IGI Global. doi:10.4018/978-1-59140-553-5.ch180

International Humanist and Ethical Union. (2012). *Freedom of thought 2012. A global report on discrimination against humanists, atheists and the nonreligious*. New York: IHEU.

International Network of Civil Liberties Organizations. (2015). *Drawing the line: Tackling tensions between religious freedom and equality*. London: INCLO.

International Organization for Migration. (2015). World Migration Report 2015: Migrants and Cities – New Partnerships to Manage Mobility. Author.

International Organization of Migration Report for the First Semester of 2016. (n.d.). Retrieved from http://dtmodk.iom.int/docs/Q2_Flows_Compilation_Report.pdf

Inter-Parliamentary Union. (2015). *Migration, human rights and governance*. Retrieved from http://www.refworld.org/docid/57b6e1697.html

Iris-Scanning Technology streamlines Refugee Registration Process. (2014). Retrieved from http://www.growthgate.com/Iris-scanning-technology-streamlines-refugee-registration-process

Irwin, W. (2005). Computers, Caves and Oracle: Neo and Socrates. In W. Irwin (Ed.), *The Matrix and Philosophy* (pp. 5–15). Chicago, IL: Open Court.

Islam, M. M., & Ehsan, M. (2013). Understanding e-governance: A theoretical approach. In M. Islam & M. Ehsan (Eds.), *From government to e-governance: Public administration in the digital age* (pp. 38–49). Hershey, PA: IGI Global. doi:10.4018/978-1-4666-1909-8.ch003

Jaeger, B. (2009). E-government and e-democracy in the making. In M. Khosrow-Pour (Ed.), *Encyclopedia of information science and technology* (2nd ed.; pp. 1318–1322). Hershey, PA: IGI Global. doi:10.4018/978-1-60566-026-4.ch208

Jaichand, V., & Suksi, M. (Eds.). (2009). *60 Years of the Universal Declaration of Human Rights in Europe*. Antwerp, Belgium: Intersentia.

Jain, R. B. (2007). Revamping the administrative structure and processes in India for online diplomacy. In A. Anttiroiko & M. Malkia (Eds.), *Encyclopedia of digital government* (pp. 1418–1423). Hershey, PA: IGI Global. doi:10.4018/978-1-59140-789-8.ch217

Jain, R. B. (2008). Revamping the administrative structure and processes in India for online diplomacy. In A. Anttiroiko (Ed.), *Electronic government: Concepts, methodologies, tools, and applications* (pp. 3142–3149). Hershey, PA: IGI Global. doi:10.4018/978-1-59904-947-2.ch233

Jakobsen, L. K. (2015). Experimentation in humanitarian locations: UNHCR and biometric registration of Afghan refugees. *Security Dialogue*, *46*(2).

Jauhiainen, J. S., & Inkinen, T. (2009). E-governance and the information society in periphery. In C. Reddick (Ed.), *Handbook of research on strategies for local e-government adoption and implementation: Comparative studies* (pp. 497–514). Hershey, PA: IGI Global. doi:10.4018/978-1-60566-282-4.ch026

Jensen, M. J. (2009). Electronic democracy and citizen influence in government. In C. Reddick (Ed.), *Handbook of research on strategies for local e-government adoption and implementation: Comparative studies* (pp. 288–305). Hershey, PA: IGI Global. doi:10.4018/978-1-60566-282-4.ch015

Jerusalem Institute of Justice. (2015). *Freedom of religion. A human rights-based approach to discrimination against religious minorities in the Palestinian Authority*. Jerusalem: Jerusalem Institute of Justice.

Jiao, Y., Hurson, A. R., Potok, T. E., & Beckerman, B. G. (2009). Integrating mobile-based systems with healthcare databases. In J. Erickson (Ed.), *Database technologies: Concepts, methodologies, tools, and applications* (pp. 484–504). Hershey, PA: IGI Global. doi:10.4018/978-1-60566-058-5.ch031

Johnson, T. (2010, June 29). *The Organization of the Islamic Conference*. Retrieved from http://www.cfr.org/religion/organization-islamic-conference/p22563

Joia, L. A. (2002). A systematic model to integrate information technology into metabusinesses: A case study in the engineering realms. In F. Tan (Ed.), *Advanced topics in global information management* (Vol. 1, pp. 250–267). Hershey, PA: IGI Global. doi:10.4018/978-1-930708-43-3.ch016

Joint Statement of Heads of Police Services from the Meeting Held in Zagreb, Croatia, on 18th February 2016. (n.d.). Retrieved from http://www.mup.hr/UserDocsImages/topvijesti/2016/veljaca/migranti_sastanak/joint_statement.pdf

Jones, T. H., & Song, I. (2000). Binary equivalents of ternary relationships in entity-relationship modeling: A logical decomposition approach. *Journal of Database Management, 11*(2), 12–19. doi:10.4018/jdm.2000040102

Journal of the Hellenic Republic Government. (2012). *Law 4075, no.89, par 59, 11/04/2012*. Retrieved from http://www.tapit.gr/attachments/nomoi/fek89-N4075.pdf

Juana-Espinosa, S. D. (2007). Empirical study of the municipalitites' motivations for adopting online presence. In L. Al-Hakim (Ed.), *Global e-government: Theory, applications and benchmarking* (pp. 261–279). Hershey, PA: IGI Global. doi:10.4018/978-1-59904-027-1.ch015

Jun, K., & Weare, C. (2012). Bridging from e-government practice to e-government research: Past trends and future directions. In K. Bwalya & S. Zulu (Eds.), *Handbook of research on e-government in emerging economies: Adoption, e-participation, and legal frameworks* (pp. 263–289). Hershey, PA: IGI Global. doi:10.4018/978-1-4666-0324-0.ch013

Junqueira, A., Diniz, E. H., & Fernandez, M. (2010). Electronic government implementation projects with multiple agencies: Analysis of the electronic invoice project under PMBOK framework. In J. Cordoba-Pachon & A. Ochoa-Arias (Eds.), *Systems thinking and e-participation: ICT in the governance of society* (pp. 135–153). Hershey, PA: IGI Global. doi:10.4018/978-1-60566-860-4.ch009

Juntunen, A. (2009). Joint service development with the local authorities. In C. Reddick (Ed.), *Handbook of research on strategies for local e-government adoption and implementation: Comparative studies* (pp. 902–920). Hershey, PA: IGI Global. doi:10.4018/978-1-60566-282-4.ch047

Kamel, S. (2001). *Using DSS for crisis management*. Hershey, PA: IGI Global. doi:10.4018/978-1-87828-961-2.ch020

Kamel, S. (2006). DSS for strategic decision making. In M. Khosrow-Pour (Ed.), *Cases on information technology and organizational politics & culture* (pp. 230–246). Hershey, PA: IGI Global. doi:10.4018/978-1-59904-411-8.ch015

Kamel, S. (2009). The software industry in Egypt as a potential contributor to economic growth. In M. Khosrow-Pour (Ed.), *Encyclopedia of information science and technology* (2nd ed.; pp. 3531–3537). Hershey, PA: IGI Global. doi:10.4018/978-1-60566-026-4.ch562

Kamel, S., & Hussein, M. (2008). Xceed: Pioneering the contact center industry in Egypt. *Journal of Cases on Information Technology*, *10*(1), 67–91. doi:10.4018/jcit.2008010105

Kamel, S., & Wahba, K. (2003). The use of a hybrid model in web-based education: "The Global campus project. In A. Aggarwal (Ed.), *Web-based education: Learning from experience* (pp. 331–346). Hershey, PA: IGI Global. doi:10.4018/978-1-59140-102-5.ch020

Kanter, J. (2016, March 18). European Union reaches deal with Turkey to return new asylum seekers. *The New York Times*.

Kaoma, J. K. (2015). *Colonizing African Values – How the US Christian right is transforming sexual politics in Africa*. Somerville: Political Research Associates.

Kap, D. (2014). Suriyeli mülteciler: Türkiye'nin müstakbel vatandaşları. *Akademik Perspektif*, *1*(3), 30–35.

Kaplan, S. (2008). Fixing Fragile States. Policy Review, 152, 63-77.

Kaplan, R. D. (1994, February). The Coming Anarchy. *Atlantic Monthly*, 44.

Karaim, R. (2011). Gay Rights. Has the movement's success sparked a backlash?. *CQ Global Researcher*, *5*(5), 107–132.

Kardaras, D. K., & Papathanassiou, E. A. (2008). An exploratory study of the e-government services in Greece. In G. Garson & M. Khosrow-Pour (Eds.), *Handbook of research on public information technology* (pp. 162–174). Hershey, PA: IGI Global. doi:10.4018/978-1-59904-857-4.ch016

Kassahun, A. E., Molla, A., & Sarkar, P. (2012). Government process reengineering: What we know and what we need to know. In *Digital democracy: Concepts, methodologies, tools, and applications* (pp. 1730–1752). Hershey, PA: IGI Global. doi:10.4018/978-1-4666-1740-7.ch086

Katsiaounis, N. (2015). *Crime and immigrant: Interview with Stefanos Rozanis*. Retrieved from http://www.kenosfakelos.blogspot.gr/2015/10/blog-post.html

Kellner, D. (2005). Baudrillard, Globalization and Terrorism: Some comments in recent adventures of the Image and Spectable on the occasion of Baudrillard's 75th birthday. *Baudrillard Studies*, *2*(1), 1–18.

Khan, B. (2005). Technological issues. In B. Khan (Ed.), *Managing e-learning strategies: Design, delivery, implementation and evaluation* (pp. 154–180). Hershey, PA: IGI Global. doi:10.4018/978-1-59140-634-1.ch004

Khasawneh, A., Bsoul, M., Obeidat, I., & Al Azzam, I. (2012). Technology fears: A study of e-commerce loyalty perception by Jordanian customers. In J. Wang (Ed.), *Advancing the service sector with evolving technologies: Techniques and principles* (pp. 158–165). Hershey, PA: IGI Global. doi:10.4018/978-1-4666-0044-7.ch010

Khatibi, V., & Montazer, G. A. (2012). E-research methodology. In A. Juan, T. Daradoumis, M. Roca, S. Grasman, & J. Faulin (Eds.), *Collaborative and distributed e-research: Innovations in technologies, strategies and applications* (pp. 62–81). Hershey, PA: IGI Global. doi:10.4018/978-1-4666-0125-3.ch003

Kidd, T. (2011). The dragon in the school's backyard: A review of literature on the uses of technology in urban schools. In L. Tomei (Ed.), *Online courses and ICT in education: Emerging practices and applications* (pp. 242–257). Hershey, PA: IGI Global. doi:10.4018/978-1-60960-150-8.ch019

Kidd, T. T. (2010). My experience tells the story: Exploring technology adoption from a qualitative perspective - A pilot study. In H. Song & T. Kidd (Eds.), *Handbook of research on human performance and instructional technology* (pp. 247–262). Hershey, PA: IGI Global. doi:10.4018/978-1-60566-782-9.ch015

Kieley, B., Lane, G., Paquet, G., & Roy, J. (2002). e-Government in Canada: Services online or public service renewal? In Å. Grönlund (Ed.), Electronic government: Design, applications and management (pp. 340-355). Hershey, PA: IGI Global. doi:10.4018/978-1-930708-19-8.ch016

Kim, P. (2012). "Stay out of the way! My kid is video blogging through a phone!": A lesson learned from math tutoring social media for children in underserved communities. In *Wireless technologies: Concepts, methodologies, tools and applications* (pp. 1415–1428). Hershey, PA: IGI Global. doi:10.4018/978-1-61350-101-6.ch517

Kingsley, P. (2016, March 9). EU-Turkey refugee deal - Q&A. *The Guardian.*

Kinninmont, J. (2015, September 8). *Why aren't Gulf countries taking in Syrian refugees?.* Retrieved from https://www.chathamhouse.org/expert/comment/why-aren-t-gulf-countries-taking-syrian-refugees

Kioupkiolis, A. (2014). Towards a Regime of Post-political Biopower? Dispatches from Greece, 2010-2012. *Theory, Culture and Society, 31.* Retrieved from http://www.tcs.sagepub.com/content/31/1/143.abstract

Kirlidog, M. (2010). Financial aspects of national ICT strategies. In S. Kamel (Ed.), *E-strategies for technological diffusion and adoption: National ICT approaches for socioeconomic development* (pp. 277–292). Hershey, PA: IGI Global. doi:10.4018/978-1-60566-388-3.ch016

Kisielnicki, J. (2006). Transfer of information and knowledge in the project management. In E. Coakes & S. Clarke (Eds.), *Encyclopedia of communities of practice in information and knowledge management* (pp. 544–551). Hershey, PA: IGI Global. doi:10.4018/978-1-59140-556-6.ch091

Kittner, M., & Van Slyke, C. (2006). Reorganizing information technology services in an academic environment. In M. Khosrow-Pour (Ed.), *Cases on the human side of information technology* (pp. 49–66). Hershey, PA: IGI Global. doi:10.4018/978-1-59904-405-7.ch004

Knoell, H. D. (2008). Semi virtual workplaces in German financial service enterprises. In P. Zemliansky & K. St.Amant (Eds.), *Handbook of research on virtual workplaces and the new nature of business practices* (pp. 570–581). Hershey, PA: IGI Global. doi:10.4018/978-1-59904-893-2.ch041

Koama, K. (2010). The US Christian right and the attack on gay in Africa. *The Public Eye Magazine*, *9*(10), 37–68.

Koh, S. L., & Maguire, S. (2009). Competing in the age of information technology in a developing economy: Experiences of an Indian bank. In S. Koh & S. Maguire (Eds.), *Information and communication technologies management in turbulent business environments* (pp. 326–350). Hershey, PA: IGI Global. doi:10.4018/978-1-60566-424-8.ch018

Kollmann, T., & Häsel, M. (2009). Competence of information technology professionals in internet-based ventures. In A. Cater-Steel (Ed.), *Information technology governance and service management: Frameworks and adaptations* (pp. 239–253). Hershey, PA: IGI Global. doi:10.4018/978-1-60566-008-0.ch013

Kollmann, T., & Häsel, M. (2009). Competence of information technology professionals in internet-based ventures. In I. Lee (Ed.), *Electronic business: Concepts, methodologies, tools, and applications* (pp. 1905–1919). Hershey, PA: IGI Global. doi:10.4018/978-1-60566-056-1.ch118

Kollmann, T., & Häsel, M. (2010). Competence of information technology professionals in internet-based ventures. In *Electronic services: Concepts, methodologies, tools and applications* (pp. 1551–1565). Hershey, PA: IGI Global. doi:10.4018/978-1-61520-967-5.ch094

Kolompar v. Belgium. (1994). [GC] No. 11613/85, ECHR. para. 123.

Korsmeyer, C. (2005). Seeing, Believing, touching, Truth. In W. Irwin (Ed.), *The Matrix and Philosophy* (pp. 41–52). Chicago, IL: Open Court.

Korstanje, M. E. (2013). The archetype of terrorism: how 11/9 changed the world?. *Sincronía*, (63), 8-22.

Korstanje, M. (2015). *A Difficult World, examining the roots of Capitalism.* New York: Nova Science Publishers.

Korstanje, M. E. (2010). Ironman. *Cultura International Journal of Philosophy of Culture and Axiology*, *7*(2), 188–203. doi:10.5840/cultura20107214

Korstanje, M. E. (2015). *A Difficult World: examining the roots of Capitalism.* New York, NY: Nova Science Pubs.

Korstanje, M. E. (2016a). *The Rise of Thana Capitalism and tourism.* Abingdon, UK: Routledge.

Korstanje, M. E. (2016b). *Tourism and Terrorism.* New Delhi: Studium Press LCC.

Korstanje, M. E., & Olsen, D. H. (2011). The discourse of risk in horror movies post 9/11: Hospitality and hostility in perspective. *International Journal of Tourism Anthropology, 1*(3-4), 304–317. doi:10.1504/IJTA.2011.043712

Korstanje, M. E., & Tarlow, P. (2012). Being lost: Tourism, risk and vulnerability in the post-9/11entertainment industry. *Journal of Tourism and Cultural Change, 10*(1), 22–33. doi:10.1080/14766825.2011.639455

Kosik, K. (2003). *The Crisis of Modernity.* Athens: Psichogios.

Kraemer, K., & King, J. L. (2006). Information technology and administrative reform: Will e-government be different? *International Journal of Electronic Government Research, 2*(1), 1–20. doi:10.4018/jegr.2006010101

Kraemer, K., & King, J. L. (2008). Information technology and administrative reform: Will e-government be different? In D. Norris (Ed.), *E-government research: Policy and management* (pp. 1–20). Hershey, PA: IGI Global. doi:10.4018/978-1-59904-913-7.ch001

Kristeva, J. (1991). Extranjeros para nosotros mismos, trad. de X. *Gispert, Barcelona, Plaza & Janes Editores (Hombre y Sociedad).*

Küçükcan, T. (1999). Re-claiming Identity: Ethnicity, Religion and Politics among Turkish-Muslims in Bulgaria and Greece. *Journal of Muslim Minority Affairs, 19*(1). Retrieved from http://s3.amazonaws.com/academia.edu.documents/36047675/Re-claiming_Identity__Ethnicity__Religion_and_Politics_among_Turkish-Muslims_in_Bulgaria_and_Gree.pdf?AWSAccessKeyId=AKIAJ56TQJRTWSMTNPEA&Expires=1467821530&Signature=ips1%2FW6wJvt3ESw%2FS18jAo4KcKA%3D&response-content-disposition=inline%3B%20filename%3DRe_claiming_identity_ethnicity_religion.pdf

Labropoulou, E., & Hunt, K. (2016). *Greece starts clearing Idomeni migrant border camp.* Retrieved from http://edition.cnn.com/2016/05/24/europe/greece-clears-migrant-camp/

Lambach, D. (2007). Close Encounters in the Third Dimension: The Regional Effects of State Failure. In State Failure Revisited I, Globalization of Security and Neighborhood Effects. Institute for Development and Peace, University of Duisburg-Essen (INEF Report, 87/2007).

Lampathaki, F., Tsiakaliaris, C., Stasis, A., & Charalabidis, Y. (2011). National interoperability frameworks: The way forward. In Y. Charalabidis (Ed.), *Interoperability in digital public services and administration: Bridging e-government and e-business* (pp. 1–24). Hershey, PA: IGI Global. doi:10.4018/978-1-61520-887-6.ch001

Lan, Z., & Scott, C. R. (1996). The relative importance of computer-mediated information versus conventional non-computer-mediated information in public managerial decision making. *Information Resources Management Journal, 9*(1), 27–0. doi:10.4018/irmj.1996010103

Lash, S. M., Urry, S. L. J., & Urry, J. (1993). *Economies of signs and space* (Vol. 26). London: Sage.

Law, W. (2004). *Public sector data management in a developing economy*. Hershey, PA: IGI Global. doi:10.4018/978-1-59140-259-6.ch034

Law, W. K. (2005). Information resources development challenges in a cross-cultural environment. In M. Khosrow-Pour (Ed.), *Encyclopedia of information science and technology* (pp. 1476–1481). Hershey, PA: IGI Global. doi:10.4018/978-1-59140-553-5.ch259

Law, W. K. (2009). Cross-cultural challenges for information resources management. In M. Khosrow-Pour (Ed.), *Encyclopedia of information science and technology* (2nd ed.; pp. 840–846). Hershey, PA: IGI Global. doi:10.4018/978-1-60566-026-4.ch136

Law, W. K. (2011). Cross-cultural challenges for information resources management. In *Global business: Concepts, methodologies, tools and applications* (pp. 1924–1932). Hershey, PA: IGI Global. doi:10.4018/978-1-60960-587-2.ch704

Lévi-Strauss, C. (2013). *Myth and meaning*. London: Routledge.

Locke, J. (1988). *Locke: Two treatises of government student edition*. Cambridge, UK: Cambridge University Press. doi:10.1017/CBO9780511810268

Longino, H. (1990). *Science as a Social Knowledge*. Princeton, NJ: Princeton University Press.

Louled Massoud v. Malta. (2010). [GC] No. 24340/08, ECHR.

Lyrintzis, C., & Nikolakopoulos, E. (2004). *Political System and Elections in Greece*. Retrieved from http://video.minpress.gr/wwwminpress/aboutgreece/aboutgreece_political_system.pdf

M.S.S. and Rahimi Groups v. Greece. (2015) Nos. 30696/09, 8687/08. Supervision of the Execution of the Court's Judgments.

Macaulay, J. R. (2008). *What the Bible says about homosexuality to Nigerian*. Retrieved April 4, 2016, from http://www.rowland-jide-macaulay/what-the-bible-says-about-homosexuality-to-nigerians.htm

Maccannell, D. (1988). Turismo e Identidad [Tourism & Identity]. In Teodorov Tzvetan. Madrid: Juncar Edition.

MacCannell, D. (1973). Staged authenticity: Arrangements of social space in tourist settings. *American Journal of Sociology*, *79*(3), 589–603. doi:10.1086/225585

MacCannell, D. (1976). *The tourist: A new theory of the leisure class*. Berkeley, CA: University of California Press.

MacCannell, D. (1984). Reconstructed ethnicity tourism and cultural identity in third world communities. *Annals of Tourism Research*, *11*(3), 375–391. doi:10.1016/0160-7383(84)90028-8

MacCannell, D. (1992). *Empty meeting grounds: The tourist papers*. London: Routledge. doi:10.4324/9780203412145

MacEoin, D. (2015, September 16). *The Arab states and the refugees*. Retrieved from https://www.gatestoneinstitute.org/6502/refugees-arab-states

Mackey, R. (2015, September 3). Hungarian leader rebuked for saying Muslim migrants must be blocked 'to keep Europe Christian'. *The New York Times*.

Magen, A. (2012). On Political Order and the Arab Spring. *Israel Journal of Foreign Affairs VI, 1*(1), 9–21. doi:10.1080/23739770.2012.11446483

Mahammad and Others v. Greece (2015) [GC] No. 48352/12, 15 April 2015, ECHR

Mahmundi and others v. Greece (2012) [GC] No 14902/10, ECHR, para. 66.

Maiani, F. (2008). *The Concept of "Persecution" in Refugee Law: Indeterminacy, Context-sensitivity, and the Quest for a Principled Approach*. Retrieved from https://dossiersgrihl.revues.org/3896#bodyftn24

Malkia, M., & Savolainen, R. (2004). eTransformation in government, politics and society: Conceptual framework and introduction. In M. Malkia, A. Anttiroiko, & R. Savolainen (Eds.), eTransformation in governance: New directions in government and politics (pp. 1-21). Hershey, PA: IGI Global. doi:10.4018/978-1-59140-130-8.ch001

Mandrou, I. (2016). *The Council of State dismissed appeal for building mosque*. Retrieved from http://www.kathimerini.gr/866601/article/epikairothta/ellada/to-ste-aperriye-prosfyges-gia-temenos

Mandujano, S. (2011). Network manageability security. In D. Kar & M. Syed (Eds.), *Network security, administration and management: Advancing technology and practice* (pp. 158–181). Hershey, PA: IGI Global. doi:10.4018/978-1-60960-777-7.ch009

Marich, M. J., Schooley, B. L., & Horan, T. A. (2012). A normative enterprise architecture for guiding end-to-end emergency response decision support. In M. Jennex (Ed.), *Managing crises and disasters with emerging technologies: Advancements* (pp. 71–87). Hershey, PA: IGI Global. doi:10.4018/978-1-4666-0167-3.ch006

Markov, R., & Okujava, S. (2008). Costs, benefits, and risks of e-government portals. In G. Putnik & M. Cruz-Cunha (Eds.), *Encyclopedia of networked and virtual organizations* (pp. 354–363). Hershey, PA: IGI Global. doi:10.4018/978-1-59904-885-7.ch047

Martin, N., & Rice, J. (2013). Evaluating and designing electronic government for the future: Observations and insights from Australia. In V. Weerakkody (Ed.), *E-government services design, adoption, and evaluation* (pp. 238–258). Hershey, PA: IGI Global. doi:10.4018/978-1-4666-2458-0.ch014

Marx, K. (1962). Frammento dell'appendice della dissertazione dottorale. In A. Sabetti (Ed.), *Sulla fondazione del materialism storico* (pp. 398–217). Florence, Italy: Observatore Romano.

Marx, K. (1973). *Grundrisse: Foundation of the critique of political economy.Trans. Martin Nicolaus*. Harmondsworth, UK: Penguin.

Mastin, L. (2011). *Arguments for atheism*. Retrieved October 16, 2016, from http://www.argument-for-atheism-mastin-luke.com

Matunhu, J. (2011). A critique of modernization and dependency theories in Africa: Critical assessment. *African Journal of History and Culture*, *3*(5), 65–72.

Mauss, M. (2000). *The gift: The form and reason for exchange in archaic societies (No. 378)*. New York: WW Norton & Company.

Mazrui, A. (1994, Fall). The Message of Rwanda: Recolonize Africa? *New Perspectives Quarterly*, 18.

Mbarika, V. W., Meso, P. N., & Musa, P. F. (2006). A disconnect in stakeholders' perceptions from emerging realities of teledensity growth in Africa's least developed countries. In M. Hunter & F. Tan (Eds.), *Advanced topics in global information management* (Vol. 5, pp. 263–282). Hershey, PA: IGI Global. doi:10.4018/978-1-59140-923-6.ch012

Mbarika, V. W., Meso, P. N., & Musa, P. F. (2008). A disconnect in stakeholders' perceptions from emerging realities of teledensity growth in Africa's least developed countries. In F. Tan (Ed.), *Global information technologies: Concepts, methodologies, tools, and applications* (pp. 2948–2962). Hershey, PA: IGI Global. doi:10.4018/978-1-59904-939-7.ch209

McCauley, C., & Moskalenko, S. (2008). Mechanisms of political radicalization: Pathways toward terrorism. *Terrorism and Political Violence*, *20*(3), 415–433. doi:10.1080/09546550802073367

McCauley, C., & Moskalenko, S. (2011). *Friction: How radicalization happens to them and us*. Oxford, UK: Oxford University Press.

Means, T., Olson, E., & Spooner, J. (2013). Discovering ways that don't work on the road to success: Strengths and weaknesses revealed by an active learning studio classroom project. In A. Benson, J. Moore, & S. Williams van Rooij (Eds.), *Cases on educational technology planning, design, and implementation: A project management perspective* (pp. 94–113). Hershey, PA: IGI Global. doi:10.4018/978-1-4666-4237-9.ch006

Melitski, J., Holzer, M., Kim, S., Kim, C., & Rho, S. (2008). Digital government worldwide: An e-government assessment of municipal web sites. In G. Garson & M. Khosrow-Pour (Eds.), *Handbook of research on public information technology* (pp. 790–804). Hershey, PA: IGI Global. doi:10.4018/978-1-59904-857-4.ch069

Memmola, M., Palumbo, G., & Rossini, M. (2009). Web & RFID technology: New frontiers in costing and process management for rehabilitation medicine. In L. Al-Hakim & M. Memmola (Eds.), *Business web strategy: Design, alignment, and application* (pp. 145–169). Hershey, PA: IGI Global. doi:10.4018/978-1-60566-024-0.ch008

Meng, Z., Fahong, Z., & Lei, L. (2008). Information technology and environment. In Y. Kurihara, S. Takaya, H. Harui, & H. Kamae (Eds.), *Information technology and economic development* (pp. 201–212). Hershey, PA: IGI Global. doi:10.4018/978-1-59904-579-5.ch014

Menninghaus, W., & Gunn, J. (2008). *Benjamin's Theory of Myth and Benjamin's Magic*. Athens: Ipsilon.

Mentzingen de Moraes, A. J., Ferneda, E., Costa, I., & Spinola, M. D. (2011). Practical approach for implementation of governance process in IT: Information technology areas. In N. Shi & G. Silvius (Eds.), *Enterprise IT governance, business value and performance measurement* (pp. 19–40). Hershey, PA: IGI Global. doi:10.4018/978-1-60566-346-3.ch002

Merwin, G. A. Jr, McDonald, J. S., & Odera, L. C. (2008). Economic development: Government's cutting edge in IT. In M. Raisinghani (Ed.), *Handbook of research on global information technology management in the digital economy* (pp. 1–37). Hershey, PA: IGI Global. doi:10.4018/978-1-59904-875-8.ch001

Meso, P. N., & Duncan, N. B. (2002). Can national information infrastructures enhance social development in the least developed countries? In F. Tan (Ed.), *Advanced topics in global information management* (Vol. 1, pp. 207–226). Hershey, PA: IGI Global. doi:10.4018/978-1-930708-43-3.ch014

Meso, P., & Duncan, N. (2002). Can national information infrastructures enhance social development in the least developed countries? An empirical investigation. In M. Dadashzadeh (Ed.), *Information technology management in developing countries* (pp. 23–51). Hershey, PA: IGI Global. doi:10.4018/978-1-931777-03-2.ch002

Middleton, M. (2008). Evaluation of e-government web sites. In G. Garson & M. Khosrow-Pour (Eds.), *Handbook of research on public information technology* (pp. 699–710). Hershey, PA: IGI Global. doi:10.4018/978-1-59904-857-4.ch063

Migdal, J. (1988). Strong Societies and Weak States: StateSociety Relations and State Capabilities in the Third World. Academic Press.

Miles, W. (2002). Auschwitz: Museum interpretation and Darker Tourism. *Annals of Tourism Research, 29*(4), 1175–1178. doi:10.1016/S0160-7383(02)00054-3

Mingers, J. (2010). Pluralism, realism, and truth: The keys to knowledge in information systems research. In D. Paradice (Ed.), *Emerging systems approaches in information technologies: Concepts, theories, and applications* (pp. 86–98). Hershey, PA: IGI Global. doi:10.4018/978-1-60566-976-2.ch006

Minister of Public Order and Citizen Protection. (2013). *Reply of the Press Office of the Minister of Public Order and Citizen Protection Mr. Nikos Dendias the statement of the Press Office of SYRIZA for events in Amygdaleza*. Retrieved from http://www.yptp.gr/index.php?option=ozo_content&lang=GR&perform=view&id=4736&Itemid=579?option=ozo_search&lang=EN&lang=GR?option=ozo_search&lang=EN&lang=GR

Mital, K. M. (2012). ICT, unique identity and inclusive growth: An Indian perspective. In A. Manoharan & M. Holzer (Eds.), *E-governance and civic engagement: Factors and determinants of e-democracy* (pp. 584–612). Hershey, PA: IGI Global. doi:10.4018/978-1-61350-083-5.ch029

Mixail, S. (1999). *Forms of Messianic*. Athens: Agra.

Mizell, A. P. (2008). Helping close the digital divide for financially disadvantaged seniors. In F. Tan (Ed.), *Global information technologies: Concepts, methodologies, tools, and applications* (pp. 2396–2402). Hershey, PA: IGI Global. doi:10.4018/978-1-59904-939-7.ch173

Mole, N., & Meredith, C. (2010). *Asylum and the European Convention on Human Rights*. Strasbourg: Council of Europe Publishing.

Molinari, F., Wills, C., Koumpis, A., & Moumtzi, V. (2011). A citizen-centric platform to support networking in the area of e-democracy. In H. Rahman (Ed.), *Cases on adoption, diffusion and evaluation of global e-governance systems: Impact at the grass roots* (pp. 282–302). Hershey, PA: IGI Global. doi:10.4018/978-1-61692-814-8.ch014

Molinari, F., Wills, C., Koumpis, A., & Moumtzi, V. (2013). A citizen-centric platform to support networking in the area of e-democracy. In H. Rahman (Ed.), *Cases on progressions and challenges in ICT utilization for citizen-centric governance* (pp. 265–297). Hershey, PA: IGI Global. doi:10.4018/978-1-4666-2071-1.ch013

Molz, J. G., & Gibson, S. (Eds.). (2012). *Mobilizing hospitality: The ethics of social relations in a mobile world*. Hampshire, UK: Ashgate Publishing, Ltd.

Monteverde, F. (2010). The process of e-government public policy inclusion in the governmental agenda: A framework for assessment and case study. In J. Cordoba-Pachon & A. Ochoa-Arias (Eds.), *Systems thinking and e-participation: ICT in the governance of society* (pp. 233–245). Hershey, PA: IGI Global. doi:10.4018/978-1-60566-860-4.ch015

Moodley, S. (2008). Deconstructing the South African government's ICT for development discourse. In A. Anttiroiko (Ed.), *Electronic government: Concepts, methodologies, tools, and applications* (pp. 622–631). Hershey, PA: IGI Global. doi:10.4018/978-1-59904-947-2.ch053

Moodley, S. (2008). Deconstructing the South African government's ICT for development discourse. In C. Van Slyke (Ed.), *Information communication technologies: Concepts, methodologies, tools, and applications* (pp. 816–825). Hershey, PA: IGI Global. doi:10.4018/978-1-59904-949-6.ch052

Morales, W. Q. (2008). *Girl Child Soldiers: The Other Face of Sexual Exploitation and Gender Violence*. Air & Space Power Journal.

Mora, M., Cervantes-Perez, F., Gelman-Muravchik, O., Forgionne, G. A., & Mejia-Olvera, M. (2003). DMSS implementation research: A conceptual analysis of the contributions and limitations of the factor-based and stage-based streams. In G. Forgionne, J. Gupta, & M. Mora (Eds.), *Decision-making support systems: Achievements and challenges for the new decade* (pp. 331–356). Hershey, PA: IGI Global. doi:10.4018/978-1-59140-045-5.ch020

Mörtberg, C., & Elovaara, P. (2010). Attaching people and technology: Between e and government. In S. Booth, S. Goodman, & G. Kirkup (Eds.), *Gender issues in learning and working with information technology: Social constructs and cultural contexts* (pp. 83–98). Hershey, PA: IGI Global. doi:10.4018/978-1-61520-813-5.ch005

Moskalenko, S., & McCauley, C. (2009). Measuring political mobilization: The distinction between activism and radicalism. *Terrorism and Political Violence*, *21*(2), 239–260. doi:10.1080/09546550902765508

Muminov v. Russia. (2008) (First Section) No. 42502/06, ECHR

Murdoch, J., & Roche, R. (2016). *The European Convention on Human Rights and Policing*. Strasbourg: Council of Europe Publishing.

Murphy, J., Harper, E., Devine, E. C., Burke, L. J., & Hook, M. L. (2011). Case study: Lessons learned when embedding evidence-based knowledge in a nurse care planning and documentation system. In A. Cashin & R. Cook (Eds.), *Evidence-based practice in nursing informatics: Concepts and applications* (pp. 174–190). Hershey, PA: IGI Global. doi:10.4018/978-1-60960-034-1.ch014

Mutharika, P. (1995). The Role of International Law in the Twenty-First Century: An African Perspective. *Fordham International Law Journal*, 17.

Mutula, S. M. (2013). E-government's role in poverty alleviation: Case study of South Africa. In H. Rahman (Ed.), *Cases on progressions and challenges in ICT utilization for citizen-centric governance* (pp. 44–68). Hershey, PA: IGI Global. doi:10.4018/978-1-4666-2071-1.ch003

Nabagesera, K. J. (2014). Exploring the intersection of religious freedom and human right. *Bombastic Magazine*, *1*, 34–35.

NAIJ. (2013). *Being gay is natural – Yemisi Ilesanmi, coordinator of the Nigerian lesbian, gay, bisexual and transsexual, LGBT community*. Retrieved October 16, 2016, from http://www.being-gay-is-natural/yemisi-ilesanmi/naij.com

Naskou-Perraki, P. (1991). *The legal status of refugees in international and Greek law*. Athens-Komotini, Ant.N. Sakkoulas.

Nath, R., & Angeles, R. (2005). Relationships between supply characteristics and buyer-supplier coupling in e-procurement: An empirical analysis. *International Journal of E-Business Research*, *1*(2), 40–55. doi:10.4018/jebr.2005040103

Ndashe, S. (2010). The battle for the recognition of LGBTI rights as human rights. *Perspectives. Political Analysis and Commentary from Africa*, *4*(10), 4–9.

Nillasithanukroh, S. (2016). Rethinking the Use of Biometric Systems for Refugee Management. *Chicago Policy Review*. Retrieved from http://chicagopolicyreview.org/2016/02/24/rethinking-the-use-of-biometric-systems-for-refugee-management/

Nissen, M. E. (2006). Application cases in government. In M. Nissen (Ed.), *Harnessing knowledge dynamics: Principled organizational knowing & learning* (pp. 152–181). Hershey, PA: IGI Global. doi:10.4018/978-1-59140-773-7.ch008

Nkhonjera, P. (1996, January). Children in Bondage. *World Press Review*, *43*, 10.

Norris, D. F. (2003). Leading-edge information technologies and American local governments. In G. Garson (Ed.), *Public information technology: Policy and management issues* (pp. 139–169). Hershey, PA: IGI Global. doi:10.4018/978-1-59140-060-8.ch007

Norris, D. F. (2008). Information technology among U.S. local governments. In G. Garson & M. Khosrow-Pour (Eds.), *Handbook of research on public information technology* (pp. 132–144). Hershey, PA: IGI Global. doi:10.4018/978-1-59904-857-4.ch013

Northrop, A. (1999). The challenge of teaching information technology in public administration graduate programs. In G. Garson (Ed.), *Information technology and computer applications in public administration: Issues and trends* (pp. 1–22). Hershey, PA: IGI Global. doi:10.4018/978-1-87828-952-0.ch001

Northrop, A. (2003). Information technology and public administration: The view from the profession. In G. Garson (Ed.), *Public information technology: Policy and management issues* (pp. 1–19). Hershey, PA: IGI Global. doi:10.4018/978-1-59140-060-8.ch001

Northrop, A. (2007). Lip service? How PA journals and textbooks view information technology. In G. Garson (Ed.), *Modern public information technology systems: Issues and challenges* (pp. 1–16). Hershey, PA: IGI Global. doi:10.4018/978-1-59904-051-6.ch001

Notten, P. W. F. V. (2014). After the Arab Spring: An opportunity for scenarios. *European Journal of Future Research, 15*(28), 1–6.

Null, E. (2013). Legal and political barriers to municipal networks in the United States. In A. Abdelaal (Ed.), *Social and economic effects of community wireless networks and infrastructures* (pp. 27–56). Hershey, PA: IGI Global. doi:10.4018/978-1-4666-2997-4.ch003

O'Flaherty, M., Kędzia, Z., Müller, A., & Ulrich, G. (2011). *Human Rights Diplomacy: Contemporary Perspectives* (pp. 101–124). Leiden: Brill Nijhoff.

Obokata, T., & OConnell, R. (2010). Ambition, achievement and potential: The UK and the Universal Declaration of Human Rights at Sixty. *International Journal of Human Rights, 14*(3), 394–406. doi:10.1080/13642980802611178

Official Journal of the European Union. (2006). *Legislation: Regulation (EC) No 562/2006 of the European Parliament and of the Council of 15 March 2006 establishing a Community Code on the rules governing the movement of persons across borders (Schengen Borders Code), L 105, vol 49, 13/04/2006*. Retrieved from http://www.eur-lex.europa.eu/legal-content/EN/TXT/HTML/?uri=OJ:L:2006:105:FULL&from=EN#L_200605EN.01000101.doc

Official Journal of the European Union. (2008a). *Council Regulation (EC) No 380/2008 of 18 April 2008 amending Regulation (EC) No 1030/2002 laying down a uniform format for residence permits for third-country nationals*. Retrieved from http://eur-lex.europa.eu/LexUriServ/LexUriServ.do?uri=OJ:L:2008:115:0001:0007:EN:PDF

Official Journal of the European Union. (2008b). *Directive 2008/115/EC of the European Parliament and of the Council of 16 December 2008 on common standards and procedures in Member States for returning illegally staying third-country nationals.* Retrieved from http://eur-lex.europa.eu/legal-content/EN/TXT/PDF/?uri=CELEX:32008L0115&from=en

OIC. (2006). *OIC ministerial conference on the problems of refugees in the Muslim world.* OIC.

OIC. (2007). *Follow-up report on cooperation between the Organization of the Islamic Conference (OIC) and the United Nations.* Jeddah: Organization of Islamic Cooperation (OIC).

OIC. (2012). *Ashgabat Declaration of the International Ministerial Conference of the Organization of Islamic Cooperation on refugees in the Muslim world.* Jeddah: Organization of Islamic Cooperation (OIC).

OIC. (2014a). *Final document of the general meeting on cooperation between the United Nations and the Organization of Islamic Cooperation.* Jeddah: Organization of Islamic Cooperation (OIC).

OIC. (2014b). *Statement of the Secretary General of the Organization of Islamic Cooperation, Iyad Ameen Madani, at the the Opening Session of the Geneva-II Peace Conference on Syria, Montreux - Switzerland.* Retrieved from http://www.oic-oci.org/oicv2/m/en/topic/?t_id=8846&t_ref=3547&lan=

OIC. (2015a). *Appeal to the international community by the OIC Secretary General to counter the Syrian refugee crisis.* Retrieved from http://www.oic-oci.org/oicv3/topic/?t_id=10404&t_ref=4107&lan=en

OIC. (2015b). Growth in Islamophobia with influx of refugees into Europe. *OIC Journal,* 38-41.

OIC. (2015c). *OIC convenes an emergency meeting to mobilize efforts to address Syrian refugee crisis.* Retrieved from http://www.oic-oci.org/oicv3/topic/?t_id=10430&t_ref=4117&lan=en

OIC. (2016). IDB Group allocates US$9 billion to support countries hosting Syrian refugees. *OIC Journal,* 15.

Okunoye, A., Frolick, M., & Crable, E. (2006). ERP implementation in higher education: An account of pre-implementation and implementation phases. *Journal of Cases on Information Technology, 8*(2), 110–132. doi:10.4018/jcit.2006040106

Olasina, G. (2012). A review of egovernment services in Nigeria. In A. Tella & A. Issa (Eds.), *Library and information science in developing countries: Contemporary issues* (pp. 205–221). Hershey, PA: IGI Global. doi:10.4018/978-1-61350-335-5.ch015

Organization for Security and Co-operation in Europe & Office for Democratic Institutions and Human Rights (OSCE/ODIHR). (2009). *Greece, Early Parliamentary Elections 4 October 2009, OSCE/ODIHR Election Assessment Mission Report.* Retrieved http://www.osce.org/odihr/elections/greece/41001?download=true

Organization for Security and Cooperation in Europe (OSCE). (2015). *Repost of the Office for Democratic Institutions and human Rights (ODIHR) on hate crime*. Retrieved from http://hatecrime.osce.org/what-hate-crime/racism-and-xenophobia#bm-reports

Orgeron, C. P. (2008). A model for reengineering IT job classes in state government. In G. Garson & M. Khosrow-Pour (Eds.), *Handbook of research on public information technology* (pp. 735–746). Hershey, PA: IGI Global. doi:10.4018/978-1-59904-857-4.ch066

Ostrand, N. (2015). The Syrian refugees crisis: A comparison of responses by Germany, Sweden, the United Kingdom, and the United States. *Journal on Migration and Human Security*, *3*(3), 255–279. doi:10.14240/jmhs.v3i3.51

Owsinski, J. W., & Pielak, A. M. (2011). Local authority websites in rural areas: Measuring quality and functionality, and assessing the role. In Z. Andreopoulou, B. Manos, N. Polman, & D. Viaggi (Eds.), *Agricultural and environmental informatics, governance and management: Emerging research applications* (pp. 39–60). Hershey, PA: IGI Global. doi:10.4018/978-1-60960-621-3.ch003

Owsiński, J. W., Pielak, A. M., Sęp, K., & Stańczak, J. (2014). Local web-based networks in rural municipalities: Extension, density, and meaning. In Z. Andreopoulou, V. Samathrakis, S. Louca, & M. Vlachopoulou (Eds.), *E-innovation for sustainable development of rural resources during global economic crisis* (pp. 126–151). Hershey, PA: IGI Global. doi:10.4018/978-1-4666-4550-9.ch011

Ozden, S. (2013). *Syrian refugees in Turkey*. Retrieved from http://www.migrationpolicycentre.eu/docs/MPC-RR-2013-05.pdf

Pagani, M., & Pasinetti, C. (2008). Technical and functional quality in the development of t-government services. In A. Anttiroiko (Ed.), *Electronic government: Concepts, methodologies, tools, and applications* (pp. 2943–2965). Hershey, PA: IGI Global. doi:10.4018/978-1-59904-947-2.ch220

Palazzani, L. (2012). *Gender in Philosophy and Law*. London: Springer.

Pani, A. K., & Agrahari, A. (2005). On e-markets in emerging economy: An Indian experience. In M. Khosrow-Pour (Ed.), *Advanced topics in electronic commerce* (Vol. 1, pp. 287–299). Hershey, PA: IGI Global. doi:10.4018/978-1-59140-819-2.ch015

Papadopoulos, T., Angelopoulos, S., & Kitsios, F. (2011). A strategic approach to e-health interoperability using e-government frameworks. In A. Lazakidou, K. Siassiakos, & K. Ioannou (Eds.), *Wireless technologies for ambient assisted living and healthcare: Systems and applications* (pp. 213–229). Hershey, PA: IGI Global. doi:10.4018/978-1-61520-805-0.ch012

Papadopoulos, T., Angelopoulos, S., & Kitsios, F. (2013). A strategic approach to e-health interoperability using e-government frameworks. In *User-driven healthcare: Concepts, methodologies, tools, and applications* (pp. 791–807). Hershey, PA: IGI Global. doi:10.4018/978-1-4666-2770-3.ch039

Papaleo, G., Chiarella, D., Aiello, M., & Caviglione, L. (2012). Analysis, development and deployment of statistical anomaly detection techniques for real e-mail traffic. In T. Chou (Ed.), *Information assurance and security technologies for risk assessment and threat management: Advances* (pp. 47–71). Hershey, PA: IGI Global. doi:10.4018/978-1-61350-507-6.ch003

Paparriga-Kostovara K. (2007). *Rape: The crime, trial, law and social perceptions.* Athens: Metaixmio.

Papp, R. (2003). Information technology & FDA compliance in the pharmaceutical industry. In M. Khosrow-Pour (Ed.), *Annals of cases on information technology* (Vol. 5, pp. 262–273). Hershey, PA: IGI Global. doi:10.4018/978-1-59140-061-5.ch017

Paris Principles. (2007). Retrieved from http://www.unicef.org/emerg/files/ParisPrinciples310107English.pdf

Parsons, T. W. (2007). Developing a knowledge management portal. In A. Tatnall (Ed.), *Encyclopedia of portal technologies and applications* (pp. 223–227). Hershey, PA: IGI Global. doi:10.4018/978-1-59140-989-2.ch039

Passaris, C. E. (2007). Immigration and digital government. In A. Anttiroiko & M. Malkia (Eds.), *Encyclopedia of digital government* (pp. 988–994). Hershey, PA: IGI Global. doi:10.4018/978-1-59140-789-8.ch148

Paterson, T. (2010). *Germany's neighbors from hell.* Retrieved from http://www.independent.co.uk/news/world/europe/germanys-neighbours-from-hell-2110303.html

Patrick, S. (2006). *Weak States and Global Threats: Assessing Evidence of 'Spillovers'.* Center for Global Development, Working Paper No: 73.

Pavlichev, A. (2004). The e-government challenge for public administration. In A. Pavlichev & G. Garson (Eds.), *Digital government: Principles and best practices* (pp. 276–290). Hershey, PA: IGI Global. doi:10.4018/978-1-59140-122-3.ch018

Penrod, J. I., & Harbor, A. F. (2000). Designing and implementing a learning organization-oriented information technology planning and management process. In L. Petrides (Ed.), *Case studies on information technology in higher education: Implications for policy and practice* (pp. 7–19). Hershey, PA: IGI Global. doi:10.4018/978-1-878289-74-2.ch001

Perrakis, S., & Mastakas, P. (2005). *Asylum- Refugees. Legislative Policy of International Organizations (UN High Commissioner for Refugees - EU - Council of Europe, etc.).* Athens: Ant.N.Sakkoula.

Pfaff, W. (1995). A New Colonialism?. Academic Press.

Piazza, J. A. (2007). Draining the swamp: Democracy promotion, state failure, and terrorism in 19 Middle Eastern countries. *Studies in Conflict and Terrorism, 30*(6), 521–539. doi:10.1080/10576100701329576

Piazza, J. A. (2008). Incubators of terror: Do failed and failing states promote transnational terrorism? *International Studies Quarterly*, *52*(3), 469–488. doi:10.1111/j.1468-2478.2008.00511.x

Planas-Silva, M. D., & Joseph, R. C. (2011). Perspectives on the adoption of electronic resources for use in clinical trials. In M. Guah (Ed.), *Healthcare delivery reform and new technologies: Organizational initiatives* (pp. 19–28). Hershey, PA: IGI Global. doi:10.4018/978-1-60960-183-6.ch002

Politico. (2016). *Imbalance of refugee*. Retrieved from http://www.kathimerini.gr/846091/article/epikairothta/kosmos/anisorropia-apo-to-prosfygiko

Pomazalová, N., & Rejman, S. (2013). The rationale behind implementation of new electronic tools for electronic public procurement. In N. Pomazalová (Ed.), *Public sector transformation processes and internet public procurement: Decision support systems* (pp. 85–117). Hershey, PA: IGI Global. doi:10.4018/978-1-4666-2665-2.ch006

Popp, M. (2011). *Right- Wing Extremism: The Village Where the Neo-Nazis Rule*. Retrieved from http://www.spiegel.de/international/germany/right-wing-extremism-the-village-where-the-neo-nazis-rule-a-737471.html

Porter, T. (2016). *Germany: Refugees hand out flowers to women in protest against New Year's Eve mass sex attacks*. Retrieved from http://www.ibtimes.co.uk/germany-refugees-hand-out-flowers-women-protest-against-new-years-eve-mass-sex-attacks-1538407

Possner, R. A. (1983). *The Economics of Justice*. Cambridge, MA: Harvard University Press.

Postorino, M. N. (2012). City competitiveness and airport: Information science perspective. In M. Bulu (Ed.), *City competitiveness and improving urban subsystems: Technologies and applications* (pp. 61–83). Hershey, PA: IGI Global. doi:10.4018/978-1-61350-174-0.ch004

Poulatzas, N. (2006). *Fascism and dictatorship: The Third International and the Problem of Fascism*. Athens: Themelio.

Poulatzas, N. (2008). *The Poulatzas Reader, Marxism, Law and the State* (J. Martin, Ed.). London: Verso.

Poupa, C. (2002). Electronic government in Switzerland: Priorities for 2001-2005 - Electronic voting and federal portal. In Å. Grönlund (Ed.), *Electronic government: Design, applications and management* (pp. 356–369). Hershey, PA: IGI Global. doi:10.4018/978-1-930708-19-8.ch017

Powell, J. (2010). Neo-liberalism and Globalization: repetitious inequalities and the implication for a global social theory. In *Sincronia: a journal of Social Sciences and Humanities*. University of Guadalajara.

Powell, S. R. (2010). Interdisciplinarity in telecommunications and networking. In *Networking and telecommunications: Concepts, methodologies, tools and applications* (pp. 33–40). Hershey, PA: IGI Global. doi:10.4018/978-1-60566-986-1.ch004

Presidential Decree No. 113/2013 on the Establishment of a Common Procedure for Identifying the Refugee Status of Foreigners and Stateless Persons or Subsidiary Protection in Compliance with Directive 2005/85/EC and Other Provisions, June 13, 2013.

Presidential Decree No. 220/2007, art. 19, para. 1, Nov. 13, 2007.

Prifti, K. (2016). *Why the Macedonian movement to close the border to Afghans can only be the first step of the "hard" European strategy*. Retrieved from http://www.huffingtonpost.gr/2016/02/25/afganoi-pgdm-synora-giati_n_9297546.html

Priya, P. S., & Mathiyalagan, N. (2011). A study of the implementation status of two e-governance projects in land revenue administration in India. In M. Shareef, V. Kumar, U. Kumar, & Y. Dwivedi (Eds.), *Stakeholder adoption of e-government services: Driving and resisting factors* (pp. 214–230). Hershey, PA: IGI Global. doi:10.4018/978-1-60960-601-5.ch011

Prysby, C. L., & Prysby, N. D. (2003). Electronic mail in the public workplace: Issues of privacy and public disclosure. In G. Garson (Ed.), *Public information technology: Policy and management issues* (pp. 271–298). Hershey, PA: IGI Global. doi:10.4018/978-1-59140-060-8.ch012

Prysby, C. L., & Prysby, N. D. (2007). You have mail, but who is reading it? Issues of e-mail in the public workplace. In G. Garson (Ed.), *Modern public information technology systems: Issues and challenges* (pp. 312–336). Hershey, PA: IGI Global. doi:10.4018/978-1-59904-051-6.ch016

Prysby, C., & Prysby, N. (2000). Electronic mail, employee privacy and the workplace. In L. Janczewski (Ed.), *Internet and intranet security management: Risks and solutions* (pp. 251–270). Hershey, PA: IGI Global. doi:10.4018/978-1-878289-71-1.ch009

Radl, A., & Chen, Y. (2005). Computer security in electronic government: A state-local education information system. *International Journal of Electronic Government Research*, *1*(1), 79–99. doi:10.4018/jegr.2005010105

Rahman, H. (2008). Information dynamics in developing countries. In C. Van Slyke (Ed.), *Information communication technologies: Concepts, methodologies, tools, and applications* (pp. 104–114). Hershey, PA: IGI Global. doi:10.4018/978-1-59904-949-6.ch008

Raine, R. (2013). A Dark Tourism spectrum. *International Journal of Culture, Tourism and Hospitality Research, 7*(3), 242-256.

Ramanathan, J. (2009). Adaptive IT architecture as a catalyst for network capability in government. In P. Saha (Ed.), *Advances in government enterprise architecture* (pp. 149–172). Hershey, PA: IGI Global. doi:10.4018/978-1-60566-068-4.ch007

Ramos, I., & Berry, D. M. (2006). Social construction of information technology supporting work. In M. Khosrow-Pour (Ed.), *Cases on information technology: Lessons learned* (Vol. 7, pp. 36–52). Hershey, PA: IGI Global. doi:10.4018/978-1-59140-673-0.ch003

Rankin, J. (2016, May 19). Human Traffickers 'Using Migration Crisis' to Force More People into Slavery. *The Guardian*. Retrieved from https://www.theguardian.com/world/2016/may/19/human-traffickers-using-migration-crisis-to-force-more-people-into-slavery

Ray, C. (2016). Homosexuality – a Sign of the End of the Age?. *Living Waters*, *16*, 23–48.

Ray, D., Gulla, U., Gupta, M. P., & Dash, S. S. (2009). Interoperability and constituents of interoperable systems in public sector. In V. Weerakkody, M. Janssen, & Y. Dwivedi (Eds.), *Handbook of research on ICT-enabled transformational government: A global perspective* (pp. 175–195). Hershey, PA: IGI Global. doi:10.4018/978-1-60566-390-6.ch010

Reddick, C. G. (2007). E-government and creating a citizen-centric government: A study of federal government CIOs. In G. Garson (Ed.), *Modern public information technology systems: Issues and challenges* (pp. 143–165). Hershey, PA: IGI Global. doi:10.4018/978-1-59904-051-6.ch008

Reddick, C. G. (2010). Citizen-centric e-government. In C. Reddick (Ed.), *Homeland security preparedness and information systems: Strategies for managing public policy* (pp. 45–75). Hershey, PA: IGI Global. doi:10.4018/978-1-60566-834-5.ch002

Reddick, C. G. (2010). E-government and creating a citizen-centric government: A study of federal government CIOs. In C. Reddick (Ed.), *Homeland security preparedness and information systems: Strategies for managing public policy* (pp. 230–250). Hershey, PA: IGI Global. doi:10.4018/978-1-60566-834-5.ch012

Reddick, C. G. (2010). Perceived effectiveness of e-government and its usage in city governments: Survey evidence from information technology directors. In C. Reddick (Ed.), *Homeland security preparedness and information systems: Strategies for managing public policy* (pp. 213–229). Hershey, PA: IGI Global. doi:10.4018/978-1-60566-834-5.ch011

Reddick, C. G. (2012). Customer relationship management adoption in local governments in the United States. In S. Chhabra & M. Kumar (Eds.), *Strategic enterprise resource planning models for e-government: Applications and methodologies* (pp. 111–124). Hershey, PA: IGI Global. doi:10.4018/978-1-60960-863-7.ch008

Reeder, F. S., & Pandy, S. M. (2008). Identifying effective funding models for e-government. In A. Anttiroiko (Ed.), *Electronic government: Concepts, methodologies, tools, and applications* (pp. 1108–1138). Hershey, PA: IGI Global. doi:10.4018/978-1-59904-947-2.ch083

Refugee Solidarity Network. (2016). *Refugees & asylum in Turkey: Legal overview*. Retrieved from http://www.refugeesolidaritynetwork.org/learn-more/turkey-asylum-basics/

Report, G. (2008). *Coalition to Stop the Use of Child Soldiers*. Child Soldiers Global Report. Retrieved from https://www.hrw.org/legacy/pub/2008/children/Child_Soldiers_Global_Report_Summary.pdf

Riesco, D., Acosta, E., & Montejano, G. (2003). An extension to a UML activity graph from workflow. In L. Favre (Ed.), *UML and the unified process* (pp. 294–314). Hershey, PA: IGI Global. doi:10.4018/978-1-93177-744-5.ch015

Riesman, D. (1961). *The Lonely Crowd: A Study of the Changing American Character. 1950*. New Haven, CT: Yale UP.

Ritzhaupt, A. D., & Gill, T. G. (2008). A hybrid and novel approach to teaching computer programming in MIS curriculum. In S. Negash, M. Whitman, A. Woszczynski, K. Hoganson, & H. Mattord (Eds.), *Handbook of distance learning for real-time and asynchronous information technology education* (pp. 259–281). Hershey, PA: IGI Global. doi:10.4018/978-1-59904-964-9.ch014

Roche, E. M. (1993). International computing and the international regime. *Journal of Global Information Management, 1*(2), 33–44. doi:10.4018/jgim.1993040103

Rocheleau, B. (2007). Politics, accountability, and information management. In G. Garson (Ed.), *Modern public information technology systems: Issues and challenges* (pp. 35–71). Hershey, PA: IGI Global. doi:10.4018/978-1-59904-051-6.ch003

Rodrigues Filho, J. (2010). E-government in Brazil: Reinforcing dominant institutions or reducing citizenship? In C. Reddick (Ed.), *Politics, democracy and e-government: Participation and service delivery* (pp. 347–362). Hershey, PA: IGI Global. doi:10.4018/978-1-61520-933-0.ch021

Rodriguez, S. R., & Thorp, D. A. (2013). eLearning for industry: A case study of the project management process. In A. Benson, J. Moore, & S. Williams van Rooij (Eds.), Cases on educational technology planning, design, and implementation: A project management perspective (pp. 319-342). Hershey, PA: IGI Global. doi:10.4018/978-1-4666-4237-9.ch017

Roman, A. V. (2013). Delineating three dimensions of e-government success: Security, functionality, and transformation. In J. Gil-Garcia (Ed.), *E-government success factors and measures: Theories, concepts, and methodologies* (pp. 171–192). Hershey, PA: IGI Global. doi:10.4018/978-1-4666-4058-0.ch010

Rorty, R. (1982). *Consequences of pragmatism: Essays, 1972-1980.* Minneapolis, MN: University of Minnesota Press.

Rosenblatt, R. (1983). *Children of War*. London: New English Library.

Ross, S. C., Tyran, C. K., & Auer, D. J. (2008). Up in smoke: Rebuilding after an IT disaster. In H. Nemati (Ed.), *Information security and ethics: Concepts, methodologies, tools, and applications* (pp. 3659–3675). Hershey, PA: IGI Global. doi:10.4018/978-1-59904-937-3.ch248

Ross, S. C., Tyran, C. K., Auer, D. J., Junell, J. M., & Williams, T. G. (2005). Up in smoke: Rebuilding after an IT disaster. *Journal of Cases on Information Technology, 7*(2), 31–49. doi:10.4018/jcit.2005040103

Rotberg, R. I. (2004). *When States Fail: Causes and Consequences*. Princeton University Press. doi:10.1515/9781400835799

Rotberg, R. I. (Ed.). (2003). *State Failure and State Weakness in a Time of Terror*. Washington, DC: Academic Press.

Royer, A. (2010). *The Council of Europe*. Strasbourg, France: Council of Europe Publishing.

Roy, J. (2008). Security, sovereignty, and continental interoperability: Canada's elusive balance. In T. Loendorf & G. Garson (Eds.), *Patriotic information systems* (pp. 153–176). Hershey, PA: IGI Global. doi:10.4018/978-1-59904-594-8.ch007

Rubeck, R. F., & Miller, G. A. (2009). vGOV: Remote video access to government services. In A. Scupola (Ed.), Cases on managing e-services (pp. 253-268). Hershey, PA: IGI Global. doi:10.4018/978-1-60566-064-6.ch017

Saekow, A., & Boonmee, C. (2011). The challenges of implementing e-government interoperability in Thailand: Case of official electronic correspondence letters exchange across government departments. In Y. Charalabidis (Ed.), *Interoperability in digital public services and administration: Bridging e-government and e-business* (pp. 40–61). Hershey, PA: IGI Global. doi:10.4018/978-1-61520-887-6.ch003

Saekow, A., & Boonmee, C. (2012). The challenges of implementing e-government interoperability in Thailand: Case of official electronic correspondence letters exchange across government departments. In *Digital democracy: Concepts, methodologies, tools, and applications* (pp. 1883–1905). Hershey, PA: IGI Global. doi:10.4018/978-1-4666-1740-7.ch094

Sageman, M. (2014). The Stagnation in Terrorism Research. *Terrorism and Political Violence*, 1-16.

Sagsan, M., & Medeni, T. (2012). Understanding "knowledge management (KM) paradigms" from social media perspective: An empirical study on discussion group for KM at professional networking site. In M. Cruz-Cunha, P. Gonçalves, N. Lopes, E. Miranda, & G. Putnik (Eds.), *Handbook of research on business social networking: Organizational, managerial, and technological dimensions* (pp. 738–755). Hershey, PA: IGI Global. doi:10.4018/978-1-61350-168-9.ch039

Sahi, G., & Madan, S. (2013). Information security threats in ERP enabled e-governance: Challenges and solutions. In *Enterprise resource planning: Concepts, methodologies, tools, and applications* (pp. 825–837). Hershey, PA: IGI Global. doi:10.4018/978-1-4666-4153-2.ch048

Sahlins, M. (2013). *Culture and practical reason*. Chicago, IL: University of Chicago Press.

Saleh, L. (2013). "We Thought We Were Playing": Children's Participation in the Syrian Revolution. *Journal of International Women's Studies*, *14*, 87.

Samuels, G. (2016). *Nottinghamshire Police to record misogyny and harassment against women as hate crimes*. Retrieved from http://www.independent.co.uk/news/uk/home-news/nottinghamshire-police-to-record-misogyny-and-harassment-against-women-as-hate-crimes-a7134306.html

Sanderson, T. (2007). Secularism holds the key to justice for all. Gay Humanist Quarterly, 2(1), 7-8.

Sanford, C., & Bhattacherjee, A. (2008). IT implementation in a developing country municipality: A sociocognitive analysis. *International Journal of Technology and Human Interaction*, *4*(3), 68–93. doi:10.4018/jthi.2008070104

Sangeeta, S., Garofalo, E., & Olimat, M. (2013). Introduction: Children and Arab Spring. *Journal of International Women's Studies*, *14*(5), 1–3.

Sather-Wagstaff, J. (2011). *Heritage that hurts: Tourists in the memoryscapes of September 11* (Vol. 4). California, CA: Left Coast Press.

Schabas, A. W. (2013). *The Universal Declaration on Human Rights: The Travaux Preparatoire.* Cambridge, UK: Cambridge University Press. doi:10.1017/CBO9781139600491

Schelin, S. H. (2003). E-government: An overview. In G. Garson (Ed.), *Public information technology: Policy and management issues* (pp. 120–138). Hershey, PA: IGI Global. doi:10.4018/978-1-59140-060-8.ch006

Schelin, S. H. (2004). Training for digital government. In A. Pavlichev & G. Garson (Eds.), *Digital government: Principles and best practices* (pp. 263–275). Hershey, PA: IGI Global. doi:10.4018/978-1-59140-122-3.ch017

Schelin, S. H. (2007). E-government: An overview. In G. Garson (Ed.), *Modern public information technology systems: Issues and challenges* (pp. 110–126). Hershey, PA: IGI Global. doi:10.4018/978-1-59904-051-6.ch006

Schelin, S. H., & Garson, G. (2004). Theoretical justification of critical success factors. In G. Garson & S. Schelin (Eds.), *IT solutions series: Humanizing information technology: Advice from experts* (pp. 4–15). Hershey, PA: IGI Global. doi:10.4018/978-1-59140-245-9.ch002

Schneckener, U. (2006). Fragile Statehood, Armed Non-State Actors and Security Governance. In *Private Actors and Security Governance* (pp. 23–41). Geneva, Switzerland: DCAF.

Schumacher, W. (2010). African churches and homosexuality. *Concordia Theology*, *36*, 77–89.

Schweitzer, A. (2012, October 22). Eastern Europe's Hard Attitude to Refugees is born out of Trauma. *The Guardian*. Retrieved from https://www.theguardian.com/world/commentisfree/2015/oct/22/refugee-eastern-europe-trauma-governments-bigotry

Scime, A. (2002). Information systems and computer science model curricula: A comparative look. In M. Dadashzadeh, A. Saber, & S. Saber (Eds.), *Information technology education in the new millennium* (pp. 146–158). Hershey, PA: IGI Global. doi:10.4018/978-1-931777-05-6.ch018

Scime, A. (2009). Computing curriculum analysis and development. In M. Khosrow-Pour (Ed.), *Encyclopedia of information science and technology* (2nd ed.; pp. 667–671). Hershey, PA: IGI Global. doi:10.4018/978-1-60566-026-4.ch108

Scime, A., & Wania, C. (2008). Computing curricula: A comparison of models. In C. Van Slyke (Ed.), *Information communication technologies: Concepts, methodologies, tools, and applications* (pp. 1270–1283). Hershey, PA: IGI Global. doi:10.4018/978-1-59904-949-6.ch088

Seaton, A. V. (1996). Guided by the dark: From thanatopsis to thanatourism. *International Journal of Heritage Studies*, *2*(4), 234–244. doi:10.1080/13527259608722178

Seidman, S. B. (2009). An international perspective on professional software engineering credentials. In H. Ellis, S. Demurjian, & J. Naveda (Eds.), *Software engineering: Effective teaching and learning approaches and practices* (pp. 351–361). Hershey, PA: IGI Global. doi:10.4018/978-1-60566-102-5.ch018

Seifert, J. W. (2007). E-government act of 2002 in the United States. In A. Anttiroiko & M. Malkia (Eds.), *Encyclopedia of digital government* (pp. 476–481). Hershey, PA: IGI Global. doi:10.4018/978-1-59140-789-8.ch072

Seifert, J. W., & Relyea, H. C. (2008). E-government act of 2002 in the United States. In A. Anttiroiko (Ed.), *Electronic government: Concepts, methodologies, tools, and applications* (pp. 154–161). Hershey, PA: IGI Global. doi:10.4018/978-1-59904-947-2.ch013

Seufert, S. (2002). E-learning business models: Framework and best practice examples. In M. Raisinghani (Ed.), *Cases on worldwide e-commerce: Theory in action* (pp. 70–94). Hershey, PA: IGI Global. doi:10.4018/978-1-930708-27-3.ch004

Sevilla-Buitrago, A. (2015). Capitalist Formations of Enclosure: Space, and the Extinction of the Commons. *Antipode, 47*(4), 829-1100. Retrieved from http://www.onlinelibrary.wiley.com/doi/10.1111/anti.12143/epdf

Shaikh, H. (2013, September 8). OIC's new mediation unit now in operation. *Arab News*.

Shareef, M. A., & Archer, N. (2012). E-government initiatives: Review studies on different countries. In M. Shareef, N. Archer, & S. Dutta (Eds.), *E-government service maturity and development: Cultural, organizational and technological perspectives* (pp. 40–76). Hershey, PA: IGI Global. doi:10.4018/978-1-60960-848-4.ch003

Shareef, M. A., & Archer, N. (2012). E-government service development. In M. Shareef, N. Archer, & S. Dutta (Eds.), *E-government service maturity and development: Cultural, organizational and technological perspectives* (pp. 1–14). Hershey, PA: IGI Global. doi:10.4018/978-1-60960-848-4.ch001

Shareef, M. A., Kumar, U., & Kumar, V. (2011). E-government development: Performance evaluation parameters. In M. Shareef, V. Kumar, U. Kumar, & Y. Dwivedi (Eds.), *Stakeholder adoption of e-government services: Driving and resisting factors* (pp. 197–213). Hershey, PA: IGI Global. doi:10.4018/978-1-60960-601-5.ch010

Shareef, M. A., Kumar, U., Kumar, V., & Niktash, M. (2012). Electronic-government vision: Case studies for objectives, strategies, and initiatives. In M. Shareef, N. Archer, & S. Dutta (Eds.), *E-government service maturity and development: Cultural, organizational and technological perspectives* (pp. 15–39). Hershey, PA: IGI Global. doi:10.4018/978-1-60960-848-4.ch002

Sharqieh, I. (2012). Can the Organization of Islamic Cooperation (OIC) resolve conflicts? *Peace and Conflict Studies, 19*(2), 162–179.

Sheller, M., & Urry, J. (2004). *Tourism mobilities: Places to play, places in play*. London: Routledge.

Shukla, P., Kumar, A., & Anu Kumar, P. B. (2013). Impact of national culture on business continuity management system implementation. *International Journal of Risk and Contingency Management, 2*(3), 23–36. doi:10.4018/ijrcm.2013070102

Shulman, S. W. (2007). The federal docket management system and the prospect for digital democracy in U S rulemaking. In G. Garson (Ed.), *Modern public information technology systems: Issues and challenges* (pp. 166–184). Hershey, PA: IGI Global. doi:10.4018/978-1-59904-051-6.ch009

Silva, E. B. (2006). *Racism without racist: Color bind racism and persistance of racial inequality in the United States*. New York: Rowman & Littlefield Publishers.

Simonovic, S. (2007). Problems of offline government in e-Serbia. In A. Anttiroiko & M. Malkia (Eds.), *Encyclopedia of digital government* (pp. 1342–1351). Hershey, PA: IGI Global. doi:10.4018/978-1-59140-789-8.ch205

Simonovic, S. (2008). Problems of offline government in e-Serbia. In A. Anttiroiko (Ed.), *Electronic government: Concepts, methodologies, tools, and applications* (pp. 2929–2942). Hershey, PA: IGI Global. doi:10.4018/978-1-59904-947-2.ch219

Singh, A. M. (2005). Information systems and technology in South Africa. In M. Khosrow-Pour (Ed.), *Encyclopedia of information science and technology* (pp. 1497–1502). Hershey, PA: IGI Global. doi:10.4018/978-1-59140-553-5.ch263

Singh, S., & Naidoo, G. (2005). Towards an e-government solution: A South African perspective. In W. Huang, K. Siau, & K. Wei (Eds.), *Electronic government strategies and implementation* (pp. 325–353). Hershey, PA: IGI Global. doi:10.4018/978-1-59140-348-7.ch014

Skoll, G. (2011). Travel Insecurity in North America: the Mexico-US border. *International Journal of Safety and Security in Tourism, 1*(1), 44-63.

Skoll, G. (2016). *Globalization of American Fear Culture: The empire in the Twenty-First Century*. New York: Palgrave-Macmillan.

Skoll, G. R. (2007). Meanings of terrorism. *International Journal for the Semiotics of Law-Revue internationale de Sémiotique juridique, 20*(2), 107-127.

Skoll, G. (2014). *The Dialectics of Social thought*. New York, NY: Palgrave-Macmillan. doi:10.1057/9781137387066

Skoll, G. R. (2008). Torture and the Fifth Amendment Torture, the Global War on Terror, and Constitutional Values. *Criminal Justice Review, 33*(1), 29–47. doi:10.1177/0734016808315585

Snoke, R., & Underwood, A. (2002). Generic attributes of IS graduates: An analysis of Australian views. In F. Tan (Ed.), *Advanced topics in global information management* (Vol. 1, pp. 370–384). Hershey, PA: IGI Global. doi:10.4018/978-1-930708-43-3.ch023

Soering v. United Kingdom (1989) 11 EHRR 439

Soloway, B. (2016). *Hajj closed to Iranians after year of discord.* Retrieved from http://foreignpolicy.com/2016/05/12/hajj-closed-to-iranians-after-year-of-discord/?utm_content=buffer6fdee&utm_medium=social&utm_source=facebook.com&utm_campaign=buffer

Somaskanda, S. (2016, September 9). Can this man save the Europe-Turkey migrant deal? *Foreign Policy.*

Sommer, L. (2006). Revealing unseen organizations in higher education: A study framework and application example. In A. Metcalfe (Ed.), *Knowledge management and higher education: A critical analysis* (pp. 115–146). Hershey, PA: IGI Global. doi:10.4018/978-1-59140-509-2.ch007

Song, H., Kidd, T., & Owens, E. (2011). Examining technological disparities and instructional practices in English language arts classroom: Implications for school leadership and teacher training. In L. Tomei (Ed.), *Online courses and ICT in education: Emerging practices and applications* (pp. 258–274). Hershey, PA: IGI Global. doi:10.4018/978-1-60960-150-8.ch020

Souliotis, G. (2016). *The Idomeni evacuation plan.* Retrieved from http://www.kathimerini.gr/860810/article/epikairothta/ellada/to-sxedio-ekkenwshs-ths-eidomenhs

Speaker, P. J., & Kleist, V. F. (2003). Using information technology to meet electronic commerce and MIS education demands. In A. Aggarwal (Ed.), *Web-based education: Learning from experience* (pp. 280–291). Hershey, PA: IGI Global. doi:10.4018/978-1-59140-102-5.ch017

Spencer, S. (2003). *The Politics of Migration: Managing Opportunity, Conflict and Change.* Oxford, UK: Blackwell Publishing.

Spitler, V. K. (2007). Learning to use IT in the workplace: Mechanisms and masters. In M. Mahmood (Ed.), *Contemporary issues in end user computing* (pp. 292–323). Hershey, PA: IGI Global. doi:10.4018/978-1-59140-926-7.ch013

Spyropoulos, K. F. (2006). *Introduction to Constitutional Law.* Athens: ANT. N. SAKKOULAS.

Starr, S. (2012). *Revolt in Syria: Eye-witness to the Uprising.* Hurst Publishers.

Statute of the Council of Europe, 87 U.N.T.S. 103, E.T.S. 1.

Stellefson, M. (2011). Considerations for marketing distance education courses in health education: Five important questions to examine before development. In U. Demiray & S. Sever (Eds.), *Marketing online education programs: Frameworks for promotion and communication* (pp. 222–234). Hershey, PA: IGI Global. doi:10.4018/978-1-60960-074-7.ch014

Stone, P. R. (2012). Dark tourism and significant other death: Towards a model of mortality mediation. *Annals of Tourism Research, 39*(3), 1565–1587. doi:10.1016/j.annals.2012.04.007

Straub, D. W., & Loch, K. D. (2006). Creating and developing a program of global research. *Journal of Global Information Management, 14*(2), 1–28. doi:10.4018/jgim.2006040101

Straub, D. W., Loch, K. D., & Hill, C. E. (2002). Transfer of information technology to the Arab world: A test of cultural influence modeling. In M. Dadashzadeh (Ed.), *Information technology management in developing countries* (pp. 92–134). Hershey, PA: IGI Global. doi:10.4018/978-1-931777-03-2.ch005

Straub, D. W., Loch, K. D., & Hill, C. E. (2003). Transfer of information technology to the Arab world: A test of cultural influence modeling. In F. Tan (Ed.), *Advanced topics in global information management* (Vol. 2, pp. 141–172). Hershey, PA: IGI Global. doi:10.4018/978-1-59140-064-6.ch009

Sugden, R. (2005). *The Economics of Rights, Cooperation and Welfare*. Hampshire, UK: Palgrave Macmillan. doi:10.1057/9780230536791

Suki, N. M., Ramayah, T., Ming, M. K., & Suki, N. M. (2013). Factors enhancing employed job seekers intentions to use social networking sites as a job search tool. In A. Mesquita (Ed.), *User perception and influencing factors of technology in everyday life* (pp. 265–281). Hershey, PA: IGI Global. doi:10.4018/978-1-4666-1954-8.ch018

Sunstein, C. R. (2002a). *Risk and reason: Safety, law, and the environment.* Cambridge, UK: Cambridge University Press.

Sunstein, C. R. (2002b). Probability neglect: Emotions, worst cases, and law. *The Yale Law Journal, 112*(1), 61–107. doi:10.2307/1562234

Sunstein, C. R. (2003). Terrorism and probability neglect. *Journal of Risk and Uncertainty, 26*(2), 121–136. doi:10.1023/A:1024111006336

Sunstein, C. R. (2005). *Laws of fear: Beyond the precautionary principle* (Vol. 6). Cambridge, UK: Cambridge University Press. doi:10.1017/CBO9780511790850

Suomi, R. (2006). Introducing electronic patient records to hospitals: Innovation adoption paths. In T. Spil & R. Schuring (Eds.), *E-health systems diffusion and use: The innovation, the user and the use IT model* (pp. 128–146). Hershey, PA: IGI Global. doi:10.4018/978-1-59140-423-1.ch008

Swim, J., & Barker, L. (2012). Pathways into a gendered occupation: Brazilian women in IT. *International Journal of Social and Organizational Dynamics in IT*, 2(4), 34–51. doi:10.4018/ijsodit.2012100103

Sylvester, J. H. (1994). *Sub-Saharan Africa: Economic Stagnation, Political Disintegration and the Specter of Recolonization.* 27 LoY. L.A. L. REv. 1299.

Tabesh v Greece (2008). No. 8256/07, ECHR.

Tamale, S. (2011). Researching and theorizing sexualities in Africa. In S. Tamale (Ed.), *African sexualities: A reader* (pp. 1–47). Kampala: Pambazuka.

Tarafdar, M., & Vaidya, S. D. (2006). Adoption and implementation of IT in developing nations: Experiences from two public sector enterprises in India. In M. Khosrow-Pour (Ed.), *Cases on information technology planning, design and implementation* (pp. 208–233). Hershey, PA: IGI Global. doi:10.4018/978-1-59904-408-8.ch013

Tarafdar, M., & Vaidya, S. D. (2008). Adoption and implementation of IT in developing nations: Experiences from two public sector enterprises in India. In G. Garson & M. Khosrow-Pour (Eds.), *Handbook of research on public information technology* (pp. 905–924). Hershey, PA: IGI Global. doi:10.4018/978-1-59904-857-4.ch076

Teale, S. (2016). *Nottinghamshire Police records misogyny as a hate crime*. Retrieved from http://www.bbc.com/news/uk-england-nottinghamshire-36775398

Teitelbaum, J. (2012). Failing States: The Real Meaning of the Arab Uprisings. In *Advancing a Free Society*. Hoover Institution, Stanford.

The flag of the German Reich was raised in the Acropolis by the "German tourists" of Golden Dawn. (2016). Retrieved from http://jungle-report.blogspot.gr/2016/02/simaia-reich.html

The Initiative for Equal Rights. (2014). *Survey on homosexuality perception in Nigeria*. Lagos: The Initiative for Equal Rights.

The Ministry Immigration Policy. (2016). There will be no rental housing for refugees in Thrace, The area is Thrace is expressly excluded from the specific program. *Ethnos*. Retrieved from http://www.ethnos.gr/koinonia/arthro/yp_metanasteutikis_politikis_den_tha_ginei_enoikiasi_katoikion_se_prosfyges_sti_thraki-64329404/

Thesing, Z. (2007). Zarina thesing, pumpkin patch. In M. Hunter (Ed.), *Contemporary chief information officers: Management experiences* (pp. 83–94). Hershey, PA: IGI Global. doi:10.4018/978-1-59904-078-3.ch007

Thomas, A. (2016). Germany Plans to Make It Easier to Deport Migrants. *The Wall Street Journal*. Retrieved from http://www.wsj.com/articles/germany-plans-to-tighten-deportation-rules-1452620702

Thomas, J. C. (2004). Public involvement in public administration in the information age: Speculations on the effects of technology. In M. Malkia, A. Anttiroiko, & R. Savolainen (Eds.), *eTransformation in governance: New directions in government and politics* (pp. 67–84). Hershey, PA: IGI Global. doi:10.4018/978-1-59140-130-8.ch004

Townsend, M. (2016, January 30). 10.000 Refugee Children are missing, says Europol. *The Guardian*. Retrieved from https://www.theguardian.com/world/2016/jan/30/fears-for-missing-child-refugees

Traverso, E. (2011). Populism and Islamophobia. ENEKEN, 19.

Treiblmaier, H., & Chong, S. (2013). Trust and perceived risk of personal information as antecedents of online information disclosure: Results from three countries. In F. Tan (Ed.), *Global diffusion and adoption of technologies for knowledge and information sharing* (pp. 341–361). Hershey, PA: IGI Global. doi:10.4018/978-1-4666-2142-8.ch015

Tunde, O. (2005). The Myth of Neo-Colonialism. *Africa Economic Analysis*, *23*, 30–49.

Turek, K. (2010). *Gay totalitarianism vs Christian liberty*. Retrieved October 18, 2016, from http://crossexamined.org/gay-totalitarianism-vs-christian-liberty/

Tyagi, Y. K. (1995). *The Concept of Humanitarian Intervention Revisited*. Michigan Journal of International Law.

Tzanelli, R. (2016). *Thana tourism and Cinematic Representation of Risk*. Abingdon, UK: Routledge.

UN. (2013). Retrieved from http://www.un.org/apps/news/story.asp?NewsID=46834#.V2E9nLuLTIU

UNHCR, Syria Regional Refugee Response, Inter-agency Information Sharing Portal. (n.d.). Retrieved from http://data.unhcr.org/syrianrefugees/country.php?id=224

UNHCR. (2001). *Interpreting Article 1 of the 1951 Convention Relating to the Status of Refugees*. Retrieved from http://www.refworld.org/pdfid/3b20a3914.pdf

UNHCR. (2007). *Advisory Opinion on the Extraterritorial Application of Non-Refoulement Obligations under the 1951 Convention relating to the Status of Refugees and its 1967 Protocol*. Retrieved from http://www.unhcr.org/4d9486929.pdf

UNHCR. (2010). *Convention and Protocol relating to the Status of Refugees*. Retrieved from http://www.unhcr.org/protection/basic/3b66c2aa10/convention-protocol-relating-status-refugees.html

UNHCR. (2014). *Greece as a Country of Asylum: UNHCR Observations on the Current Asylum System in Greece*. Geneva: UNHCR.

UNHCR. (2015). *Greece as a Country of Asylum: UNHCR's Recommendations*. Geneva: UNHCR.

UNHCR. (2015). *Refugee Status Determination, Identifying who is a refugee*. Office of the UNHCR.

UNHCR. (2016). *Stories from Syrian refugees*. Retrieved from http://data.unhcr.org/syrianrefugees/syria.php

UNHR. (1996). *International Covenant on Civil and Political Rights*. Retrieved from http://www.ohchr.org/en/professionalinterest/pages/ccpr.aspx

UNHR. (2013). *Addendum-Mission to Greece, 2013 23rd session HRC, A/HRC/23/46/Add.4*. Retrieved from http://www.ohchr.org/EN/Issues/Migration/SRMigrants/Pages/AnnualReports.aspx

United Nations Convention relating to the Status of Refugees, 189 U.N.T.S. 150, entered into force April 22, 1954.

Urry, J. (2002). *The Tourist Gaze*. London: Sage.

Urry, J. (2007). Introduction: Mobile cultures. *Viajes y Geografías*, 17–32.

Urry, J., & Larsen, J. (2011). *The tourist gaze 3.0*. London: Sage. doi:10.4135/9781446251904

v Greece, R. T. (2016). *No. 5124/11*. ECHR.

Vafiadis, N. (2014). *The Evros is no longer "an unfenced vineyard"*. Retrieved from http://www.kathimerini.com.cy/index.php?pageaction=kat&modid=1&artid=179753

Vale, P. (1995). Engaging the World's Marginalized and Promoting Global Change: Challenges for the United Nations at Fifty. *HARV. INT'L L.J., 36*(283).

Van Creveld, M. (1982). *Fighting Power: German and US Army Performance, 1939–1945*. Westport, CT: Greenwood.

Van Creveld, M. (1991). *Technology and War from 2000 BC to the Present*. London: Brassey's.

Van de Berg, M., Bos, D. J., Derks, M., Ganzevoort, R., Jovanovic, M., Korte, A. M., & Sremac, S. (2014). Religion, Homosexuality and Contested Social Orders in the Netherlands, the Western Balkans and Sweden. In *Religion in Times of Crisis* (pp. 116–134). Boston: Brill. doi:10.1163/9789004277793_008

Van Dijk, T. (2001). *Critical discourse analysis. In The handbook of discourse analysis*. Oxford, UK: Blackwell Publishing.

Van Dijk, T. (2005). *Racism and discourse in Spain and Latin America*. Amsterdam: John Benjamins Publishing Co. doi:10.1075/dapsac.14

van Grembergen, W., & de Haes, S. (2008). IT governance in practice: Six case studies. In W. van Grembergen & S. De Haes (Eds.), *Implementing information technology governance: Models, practices and cases* (pp. 125–237). Hershey, PA: IGI Global. doi:10.4018/978-1-59904-924-3.ch004

van Os, G., Homburg, V., & Bekkers, V. (2013). Contingencies and convergence in European social security: ICT coordination in the back office of the welfare state. In M. Cruz-Cunha, I. Miranda, & P. Gonçalves (Eds.), *Handbook of research on ICTs and management systems for improving efficiency in healthcare and social care* (pp. 268–287). Hershey, PA: IGI Global. doi:10.4018/978-1-4666-3990-4.ch013

Vautravers, A. J. (2008). Why Child Soldiers are such a Complex Issue. *Refugee Survey Quarterly, 27*(4), 96–107. doi:10.1093/rsq/hdp002

Veith, G. (2011). *Gay marriage & totalitarianism*. Retrieved October 18, 2016, from http://www.patheos.com/blogs/geneveith/2011/07/gay-marriage-totalitarianism/

Velloso, A. B., Gassenferth, W., & Machado, M. A. (2012). Evaluating IBMEC-RJ's intranet usability using fuzzy logic. In M. Cruz-Cunha, P. Gonçalves, N. Lopes, E. Miranda, & G. Putnik (Eds.), *Handbook of research on business social networking: Organizational, managerial, and technological dimensions* (pp. 185–205). Hershey, PA: IGI Global. doi:10.4018/978-1-61350-168-9.ch010

Villablanca, A. C., Baxi, H., & Anderson, K. (2009). Novel data interface for evaluating cardiovascular outcomes in women. In A. Dwivedi (Ed.), *Handbook of research on information technology management and clinical data administration in healthcare* (pp. 34–53). Hershey, PA: IGI Global. doi:10.4018/978-1-60566-356-2.ch003

Villablanca, A. C., Baxi, H., & Anderson, K. (2011). Novel data interface for evaluating cardiovascular outcomes in women. In *Clinical technologies: Concepts, methodologies, tools and applications* (pp. 2094–2113). Hershey, PA: IGI Global. doi:10.4018/978-1-60960-561-2.ch806

Villanger, E. (2007). Arab foreign aid: Disbursement patterns, and policies and motives. *Forum for Development Studies, 34*(2), 223–256. doi:10.1080/08039410.2007.9666378

Vilvarakah and Others v. the United Kingdom. (1991). [GC] Nos. 13163/87; 13164/87; 13165/87; 13447/87; 13448/87, ECHR. para. 102.

Virilio, P. (2010). *The University of Disaster.* Cambridge, UK: Polity Press.

Virkar, S. (2011). Information and communication technologies in administrative reform for development: Exploring the case of property tax systems in Karnataka, India. In J. Steyn, J. Van Belle, & E. Mansilla (Eds.), *ICTs for global development and sustainability: Practice and applications* (pp. 127–149). Hershey, PA: IGI Global. doi:10.4018/978-1-61520-997-2.ch006

Virkar, S. (2013). Designing and implementing e-government projects: Actors, influences, and fields of play. In S. Saeed & C. Reddick (Eds.), *Human-centered system design for electronic governance* (pp. 88–110). Hershey, PA: IGI Global. doi:10.4018/978-1-4666-3640-8.ch007

Wallace, A. (2009). E-justice: An Australian perspective. In A. Martínez & P. Abat (Eds.), *E-justice: Using information communication technologies in the court system* (pp. 204–228). Hershey, PA: IGI Global. doi:10.4018/978-1-59904-998-4.ch014

Wang, G. (2012). E-democratic administration and bureaucratic responsiveness: A primary study of bureaucrats' perceptions of the civil service e-mail box in Taiwan. In K. Kloby & M. D'Agostino (Eds.), *Citizen 2.0: Public and governmental interaction through web 2.0 technologies* (pp. 146–173). Hershey, PA: IGI Global. doi:10.4018/978-1-4666-0318-9.ch009

Wangpipatwong, S., Chutimaskul, W., & Papasratorn, B. (2011). Quality enhancing the continued use of e-government web sites: Evidence from e-citizens of Thailand. In V. Weerakkody (Ed.), *Applied technology integration in governmental organizations: New e-government research* (pp. 20–36). Hershey, PA: IGI Global. doi:10.4018/978-1-60960-162-1.ch002

Wassenberg, B. (2013). *History of the Council of Europe* (pp. 13–15). Strasbourg: Council of Europe Publishing.

Waterfield, B. (2015). *Greece's defence minister threatens to send migrants including jihadists to Western Europe.* Retrieved from http://www.telegraph.co.uk/news/worldnews/islamic-state/11459675/Greeces-defence-minister-threatens-to-send-migrants-including-jihadists-to-Western-Europe.html

Weber, A. (2009). *Manuel on hate speech.* Strasbourg: Council of Europe Publishing.

Wedeen, L. (1999). *Ambiguities of Domination: Politics, Rhetoric, and Symbols in Contemporary Syria*. Chicago: University of Chicago Press.

Wedemeijer, L. (2006). Long-term evolution of a conceptual schema at a life insurance company. In M. Khosrow-Pour (Ed.), *Cases on database technologies and applications* (pp. 202–226). Hershey, PA: IGI Global. doi:10.4018/978-1-59904-399-9.ch012

Whybrow, E. (2008). Digital access, ICT fluency, and the economically disadvantages: Approaches to minimize the digital divide. In F. Tan (Ed.), *Global information technologies: Concepts, methodologies, tools, and applications* (pp. 1409–1422). Hershey, PA: IGI Global. doi:10.4018/978-1-59904-939-7.ch102

Whybrow, E. (2008). Digital access, ICT fluency, and the economically disadvantages: Approaches to minimize the digital divide. In C. Van Slyke (Ed.), *Information communication technologies: Concepts, methodologies, tools, and applications* (pp. 764–777). Hershey, PA: IGI Global. doi:10.4018/978-1-59904-949-6.ch049

Wickramasinghe, N., & Geisler, E. (2010). Key considerations for the adoption and implementation of knowledge management in healthcare operations. In M. Saito, N. Wickramasinghe, M. Fuji, & E. Geisler (Eds.), *Redesigning innovative healthcare operation and the role of knowledge management* (pp. 125–142). Hershey, PA: IGI Global. doi:10.4018/978-1-60566-284-8.ch009

Wickramasinghe, N., & Geisler, E. (2012). Key considerations for the adoption and implementation of knowledge management in healthcare operations. In *Organizational learning and knowledge: Concepts, methodologies, tools and applications* (pp. 1316–1328). Hershey, PA: IGI Global. doi:10.4018/978-1-60960-783-8.ch405

Wickramasinghe, N., & Goldberg, S. (2007). A framework for delivering m-health excellence. In L. Al-Hakim (Ed.), *Web mobile-based applications for healthcare management* (pp. 36–61). Hershey, PA: IGI Global. doi:10.4018/978-1-59140-658-7.ch002

Wickramasinghe, N., & Goldberg, S. (2008). Critical success factors for delivering m-health excellence. In N. Wickramasinghe & E. Geisler (Eds.), *Encyclopedia of healthcare information systems* (pp. 339–351). Hershey, PA: IGI Global. doi:10.4018/978-1-59904-889-5.ch045

Widner, J. (1995). States and Statelessness in Late Twentieth Century Africa. *Daedalus*, *124*(3), 129-153.

Wike, R., Stokes, B., & Simmons, K. (2016). *Europeans fear wave of refugees will mean more terrorism, fewer jobs.* Retrieved from http://www.pewglobal.org/2016/07/11/europeans-fear-wave-of-refugees-will-mean-more-terrorism-fewer-jobs/

Williams, E. (2015). *Children of ISIS*. Retrieved from http://www.pbs.org/wgbh/frontline/film/children-of-isis/transcript/

Wren, K. (2001). Cultural racism: Something rotten in the state of Denmark? *Social & Cultural Geography*, *2*(2), 141–162. doi:10.1080/14649360120047788

Wyld, D. (2009). Radio frequency identification (RFID) technology. In J. Symonds, J. Ayoade, & D. Parry (Eds.), *Auto-identification and ubiquitous computing applications* (pp. 279–293). Hershey, PA: IGI Global. doi:10.4018/978-1-60566-298-5.ch017

Yaghmaei, F. (2010). Understanding computerised information systems usage in community health. In J. Rodrigues (Ed.), *Health information systems: Concepts, methodologies, tools, and applications* (pp. 1388–1399). Hershey, PA: IGI Global. doi:10.4018/978-1-60566-988-5.ch088

Yasu, R. (2010). Identity, law, justice. Thinking about sexual rights and citizenship in post-apartheid South Africa. *Perspectives, Political Analysis and Commentary from Africa*, *4*(10), 18–23.

Yazbek, S. (2012). A Woman. In *The Crossfire: Diaries of the Syrian Revolution* (p. 113). London: Haus Publishing Ltd.

Yee, G., El-Khatib, K., Korba, L., Patrick, A. S., Song, R., & Xu, Y. (2005). Privacy and trust in e-government. In W. Huang, K. Siau, & K. Wei (Eds.), *Electronic government strategies and implementation* (pp. 145–190). Hershey, PA: IGI Global. doi:10.4018/978-1-59140-348-7.ch007

Yeh, S., & Chu, P. (2010). Evaluation of e-government services: A citizen-centric approach to citizen e-complaint services. In C. Reddick (Ed.), *Citizens and e-government: Evaluating policy and management* (pp. 400–417). Hershey, PA: IGI Global. doi:10.4018/978-1-61520-931-6.ch022

Younes, A.-E. (2015). *Islamophobia in Germany, National Report 2015* (E. Bayrakli & F. Hafez, Eds.). Istanbul: SETA.

Young-Jin, S., & Seang-tae, K. (2008). E-government concepts, measures, and best practices. In A. Anttiroiko (Ed.), *Electronic government: Concepts, methodologies, tools, and applications* (pp. 32–57). Hershey, PA: IGI Global. doi:10.4018/978-1-59904-947-2.ch004

Yücebaş, M. (2015). Gaziantep yerel basınında Suriyeli İmgesi: Yeni taşranın yeni suskunları: Suriyeliler. *Birikim Dergisi*, *311*, 38–47.

Yun, H. J., & Opheim, C. (2012). New technology communication in American state governments: The impact on citizen participation. In K. Bwalya & S. Zulu (Eds.), *Handbook of research on e-government in emerging economies: Adoption, e-participation, and legal frameworks* (pp. 573–590). Hershey, PA: IGI Global. doi:10.4018/978-1-4666-0324-0.ch029

Yuval, S. (2006). Toward a General Margin of Appreciation Doctrine in International Law?. *The European Journal of International Law*, *16*(5). Retrieved from http://www.ejil.org/pdfs/16/5/330.pdf

Zhang, N., Guo, X., Chen, G., & Chau, P. Y. (2011). User evaluation of e-government systems: A Chinese cultural perspective. In F. Tan (Ed.), *International enterprises and global information technologies: Advancing management practices* (pp. 63–84). Hershey, PA: IGI Global. doi:10.4018/978-1-60960-605-3.ch004

Ziter, E. (2013). The Image of the Martyr in Syrian Performance and Web Activism. *The Drama Review, 57*(1), 116-136.

Žižek, S. (2001). Have Michael Hardt and Antonio Negri rewritten the Communist Manifesto for the twenty-first century? *Rethinking Marxism, 13*(3-4), 190–198. doi:10.1080/089356901101241875

Zmirak, J. (2015). Gay totalitarianism and the upcoming persecution of Christians. *The Stream, 19*, 43–67.

Zuhur, S. (2011). *Saudi Arabia*. Santa Barbara, CA: ABC-CLIO.

Zuo, Y., & Hu, W. (2011). Trust-based information risk management in a supply chain network. In J. Wang (Ed.), *Supply chain optimization, management and integration: Emerging applications* (pp. 181–196). Hershey, PA: IGI Global. doi:10.4018/978-1-60960-135-5.ch013

About the Contributors

Christina M. Akrivopoulou holds the post of committee President in the Greek Refugee Appeals Authority. She has a PhD in Constitutional Law and has been a Postdoctoral Researcher in the Greek Scholarship Foundation and the Aristotle University Research Committee. Her main research interests concern human and constitutional rights, the protection of the right to privacy, data protection, the private-public distinction, asylum and citizenship. She has lectured in the Faculty of Political Sciences of Democritus University of Thrace, in Hellenic Open University, in Aristotle University of Thessaloniki and in the EMA Unesco Chair inter-university master class. She also works as an Attorney-at-Law at the Thessaloniki Law Bar Association. She is collaborating with several Greek law reviews and she is an active member of many non-governmental human rights organisations in Greece and abroad.

* * *

Zahid Shahab Ahmed is a postdoctoral fellow at Deakin University in Australia focusing on peace and security in the Muslim world. His work examines the impacts of sectarianism and violent extremism on domestic, regional and global peace and security. He is also engaged in research and educational projects on countering violent extremism in Pakistan. During 2013-2015, he served as Assistant Professor at the Centre for International Peace & Stability (CIPS), National University of Sciences and Technology (NUST) in Islamabad. He has worked on numerous research assignments with Die Deutsche Gesellschaft für Internationale Zusammenarbeit (GIZ), Friedrich Ebert Foundation, Commonwealth Foundation, United States Institute of Peace, Transparency International, Global Integrity, and International Centre for Nonviolent Conflict during a decade long engagement with the development sector. Dr Ahmed received his PhD in the area of Political and International Studies from the University of New England (UNE) in Australia. He has an MA in Peace Education from the United Nations mandated University for Peace (Costa Rica), and an MA in Sociology from the University of Agriculture Faisalabad (Pakistan).

He has an excellent record of publications. In 2010, he co-authored with Balasubramanian R. a study entitled "Extremism in Pakistan and India: The Case of the Jamaat-e-Islami and Shiv Sena". Among his prominent publications is a following contribution: Ahmed, Z.S. 2012, 'Political Islam, Jamaat-e-Islami, and Pakistan's Role in the Afghan-Soviet War, 1979-1988', in Religion and the Cold War: A Global Perspective, P. Muehlenbeck (ed), Vanderbilt University Press, Tennessee, pp.275-296. In 2013, Routledge published his following book "Regionalism and Regional Security in South Asia: The Case of SAARC".

Endong Floribert Patrick Calvain (Ph.D) is a research consultant in the humanities and social sciences. His areas of interest include sexuality, culture, religion, gender, media communication, religious communication and international relations. He is author of numerous peer-reviewed articles and book chapters in the above-mentioned areas.

Bulut Gurpinar received her Bachelor of Science and her Ph.D degree in International Relations from Istanbul University, Faculty of Political Sciences. She performed her postdoctoral training in foreign policy at Bilgi University. She was recruited to Gebze Technical University as a research assistant. Her research interests focus on foreign policy, civil society and international relations. Her current projects include Muslim Brotherhood and Syria.

Nurhan Kavakli is a PhD student in Journalism at the Faculty of Communication at Ankara University, Turkey. Her dissertation research focuses on the Internet as a public sphere and consists of a comparison of old media and the Internet. Her research interests include the media and globalization, the history of Turkish journalism and new media and journalism. She is the author of *The History of a Newspaper: Aksam* and she has published several papers in Turkish academic journals, including *Culture and Communication* and *Social History*. She holds two MA's, one in journalism from Northeastern University (Boston), and another in Broadcasting and Communication from Marmara University (Istanbul). She received her BA from the Faculty of Communication at Istanbul University. Before starting her doctorate study, she worked as a journalist at *Cumhuriyet*, a national daily newspaper in Turkey. Nurhan Kavaklı is an assistant professor at Üsküdar University, Turkey. She is the author of *Public Sphere and New Media* and *The History of a Newspaper: Aksam*. Kavaklı earned a PhD in Journalism at Ankara University. Before starting her doctorate study, she worked as a journalist at *Cumhuriyet*, a national daily newspaper in Turkey. She holds two MA's, one in journalism from Northeastern University (2000/Boston), and another in Broadcasting and Communication from Marmara University (1995/Istanbul). She received her bachelor's degree in Broadcasting and Communication from Istanbul University. Her research interests include new media, social media, journalism, global media and political communication.

Maximiliano Korstanje is editor in chief of International Journal of Safety and Security in Tourism (UP Argentina) and International Journal of Cyber Warfare and Terrorism (IGI-GlobalUS). Besides being Senior Researchers in the Department of Economics at University of Palermo, Argentina, he is a global affiliate of Tourism Crisis Management Institute (University of Florida US), Centre for Ethnicity and Racism Studies (University of Leeds), The Forge (University of Lancaster and University of Leeds UK) and The International Society for Philosopher, hosted in Sheffield UK. With more than 700 published papers and 25 books, Korstanje was awarded as Outstanding Reviewer 2012. International Journal of Disaster Resilience in the Built Environment. University of Salford, UK, Outstanding Reviewer 2013. Journal of Place Management and Development Institute of Place, Manchester Metropolitan University, UK and Reviewer Certificate of Acknowledgement 2014. International Journal of Contemporary Hospitality Management (IJCHM), University of Central Florida, US. Now he co-edits almost 10 specialized journals in such themes as human rights, mobility, tourism and terrorism. Korstanje is subject to biographical records for Marquis Who`s Who in the World since 2009. He had nominated to 5 honorary doctorates for his contribution in the study of the effects of terrorism in tourism. In 2015 he was awarded as Visiting Research Fellow at School of Sociology and Social Policy, University of Leeds, UK and the University of La Habana Cuba. In 2017 is elected as Foreign Faculty Member of AMIT, Mexican Academy in the study of Tourism, which is the most prominent institutions dedicated to tourism research in Mexico.

Iliana Kynigopoulou is a postgraduate student in Public International Law at the School of Law of the National and Kapodistrian University of Athens (Athens, Greece). Her first degree was in International and European Studies, specializing in Political Studies and Diplomacy. She has been awarded with a scholarship and an award by the State Scholarships Foundation of Greece. Her research interest focuses on different human rights aspects, such as human rights of refugees and immigrants, the phenomenon of female genital mutilation, human rights within the Middle East countries, the crime of genocide and the crime of apartheid. She has worked voluntarily for several non-governmental human rights organizations.

Anastasia Pitsou is a political scientist and she undertook a traineeship in the Centre of International and European Economic Law (CIEEL). She has a BA in Balkan Studies from the Aristotle University of Thessaloniki and in Political Science and Public Administration from the National and Kapodistrian University of Athens. Additionally, she has an MSc in Cultural Studies (Semiotics, Structures and Practices) from the University of Western Macedonia and also she has an MSc in Philosophy from the Aristotle University of Thessaloniki.

Zafeiris Tsiftzis (Ph.D, LL.M, BSc) is a legal practitioner and he has completed his Ph.D. studies in International Human Rights Law (School of Law, University of Bolton, United Kingdom). His research interests are based on human rights law and humanitarian law and also on international law and international criminal justice. His doctoral research is on the international preventive framework for human rights abuses committed by private military and security companies (Private Military and Security Companies: Options for Regulation under Human Rights Law).

Index

I

L

M

N

O

R

S

T

U

V

CPSIA information can be obtained
at www.ICGtesting.com
Printed in the USA
BVOW10*1706021117
499179BV00006B/24/P

9 781522 528173